Advance Praise for
## *Enacting Critical Pedagogy Online*

"*Enacting Critical Pedagogies Online* is a timely publication that serves as an essential resource for instructor training, instructor onboarding, teacher preparation programs, and annual assessment of programs responsive to the call for curricular diversification.

This compilation focused on the central question of how to honor principles of critical pedagogy in computer mediated learning and offers examples of transformative classrooms and culturally sustaining pedagogies through consideration of theory and practice.

Central to both critical pedagogy and quality online instruction is the creation of community, and conscious engagement with content, peers, and instructors. Challenges that arise include designing content that promotes and balances meaningful communication and providing opportunities for application beyond the classroom.

The contributing authors share theoretically grounded and practical examples of how they have advanced genuine and mindful engagement in online learning where critical pedagogy content is central. Sample cases include online and hybrid modalities, learner experiences, and full-time instructor and adjunct perspectives on enacting critical pedagogies online."

—Melisa Fiori, Associate Professor of Spanish, Daemen University

# Cover Artist Statement

The use of flowers and plants as symbols for human emotion is nothing new. Botanical metaphors can be found in the art and artifacts of cultures from all over the planet. Humans have often used flowers and plants to underscore emotion or state what they could not say aloud. With their ability to stimulate all our senses, flowers can be used to soothe and inspire as well as trigger a major allergic reaction. Some can heal, while others kill. They can herald our birth or share the pain of our death.

As a metaphor for the online classroom community studying diversity, the flowering plants on the cover represent the complexity of that diversity. They also represent the struggles of a classroom community trying to come together to learn and grow. From the student being choked out of the discussion to the student struggling to move past their toxicity to the student easily thriving in the electric environment — each are meant to break free together. Each need to move past constructed barriers to a place where their collective diversity serves to enrich instead of eradicating, to equalize instead of dominating. Each must strive to see that, in the words of my grandmother, "Il giardino è bellissimo con molti fiori."

Cynthia Clabough
cynthia.clabough@oswego.edu

# Enacting Critical Pedagogy Online

# Studies in Criticality

Shirley R. Steinberg
*General Editor*

Vol. 533

The Counterpoints series is part of the Peter Lang Education list.
Every volume is peer reviewed and meets
the highest quality standards for content and production.

PETER LANG
New York • Berlin • Brussels • Lausanne • Oxford

# Enacting Critical Pedagogy Online

Edited by
Erin Mikulec and Tania Ramalho

PETER LANG
New York • Berlin • Brussels • Lausanne • Oxford

Library of Congress Cataloging-in-Publication Control Number: 2022007193

Bibliographic information published by **Die Deutsche Nationalbibliothek**.
**Dsie Deutsche Nationalbibliothek** lists this publication in the "Deutsche Nationalbibliografie"; detailed bibliographic data are available on the Internet at http://dnb.d-nb.de/.

ISSN 1058-1634
ISBN 978-1-4331-9410-8 (hardcover)
ISBN 978-1-4331-9409-2 (paperback)
ISBN 978-1-4331-9406-1 (ebook pdf)
ISBN 978-1-4331-9407-8 (epub)
DOI 10.3726/b19369

© 2022 Peter Lang Publishing, Inc., New York
80 Broad Street, 5th floor, New York, NY 10004
www.peterlang.com

All rights reserved.
Reprint or reproduction, even partially, in all forms such as microfilm, xerography, microfiche, microcard, and offset strictly prohibited.

# Table of Contents

List of Figures ix
List of Tables xi

Introduction 1
    Erin Mikulec and Tania Ramalho

Chapter One  What Would Paulo Freire Think of Blackboard™: Critical
    Pedagogy in an Age of Online Learning 13
    Drick Boyd

Chapter Two  Teaching Critical Pedagogy Online: What Would
    Paulo Freire Say? 31
    Tania Ramalho

Chapter Three  Online Engagement with Critical Pedagogy 53
    Tina Wagle

Chapter Four  (Digital) Media as Critical Pedagogy 75
    Maximillian Alvarez

Chapter Five  Teaching and Learning in Hybrid Environments: Professor
    and Student Perspectives 101
    Delores D. Liston and Heather M. Huling

Chapter Six  Promoting Transformative Learning Using Critical Pedagogy
and Moore's Theory of Transactional Distance                                    119
  Sara Donaldson, Heather Yuhaniak, Carey Borkoski, & Yolanda Abel

Chapter Seven  Creating Community Through Meaningful Interactions: A
Framework to Support Critical Pedagogy and Social Justice                       141
  Brianne Morettini

Chapter Eight  COVID-19 and the Exacerbation of Educational Inequalities
in New Zealand                                                                  159
  Carol A. Mutch

Chapter Nine  Teaching for Social Justice: Online Classes at Historically Black
Colleges and Universities                                                       181
  John Bannister, Anita Bledsoe-Gardner, & Mary Holiman

Chapter Ten  Knowledge Production and Power in an Online Critical
Multicultural Teacher Education Course                                          193
  Ramona Maile Cutri, Erin Feinauer Whiting, & Eric Ruiz Bybee

Chapter Eleven  Critical Pedagogy and Online Discussions in a Multicultural
Education Teacher Preparation Course                                            207
  Jessamay T. Pesek

Chapter Twelve  Evolving Toward Critical Social Justice Online: A Rogerian-
Based Theoretical Model                                                         227
  Jennifer L. Martin and Denise K. Bockmier-Sommers

Chapter Thirteen  Ignatian Pedagogy Online                                      241
  Margaret Debelius, Kimberly Huisman Lubreski, Mindy McWilliams,
  James Olsen, Lee Skallerup Bessette, & Yianna Vovides

Chapter Fourteen  Educating Awareness in an Online Reflective Practice
Course: Becoming Aware of Implicit Biases and Leaps to Judgment                 263
  Robyn Ruttenberg-Rozen, Sahana Mahendirarajah, & Brianne Brady

Chapter Fifteen  Reaching Critical Depths: Engaging Teacher Candidates in
Critical Pedagogy Online                                                        281
  Vicki A. Hosek and Jay C. Percell

Chapter Sixteen  Converting Research Efforts to Improve Equitable Student
Achievement from Professional Development Program to Online
Course: GESA (Still) Works!                                                     299
  Dolores A. Grayson

Chapter Seventeen  Adjunct Online Instruction in Higher Education: Are
    Piece-Work Professors Able to Teach Critically Under Virtual
    Panopticism?                                                        319
    Batya Weinbaum

About the Authors                                                       329

# List of Figures

| | | |
|---|---|---|
| Figure 6.1 | Hypothesized Conceptual Framework | 126 |
| Figure 6.2 | Study Outcomes: Trends in Participants' Course Experiences | 134 |
| Figure 7.1 | Pedagogical Methods to Structure an Online Community of Practice | 147 |
| Figure 7.2 | Integrated Feedback and Student Voice Represented by a Word Cloud | 149 |
| Figure 12.1 | Evolving Toward Critical Social Justice: A Theoretical Model | 231 |
| Figure 13.1 | Intersections of Critical Pedagogy and Ignatian Pedagogy | 245 |
| Figure 16.1 | GESA Strands | 304 |
| Figure 16.2 | Observation Chart Based on Submission by K. Jacobson | 311 |

# List of Tables

| | | |
|---|---|---|
| Table 6.1: | Participant Characteristics (N = 14) | 125 |
| Table 6.2: | Overview of Course Design Changes in Terms of Opportunities for Course Interactions | 128 |
| Table 6 Appendix: | Types of Learning Interaction | 136 |
| Table 8.1: | COVID-19 in New Zealand from First Infections to First Lockdown | 161 |
| Table 8.2: | Timeline Outlining the Impact of COVID-19 on the Education System | 164 |
| Table 8.3: | Summary of Studies Conducted During or After the National Lockdown | 166 |
| Table 8.4: | Continuum of Lockdown Learning in New Zealand | 167 |
| Table 13.1: | Comparing the Critical Pedagogy and Ignatian Pedagogy Cycles | 244 |
| Table 15.1: | Student Demographic Information | 287 |

# Introduction

The spark for this project ignited in Bilbao, Spain, capital of the historically resistant Basque region. The idea came to fruition at a bench outside of the architecturally exquisite Guggenheim Museum Bilbao, where a group of Critical Pedagogy and Transformative Leadership Congress had just visited an exhibit of the monumental works of Portuguese feminist artist, Joana Vasconcelos. Earlier that day we had delivered a presentation on the work we were doing with our own online courses, the challenges we faced and the successes we enjoyed, teaching controversial content online. Congress founder and leader, Shirley Steinberg, approached us with the suggestion, "Why don't you work on a book on teaching Critical Pedagogy online?"

We had met at the previous gathering of the Congress in Turin, Italy. There we committed to present our work on online teaching at the upcoming *International Conference Paulo Freire: The Global Legacy* in Belo Horizonte, Brazil. We were in support of the efforts of the Federal University of Minas Gerais' conference organizers to keep alive the tenets of the *Pedagogy of the Oppressed* in face of the political pendulum moving dangerously to the right. The conference turned out to be the perfect setting to discuss the emergence of critical pedagogy-inspired teaching online, as our presentation took place in a room full of engaged students and scholars, Brazilian and from other countries, including Colombia, Israel, and Norway. Our session yielded a rich conversation, mediated through several languages and translations, that led to the same conclusions. While online learning provided access to more students, the distance created by virtual walls did not always facilitate genuine engagement. Furthermore, the challenge to establish an environment in which difficult conversations could be had with mindful intention was all the greater. In an online setting, our students either felt emboldened by the ability to remain shielded by the lack of humanity that asynchronous environments create, or the opposite, they were in fact too timid to express any thoughts or ideas out of fear of being perceived a certain way by others. As all our students were preservice or practicing teachers in an online environment, they were aware of what they themselves had told their own students: once you write something on the internet, it is there to stay. Although this was something that was never discussed, we came to understand the effect it had on the climate in our online courses.

Curious to understand and share the experiences of others, the call for proposals went out. We received many responses, with proposals falling both close to and far from our vision for the book, and some surprising. The global pandemic hit, disrupting work routines and all lives, adding some delays to the process. Nonetheless, the project proceeded. The final product, which we highlight in this introduction, attests to the diversity of scholars engaging with critical pedagogy online in various forms, their practices, and narratives, in the United States, Canada, and New Zealand. Before Covid-19, teaching online from a critical pedagogical perspective seemed to be pioneering experiences needing to be documented. Since, online teaching in general has become commonplace not only in higher education but at all levels of schooling, even kindergarten. Therefore, although the pandemic has at times brought about frustration with the process of bringing this project to a close, it has also proven to emphasize the timeliness of its completion.

In *Enacting Critical Pedagogy Online*, seventeen chapters span theory and practice of critical pedagogy in online spaces. Each author brings a unique online teaching experience of courses about or related to critical pedagogy. The community of scholars in this book share practices, theories, resources, as well as challenges they face in online teaching enacting critical pedagogical principles.

The book opens with activist professor Drick Boyd (Eastern University), whose 2016 paper, *What Would Paulo Freire Think of Blakboard TM: Critical Pedagogy in an Age of Online Learning*, is reprinted here from the International Journal of Critical Pedagogy. He writes,

> While Paulo Freire formulated his ideas about teaching in a pre-Internet era, he did not object to the use of technology in the teaching-learning process. He urged educators to think critically about the use of technology and to find new ways of seeking and creating knowledge with the aid of technology (p. 14).

Is it possible to follow critical pedagogical principles in online teaching? Boyd did it, as others in this book, in trial-and-error fashion. He called particular attention to Freire's deeply interpersonal "situated pedagogy," intuitively resembling Vygotsky's, requiring the teacher to know and to work with the students' very languages and cultures. He also examined Feenberg's critical theory of technology, contending that much like schooling, technology is not politically neutral as it affects our understanding of self and the world. Computer-mediated education represents an "all-encompassing environment managing and controlling access to information, structuring relationships, and redefining individual identities" (p. ;171). Boyd identifies conditions that facilitate and constrains Freirean concepts in online teaching, concluding with five problem-posing questions and pointing to future research and practice of online educators: avoiding the banking model of education (content transmission), creating community, leading students to understand the contexts of cyberculture and of neoliberal culture; and providing opportunity for action.

Boyd's initial question also informs Chapter Two, by Tania Ramalho (SUNY Oswego), *Teaching Critical Pedagogy Online--What would Paulo Freire say*? She acknowledges writing it without the knowledge advanced in his pioneer paper, and indicates the happenstance circumstances by which she came to teach online the master's level course, Critical Pedagogy. Freire's standpoint informs the course's main goal: "to empower the development of students as subjects through understanding and enacting critical consciousness in their concrete existential conditions, in interconnect personal and occupational everyday life" (p. 32). She expects students to undergo conscientization, becoming critically aware of contextual "specs"—the historical social, political, economic and cultural systems shaping lives—while also entertaining the possibility of becoming critical pedagogy-informed teachers.

The "critical" is also a political perspective that developed modernly, more so following Marx's posing of historical materialism. Marxist scholars, including from the Frankfurt School, have continued to put it forth as a basis for understanding and guiding human evolution through revolutionary praxis. Ramalho's students compare and contrast conservative, liberal and critical political traditions, and examine the platforms of main American political parties and their views on education and schooling. They study critical pedagogical principles and practices and are urged to consider them in their own teaching and relationships with their students, parents and school communities.

Tina Wagle (SUNY Empire) writes about her Introduction to Critical Pedagogy course in Chapter Three, *Online Engagement with Critical Pedagogy*, departing from the premise, "an instructor should be able to deliver the content s/he wants to convey regardless of mode of instruction" (p. 54). Given that most social justice-oriented courses have been, until recently, taught face-to-face, she understands the uniqueness of this new technology-infused critical pedagogical teaching. As one of the core courses of a master of education program, Wagle's Introduction to Critical Pedagogy is "designed to create a discourse community that questions hegemonic social practices and contributes to a larger collective conversation" (p. 56). The course content includes a module on educational ethnography. She showcases a program and course unique online model of virtual residency bridging university and communities, which undergraduate, graduate and international education students attend. In 2018, the theme for this three-week virtual residency was Indian Education and Indigenous Knowledge. Students were immersed in related reading, watching and responding to documentaries, and attending a lecture by an activist and cultural expert. For the course's final project, following a framework for community activism, students are asked to develop a plan for change that also engages school and community partnerships.

In Chapter Four, *(Digital) Media as Critical Pedagogy*, Maximilian Alvarez explores the paradox that technology presents in the context of teaching and learning. Alvarez argues that in contrast to the promise of creativity and expression that technology-enhanced learning purports, ultimately, teachers and students alike "perform what the programmers of said technology have determined learning to be" (p. 79). Through this lens, technology only offers the illusion of choice and agency, and by encouraging multimodal demonstrations of learning, students and teachers are still at the mercy of what the original designers intended but now believe they are somehow empowered with the very opposite. Alvarez further examines these concepts through the work of Freire, Giroux, Kincheloe, and others and call for a critical evaluation of ready acceptance of technology as positive progress in education.

Delores D. Liston (Georgia Southern University) pairs with doctoral student Heather M. Huling to reflect about two second-year hybrid courses in a Curriculum Studies E.D. program: a critical pedagogy introductory course, Inquiry and Development into Educational Practice; and a second one, Advanced Critical Pedagogy. In Chapter Five, *Teaching and learning in hybrid environments: Professor and student perspectives*, Liston explains the courses' objectives and assignments. In the first course, students reflect and write autobiographically about gender, social class and race. Other projects, which receive feedback from instructors, are a grant proposal and a bibliographical review. The second course addresses the perspectives of diverse critical pedagogy scholars in greater depth.

Huling, Liston's doctoral student, writes about the benefits of the hybrid format of the courses and the constructive feedback on assignments she received. Testifying about the prevailing social dynamics, she writes:

> The acts of writing about our personal experiences, reading about the family experiences of our classmates, and then, engaging in in-person conversations about our different experiences pushed us into uncomfortable dialogues with one another. These rich conversations about our autobiographies sparked personalized discussions about critical pedagogy and how *we* acknowledge our biases as educators (p .107).

Huling witnesses the student-focused, transmission-avoiding nature of these critical pedagogy courses at the doctoral level.

Jack Mezirow's adult learning and development theory; Paulo Freire's concept of critical consciousness and critical pedagogy; and Michael G. Moore's transactional distance theory are connected in Chapter Six, *Promoting transformative learning using critical pedagogy and Moore's Theory of Transactional Distance*. The research team, Sara Donaldson and Heather Yuhaniak (Wheaton College), and Carey Borkoski and Yolanda Abel (John Hopkins University), investigates how online instructional design affects doctoral students' critical reflection.

A multicultural teacher education doctoral course' structure was redesigned to decrease transactional distance (TD) by offering more opportunities for synchronous dialogues, hypothesized to increase opportunity for critical reflection. The authors describe the changes made to the course and the emerging patterns of transformation in student experiences, ranging from simply informative, intensifying, to transformative, noting that the latter was different for student members of dominant and non-dominant groups. They found that the "relationship between TD and critical reflection may be more nuanced" and that "conditions leading to transformative learning differ based on individuals' backgrounds" (pp. 133–134).

Brianne Morettini (Rowan University) presents *Creating community through meaningful interactions: A framework to support critical pedagogy and social justice* in Chapter Seven. She reflects on the first-year undergraduate online course, Foundations and Philosophies of Education, part of an inclusive education program. She starts by situating herself as instructor: "I view myself as a critical mentor and facilitator of learning and growth" (p. 143). She explicitly models vulnerability and trust, and the sense of importance of the work with young diverse learners that requires cultural competence. Vygotsky's sociocultural approach, Wenger's communities of practice, and Freire's praxis principle inform her views on teaching and learning. She writes, "My felt obligations, then, as an instructor in an asynchronous online learning space are to foster meaningful interactions *with* students and *among* students so they can begin to cultivate meaning and participate in a community of practice" (p. 145).

The model Morettini uses to create an online community of practice that structures student access comprises course assignments, virtual office hours, learner autobiographies, integrated feedback and student voice. A sense of belonging and community is necessary for participants' calling on each other's biases, in order for understandings of social justice issues develop. The author is available for individual communication and uses autobiographical video for introductions. She creates many opportunities for student interaction through three main course assignments—critical friend, community engagement, personal teaching philosophy. "Critical friend" requires pairs of students to follow each other's posts, and at the end of the course they write about what they learned from the other.

Carol A. Mutch explores how the Covid-19 pandemic laid bare the lack of access to educational resources and deepened the socio-economic divide in *Covid-19 and the exacerbation of educational inequalities in New Zealand* in Chapter Eight. Providing a detailed timeline of events following the arrival of Covid-19 and responses from the Ministry of Education, along with a review of studies conducted during this time, Mutch identifies the many challenges faced by teachers and parents in having to navigate digital platforms seemingly overnight while maintaining regular work and family life. Mutch also discusses the social, emotional, and educational effects on students. The piece is further substantiated by the student voices showcased within from Mutch's own study. The chapter concludes with an optimistic outlook for the future based on the lessons learned and the Māori proverb: kia kaha, kia maia, kia manawaui — be strong, be brave, be steadfast (p. 175).

John Bannister, Anita Bledsoe-Gardner, and Mary Holiman provide a framework for expanding coursework beyond the online platform in Chapter Nine, *Teaching for social justice: Online classes at Historically Black Colleges and Universities.* Reflecting on the influence of social media and hashtag activism, the authors discuss the power of online classes as spaces to center culturally responsive teaching, where "topics once taboo, such as feminism and police brutality, now have a strong presence" (p. 186). Beyond serving as a platform for culturally responsive teaching, the chapter also explores how online social justice classes can utilize social media as means of reaching vast audiences and to connect with community leaders and activists to enrich and further course content and dialogue. Furthermore, the authors as instructional designers encourage others to consider how traditional online course formats might be integrated with Massive Open Online Courses (MOOCs) to engage an even wider group of students in dialogue about issues of social justice.

Ramona Maile Cutri, Erin Feinauer Whiting, and Eric Ruiz Bybee (Brigham Young University) ask "What are the motivations, experiences, and insights of a teacher educator designing an online course with the intention of sharing the production of knowledge with her students?" (p. 194) in Chapter Ten, *Knowledge production and power in an online critical multicultural teacher education course*, a reflexive inquiry into their practice. The teacher education course aims to engage students intellectually and emotionally in the examination of issues of equity and social justice. The authors seek to understand how this can be accomplished online by creating new practices of shared knowledge construction and the expertise and authority that come with it. With that purpose in mind, the instructors developed an assignment where students bring media content illustrating central course concepts such as ideology, hegemony, and oppression. The authors discuss contradictions, pedagogical risks, and tensions that arise from this online teaching model where "the power relations […] shifted away from the teacher educator as the sole expert in the classroom" (p. 203).

Jessamay T. Pesek also discusses the importance of empowering students in online spaces for effectives pedagogical spaces in Chapter Eleven, *Critical pedagogy and online discussion in a multicultural teacher education preparation course*. The author focuses on strategies for building a course that centers student voices, however acknowledges that rich and meaningful discussion is the result of purposeful planning on the part of the instructor. Pesek also emphasizes the role of the instructor in crafting online discussion "with and for critical pedagogy" (p. 213). The author describes how discussion lends itself not only as a platform for students to show what they know, but also as a means of discovery and process through which to shift their own ideas and perspectives. The chapter provides practical and actionable strategies for designing discussion-based instruction.

In *Evolving toward critical social justice online: A Rogerian-based theoretical model*, Chapter Twelve, Jennifer L. Martin and Denise K. Bockmier-Sommers (University of Illinois Springfield) offer a model for online teacher and social services education based on Carl Rogers' principles, or conditions, for productive dialogues between instructors and students. Educators' empathy, genuineness, and unconditional positive regard toward students create a safe environment that make addressing controversial and difficult topics possible. The authors discuss their approach to anti-racism education, departing from the dominant ideas on how present society has overcome racism, and colorblindness and meritocracy are fair and just. They offer counter-narratives that "allow the story of the more vulnerable person to override the stereotypes held by the more hegemonic reader" (p. 236).

A time-tested pedagogy named after the Jesuit order's founder, Saint Ignatius of Loyola adapted to online teaching is the topic of Chapter Thirteen, *Ignatian pedagogy online*, by Margaret Debelius, Kimberly H. Lubreski, Mindy McWilliams, James Olsen, Lee S. Bessette, and Yianna Vovides (Georgetown University). Not formalized until 1993, Ignatian pedagogy includes five elements—context, experience, reflection, action, and evaluation—applied across disciplines. The authors compare it to Freire's critical pedagogy, showing commonalities and differences. They argue that "the Ignatian pedagogical elements and approach can be used by instructors designing their online courses, with the explicit aim of transformation and social justice" (p. 246). The design elements indicated are: 1. Analyze human learning experience online/offline; 2. Establish relationships of mutual respect online/offline; 3. Tap into learner's prior knowledge & experience; 4. Design optimal learning experience for the whole person; 5. Assimilate new information; 6. Transfer learning into lifeworld; 7. Encourage lifelong learning & reflections beyond self-interest; and, 8. Learners become contemplatives in action. These aspects are examined closely in two case studies of the undergraduate courses, Introduction to Ethics (online) and Gender, Immigration and Social Justice (hybrid).

Teacher educators, Robyn Ruttenberg-Rozen, Sahana Mahendirarajah, and Brianne Brady (Ontario Tech University) describe their work in support of critical consciousness development through questioning "leaps of judgment" with implicit biases and "in-the-moment decisions" that teachers make in complex, fast-paced, classroom interactive contexts. In Chapter Fourteen, *Educating awarenesses in an online reflective practice course: Becoming aware of implicit biases and leaps to judgement*, they study Canadian teacher candidates attending an online reflective practice and action research course. The main activity includes 1. Reading about ethnography and the practice of notetaking (strictly observations) and notemaking (comments on the observations); 2. A 45-minute observation and reflection on a familiar environment; 3. Feedback from the instructor focused on the leaps of judgment and implicit biases evident in the notes taken; 4. Reiteration of the process, with reflection on what was learned from the first assignment/feedback, and on implications for teaching practice. They write, "We found that through creating a transformative space, the online classroom can be a powerful conduit for learning about social justice issues. […] The flexibility of the online environment afforded each preservice teacher to be on a different path and trajectory" (p. 277).

In Chapter Fifteen, Vicki A. Hosek and Jay C. Percell (Illinois State University) offer *Reaching critical depths: Engaging teacher candidates in critical pedagogy online*, about the undergraduate course, The Teaching Profession in Secondary Schools. Hosek, too, faced challenges when developing the course's online version. Hosek presents an honest and authentic account of translating her face-to-face

Socratic practice to approach core course concepts to an online space. Centering on students' access to the instructor and to each other, she created spaces for reflection and dialogue in private journals, to which she vigilantly responds. The authors examine students' reflections on course readings and experiences in schools. In their experience, "a personal and private dedicated digital space for each student is necessary to both individualize student learning and develop personal instructor-student connections" (p. 295). They note the importance of appropriate sequencing of materials and critical reflection opportunities.

In *Converting research efforts to improve equitable student achievement from professional development program to an online course: GESA (still) works*, Dolores A. Grayson (SUNY Oswego) brings us in Chapter Sixteen her time-tested Generating Expectations for Student Achievement (GESA). GESA asks teachers to entertain five areas of disparity and work on instructional strategies to address them: 1. Instructional Contact/Engagement, related to response opportunities and acknowledging students and providing feedback; 2. Grouping/Organization of the classroom, with particular attention to proximity and wait time; 3. Classroom Management/Discipline, involving reproof and the need to collect discipline data; 4. Student Self-Esteem/Self-Concept/Self-Efficacy, listening and probing students; and, 5. Evaluation of Student Performance, which take into consideration higher level questioning on the part of the teacher and the ability to provide analytical feedback to students.

When teachers become critically aware of these professional skills and hone them, the quality of interaction with students from diverse backgrounds improve, they are more likely to use culturally relevant materials and activities, and overall students' achievement scores rise. Grayson provides a history of GESA and its national and international reach, and discusses in detail the online course, including main assignment relevant to the areas of disparity. Grayson concludes, "GESA continues to work. It raises teachers' consciousness and shapes effective action in classrooms. GESA online empowers teachers to make rich, critical knowledge-informed pedagogical decisions, and engage in meaningful dialogues in school communities" (p. 316).

Finally in Chapter Seventeen, *Adjunct online instruction in higher education: Are piece-work professors able to teach critically under virtual panopticism?* by Batya Weinbaum (American Public University System and Kent State Stark), offers two perspectives on online teaching. First, she speaks out bravely from the point of view of an adjunct instructor, or, "piece-work professor." She also describes her interactions with and for students and critical pedagogical approaches. Of her experience as contingent university employee, she testifies to the continuing replacement of full-time for "piece-work" academic positions; extra-work not accounted for in salaries; surveillance by online administrators monitoring curriculum and instructors' behavior; not being re-hired after questioning administrators' decisions, and facing the impossibility of receiving unemployment compensation. She indicts:

> Criticizing the institutions in which we try to carry out critical pedagogy and the society those institutions are serving, we might end up not getting to do pedagogy of any kind in the first place, and society stays dumbed down, unless we minister through poetry, alternative networks we create on our own, or in churches (p. 322).

Weinbaum implies that online administrators may be functioning as masters of banking education who impose acritical curricula, instruction, and evaluation. Her courses, on the other hand, follow ten pedagogical principles and aim at creating critical communities and model how scholars engage in dialogue, which students can apply to other online courses.

Each of the authors in this collection affirm the central importance of dialogue in their courses, at the undergraduate, master's and doctoral levels, as demonstrated in these readings. Transactional *closeness*, decreased transactional distance, is the core element in critical pedagogical teaching, face-to-face or online. It cannot be replaced. Critical instructors have one-to-one, small and large group interactions with students, who also interact with each other in activities that increase contact and communication in hybrid or asynchronous courses. Establishing opportunities for interaction and dialogue between all members of the online community is the number one design component in critical pedagogy-informed online courses.

Escaping banking education, a second aspect of design has to do with the importance of seeking the contribution of students as co-constructors of knowledge. This too can be done in different ways, beyond knowledge generated in conversations and dialogues. Students may actively seek real-life examples in media portrayals of critical, social justice-related concepts and perspectives on self and society; or, engage in ethnographical observations of spaces outside the online or media environments, which are then shared and discussed.

Beyond Paulo Freire and other critical pedagogical intellectuals, ideas from other critical educators and scholars can be fruitful to online critical pedagogy. The enduring contribution of Aquinas to religious and secular education aimed at self and social development; Carl Rogers' conditions for authentic relationships with maturing young learners; and, Mezirow's powerful understandings of transformative learning; each has brought a new dimension to now online approaches to critical pedagogy. Undoubtably, others can be studied for their power to shed light and enhance online interaction and communication. This constitutes a call for future investigation of this kind.

Finally, our contributors wrote independently and in teams of scholars. Especially since the pandemic started in 2020, which is still with us, many more instructors have moved to the required mode of online teaching. What has been their personal experience with critical pedagogical approaches online during this time? What can we learn, individually and collectively, from this period of restraint in terms of liberatory and social justice-enhancing knowledge in online environments? We, Erin Mikulec and Tania Ramalho, only hope our edited text helps this complex field forge ahead as it inspires writers everywhere.

CHAPTER ONE

# What Would Paulo Freire Think of Blackboard™: Critical Pedagogy in an Age of Online Learning

DRICK BOYD

During a recent faculty training event, as I listened to a presentation of how to teach effectively on Blackboard™, an online platform used by my university, I reflected on my struggles to employ a critical pedagogy in the increasingly assessment-oriented, outcomes-based environment in which I find myself as a university professor. As my university has turned to online delivery systems as a way to attract students not able to attend or interested in a residential campus experience, I wonder about the nature of their learning experience. While designed to make teaching in the online environment more efficient, these systems confront the critical pedagogue with challenges to create a teaching-learning environment that promotes critical reflection not only on the content of a course but on the very way in which content is delivered. So, I mused: "What would Paulo Freire think of Blackboard™?"

I have been teaching online courses for over fifteen years, including accelerated courses with undergraduate adults, semester courses with graduate students, and blended or hybrid courses conducted in both a traditional classroom and online. Since I began teaching online, the technology has greatly improved. Furthermore I have learned, along with others, that teaching in cyberspace requires a different teaching paradigm altogether (Harasim, 2000; Palloff & Pratt, 2007).

I am also deeply committed to critical pedagogy, particularly as articulated in the writings of Paulo Freire. Because most of the literature on critical pedagogy assumes a traditional classroom, I have largely had to apply the principles of Freirean pedagogy in a trial and error manner, often wondering if teaching like Freire online was even possible.

Freire's pedagogical concepts, such as problem posing, dialogue, praxis, *conscientization* and the politics of education, were developed in a pre-Internet era. His work in popular education was deeply interpersonal and involved spending significant time in a community becoming familiar with the culture, linguistic patterns, and lifestyle of the people before ever embarking on teaching. He practiced a "situated pedagogy" in which it was essential to teach in the vernacular of the people and use cultural symbols and forms familiar to them. Freire believed the educator must first seek to understand reality from the perspective of the students before he/she could encourage them to resist and transform their reality (Shor & Freire, 1987). For these reasons it is hard to imagine how Freire would react to a teaching-learning environment where instructor and student are geographically separated from one another, only connected by the electronic impulses of a computer network.

Nevertheless, Freire (2014) did not object to the introduction of technology into the practice of teaching. While he recognized the dangers of the "relegation of education to a mere exercise of technology," he also believed "that the use of technical aids and materials is indispensable" to the educational process (p. 75). He urged educators to think critically about the use of technology in teaching and "to create new channels of knowledge, new methodologies, new relationships between the subjects who seek knowledge and the most advanced technological innovations that we have at our disposal" (pp. 74–75). With this caveat in mind I want now to take a critical look at how Freirean critical pedagogy can be practiced in the online environment.

After giving a brief history of the development of online learning, I review Feenberg's Critical Theory of Technology (CTT). Then I examine the practice of online teaching and learning through the lens of selected Freirean concepts, identifying areas where I believe he would be troubled and others where he might sense the ways online learning can enhance the learning process. I then close with a series of problem-posing questions which guide our exploration moving forward. The purpose of this analysis is not to dismiss the contributions of online learning, but to raise fundamental questions that critical educators can and must address.

## Online Learning

The first experiments in online learning occurred in the mid-1970s when computers were used for email, crude forms of computer conferencing, and computer-mediated instruction for skill development and simple knowledge-based instruction. Early online tools such as email supplemented in-class instruction and the correspondence course style of distance education. Corporations and universities in the United States and Canada experimented with various formats for delivering education in an online format. In 1981 the first totally online courses developed were non-credit mini-courses offered by educational institutions and executive training programs in the corporate sector (Harasim, 2000).

In 1996, eleven U.S. state governments pledged $100,000 each to launch Western Governor's University (WGU), the first virtual university in the United States. Initially, WGU did not create its own courses, but served as an access point for potential students to take online courses from several state universities in the western States. Each course had a list of competencies that had to be mastered, and when those competencies were achieved, the student "passed the class." Based on their past experience, previously developed skills and knowledge, and diligence, students progressed at different paces. Eventually, WGU moved out of its role as an education "broker" and began to hire its own content experts to identify key competencies for courses, which they then offered as a separate institution (Meyer, 2009).[1]

Soon several other state university systems developed online offerings gleaned from existing courses at their state-funded institutions. Heavily dependent on state funding, these initiatives were eventually absorbed into existing schools or faded away. Like WGU, these early online courses tended to be competency-based, relying on testing as the primary mode of assessment. While WGU's goal was to create a virtual university, the goal of the other early efforts was more modest, in that they created opportunities for students unable to attend a place-based university to take university courses (Garn, 2009).

The push for the development of online education came largely from government and business interests. States often used a carrot-and-stick approach with educational institutions, insisting upon the further development of online options while offering grants for training future teachers in the use of technology. Corporate entities like Microsoft, Apple, and various software companies promoted their products as a means to more effective teaching and learning. The overall message was that society was becoming more technology-based and therefore education had to change with this cultural shift or become irrelevant. Accrediting agencies required university faculty to create quantifiable learning outcomes to justify and validate their students' learning (McCurry, 2000). While the language spoke of being "learner-centered," most educators still felt these directives were top-down oriented and undermined their primary role in the teaching-learning process. Thus, essentially online learning did not come into being because educators found a more effective way to teach, but rather because they were forced to adapt due to the political and economic interests that pushed and promoted it in their institutions.

Since the early 2000s the pervasiveness of online programs in the United States has continued to grow. Between 2002 and 2011 the percentage of students enrolled in online courses at colleges and universities grew from 9.6% to 32%. In 2002, 1.6 million students reported taking at least one online course, and by 2012 the number was 6.7 million. One of the largest areas of growth was in the development of programs offered completely online. In 2012, 62.4% of institutions offered at least one degree program completely online compared to only 34.5% in 2002. Furthermore the confidence of both students and teachers in the quality of education being offered increased significantly (Allen & Seaman, 2003, 2013). While administrators have generally had a positive attitude toward online learning, by 2012 only 30% of chief academic officers reported their faculty had accepted the value and legitimacy of online learning. Retention rates in online courses were significantly lower than in face-to-face courses, and only 40% of academic leaders believed potential employers saw online degrees as equivalent to degrees earned in the traditional face-to-face classroom (Allen & Seaman, 2013).

Since its beginning, when online learning involved cumbersome software and was dependent on bandwidth often beyond the reach of many users, "e-learning" has come a long way. Now learning management systems (LMS) create relatively easy-to-use platforms for organizing and delivering course content through the use of text-based and virtual face-to-face options for instruction. While in the beginning online instructors often just posted lectures previously delivered in traditional classrooms, now many practitioners have discovered innovative, discussion-based constructivist methods for teaching online (Palloff & Pratt, 2007). Moreover, larger universities like MIT, Stanford, Yale, and Duke have experimented with MOOCs (Massive Open Online Courses), offering online lectured-based courses for no or low cost to existing and potential students (Allen & Seaman, 2013).

Regardless of one's perspective on online learning, unquestionably in the last twenty-five years the paradigm of university education has shifted. Driven by economic and political forces, most universities now regard online education as an important component of their course offerings. Moreover, by and large this paradigm shift has occurred primarily for non-pedagogical reasons, forcing those entrusted with the responsibility of creating meaningful, transformative learning experiences to adjust to the new paradigm (Harasim, 2000).

## Critical Theory of Technology

Reflecting on this incorporation of online learning technologies into the educational sector, Feenberg (2009) developed the Critical Theory of Technology (CTT), which rejects the "techno-utopianism" of those who assume there is a technical solution for all challenges and barriers facing teachers. From the perspective of CTT, "technologies are not separate from society but are adapted to specific social and political systems" and in their use promote and reinforce the values, beliefs, and "truths" of those systems. Thus, technology is not regarded as economically or politically neutral. From a CTT perspective technologies are environments that shape the values and worldviews of their inhabitants. Technological environments redefine the way human users understand themselves and their relationship to the world and operate at the level of meaning and ethics. Like the common in the middle of a New England town, today the Internet is regarded as a common space to which all persons regardless of rank or position should have access.

Rather than being value-neutral, CTT posits that embedded in all technologies are implicit values and principles referred to as "technical codes." Technical codes describe "the congruence of a social demand and a technical specification" (Feenberg, 2009, p. 151), in the process redefining basic values and social principles. For example, when the U.S. government required all automobiles to be built with seatbelts and airbags (technologies), the meaning of auto safety (a value) was redefined. From the perspective of CTT these technical codes "are always biased to some extent by the values imposed by the dominant actors" (p. 152), thus making them essential to hegemonic control by those dominant actors on the wider society.

As outlined by CTT, technology creates a cyber culture that redefines human identity and the meaning and means of human interaction (Gomez, 2009). When viewed through this lens, online education is not simply another tool for the promotion of learning, but rather an all-encompassing environment managing and controlling access to information, structuring relationships, and redefining individual identities. Accompanying and contributing to this rise in online education, an education technology industry has emerged, comprised of LMSs, content providers, information database providers, computer software, e-books, and the like. While masquerading as efforts to enhance student learning, these industries are clearly profit-oriented. Knowledge has become a commodity, students have become consumers, faculty have become content providers, and schools operate as businesses. In the cyber culture these changes are seen as necessary and normal and are not to be challenged or questioned.

However, it is precisely because of this overarching and rapid transformation of the culture of higher education that a critical perspective is needed. The key question CTT asks is: What are the underlying values and beliefs embedded in a given technology and for which it is designed (Feenberg, 2009; Hamilton & Feenberg, 2005)? Freire's critical pedagogy, informed by the insights of CTT, helps expose these underlying values and raises important questions as to the role online learning plays and should play in the teaching-learning process.

## Freire and Online Learning

Freire stressed that he offered a philosophy rather than a methodology of teaching and believed the appropriate application of that philosophy had to be recreated in every context. For Freire, context is critical in determining the manner in which the instructor will conduct his/her teaching. Thus, I take a critical look at teaching and learning in the online environment and examine it from a Freirean critical perspective. In particular, I have chosen to focus on those aspects of Freire's educational philosophy that critique the dominant values in online learning, and which empower educators and their students to recreate the learning environment in a way that is liberatory for those often marginalized by the educational system and equitable for all who participate in it.

### The Politics of Education

Essentially, Freire understood education as inherently political and believed its central goal to be the liberation of those who are politically marginalized and impoverished. Liberatory education is humanizing because it dignifies people and empowers them to shape their destinies and their world. In Freire's words, they move the oppressed from being objects to subjects of their experiences (Freire, 2007). Freire wrote: "A humanizing education is the path through which men and women can become conscious about their presence in the world" (as cited in Macedo, 1998, p. xiii). By contrast those educators who claim their teaching is apolitical by default align themselves with the status quo and reinforce conditions leading to the dehumanization and marginalization of their students. While Freire acknowledged that education should help students develop skills and knowledge to be able to survive economically, he also insisted education should challenge students to question the very capitalistic enterprise for which they are preparing (Escobar et al., 1994).

Freirean critical pedagogy views education as a "form of social and cultural criticism" (McLaren, 1994, p. xvi), with a vision toward creating a politically democratic, racially inclusive, economically just social order replacing the hierarchical, exclusive powers currently dominating the social and political world. Likewise, Freire believed education must take into account both the social, political, and economic context in which it occurs and also the vision (Freire used the word "utopia") toward which it strives. Like Feenberg (2009), Freire would be concerned with the values and principles embedded in the technology of online learning, as well as the cyber culture it has created. As Feenberg (2009) has shown, technology is more than a tool for transmitting education; it is an environment which must be critically analyzed for its underlying values and assumptions.

Therefore, our discussion of Freire and online learning must begin with the origins of online learning. As has already been noted, the primary impulse for the expansion of online learning in higher education was due to economic and political interests, rather than pedagogical ones. Schools did not venture into online learning because they thought it was a better way to teach, but rather because they saw it as a way to reach unreached student populations with the promise of offsite educational offerings. Only later was attention given to developing online pedagogies.

At the same time online programs were being developed, colleges and universities adopted a business model with a primary focus on the financial bottom line and preparing graduates for the job market. As recent criticisms of higher education have indicated, students are now seen as educational consumers who expect a return on investment in terms of employable skills. Online learning is seen as a cost-effective and efficient way for students to get an education. Whereas education in the United States was originally viewed as a way to prepare students for effective citizenship, now it is seen as a way to develop loyal and capable employees of their corporate overlords. As a result, those academics who do seek to practice critical pedagogy find their efforts significantly compromised by an insistence on content standards and pre-determined learning outcomes (Martin & Riele, 2011).

Those who teach in an online setting must be aware of this larger social and political context, for as McLaren (1994) writes, they "must have a vision that is not content with adapting individuals to a world of oppressive social relations but [be] dedicated to transforming the very conditions that promote such conditions" (p. xxxii). In practical terms, this means teachers committed to critical pedagogy must develop exercises and assignments that challenge students to examine their social and cultural contexts, including the technological environment in which their class is being conducted. However, to do so may cause these teachers to become suspect to those who expect faculty and their students to simply fit into their corporately-directed niche.

## Online Banking

A second area of concern is the banking nature of the LMSs. One of the underlying assumptions of an LMS like Blackboard™, Moodle™, or Brightspace™ is that the online platform is a repository of resources for teaching and learning. Some forms of online learning go so far as to design learning modules, which when completed, certify the student as having developed certain skills or mastered certain content areas.

The latest expression of this banking orientation is the development of MOOCs, large online courses offered by major universities with so-called "experts in their field." MOOCs were originally believed to be a way to provide "universal access to free, high-quality, impeccably branded online courses" (Carey, 2012) and are characterized by massive number of students watching short video lectures combined with short quizzes, automated assessments, and optional peer discussion formats for answering questions. Largely patterned after traditional lecture-style courses, MOOCs were initially developed by computer programmers and content experts with little attention paid to the unique challenges of teaching in the online environment. Even by their own standards, MOOC providers have reported mixed results on student learning and engagement, with roughly only 15% of the students who start courses completing them. Promoted as efficient and simple means of delivering education, MOOCs offer little opportunity for students to engage in critical reflection, focusing mostly and information retrieval and concept mastery. Furthermore, while promoted as a way to provide higher education for low income and less educated students, the primary MOOC user has been the individual who has already earned a higher education degree (Adair et al., 2014; Baggley, 2013; Carey, 2012; Glance et al., 2013).

Freire vehemently rejected this banking approach to education because it did not recognize or encourage the student's creative, exploratory, and critical abilities. In the banking model the teacher is regarded as the holder and transmitter of knowledge, which is then imparted to the student. The banking model assumes the student is an empty vessel and does not value or recognize the student's experiential and cultural knowledge. Moreover, it leaves the student in the role of passive recipient rather than active creator of knowledge (Freire, 2007).

By contrast Freire argued for a problem-posing, constructivist approach that invites students to critically engage their world and one another. In the critical classroom, the student at times takes on the role of teacher and the teacher becomes a learner, inviting a sharing of power and mutual learning. While this approach can be carried out to an extent online, the LMS is set up to be the primary source of information in a course, and the teacher is assigned as the expert designer of the learning experience, thus limiting the constructivist nature and mutuality of the learning process.

The Digital Divide

A third area of concern is the limited access to online learning to large sectors of society. While e-learning advocates tout the greater access to learning provided by online learning (Goral, 2013; Kashi & Conway, 2010), the digital divide is a reality impacting millions of students. While 95% of households in the United States have access to broadband and therefore the Internet, only 68% actually have Internet in their homes. In 2009, a study found that 35% (or 80 million) of U.S. adults (not counting children) did not use broadband in their homes (Congressional Digest, 2013). Moreover, a 2013 Pew Research Center study found lower rates of usage among low income families and among Blacks and Hispanics than the general population (Zickhur, 2013). Recent studies (Anderson 2014; Mossberger et al., 2014) have indicated that the gap may be closing slightly with the increased use of smart phones by low income Blacks and Latinos, but often this is more for communication than academic purposes. These statistics suggest that a significant number of students have no access in their homes to online education. Lack of access to digital technology tends to be located in areas of concentrated poverty and racial/ethnic segregation. Thus, the disparities in health care, adequate housing, social services, economic opportunity, and quality education also include technological deprivation. As more public services go online, including education, these communities become increasingly disenfranchised (Mossberger et al., 2006).

With the digital divide comes digital illiteracy, which is the in-ability to find, assess, and construct knowledge in the digital realm (Bawden, 2008). In practical terms, effectiveness in the online learning process requires facility with information technology and digital literacy. A recent study found huge disparities between wealthy suburban and poor urban school districts in terms of their access to and use of computer technology (Education Week, 2014). This has translated into a notable disadvantage for first-generation college students who, even if they have access to information technology, lack the knowledge and ability to effectively use information and communicate online (Fleming, 2012).

Freire was particularly focused on empowering those who have been socially and economically marginalized and oppressed. A learning environment that by its very nature is unavailable to a significant percentage of the population and whose presence tends to increase economic and racial disparities is inherently problematic. Moreover, students coming into higher education from technology-impoverished high schools find themselves at a disadvantage in an age of online learning. Unless teachers and educational institutions are consciously committed to closing the digital literacy and access gap, the very presence of online education contributes to increasing disparities not only in the educational present, but also in the future possibilities for those students to whom access is denied.

### Disembodied Learning

A final area of concern is the disembodied nature of the online learning process. One of the major attractions of online learning to potential students is the freedom from having to be in a classroom in a particular time or place. In online courses information is shared via articles and presentations posted on an LMS, and students are required to read or view these resources in a particular period of time. Then students interact with the instructor and classmates through an electronic discussion format where they write responses to prompts and respond to the posting of other students. Often to augment these asynchronous interactions, online courses will include synchronous sessions using video-conferencing software that enables students and instructor to be in a virtual classroom together for short periods of time. However, overall the modality of interaction online is highly focused on textbased communication.

Because the primary medium is text-based, this tends to encourage a cognitively-oriented learning process. However, Freire (1988) believed learning was to be holistic. As he saw it, a key component of the teaching-learning process was the demonstration of love and the cultivation of community among the instructor and students. For Freire, love was not simply a virtue to be followed, but an embodied emotion to be expressed. He writes "… we study, we learn, we teach, we know *with our entire body* [emphasis mine]. We do all of these things with feeling, with emotion, with wishes, with fear, with doubts, with passion and also with critical reasoning" (p. 3).

Embodied learning means students must not only engage the cognitive dimension (thinking and reflection), but also partake in concrete action. This action in reflection, and reflection in action, referred to as praxis, involves acting on and in the world as one is seeking to learn about and transform the world. For Freire, the willingness to act on what one is studying is absolutely critical to learning; we learn as we do, and we do as we learn. To limit education to the transmission and reception of text-based knowledge without action undermines the entire learning process (Escobar et al., 1994). The nature of online learning technology strongly leans toward this disembodied form of learning and mitigates against the holistic, praxis-oriented learning process Freire promotes.

Dialogue Online

Despite the challenges created by the online learning environment, there are ways I believe Freire would find the online environment enhances the teaching-learning experience. The first way in which online learning coincides with a Freirean pedagogical approach is its capacity to facilitate meaningful dialogue.

Freire believed dialogue begins not with what the teacher professes to know, but with the student's experience and knowledge. Ever aware of the power dynamics between teacher and student in the educational space, the teacher enters into an exploration with student of the subject at hand. In this process students become subjects of their own learning, developing the capacity to name their own reality. As Freire (2007) writes: "Dialogue is the encounter between [persons], mediated by the world, in order to the name the world" (p. 88). For Freire, dialogue must not be manipulative and must be carried out with "profound love" and respect for the other, especially when the other holds views and perspectives different than one's own. Through dialogue, both within oneself and with other learners, Freire believed one could come to a critical consciousness (*conscientization*) of one's place in the social, political, and economic context.

Dialogue is not simply a teaching technique, but also a process essential to the nature of human beings. We come to know the world and ourselves in and through our interaction with others; knowledge is created in the dialogical encounter. Moreover, this knowledge is not something held by an individual but is held corporately by those in the dialogue. This includes even the instructor who by virtue of previous study and teaching has a certain level of understanding greater than the students. However, in the dialogue even the instructor re-learns the subject matter in a way that transforms him/her as well as the students. In this way, instructors become teacher-learners and students become learner-teachers (Freire, 1988; Shor & Freire, 1987).

The tool often used to facilitate online dialogue is called computer conferencing, which is "distributed, asynchronous, text-based communication" in an online course (Hamilton & Feinberg, 2005, p. 109). In a computer conference the instructor may post one or more discussion questions, and then over the course of a designated time (usually a week or two), students interact with the instructor and one another around a designated topic or set of assigned readings. At times the instructor may add or provide direction to relevant information missing in the discussion or encourage the students to reflect on a particular issue at hand. Thus, effective online discussion in this mode is not just free-flowing but has a particular focus and direction. When done well, these discussions can lead to a greater depth of understanding and connection between participants. The extended nature of the online dialogue allows for deeper inquiry and reflection often absent in a time-bound classroom setting (Hamilton & Feenberg, 2005; Palloff & Pratt, 2007).

For Freire, the building of a learning community is essential to creating meaningful dialogue; this is also true for those who seek to teach effectively online. Palloff and Pratt (2007) contend that all online teaching must begin with building community and stress that a carefully constructed online learning community provides a space for students to test ideas, get feedback, and create a collaborative learning experience. Freire regarded the learning community as the container in which knowledge is held jointly by the group. For Freire, learning was a social and democratic event where authoritarianism and control of the learning process are minimized. In dialogue "the object to be known is not an exclusive possession of one of the subjects doing the knowing, one of the people in the dialogue. …. [Rather] they meet around it and through it for mutual inquiry" (Shor & Freire, 1987, p. 99).

The goal of this dialogical encounter is greater comprehension of one's experience not only on a personal level, but also in the sociopolitical and economic dimension as well. This is what Freire (1988) called "reading the world," or *conscientization*, that is, understanding the larger political context in which experience occurs and knowledge is situated. In the current era of Facebook, Twitter, instant message, and other social media, in-depth discussion and analysis is often absent in favor of brief, often innocuous statements and personal opinions. If done effectively, online discussions can push students and teachers beyond a superficial level to an expanded understanding of the context in which this knowledge is being created. Instead of giving into the pattern of shallowness created by contemporary tendencies of computer-mediated communication, online teachers can use the online discussion to reach toward a greater critical consciousness.

Online Access to Information

A second way online environments can facilitate a critical approach to teaching-learning is through greater access to information on the Internet. Through online academic databases, students have easy access to far more sources of information than previous generations. Furthermore, search engines like Google, Bing, and the like bring students in contact with remote sources, organizations, and individuals instantly.

In addition to proprietary information, open sources of information are also available, such as online journals, multimedia databases, YouTube channels, Open Universities, and even MOOCs. With this increased access to information, comes the ability to act on what is learned in new and refreshing ways. One only has to look at how the 1999 WTO demonstrations in Seattle, the 2011 Arab Spring uprisings in Tunisia and Egypt, and the 2011 Occupy Wall Street Movement used cyber technologies to connect previously unconnected individuals toward a common social goal (Carroll-Miranda, 2011). In 2015, *Black Lives Matter* did the same.

However, recent revelations of extensive government surveillance on private citizens demonstrate how government and corporate elites are using their extensive power to suppress free expression of ideas. Moreover, telecommunications companies have aggressively sought government-sanctioned license to create a multi-tiered internet, thereby limiting optimum bandwidth to an elite few. While the Internet remains a virtual public square, if the corporate elites get their way, the open access of the Internet could be greatly curtailed (Clement, 2014; Galloway, 2014).

Despite these concerns, the online environment offers tremendous opportunities to remote and marginalized communities to gain access to previously unavailable information. For example, Srinivasan (2006) highlights remote communities in Brazil and India who have promoted their cultural and political agendas through the use of information technology. These examples illustrate tremendous potential for Freire's vision of praxis and social learning to be realized and the development of oppressed and marginalized communities to be advanced. For students in an online learning context, particularly those students from marginalized communities, this open access to information has revolutionary possibilities.

However, the challenge is not only the accessing of information, but also encouraging students to become discerning purveyors of information—to develop "critical digital literacy," the capacity to effectively and critically navigate the databases and myriads of potential sources (Poore, 2011). The sheer magnitude of the information available to students often is overwhelming such that they have difficulty prioritizing and evaluating their search results. Often educators are not much further ahead of their students in terms of digital literacy and so are limited in their ability to help their students in this regard. Thus, an essential component of student and faculty preparation for online education must strengthen instructor digital literacy skills. In this way, the potential for freer and more democratic access to previously privileged information can be maximized.

## Conclusion

What would Paulo Freire think of Online Learning? In the end the answer to that question hinges on several inter-related questions. Thus, in the problem-posing manner endorsed by Freire, I conclude with a series of questions for practitioners of critical pedagogy who teach in the online environment to consider.

- How can online educational technologies be employed to counter a top-down, banking-oriented approach to learning and be used to create constructivist, democratic classrooms where students and teachers interact in collaborative production of knowledge?
- How can online education be used to create communal connections across geography, culture, and worldviews thereby countering the tendency to atomize learners in their individualistic and isolated learning modes?
- How can online instructors help their students recognize how online teaching and learning occurs within a cyberculture, which itself implies certain values, beliefs and life principles?
- How can online educators encourage their students to interrogate the neoliberal, capitalistic context which has given rise to and continues to shape online education and challenge its assumptions in the pursuit of a more equitable and just society?
- What are creative methods online instructors can employ to help their students embody their learning by engaging in embodied praxis-oriented activities as part of their learning efforts?

Given the explicit and implicit investment both students and teachers have in their economic and social survival, this process of liberating education is always at best a compromised enterprise (Carroll-Miranda, 2011). As employees of the university whose mission is to enable students to fit and thrive in the dominant system, faculty face the temptation to compromise their essential academic and pedagogical values. Likewise, because most students attend the university in order to become employable, even the most critically and socially conscious learners can find themselves caught between their need for a job and their desire to do the "right thing." Thus the challenge for critical pedagogues is to maintain a clear fixation on their revolutionary values and social vision, while working in the spaces allowed by academic freedom and seeking to "[fill] the concepts of [one's] pedagogy with liberating forces" (Escobar et al., 1994, p. 87).

Ultimately, a tension exits between the tendency of technology to supersede the learning process and the creativity of teachers and learners to subvert the very environment designed to pacify and subordinate them. Like it or not, critical educators find themselves in a world largely defined and shaped by telecommunication technologies. The challenge in our time is to turn those technologies toward the pursuit of social and political liberation, so they can become the tool for empowering engaged citizens committed to creating a more equitable and just world in which to live, work, and learn.

This article has been reprinted with permission from *The International Journal of Critical Pedagogy*.

Boyd, D. (2016). What would Paulo Freire think of Blackboard™: Critical pedagogy in an age of online learning. *The International Journal of Critical Pedagogy*, 7(1), 165-186.

## Note

1. See also Western Governors University website: www.westgov.org

## References

Adair, D., Alman, S., Budzick, D., Grisham, L., Mancini, M., & Thackaberry, A. S. (2014). Many shades of MOOCs. *Internet Learning*, 3(1), 53–72.

Allen, I. E., & Seaman, J. (2003). *Sizing the opportunity: The quality and extent of online education in the United States, 2002 and 2003*. The Sloan Consortium. Retrieved at http://sloancon sortium.org/ publications/survey/sizing_the_opportunity2003

Allen, I. E., & Seaman, J. (2013). *Changing course: Ten years of tracking online education in United States*. Babson Survey Research Group and Quahog Research Group, LLC. Retrieved at http://sloanconsortium.org/publications/survey/changing_ course_2012

Anderson, J. (2014). The second digital divide: The effects of ethnicity and socioeconomic status on student technology access and use outside the school day (Doctoral Dissertation). Retrieved at http:// paperroom.ipsa.org/papers/paper_36182.pdf

Baggaley, J. (2013). MOOC rampant. *Distance Education*, 34(3), 368378.

Bawden, D. (2008). Origins and concepts of digital literacy. In C. Lankshear & M. Knobel (Eds.), *Digital literacies: Concepts, policies and practices* (pp. 17–32). New York: Peter Lang.

Carey, K. (2012, Sept 7). Into the future with MOOC's. *Chronicle of Higher Education*, 59(2) Retrieved from EBSCOHost.

Carroll-Miranda, J. (2011). Emancipatory technologies. In C. Mallott & B. Porfilio (Eds.), *Critical pedagogy in the twenty-first century: A new generation of scholars* (pp. 521–539). Charlotte, NC: Information Age Publishing.

Clement, C. (2014). Can we keep the internet free? *YES! Magazine.* Retrieved at http://www.yesmagazine.org/issues/the-power-ofstory/can-we-keep-the-internet-free?utm_source=YTW&utm_ medium=Email&utm_campaign=20140516

Congressional Digest. (2013). Access to telecommunications technology: Bridging the digital divide in the United States. *Congressional Digest, 92*(4), 2–5.

Education Week. (2014). Vast digital divide found in nation's schools. *Education Week.* Retrieved at EBSCOHost.

Escobar, M., Fernandez, A., Guevara-Niebla, G., & Freire, P. (1994). *Paulo Freire on higher education: A dialogue at the National University of Mexico.* Albany, NY: State University of New York.

Feenberg, A. (2009). Critical theory of technology. In J. Olsen, S. Pederson, & V. Hendricks (Eds.), *A companion to the philosophy of technology* (pp. 146–153). Malden, MA: Wiley-Blackwell.

Fleming, N. (2012). Digital divide strikes college-admissions process. *Education Week, 32*(13). Retrieved at EBSCOHost.

Freire, P. (1988). *Teachers as cultural workers: Letters to those who dare to teach* (D. Macedo, D. Koike, & A. Oliveira, Trans.). Boulder, CO: Westview Press.

Freire, P. (2007). *Pedagogy of the oppressed, 30$^{th}$ Anniversary Edition.* New York: Continuum Press.

Freire, P. (2014). *Pedagogy of commitment* (D. Brookshaw & A. Oliveira, Trans.). Boulder, CO: Paradigm Publishers.

Galloway, A. (2014, July 2). *FCC plan could make Internet gated community, advocates say.* VTDIGGER. https://vtdigger.org/2014/07/02/fcc-plan-make-internet-gated-community-advocates-say/

Garn, M. (2009). On the edge of innovation: Transition and transformation in statewide administrative models for online learning. *New Directions for Higher Education, 146*(Summer 2009), 55–64.

Glance, D. G., Forsey, M., & Riley, M. (2013). The pedagogical foundations of massive open online courses. *First Monday, 18*(5). Retrieved at http://firstmonday.org/ojs/index.php/fm/rt/printerFriendly/4350/3673

Gomez, M. V. (2009). Emanuel Levinas & Paul Freire: The ethics of responsibility for the face-to-face interaction in the virtual world. *International Journal of Instruction, 2*(1), 27–58.

Goral, T. (2013). A conversation with Tony Bates. *University Business, 16*(2), 44–45.

Hamilton, E., & Feenberg, A. (2005). The technical codes of online education. *E-Learning, 2*(2), 104–121.

Harasim, L. (2000). Shift happens: Online education as a new paradigm of learning. *The Internet and Higher Education, 3*(1–2), 41–61.

Kashi, S., & Dessinger, J. C. (2010). Paulo Freire's relevance to online instruction and performance improvement. *Performance Improvement, 49*(2), 17–21.

Macedo, D. (1998). Foreword. *Teachers as cultural workers: Letters to those who dare to teach* (pp. ix–xx). Boulder, CO: Westview Press.

Martin, G., & Riele, K. (2011). A place-based critical pedagogy in turbulent times: Restoring hope for alternative futures. In C. Malott & B. Porfilio (Eds.), *Critical pedagogy in the twenty-first century: A new generation of scholars* (pp. 23–52). Charlotte, NC: Information Age Publishing.

McCurry, D. (2000). Multimedia knowledge and culture production: On the possibility of critical and ethical pedagogy resulting from the current push for technology in the classroom. *Bulletin of Science Technology & Society, 20*(2), 100–105.

McLaren, P. (1994). Foreword. *Paulo Freire on higher education: A dialogue at the National University of Mexico* (pp. ix–xxxiii). Albany, NY: State University of New York.

Meyer, K. (2009). Western Governors University: Creating the first virtual university. *New Directions for Higher Education, 146*(Summer 2009), 35–43.

Mossberger, K., Tolbert, C., & Anderson, C. (2014). Digital citizenship: Broadband, mobile use, and activities online. Paper presented at the International Political Science Association Conference, Montreal, Canada. July 2014.

Mossberger, K., Tolbert, C., & Gilbert, M. (2006). Race, place and information technology. *Urban Affairs Review, 41*(5), 583–620.

Palloff, R., & Pratt, K. (2007). *Building online learning communities: Effective strategies for the virtual classroom.* San Francisco: Jossey-Bass.

Poore, M. (2011). Digital literacy: Human flourishing and collective intelligence in a knowledge society. *Literacy Learning: The Middle Years 19*(2), 20–26.

Shor, I., & Freire, P. (1987). *A pedagogy for liberation: Dialogues on transforming education.* Westport, CT: Bergin & Garvey.

Srinivasan, R. (2006). Where information society and community voice intersect. *The Information Society, 22*, 355–3675.

Zickhur, K. (2013). Who's not online and why. *Pew Research Center Internet & American Life Project*, Washington, D.C.

CHAPTER TWO

# Teaching Critical Pedagogy Online: What Would Paulo Freire Say?

TANIA RAMALHO

Knowing is the task of Subjects, not of objects. It is as a Subject, and only as such, that a man or a woman can really know. In the learning process the only person who really learns is s/he who appropriates what is learned, who apprehends and thereby re-invents that learning: s/he who is able to apply the appropriated learning to concrete existential situations. On the other hand, the person who is filled by another with "contents" whose meaning s/he is not aware of, which contradict his or her way of being in the world, cannot learn because s/he is not challenged. Thus, in a situation of knowing, teacher and student must take on the role of conscious Subjects, mediated by the knowable object that they seek to know (Freire, 2007, p. 93).

I depart on this journey of describing and reflecting on my online course—Critical Pedagogy—from this quote by Freire (1974/2007) in *Education for Critical Consciousness*. He intimates a core condition for learning: the learner must be a subject, an agent in the pedagogical experience. The learner cannot be an object, a passive recipient of someone's action of imparting knowledge. The learner subject recreates knowledge by acting consciously within the context of his or her life as an individual and as a member of communities.

My students are teachers pursuing a master's degree, as required for K-12 permanent teacher certification in the state of New York. Computer technology affords a distance that makes it easier and less expensive to take classes outside of the traditional in-person classroom. It does not allow, however, for the type of personal interaction between bodies where instructor and students are able to more immediately respond to shifting energy levels, emotional states, subtle gestures, impromptu questions, answers, and suggestions. When teaching online, most of the time I interact with a name on the screen. I relate to what and how this student can convey a message in writing, and with my own background, always in check, and imagination.

Given the distance, it is not easy for me to assess students' maturity as subjects—the important condition of knowledge that Freire assumes. I do know most have been through a public educational system that affords minimal opportunity to consider critical perspectives about United States society and history (Rivage-Seul, 2018). I consider the higher education experience, where attending a critically-informed course depends on the luck of a draw for most majors. The American educational system is "hard wired" to keep people outside of the country elites as objects, in the shape of obedient future workers, more precisely (McLaren & Jandrić, 2020).

The pressure of objectification forces continues when my students take their first teaching jobs, mostly in public schools in New York State but also in other states, particularly in the warmer South. It is clear: limited agency is afforded to teachers in public schools nationwide, including those serving the poor and racialized minorities (Davidson, 2009; Wright et al., 2018). Teachers are to follow orders of district and schools that in recent times have increasingly worked against the developmental capacities, needs, and interests of the children and adolescents they are supposed to be serving. The influences on education of "educational" corporations and their ethos, along with a generalized culture of consumerism, have expanded since the 1980s, under the neoliberal political-economic order (Bailey, 2013; Giroux, 2004, 2008, 2012; Ravitch, 2014). Opportunities for academic freedom and democratic practices in teaching have all but vanished under the smokescreen of "proof" and "accountability," shaping and reinforcing authoritarian—necrophilic (Fromm, 1964)—public school cultures.

Teaching critical pedagogy, online or in the classroom, I assume that my young adult students are still struggling with the terms of becoming subjects. Most are women under the lingering impact of a sexist culture that intensifies the forces of objectification. Following Freire's critical pedagogical standpoint, my principal course objective is to empower the development of students as subjects through understanding and enacting critical consciousness in their concrete existential conditions, interconnecting personal and occupational everyday life. In this paper, I offer a history and rationale of the critical pedagogy curriculum I developed for this purpose, and examples of assignments and assessments, with a greater focus on online course discussions. After such reflections, based on Freirean thought and the testimonies about who he was as a human being, I conclude with a hypothetical answer to the questions: What would Paulo Freire have to say about teaching critical pedagogy online? What suggestions would he make to a progressive online educator?

## Background

When I took the job at SUNY Oswego in 2000, the then strong and popular Literacy graduate program was undergoing restructuring. The coordinator, Dr. Claire Putala, asked me to teach a new foundations of education course, LIT 500, Critical Pedagogy (this title was later changed to Critical Literacy and Pedagogy to satisfy outside evaluators who could not realize the connection between critical literacy and critical pedagogy). Professors in the program sought a Freirean approach to support the Foundations of Literacy and other courses, guided by an overall commitment to social justice education (SUNY Oswego's School of Education Conceptual Framework, n.d.). For me, it was a challenge and a dream come true to have the honor of engaging students with the seminal work of Freire, a Brazilian like me, and his American critical scholar friends, Macedo, Giroux, McLaren, Horton, Shorr, Kincheloe and Steinberg, hooks, Darder, and others. The course became a requirement for both master's programs, in Literacy and in Curriculum and Instruction.

Excitement notwithstanding, I have had a lot to learn from my students since the beginning of Critical Pedagogy, until today, teaching it online. The course has changed and still changes depending on the students, though its central structure—and some of its related texts—have remained stable over time. As an example of a challenge, I was not successful in teaching the full text of Freire's (1970) work, *Pedagogy of the Oppressed*[1] to beginning graduate students. They resisted it, saying it was a difficult, challenging, and slow reading This was much before Darder's (2018) book that provides background concepts needed for American students to fully understand Freire, or the detailed LitCharts (n.d.) summary and explanation of the book presently available online.

My first few sections of Critical Pedagogy in the face-to-face classroom yielded similar observations in student evaluations, which indicted me in their too frequent question: What does this (course content) have to do with *actual teaching*? Obviously, I was not being successful in connecting critical theoretical concepts to everyday life in K–12 classrooms. A summary of my untested reasons for my students' perceptions are as follows:

1. Some of the critical pedagogical concepts (dialectic, consciousness and conscientization, hegemony, and oppression, for example), especially when working with white female students, can be challenging. Most even tend to avoid uttering or writing down ordinary words such as "racism" and "sexism."
2. Such concepts do not seem to be relevant or interesting to beginner teachers because they have no currency or immediacy in day-to-day life within conservative capitalist schooling and are largely absent from mass entertainment culture (Chomsky, 2002; Post, 1985);
3. On top of the difficulty, sadly I assume that most—not all—students face difficulties with reading itself. Reading in general requires effort, attention, and habit. Reading to study is work. It requires some level of ability, including comprehension, which vary widely among my students. My enduring concern—how can I support students in this reading?
4. Most of my students have little time (or interest) to dedicate to studying outside the classroom because they must work; many are teaching or substitute-teaching full-time, while pursuing a master's degree. Some try to pile graduate courses because of financial constraints or because they "want to get it over with" and "move on." A master's degree in education is regarded primarily as a requirement to achieve permanent employment, not necessarily as an opportunity to learn and grow as a professional and person, despite some acknowledging "learning a lot." Above all, students' lives include relationships, spouses and children who demand attention. The myth that a three-hour graduate credit requires at least nine hours of study outside the classroom is largely that, an academic myth. We make do.

How did I solve the problem of demonstrating the connection between the theories in support of critical pedagogy and their application to everyday teaching practice? I found a textbook that solved this puzzle to a great extent—*Critical Pedagogy, Notes from the Real World*, by Professor Joan Wink (2011). The numerous examples of critically-informed teachers' actions in her book saved the day. I also developed "what you can do" lists for every social justice-related issue we discussed.

With Wink's book by my side, I established myself as the professor of Critical Pedagogy. In the first few academic years the program served up to sixty or more graduate students. Unfortunately—or fortunately, depending on how we argue—times and conditions have since changed. It is no news that the number of young people who want to become teachers has dwindled nationwide (Flannery, 2016; Parterlow, 2019). Supporting evidence also comes from the 2018 PDK poll uncovering for the first time that fifty-four percent of American parents do not wish their child to become public-school teachers (p. K 7), the highest percentage since 1969, when the first poll was taken.

The reasons for decreasing numbers of teacher candidates are complex and telling. On one hand, we face a demographic shift (Hamilton et al., 2020), with declining birth rates. With better paying jobs available to choose from, teaching does not seem to have the same appeal as before. In addition, students have just left a public school environment where they witness teachers being disrespected, feeling stressed, and burnt-out. Teachers are submitted to whims of corporations selling curriculum materials to districts, which then they are obliged to follow, oftentimes in lockstep, to prepare students for what many regard as meaningless standardized tests. Additionally, under neoliberal schooling exemplified in No Child Left Behind (2002) and Race to the Top (2009) national policies, American youth continues to be treated instrumentally as future workers who will compete in the global economy—not as complex, cooperative, human beings and citizens with a say in democracy (Dewey, 1916; Giroux, 2008, 2009; Noddings, 2013).

For future workers, skills in numeracy, regimented reading, and pre-formatted writing, carefully assessed through an array of corporate-issued tests, have been the focus of a narrower, skills-based, curriculum. Students have little chance to engage in critical discussion of social, political, and economic issues of the age—less likely to be on the test—along with diminished opportunities for creative thought and action through increasingly limited offerings in the arts, music, and sports (Beyerbach et al., 2017; Noddings, 2013). The Internet, social media, and games have reigned over young lives, with the latest drama, celebrities, Hollywood fare, and other highlights of popular culture taking center stage (Drotner & Livingstone, 2008; Ruddock, 2013; Valkenburg & Piotrowski, 2017). Public school teaching is no longer an enticing occupation. On our campus, communications and business strands are the preferred majors.

As a result of overall declining numbers of the student population, numbers of enrollees in the undergraduate teacher education program have decreased accordingly, reflecting a national trend (U.S. Department of Education, 2015). Because historically our graduates used to feed the enrollments in our graduate programs, numbers here have declined there as well. Our established, face-to-face, and rigorous Literacy and Master's in Education programs, of which the department has been so proud, now attract fewer students. One strategy to counteract declining numbers has been to offer at least some online courses, which other institutions in the SUNY system moved to adopt sooner, including offering fully online literacy programs.

My chairperson asked me to make the move to online teaching of Critical Pedagogy for the Master's in Education; the Literacy program continued in the classroom, but, presently, it too is being restructured. Wanting to support the department, I agreed. The point here is that I did not create the online course from scratch; I adapted the course from the classroom setting to the online environment. A related point is that I was already using the online platform at the time, ANGEL, mostly as assignment depository and means of group communication. To develop the fully online course, I had some technical support, but I wish I had been more proactive in reading and experimenting with online course design literature. Still, I adapted the content and went live. After a few semesters, campus changed platforms to Blackboard, where we are still working. This change was relatively smooth.

I will discuss my critical pedagogy curriculum next, before delving into details of the online course structure.

## Critical Pedagogy Course Curriculum Content

This section provides a summary narrative of the critical pedagogy curriculum I have created with these aims in mind for my students: to become critically aware subjects and to consider teaching from a critical pedagogy-informed stance. The two purposes are interconnected; one cannot teach critically without becoming a critically conscious subject; both are also life-long developmental tasks. In other words, this is a path to follow, not a destination at which to arrive, or yet another teaching method to adopt. I am also clear about this curriculum being just one the many possible ways to approach this complex field. It reflects, above all, not the way I personally learned critical pedagogy, but a possible way to organize it for my students to scaffold future learning.

There are four points of entry to my curriculum approach. First, a discussion on the concept of power and the social dynamics of domination and subordination; second, how power plays out in models of teaching. A unit on understanding political perspectives and visions for education of three mainstream American political parties follows. Finally, we study the tradition of critical pedagogy and on how to conduct critically-informed classrooms.

To become critically conscious, a person needs to examine power issues stemming from the normative social dynamics of domination and subordination, the landscapes of the oppressed and oppressor relations in society, in Freire's terms. Domination and subordination take place in human relationships at interlocked individual and social group levels. Historically dominant and subordinate groups and individuals demonstrate learned behavioral and attitudinal characteristics, which are also interconnected. For example, dominants believe in their superiority.

They are supposedly "naturally" better, more knowledgeable, and correct than the subordinated, always a "lesser." Uncritically, subordinates learn to accept such portrayal and condescending treatment until (and if) coming to understand his or her own situation of subordination not as "natural" but as socially constructed. Every human being experiences dominant and subordinate positions from birth, at different ages, and as members of groups, according to the relations of gender, sexuality, "race"/ethnicity, social class/occupational group, age, and ability, in their societies.

Domination—being in a place of power over others directly or indirectly through the benefits of discriminatory laws and social customs—may result in temporary or even permanent inequality between parties, an eminent distinction that Jean Baker Miller (1976) makes in her classical text, *Toward a New Psychology of Women*. Temporary relations of domination, which create temporary inequality, aim at ending domination as the subordinate grows and matures and becomes a subject under the guidance of the "dominator," an older, more mature, knowledgeable, and experienced person or group, or someone provisionally privileged for contingent reasons. Ideally, the relations between parent and child or of a teacher and student serve as example—the more mature adult cares that the young become equally knowing, capable, and independent, a being for him/herself—a subject.

In counter position to temporary inequality, in "permanent" relations of domination, the dominator oppresses the subordinate through complex mechanisms of exploitation, marginalization, disempowerment, cultural imperialism, and violence (Young, 1990). Sexism, heterosexism, white supremacism, racism and ethnocentrism, classism and elitism, ableism and adultism are expressions of interlocking differences, inequalities, and oppressions that progressive humans historically have been working to eliminate by envisioning and enacting just relations based on reciprocity, cooperation, mutuality, equity, and equality.

Teachers have an important role to play here. We must understand and enact our relationship to students as a temporary inequality; we contribute individually and as members of the occupational class of teachers toward the growth and development of society's young, hopefully empowering them to become subjects. As teachers—contingent "dominators"—we are to avoid the mode of relating of permanent domination which permeates society and with which we are well too familiar, consciously, or not. We must resist subordinating our students through oppressive practices I call "teacher terrorism," as they can strike students unexpectedly, such as harsh or inappropriate punishments, silencing, ignoring, condescending treatment, doubting, tracking, low expectations, derisory curricula and instruction, and even the implementing of curricula and tests enforced by outsiders of the relation teacher-student. In fact, critically-informed teachers, beyond the enactment of just relations with students, must work counter- hegemonically in classrooms and schools, confronting the "isms" of the interlocking oppressions outlined above—in themselves, in school, and community.

Related to the dynamics of power, domination, subordination, and inequality described, the second initial strand in this critical pedagogy curriculum comes from the comparison of three ideal models of teaching: transmission, generative, and transformative (Wink, 2011). In the traditional and still most prevalent model of teaching, transmission—or, in Freire's (1970) words, "banking education"—the teacher is the knower who conveys knowledge to student-depositories, in an active to passive oppressive relation. In the generative (constructivist-based) model, teachers organize students to work together to learn the material cooperatively and actively. In the transformative, or critical pedagogical model, teacher and students go further, they pose critical questions related to their real lives in community, conduct research to understand problems better, and take action to solve them. This questioning and action contribute to changing participants' personal and social circumstances as well as the development of democratic subjects.

The three models of teaching—transmission, generative and transformative—are interconnected. The social justice-oriented critical pedagogical model is slowly evolving as teachers learn about it, become politically conscious, and encounter circumstances that demand its use. From such understandings, the course proceeds to examine briefly what "critical" in critical pedagogy means as a political-philosophical stance within the history of Western thought, with an impact on education. Arbitrarily, I place the idea of "critical" in Karl Marx, followers of the Frankfurt School, and others. Critical views about the individual, society, legitimate sources of knowledge, the state and government, the economy, and the role of education are then compared to views in the tradition of Liberalism, with its right and left wings. More concretely, students move to read the platforms of three U.S. parties, which to a greater or lesser extent represent political perspectives (conservative-liberal and critical)—Republican, Democratic and Green parties, with a focus on proposed education policies.

The emphasis on political perspectives in the course aims to educate politically for greater recognition of the importance of understanding their impact on educational policy—for example, the conservative nature of No Child Left Behind, Race to the Top, and former Secretary of Education, Betsy DeVos' signature program, Education Freedom Scholarship. This political knowledge is required of citizens in a democratic society, particularly those who function as role models—teachers—and is also necessary to critical literacy. One needs to be able to identify the political perspectives behind texts, from newspaper articles, to educational policies and entire curricula.

The fourth and last strand in this critical pedagogy curriculum comprises the historical and theoretical foundations of critical pedagogy, and "how to do" critical pedagogy, following in the steps of Joan Wink (2011), and texts by Freire, Giroux, and McLaren. We examine steps in problem-posing (Freire, 1970), and discuss teacher relationships with students and parents. We also look at media influence on children and youth cultures, using the Walt Disney Corporation as an example of deep political implications of corporate-shaped imagination prevailing in children's culture, from pretty princesses and handsome princes, to "evil" Middle Eastern men (Giroux, 1995). This I also find essential to the development of critical literacy. Manufactured media images especially impact the subjectivities of young female teachers.

The course ends with students challenged to put it all together in a text with their course-materials-informed definitions and explanations about critical pedagogy and what it requires from teachers, students, parents, and communities.

## Online Course Structure, Assignments and Assessment

On the Blackboard platform there are two important links I utilize most: *Course Information* and *Content*. Under *Course Information*, I include a letter of welcome; a conventional syllabus, with course description, objectives, readings, assignments with percentage point distribution, and grade scale from A to C and E, failure; the schedule with topics and readings; rubrics for writing and discussion; and required university policies about intellectual integrity and non-discrimination.

I also include a one-page hand-out, *how to read and explain complex material*, which communicates ways to approach challenging readings. As already mentioned, some graduate students still struggle with college-level reading and writing. I am sensitive to this due to my own struggles as an English language learner, being aware of comprehension challenges, especially in the less familiar, more abstract critical theoretical texts. Part of the issue is the students' biographies as readers and difficulties they have faced in developing reading skills. More importantly, how much actual reading do they do, for what purposes, and how much interest in reading, outside of social media, do they display? I try to gage answers from students' posts or ask them directly in conversation. I always indicate privately and publicly that, if we tend to them, reading and writing are life-long developing skills that enhance the quality of one's life, personally and professionally.

While the *Course Information* link houses general material, *Content* includes weekly folders related to specific topics or modules of the curriculum. Week 1 is a *Welcome to Critical Pedagogy* folder. It includes a *To Do* List that refers students back to the *Course Information* page and contains a link for personal introductions. I take these seriously; when I read students' introductions, I keep short notes which become helpful reminders of some of their traits, life situations and experiences for when I need a refresher as I read later posts. I ask them to take the introductions seriously as well. I ask them to write about family, community background, and significant others, including pets; education in general, teacher education preparation, teaching, and other work experience; hobbies, travel, media tastes, and anything else about themselves they wish to share with the class. I usually also ask an ending question—for example, "If you had to summarize one principle from which to live the good life, what would it be?"

Besides submitting introductions, I ask course participants to read and comment on everyone's submissions. Personal introductions represent an important aspect of social presence online. Often, class members find out they know each other from other courses, have attended or taught in the same schools, come from the same or neighboring communities, or identify common interests and backgrounds. Besides offering the opportunity to get to know the students individually at some level, introductions are also instrumental to organizing work or discussion groups.

After the introductory module and to the end of the term, each week's folder includes two documents entitled, *Overview and Objectives* and *To Do List*. Respective links to discussions and other assignments also appear here. In *Overview and Objectives*, I briefly summarize the topic addressed and its explicit learning objectives. The idea is to make the student aware of the specific concepts they should acquire from the readings. I assess this knowledge perfunctorily through discussion posts and a reaction-paper type of assignment. The *To Do List* aims to be very explicit about what I expect students to perform during the week. Number 1 starts, "read *Overview and Objectives* above." Assuming that students may look to cut corners to save time, I clearly point out what my expectations are.

Each word in each prompt has to be carefully thought out and clearly written. In new iterations of the course, I often find myself changing phrases to make directions and statements clearer to students and myself. I keep in mind that the written word on an electronic page is the principal way of communication in an online asynchronous course. Clarity of expression and appropriate tone of prompts, and, more important, of personal and public messages, are central to the work of the online instructor. These require clarity and thoughtfulness, and they can be improved from one semester to the next.

Among the instructional activities, discussion and dialogue are central to critical pedagogy and will be discussed in detail in the next section. Alternatively, I ask students to write response papers, oftentimes as part of a discussion strand. Response papers ask for students' thoughts and feelings concerning the topic and connections to a teacher's experience. They are different than summarizing concepts and arguments in short papers, which I use to check for understanding of more complex content. Assignments may depend on the topic, or other reasons affecting the course, such a longer than usual required reading assignment. Truthfully, sometimes my personal workload is too heavy with other courses or departmental demands, and I decrease the online students' load so I can respond to them when I have more time. Teaching online requires more work on the part of the instructor—let me make this very clear.

Another type of assignment is the web quest. In Critical Pedagogy, the quest is always about authors we read. I ask for the student to find any type of material, including articles about or by the author, video interviews, or educational videos; then, they must write no more than two strong paragraphs describing what they learned and providing the web link so that others can access the site.

Authors for the web search include Freire; students are surprised to find out about the extent of his global influence as well as his personal biography, having been in exile during the U.S.-sponsored military dictatorship in Brazil (1964–1984). Though now retired, Joan Wink, the author of the book we read, still maintains an excellent website which includes very useful materials for K-12 teachers, and, particularly, bilingual education teachers. Wink is a true source of inspiration for teachers.

Other authors include Henry Giroux, who we read for his understanding of popular culture's influence on children and youth culture, Disney, in particular (Giroux, 1995). Peter McLaren (2003) also maintains a personal-professional website that surprises students from upstate New York for content they view as radical and revolutionary. In all four authors, students find examples of people who started their professional lives as teachers who advocated for their students and became leading critical pedagogy scholars in their work to change the world.

As each week progresses, students establish a schedule where the week's work is open on Blackboard on Sunday evening. They are supposed to read assigned texts and write a reaction paper by Thursday evening, in preparation for the discussion. They engage in the discussion from Thursday until Sunday evening. I monitor the discussion and contribute as I find pertinent, always with intent to clarify or reinforce concepts in the readings. I check and read reaction papers on Fridays and all contributions to the discussion on Monday. I then summarize the main points of the discussion, hoping to reinforce main ideas, copying short passages from the students' discussion posts, and identifying the writer. This functions as assemblage of ideas about the topics, and hopefully, also contributes to social presence. I send this summary in an email to the class, usually with a message of encouragement and thanking students for their work—each based on my real feelings of respect for their efforts, as I am aware of their complex, often challenging, lives as young adults.

For assessment, I use two rubrics, a writing rubric for papers and a discussion post rubric. For the summative assessment, discussions and final integrative papers weigh the most, and reaction papers, midterm, and web quests weigh relatively less. I put a premium on how they present arguments in the discussion—reflective of knowledge learned from the readings and personal inquiry; how they respond to their colleagues; and on their ability to integrate the concepts in the course in a coherent and hopefully compelling manner in competent writing.

## Online Discussions

Communication among members of a classroom community is the essential critical pedagogical educational strategy, online and in the classroom. The word "discussion" is more commonly used to name communicative exchange about a topic in an online course. Freire (1970) used "dialogue" in developing his pedagogy of the oppressed. While communications specialists distinguish between the two concepts, discussion and dialogue (Garmston & Wellman, 1999), in my course, I use the terms interchangeably. In online communication, sometimes *discussion* takes places (examination of issues that may evolve into debate, where one is vying to have a point-of-view demonstrated and accepted), and, at other times, *dialogue* (joint examination of or inquiry about a topic) happens. Distinguishing further, *conversation* (freer com exchange of ideas about personal or professional matters) frequently comes about. All three represent communication between class participants and contribute to the creation of the shared flow of knowledge in critical pedagogy.

I use three types of discussion prompts: choose your own topic to discuss; summarize a section of the reading and discuss it; and discuss a particular topic in the reading. Each serves a particular purpose. When I ask for a summary of a particular argument or concept in the reading and discussion about it, my first concern is students' understanding of the point the author was making; then, I want them to apply what they understood to a new situation.

For example, as already indicated, it is important for teachers to understand the distinction between permanent and temporary inequalities (Miller, 1976) resulting from the dynamics of domination and subordination. Under conditions of permanent inequality between males and females, the interest (in the abstract, cf. Habermas, 1971) of the male dominator is to keep females subordinate through the interconnected faces of oppression (exploitation, marginalization, disempowerment, cultural imperialism, and violence). Gender justice—respect, reciprocity, equity and equality between man and woman—only develops through women's struggles of liberation in everyday life, through history. The ordinary school classroom reflects sex and gender disparity, with teachers often unconsciously and unknowingly treating male, female students, trans, and nonbinary students in ways that aid to the persistence of sexism, heteronormativity, or transphobia.

For a counterhegemonic effect, teachers' praxis needs to be conscious and resisting of the intersectionality of all the "isms," racism, classism, sexism, heterosexism, etc., working against the grain of each permanent inequality and their oppressive dimensions as manifested in classrooms. This includes violence in all forms (physical, emotional, and cognitive) embedded in "teacher terrorism." At the same time, teachers need to understand their own relationship of inequality vis-à-vis students as terminating at the end of the school term, from the perspective of the individual teacher; the relationship ends again when students eventually graduate, from the perspective of the collective of teachers who contributed to the students' education along the years of schooling. When teachers are conscious of the temporary nature of relations with their students, they hopefully keep in check personal attitudes and behaviors that reproduce in classrooms oppressive permanent inequalities due to social class, race, gender, or ability differences. Teachers' practices then may become focused on empowerment of all students.

Given the critical nature of the content just discussed, my prompt for online discussion of temporary and permanent inequalities asks students to write two posts—a summary of the issue of inequality as Miller developed, and an answer the application question: Why is important to teachers to know the distinction between temporary and permanent relations of inequality? As ideas flow, I can verify students' understanding of the concept.

I write prompts asking students to discuss a topic in the reading directly as it relates to their teaching experience, without preoccupation about summarizing related content in the readings. After examining notions of power and empowerment, for example, I enquire—Which forms of empowerment do you facilitate in your classroom? This question, like others of its kind, generates opportunities for the class to reflect and share approaches to teaching practice. I offer three forms of power:

Power *over*, found in any scenario of control and domination;
Power *with*, power generated through cooperation between actors; and,
Power from *within*, individually embodied power reflecting body-mind capacities, such as intelligence, physical fitness, skills, voice, spirituality, social ethical traits, value sets, and so on.

This simple categorization of types of power, with obvious expressions in classrooms and elsewhere, is just one way of looking at this concept which many thinkers have studied extensively (Hobbes, Nietzsche, Foucault, and others). Again, students in the online course learn to regard and name their actions in classrooms as exercises in teacher power, and empowerment (or disempowerment!) of students.

The third type of prompt leaves students free to discuss anything they wish based on ideas from the readings. As a result, they tend to share ideas that intuitively speak to them. A student observed (Fall semester, reinforcing my belief in open discussions in critical pedagogy:

> I appreciate the opportunity to have an open discussion this week. With so many things going on in our country that relate to these readings, I believe we won't have any shortage of topics to discuss.

In the chapter about capitalism, poverty, and elitism, students were concerned about the abuse of the natural environment; about how capitalist culture teaches people to want to imitate the unsustainable life of the rich and famous; and the circumstance of lower pay for workers who care for or teach children, including teachers.

To recapitulate the ideas on online discussions, to fashion adequate prompts the instructor-facilitator needs to be clear about what critical pedagogical objectives are to be addressed—those relevant to content and those relevant to the experience of teachers as well as understandings about larger social issues and their effects on individuals and cohorts. I am not afraid of changing prompts and even of saying, after the fact, that I had not been clear or explicit enough. In this process, I also learn as a teacher; Freire says, there is no teaching without learning and no learning without teaching.

In terms of assessing discussion posts, there is always room for doubt relative to judgment. I have used a four-point scale—below, average, above average, and excellent—that recognizes two aspects of students' posts, quality of writing and content, implying contribution to the flow of critical ideas. A student may offer an excellent contribution to the discussion, making text-to-text connections in ways that open paths to thinking about the topic; still, the writing may contain mistakes. My students' most consistent writing mistake has to do with organization of the text where a traditional introduction, topical paragraphs, and a conclusion are missing, or where there is careless repetition of the same ideas. Students know that I do not support submissions of one long paragraph posts, with twenty or more lines with no breaks and addressing many topics. I insist on clarity. I urge them to think critically about their own and others' writing, always keeping in mind they are improving.

By the eighth week of the semester, most students can shape what I consider above average to excellent posts with strong ideas, often with connections to outside sources relevant to content. These serve as a basis for others to comment, their contributions turning into dialogue, discussion, and conversation. Sometimes there is a tendency for participants to offer conversation about personal issues, especially in the beginning of the course. Unfortunately, trite content sometimes masks avoidance of the topics when students hurry through or do not read assigned texts. Substantive, more real, communication does take place by the end of the course. One student sent me the following message in an email at the course's conclusiom in the Fall 2019:

> The community you created from an online course was incredible and I'm so happy to have been a part of it. The perspective I gained has now followed me into teaching and beyond as I question the way I perceive and present information. Thank you for all you did last semester and pushing me to be a better writer and better critical thinker.

Unsolicited, this student provided me with reassurance.

## Am I Doing Critical Pedagogy? What Would Freire Have to Say?

From reading Freire's words, and testimonials from his students, co-workers, and fellow scholars (Gadotti, 1996), I dare to affirm that Freire beyond doubt would have approved the use of computer technology for teaching critical pedagogy online. He would have been intrigued and questioned its implications for liberation and humanization. Freire would have embraced the change. There were no dogmas for him, except his staunch humanism. He lived his beliefs pragmatically, facing situations guided by praxis—the dialectic between reflection and action, theory, and practice.

Do universities need to offer flexibility to students through long distance learning? Yes. This answer can be reduced to a question of supply and demand. However, as scholars have done recently (Andreotti et al., 2016), Freire (1998) would scrutinize the ethical dimensions of online teaching taking place in global higher education in the contexts of what he called the "mean ethos of neoliberalism" (p. 59), and of the more recent Covid-19 pandemic. He would examine online course format and pedagogy, the qualities of the teacher-student relationship, of teaching, content, and of rigorous computer-mediated study.

In *Teachers as Cultural Workers: Letters to Those Who Dare Teach*, published posthumously, Freire (1998) discusses issues relevant to online teaching. He does not provide teachers "how to" assistance on "methods"—recipes for teaching—based on a technical-instrumental interest of knowledge (Habernas, 1971). He provides guidelines based on three other types of human knowledge interests. The first two are Habermas's (1971) practical and emancipatory interests of knowledge (respectively, knowledge needed for communicative or social interactive action; and knowledge required for surmounting oppression). The erotic represents a third interest—life-expanding knowledge of love, beauty, and pleasure (Ramalho, 1985; inspired in Audre Lorde, 1984), ever present in Freire's work.

In his Fourth Letter, Freire (1998) makes clear the seven attributes he expects of progressive teachers—those who care about emancipation of self and of students as subjects (p. 39). These interrelated practical, emancipatory, and biophilic qualities are acquired and honed through the practice of humility; lovingness; courage; tolerance; decisiveness and security; patience-impatience; and joy of living.

Humility heads the list because "no one knows it all" (Freire, 1998, p. 39). It requires courage, self-confidence, self-respect, and respect for others. For Freire, humility is required for listening to others and dialoguing. Humility is obviously necessary to online teaching, due to its extensive efforts in written communication. As an online instructor, I am always "listening" to what students express in their posts and papers and making decisions about when and how to respond. I take the labor intensity of the reading-responding task into consideration, especially in large classes (more than twelve students, in my experience). Common sense, says Freire (1998), is the answer when we are too close to getting lost and too "entrenched in the circuit of [one's] own truth" (p. 40).

Lovingness—loving your students as well as loving teaching, both pleasurable—is indispensable. Freire (1998) refers to such love as "armed love," necessary to face the struggles that teachers experience. Truthfully, as a tenured professor, I do not face struggles such as those Dr. Batya Weinbaum describes in this book about academic contingent labor (Chapter Seventeen), including surveillance, interference with academic freedom, low pay without benefits, and employment instability. I do need, however, the next related quality—courage—to conquer fears arising from concern about student learning and decision-making processes involved in online teaching, such as choice of readings, participation in discussions, grading students' work, and dealing with the various ways in which they resist ideas and the course work itself. Freire (1998) shows the importance of educating one's fears; it is from control of fear that courage there arises.

Concerning tolerance, Freire (1998) writes:

> Being tolerant does not mean acquiescing to the intolerable; it does not mean covering up disrespect; it does not mean coddling the aggressor or disguising aggression. Tolerance is the virtue that teaches us to live with the different. It teaches us to learn from and respect the different. (p. 42)

Setting limits is not outside of tolerance, which "requires respect, discipline, and ethics" (Freire, 1998, p. 42). As indicated before, I require rigor in writing submissions, which demands serious attention to the readings. This does not make me intolerant. This shows decisiveness and security in my own pedagogical principles, a confidence that reveals competence in my field of knowledge, political clarity, and ethical integrity.

I am clear that all my students are different from me, a Brazilian immigrant to the United States, now a senior and critical scholar. With rare exceptions, they have been raised as English-speaking Americans, and they are young. Most identify as coming from political, if not religious, conservative backgrounds. When political discussions take place, I reinforce the idea that I genuinely respect where they stand in their present perspectives. I remind them that they can, and likely will, change over their lifetimes. I also say that I do expect that they really learn to compare the three political perspectives—conservative, liberal, and critical. Upon examining these closely, beyond parties and personalities, over the years, several students have changed political positions while taking the course, disclosing that they now identify as liberal, even occasionally as wholly critical.

Freire (1998) refers to the tension between patience and impatience, and he favors verbal parsimony that characterizes the balance between the two qualities (p. 44). I tend to write parsimoniously when participating in discussions, letting students develop dialogues among themselves. Nonetheless, I write more to reinforce central issues they raise in their posts, while underscoring important critical pedagogy concepts that do not appear yet in their discourse. Here, it is interesting to note that many students may clearly describe but fail to name, for example, the "isms." In face-to-face teaching, in jest, I have had groups repeat aloud together words such as "racism" and "sexism," to give them courage to utter the challenging terms.

The biggest challenge to impatience, for me, has to do with students who take longer to become aware of their writing, who appear to write the first thing that comes to their minds just to finish the task, and do not take time to revise their work with care and attention. Also, in every class there is a student expert in "sausage filling." This is a Brazilian expression describing abundance of talk (or text) but emptiness of meaning. This increases the workload of online teaching and makes me aware of the tension between patience-impatience.

Each of Freire's dispositions leads to the ultimate liberatory and biophilic aims of critical pedagogy—facilitating the development of students as subjects as they become critically conscious about society and their place in it as teachers and encouraging them to do the same for their own students. I have not researched the impact of my Critical Pedagogy course beyond the immediate semester to verify the degree of success in achieving these aims long term. I know that other factors are at play because my course is just one of the many sites of learning my students have experienced over their lifetimes. Immediate feedback that speaks to course impact only takes place at the end of the semester, when I ask students to discuss three things they have learned personally or professionally as participants. In the Fall (2018) semester, a student wrote:

> This course reached me in a specific place of my heart and has opened my mind in new ways of thinking. What this class has taught me is that if I want to be a good teacher, I will always have to be a student. As progressive teachers today, we must be a student in our own career pathway. This is not only in regard to curriculum, classroom management, and teaching methods, but we must be a student of the world. We need to be up to date on current events, participate in local government, being sure that we have a representing voice in education. Although there are many aspects to politics in society, what are those politics going to do for our educational system? Are we collecting data, feedback, and talking to our students as if they are humans? What are we learning, what are we teaching in our classrooms, in society, and in the world? To do critical pedagogy means all these things. It is not only an attempt to know the information available to us, but always keeping an open, malleable mind for the information that will come.

As I read this clearly critical, inquiring, student's passage, I thought, "I would only hope so!"

## Final Thoughts

Writing this chapter gave me the opportunity to express my experience as an online educator in critical pedagogy, as I questioned if I was doing the right thing, if my teaching critical pedagogy online has integrity, and what Paulo Freire would have to say about it. I started by revealing that I was asked to offer the asynchronous course as a response to the changing context of higher education, particularly in teacher education. Like many tasks in higher education, resources were limited, especially time. I had to develop the course rather quickly; time to tweak has happened as I teach or before the next semester is upon us. I do not think these circumstances are unusual at academic workplaces.

I also explained the curriculum I shaped over the years, always wishing I had Critical Pedagogy I and II courses to fully offer the rich content and engage the students for a longer period . As I said, it is not a perfect curriculum. It keeps evolving. However, at the end, students do get a greater sense of where they fit in the world vis-à-vis others, and I want to think that the topics affect their personal decolonial processes as individuals and as teachers.

I described in greater detail the workings of the online course on Blackboard. Here I had to be careful to choose what to include and for which purpose. Reflecting about what I do as an online instructor in terms of "methods" can lead me to many directions because so much is happening. My bigger focus was on online discussions—the best approximation to dialogue—the communicative process at the core of critical pedagogy, which for Freire was face-to-face or through letters, his preferred writing genre, not in virtual space.

In the last section, I try to respond to the questions that led my co-editor Erin Mikulec and I to taking on this project. Are we "doing" critical pedagogy? Is teaching critical pedagogy online fostering the aims of critical pedagogy? Consulting what we can read and learn from Paulo Freire provides us the answer: Yes! Furthermore, the chapters of our colleagues describing their inspiring work reaffirm this answer. Critical pedagogical practices are possible online. Not unflawed, not with absolute precision, but as a road to be made by walking (Horton & Freire, 1990).

## Note

1. I had introduced the *Pedagogy of the Oppressed* as I would have introduced any other book. I talked about Freire and his background as a Brazilian, exiled by a military dictatorship for many years because of his beliefs and actions educating illiterate adults. I described the social context in which the book was written, a historical phase when Latin-American countries were struggling for self-determination that clashed with the imperialist interests of the United States government in the aftermath of the Cuban Revolution. Freire's book had a global impact, including in the United States, where he taught at Harvard and developed connections with Civil Rights leaders. *Pedagogy of the Oppressed* can be considered a philosophical primer for the ensuing field, critical pedagogy. Finally, I also advised students about the book's language, a translation from the original in Portuguese. It requires effort to read and make sense of some of its denser passages, many connecting back to previous passages, in a spiral format that mimics Freire's speech grounded in the life and culture of the Brazilian Northeast.

But I hit an unproductive wall, particularly time limitations that restricted going into depth of analysis required in each chapter. I eventually settled for Chapter Two, where Freire discusses "banking" education. My students got that one clearly—it was relevant to their experience as students themselves and as teachers. In later renditions of the course, I brought in my own summaries of main chapter themes and had students do web searches on Freire and write about what they learned. I still recommend that students make the effort to read the Freire's masterpiece, as we reaffirm the importance of literacy in shaping our subjectivities as individuals and as teachers, which hooks (Hirshorn et al., 1997) also underscores. (As I revise this chapter in February, 2021, a student just let me know she has read Freire and developed a presentation on his work for residents at the hall she directs on campus.)

## References

Andreotti, V., Stein, S. Pashby, K. & Nicholson, M. (2016). Social cartographies as performative devices in research on higher education. *Higher Education Research and Development, 35*(1), 84–99.

Bailey, N. E. (2013). *Misguided education reform*. Rowman & Littlefield Education.

Beyerbach, B., Davis, R. D., & Ramalho, T. (2017). *Activist art in social justice pedagogy. Engaging students in glocal issues through the arts*. Revised edition. Peter Lang.

Chomsky, N. (2002). *Understanding power: The indispensable Chomsky*. The New Press.

Darder, A. (2018). *The student guide to Freire's pedagogy of the oppressed*. Bloomsbury Academic.

Davidson, K. V. (2009). Challenges contributing to teacher stress and burnout. *Southeastern Teacher Education Journal, 2*(2), 47–56.

Dewey, J. (1916). *Democracy and education*. https://en.wikisource.org/wiki/Democracy_and_Education

Drotner, K., & Livingstone, S. (2008). *International handbook of children, media and culture*. SAGE Publications.

Flannery, M. E. (2016, March 15). *Survey: Numbers of future teachers reach all-time low*. NEA. http://neatoday.org/2016/03/15/future-teachers-at-all-time-low/

Freire, P. (1970). *Pedagogia do oprimido* [Pedagogy of the oppressed]. Editora Paz e Terra.

Freire, P. (1998). *Teachers as cultural workers: Letters to those who dare teach*. Westview Press.

Freire, P. (2007). *Education for critical consciousness*. Continuum. (Original work published 1974).

Fromm, E. (1964). *The heart of man, its genius for good and evil*. Harper & Row.

Gadotti, M. (1996). Paulo Freire: Uma biobibliografia [Paulo Freire: A biobibliography]. Cortez Editora/Instituto Paulo Freire.

Garmston, R. J., & Wellman, B. M. (1999). *The adaptive school: A sourcebook for developing collaborative groups*. Christopher-Gordon Publishers.

Giroux, H. (1995). Animating youth: The disnification of children's culture. *Socialist Review, 24*(3), 23–55.

Giroux, H. (2004). *The terror of neoliberalism: Authoritarianism and the eclipse of democracy*. Paradigm Press.

Giroux, H. (2008). *Against the terror of neoliberalism: Beyond the politics of greed.* Paradigm Publishers.

Giroux, H. (2009). *Youth in a suspect society: Democracy or disposability?* Palgrave Macmillan.

Giroux, H. (2012). *Education and the crisis of public values.* Peter Lang.

Habermas, J. (1971). *Knowledge and human interests.* Beacon Press.

Hamilton, B. E., Martin, J. A., M. P. H., & Osterman, M. J. K. (2020). *Vital statistics rapid release report no. 008 v May 2020 births: Provisional data for 2019.* https://www.cdc.gov/nchs/data/vsrr/vsrr-8-508.pdf

Hirshorn, H., Patierno, M., Talreja, S., & Jhally, S. (Directors). (1997). *Cultural criticism and transformation* [video]. Media Education Foundation.

Horton, M., & Freire, P. (1990). *We make the road by walking: Conversations on education and social change.* Temple University Press.

LitCharts. (n.d.). *Pedagogy of the oppressed study guide.* https://www.litcharts.com/lit/pedagogy-of-the-oppressed

Lord, A. (1984). *The uses of the erotic: The erotic as power.* Crossing Press.

McLaren, P. (2003). Critical pedagogy: A look at the major concepts. In A. Darder, M. Baltodano, & R. D. Torres (Eds.), *The critical pedagogy reader* (pp. 69–96). RoutledgeFalmer.

McLaren, P., & Jandrić, P. (2020). *Postdigital dialogues on critical pedagogy, liberation, theology and information technology.* Bloomsbury Academic.

Miller, J. B., M.D. (1976). *Toward a new psychology of women.* Beacon Press.

Noddings, N. (2013). Standardized curriculum and loss of creativity. *Theory Into Practice, 52*(3), 210–215. https://doi.org/10.1080/00405841.2013.804315

Paterlow, L. (2019 December 3). *What to make of declining enrollment in teacher preparation programs.* Center for American Progress. https://www.americanprogress.org/issues/education-k-12/reports/2019/12/03/477311/make-declining-enrollment-teacher-preparation-programs/

Post, N. (1985). *Amusing ourselves to death: Public discourse in the age of show business.* Penguin.

Ramalho, T. (1985). *Towards a feminist pedagogy of empowerment: The male and female voices in critical theory* (Electronic Thesis or Dissertation). https://etd.ohiolink.

Ravitch, D. (2014). *Reign of terror: The hoax of the privatization movement and the danger to America's public schools.* Vintage.

Rivage-Seul, D. M. (2018). *The magic glasses of critical thinking: Seeing through alternative facts & fake news.* Peter Lang.

Ruddock, A. (2013). *Youth and media.* SAGE Publications.

SUNY Oswego School of Education (n.d.). *Conceptual framework.* https://www.oswego.edu/education/conceptual-framework

U.S. Department of Education. (2015). *Enrollment in teacher preparation programs.* Higher Education Act. https://title2.ed.gov/Public/44077_Title_II_Issue_Brief_Enrollment_V4a.pdf

Valkenburg, P. M., & Piotrowski, J. T. (2017). *Plugged in: How media attract and affect youth.* Yale University Press. https://yalebooks.yale.edu/sites/default/files/files/Media/9780300228090_UPDF.pdf

Wink, J. (2011). *Critical pedagogy: Notes from the real world.* Pearson.
Wright, K. B., Shields, S. M., Black, K., Banerjee, M., & Waxman, H. C. (2018). Teacher perceptions of influence, autonomy, and satisfaction in the early Race to the Top era. *Education Policy Analysis Archives, 26*(62), 2–29.
Young, I. M. (1990). Five faces of oppression. In I. M. Young (Eds.), *Justice and the politics of difference* (pp. 39–65). Princeton University Press.

CHAPTER THREE

# Online Engagement with Critical Pedagogy

TINA WAGLE

In her article, Mary Breuing (2011) explains that critical pedagogy is a challenging term to define, even among self-identified critical pedagogues, because of overlapping yet divergent roots of the field. However, they tend to agree on critical pedagogy's commitment to raising awareness about social inequality and oppression and the need for social transformation. Though there is not one commonly used definition, there are many overlapping ideas and themes that emerge from the term, *critical pedagogy*. They include "a sociocultural examination of schools" (Breung, p. 11) and students evaluating their own positionality in terms of race, class, gender, socioeconomic status, sexuality, and ability. According to Burbules and Burk (1999),

> Critical pedagogues are specifically concerned with the influences of educational knowledge, and of cultural formations generally, that perpetuate or legitimate an unjust status quo; fostering a critical capacity in citizens is a way of enabling them to resist such power effects. (p. 46)

Critical pedagogy involves awareness of power dynamics, the understanding of inequality and social justice, and of one's position in the context of schools, communities, and the economy. Breuing (2011) explains that the definition of the term aligns closely with its aims, which include critical understanding of one's surroundings and becoming agents of change.

In this piece, these aims are central course objectives in an Introduction to Critical Pedagogy course at the master's level that happens to be taught online. The term "online" in this context means a fully remote learning experience wherein students utilize a learning management system, Moodle, to complete the course. While a text-based course reading anthology is a required resource, all other course learning materials are available through the internet. Though a fully interactive course, there are no synchronous meetings so that students can work according to their personal schedules within course assignment deadline parameters. The delivery of an online course is necessarily different than in a face-to-face setting; however, that does not indicate any less learning or mastery of subject matter. A different delivery mode of instruction does not weaken the content nor the pedagogy of a course.

Dell et al. (2010), for instance, conducted a study comparing student achievement in three sections of an educational psychology course, two face-to-face and one online, finding no significant differences. Their results suggest that the mode of delivery is not as important as the teaching methods. Instructors should be able to deliver the content they want to convey regardless of mode of instruction. This concept weighed heavily into the development of Introduction to Critical Pedagogy, as social justice-oriented courses are often taught in a face-to-face setting. Thus, the program faculty, including the main course developer, needed to ensure the heart of the foundational core was retained in the creation of the online critical pedagogy course.

## Online Courses: Pedagogical Resources

Work in a teacher education program offers many resources to support good pedagogical practices. The literature is vast with references (Bloom et al., 1969; Gregory & Kuzmich, 2014; Tileston, 2005; Wong, 2009) to research-based teaching strategies and classroom management techniques for face-to-face courses. Good pedagogy includes a variety of methods including techniques that support student engagement. In addition, collaboration, differentiation, and culturally-responsive pedagogy are all themes that should be woven into classroom practice (Danielson, 2013). Danielson (2013) also suggests that a key component of solid pedagogy is a well-managed classroom, which Wong (2009) describes as a teacher's ability of keeping the class in order, engaging students, and having student cooperation. Classroom management is one of the more challenging aspects for a teacher to master but often improves as one's self-efficacy grows (Marashi & Azizi-Nassab, 2018). All of these characteristics help make any classroom run smoothly, thereby offering a space for good pedagogy. When it comes to best practices in online teaching, however, the research is newer and still evolving. Yet, common themes have found to be stated consistently.

In 2002, the Sloan Consortium (now known as the Online Learning Consortium) developed its quality framework for institutions to identify and monitor online learning goals. This framework includes five pillars on which online education should be established: Learning Effectiveness, Access, Scale, Faculty Satisfaction, and Student Satisfaction. The Learning Effectiveness pillar is the most relevant here, as it includes effective practices such as,

> Course Design, Learning Resources. Faculty Development, Learner Characteristics, Pedagogy, Interaction (e.g., with content, faculty, other students; development of learning communities, etc.), Assessment, and Learning Outcomes (e.g., student satisfaction, retention, achievement, performance, etc.) (Online Learning Consortium, n.d.).

Similarly, eight best practices emerged from a study by Grant and Thornton (2007) that includes contact between faculty and student; cooperative learning; active learning; prompt feedback; deadlines; high expectations; respect for diverse learning styles; and overall good pedagogy in their inventory. Sloan's learning effectiveness pillar underscores the essential components to create a high-quality course with informed instruction practices, impactful content, and intentional strategies.

In developing Introduction to Critical Pedagogy (ICP), the University of Central Florida's best pedagogical practices of online or blended learning were followed. They suggested organizing a course around three categories: course content, interaction, and assessment. Course content includes the course organization, frequently referred to as modules, organizers, images, and guides. Interaction includes discussions and messaging. Finally, assessment includes formative and summative evaluation incorporating the use of rubrics. The teaching of an online course is necessarily different from teaching in a face-to-face mode, but key components of good instruction remain.

## The Master in Education: Curriculum and Instruction Program

SUNY Empire State College was founded in 1971 as a non-traditional institution serving adult learners across New York State and beyond. The Master in Education Program began enrolling students in 2011 and is, thus, nearly a decade in existence. It is a completely online degree whose clients are mainly P-12 teachers obtaining their professional certification, a requirement of educators in New York State. They are early and mid-career educators with a median age of 34. Offering admission twice a year, fall or spring, the program enrolls cohorts of 25–50 students. Having cohorts supports student camaraderie, as they take most of their core courses together as sequenced (Conrad, 2005; Whisker et al., 2007). Moreover, students who choose the same concentration also take electives together, so there is comfort and familiarity borne of the cohort structure.

The program, and the Introduction to Critical Pedagogy (ICP) course within it, are designed to create a discourse community that questions hegemonic social practices and contribute to a larger collective conversation. Other core courses include New Media and New Literacies, Contemporary Issues in Teaching and Learning, and Leading in a Learning Environment. These are designed to provide students with a foundation in understanding and utilizing appropriate technologies for instruction, the importance of current educational and social contexts, and the complex dynamics of both administrative and teacher leadership. Besides core courses, students also take four electives to make up their concentration, either Literacy or Foundations of Teaching. Students have a further option of creating a self-selected concentration based on related electives that make sense grouped together, such educational technology, child activism or even a content area like mathematics. The degree represents the additional learning, development, and practice needed to enhance their pedagogical skills in the classroom.

## Program and Course Learning Outcomes: Alignment and Design

A theme woven throughout the Master of Education: Curriculum and Instruction courses is the practical application of social justice-informed research and work. After the program was mapped through the specific core and research courses, each individual course was then developed taking into consideration the overall program learning outcomes as a point of departure. Thus, each course generated its specific learning outcomes aligned with the broader outcomes of the program, which include:

- Compare and contrast various perspectives and applications of critical pedagogy.
- Collaborate in creating a process for reflection and action in a community of learners.

- Generate ideas for programs and policies that develop effective learning communities.
- Create a learning reform model that takes into account developments in policies, research, technology, employment, and culture.
- Develop learning activities that utilize new media to foster the development of theories and methods that impact creative expression and communication across modalities and genres.
- Develop strategies to effectively infuse social media into the work of communities of learning.
- Adapt instructional strategies in response to institutional and systemic changes while developing students' capacity to become change agents toward a more just and democratic society.
- Analyze and critique educational research studies including identifying components, methodologies, variables, theoretical frameworks, and ethical issues.
- Design a curricular or community-based project based on researching best practices that can enhance P-20 learning.
- Evaluate how the roles of educational researcher and reflective practitioner contribute to students' identities as educators.

Given the outcomes above, the central objective of the ICP course is to understand how critical pedagogy is defined and how it can be applied to any learning or work environment. (Please see Appendix A for a complete curriculum map). Specific ICP course objectives include students' ability to:

- Understand definitions and perspectives of critical pedagogy.
- Deconstruct how each attribute of diversity such as race, class, and gender stands alone as a unique social construct and how different attributes are inextricably linked to each other.
- Analyze and critique published critical ethnographies and write a literature review.
- Collaborate in developing an idea for a new critical ethnography.
- Generate a process of reflection and action that could effect change.

A small core group of faculty with one lead course developer comprised the curricular experts in critical pedagogy who designed the ICP course. After the outcomes above were generated, backward design was then used to ensure that students meet them. This process entailed three steps: identifying desired results, determining acceptable evidence, and planning learning experiences and instruction (Wiggins & McTighe, 1998, p. 10). Key assignments and assessments were generated, beginning with the final course project, which asks how students can be an agent of change in their school and/or community. Other key assignments include an analysis of an ethnography and research-based articles, the development of a lesson plan incorporating critical pedagogy, participation in virtual residencies when applicable, and response papers and discussion to various videos and prompts. An annotated bibliography about Holocaust propaganda was recently added to the course in order to help scaffold the development of a full literature review, a key assignment in the Research Design course.

The final project utilizes the Joyce Epstein (2018) framework as a guide for community activism and asks students to develop a plan through which they can be agents of change. Epstein's model incorporates school and community partnerships. Students follow her framework which includes parenting, communicating, volunteering, learning at home, decision making, and collaborating with community. The importance of this particular framework in the ICP course is that the students need to find a meaningful way to incorporate community and family into their teaching. This partnership enhances pedagogical practice and, ideally, student achievement.

Additional assignments were added to address the remaining course objectives. These include having students select an ethnography, writing an analysis of the work, and using a data related protocol. Students read selections from the main text and write written response papers according to pertinent topics related to critical pedagogy. They are given learning guides to help scaffold their understanding of certain topics like critical race theory and critical literacy.

Students are also asked to write a lesson plan incorporating critical pedagogy and to implement it in their P-12 teaching. This particular assignment gets to the application of theory and other learning obtained throughout the course. There are also videos students are asked to watch and write a response with a critical perspective, such as Suli Breaks (2012), *Why I Hate School but Love Education*. Finally, there are discussions in every module throughout the course through which peers can interact, engage, and help each other understand concepts and offer multiple perspectives. These smaller assignments build students' foundations in critical pedagogy, which inform their final project rooted in social justice. At the end of the course, students share their final projects with each other and must comment on them, thus supporting the online learning community dimension of the course (Online Learning Consortium, n.d.).

## Introduction to Critical Pedagogy: Content and Resources

Introduction to Critical Pedagogy is divided into seven modules: the Introduction, Definitions and Perspectives of Critical Pedagogy, Diversity in Critical Pedagogy I and II, Critical Pedagogy Today: Is there "New Knowledge"?, Research and Ethnography, and finally, Reflection and Agency. Each module lasts approximately two weeks, as the term is a fifteen-week semester. Serving as important background to the course, there are also key academic pieces, the course syllabus, a schedule of assignments, learning contract[1], a guide to the American Psychology Association (APA) formatting with a writing sample, and the college policy on academic integrity. These course components are important to ensure student understanding of expectations both in the course and as students at the college.

In the Introductory module, students present themselves to build community and camaraderie with each other. They also are asked to complete a K-W-L graphic organizer, filling out what they "K" (Know) about critical pedagogy and what they "W" (Want) to know about the topic. At the end of the course, students complete the chart with what they have "L" (Learned) about critical pedagogy.

Often utilized as a reading strategy, a K-W-L organizational chart serves three main purposes: it elicits students' prior knowledge of the topic; it sets a purpose for learning the topic; and helps students self-assess or monitor their comprehension (National Education Association, n.d.). In other words, in this application of the tool, the K-W-L chart asks the student to state where they are with their current knowledge. In addition, it lets the faculty member know what students would like to gain out of the course, which then may lead to altering subsequent readings or assignments[2]. Finally, it asks students to reflect on their learning at the end of the course. This reflection is vital to thoughtful application (Hoffman-Kipp et al., 2003).

For the modules on diversity in critical pedagogy, students are asked to read several selections from the main text reader. Quality resources represent a key component to any course, and while the instructors of ICP continue to look for suitable Open Educational Resources (OER), *The Critical Pedagogy Reader* is still used. Editors Darder et al. (2017) state that the intention behind this distinctive pedagogy is "to link practices of schooling to democratic principles of society and transformative social action in the interest of oppressed communities" (p. 2).

*The Critical Pedagogy Reader* is a comprehensive collection of important essays directly related to the understanding of critical pedagogy. Its early introduction is a collection of quotations from educational and philosophical giants whose deep influence on critical pedagogy remains today. At the heart of ICP is the effort to help students understand the approach behind critical pedagogy and this understanding of the role in education. This anthology encapsulates this concept, which is why it serves as a central resource in the course. However, as good online instruction cannot be text-based alone, additional resources are added. Learning guides, for instance, are included in many modules with text-based information as are links to news stories via YouTube or other outlets, for example, TED Talks and videos, such as one by Sir Ken Robinson (2010) on *Changing Paradigms*. This video includes interesting graphics where visual learners can follow along in a different manner to stimulate learning.

Throughout the course, students are prompted to write asynchronous discussion posts on a given topic, one of which on the *Changing Paradigms* video. An open-ended prompt requires that students formulate their own, original responses. There is no right or wrong answer, but their posts should include evidence from the video or additional sources to support their views. From an instructor's perspective, it is important to be present in the discussion boards but allow the students enough space for interpersonal dialogue, which enriches community and collaboration. Discussions also offer the opportunity for invaluable peer-to-peer learning, as Boud et al. (2013) indicate:

> The advantage in learning from people we know is that they are, or have been, in a similar position to ourselves. Not only can they provide each other with useful information but sharing the experience of learning also makes it less burdensome and more enjoyable. (p. 10)

As P-12 teachers, the majority of program enrollees share similar experiences of teacher preparation and classroom teaching, which serve as a rich backdrop for online discussions. Discussion forums allow participants to reflect on the readings, write an initial, thoughtful post, then reflect on what others write to respond, thus creating an important dialogue even asynchronously. Referring back to Hoffman-Kipp et al. (2003), reflection is a mechanism for growth and professional development, particularly for teachers.

While instructors may take a backseat in these discussions, students also need to know they are being held accountable for their contributions. Therefore, expectations about discussions are posted, including dates by which to publish both initial and response posts, and the frequency with which to post to a given forum. Written assignments throughout the semester ask students to delve deeper into the concept that has been presented, utilizing higher-level critical thinking to analyze, evaluate, and synthesize relevant material. Discussions are graded along with written assignments and the capstone assignment (See Appendix B for a list of assignments).

## Challenges of Teaching Critical Pedagogy Online

One could argue that teaching critical pedagogy online is unique and challenging. A strong, foundational course such as this is often taught in a traditional face-to-face mode. Even though the course design may be excellent, one is still interfacing with a machine, not other human beings. In an online platform, one cannot read body language, cannot see inflection. These dynamics can lead to misinterpretation of texts and statements and can limit one's ability to express oneself. Academics may struggle to teach in an online format about topics that include critical discussions about marginalization and oppression, themes common to critical pedagogy. The potential for misunderstanding and misinterpretation may be greater in an online platform, especially one that is asynchronous. In a face-to-face setting, on the other hand, students and faculty are able to look into each other's eyes, to see reactions including shock, confusion, even disgust at a controversial statement. While a student in an online class is able to respond to such comments in writing, a live setting does provide for more immediate discussion, questioning, and clarification.

Critical pedagogy necessarily involves critical thinking, debating hard, controversial ideas, and putting them into practice, which may be quite engaging in a traditional face-to-face classroom setting. In a hybrid model, students frequently comment that their best learning experiences for pedagogical application happen face-to-face. They enjoy the energy offered in a face-to-face session and the greater ability to develop community. One pitfall to try to avoid in online courses is the potential feeling of isolation (Dolan, 2011; McDonald et al., 2005). Hence, some may argue that an online platform may not be the best venue for teaching critical pedagogy. However, course design and subsequent competent teaching can be effective in sharing critical pedagogical knowledge.

Offering a variety of learning forums is important; however, one must also be cognizant of accessibility and remain in compliance with accessibility mandates for online teaching. Photographs and other images can convey concepts effectively and provide visual interest in course materials. There are copyright, intellectual property, and accessibility issues to consider here, in order to use images appropriately. For instance, "copyright law [is] a potential liability for both the faculty member and the institution" (Diaz et al., 2009, p. 9,). Faculty at SUNY Empire State College work closely with educational technologists and instructional designers to ensure compliance with accessibility related to visual and other resources. If this kind of support is not available at a given institution, it is still incumbent upon the course developer to ensure compliance with accessibility.

As noted in the course content outline, there is a module on Research and Ethnography. It is important to remember, at least in this specific context, that ICP is one of many other courses in a larger education program. It is a challenge to ensure fit and purpose of a course and its contents into the broader degree. The entire core faculty was involved in backwards design not just for the development of this course but also when mapping the entire curriculum of the program.

The faculty decided it would be helpful for students to be exposed to various research techniques and methodologies throughout the program. When they reach the final capstone project, which includes a research project, they are more knowledgeable and experienced researchers. Thus, this assignment helps scaffold the broader capstone project by introducing students early on to research-based articles, annotated bibliographies, and ethnography. Ethnography is an important qualitative research methodology that aligns well with critical pedagogy. In this module, students select an ethnography of their choice from a provided list and analyze it critically. The intention in explaining this research module is to demonstrate that while a particular topic is central to online course development, it is helpful to consider where and why the course is situated in the broader context of the degree.

## New Developments for Critical Pedagogy Online: Virtual Residencies

The key to quality online course development and teaching is currency. While writing this piece, it was important to review some of the dates of the current course readings and supplementary materials. In today's fast paced world, technology changes daily, as do resources. One needs to continue to revise courses with new materials, yet we must remain steadfast in the vetting of such materials to maintain quality. New enhancements to courses are important as well. One such example of this is when this course was taught in the fall of 2018, and I encountered the following offer to participate in a new endeavor of a Virtual Residency:

> SUNY Empire State College has recently incorporated "virtual residencies" as a mechanism to bring communities together in a learning environment. Virtual Residencies (VR) at SUNY Empire State College connect undergraduate, graduate, and international education courses via a three-week collaborative online module, which usually

consists of joint asynchronous discussions, joint asynchronous assignment(s), and a synchronous/asynchronous keynote address by an expert in the thematic field for that term.

The theme of the fall 2018 Virtual Residency was Indian Education and Indigenous Knowledge. Colleagues associated with Graduate Studies at the college were asked to participate. The Introduction to Critical Pedagogy instructor took part in this residency, as the theme aligned well with some of the offerings in this course. In this VR module, students were asked to watch a variety of videos on Native Boarding Schools, Indian Languages, and lectures from educational experts in the field. The module culminated with a keynote address from Mr. Roberto Mukaro Borrero, a cultural consultant, advisor, human rights advocate, writer, historian, artist, and musician who offers particular expertise in Caribbean and other Indigenous Peoples' issues. Students were asked to join this keynote live, but due to scheduling issues, the session was recorded so that they could watch later if they were not able to attend synchronously.

Participation in this virtual residency was a tremendous experience for the students, as they were in a module with peers from all over the country, and an institution in Lebanon, with whom they were able to exchange thoughts and ideas. In this module, students had a discussion, a written assignment tying the theme back to the critical pedagogy course, as well as a residency reflection essay, which served as an important assessment on the residency itself. The Virtual Residency is just an example of how courses may change and include engagement from other sources. Again, the important takeaway is to revise online courses to remain current and interesting. To that end, the next Virtual Residency to take place in which the ICP course may participate is on Holocaust Education, which would dovetail nicely with the section on critical literacy and social justice praxis.

## Faculty and Student Engagement and Satisfaction

While student engagement is critical in teaching an online course, faculty engagement is just as important. According to Bolliger and Wasilik (2009), there are multiple factors that influence faculty satisfaction with online teaching. These include student performance, promoting positive student outcomes, recognition for their work, and institution values and supports the faculty (p. 106). In their article, *"Faculty influencing faculty satisfaction with online teaching and learning in higher education,"* they cite the National Education Association (NEA)'s research findings that "75% of faculty surveyed felt positively about distance education" (p. 105).

They also state that "83.4% of instructors were satisfied with teaching fully online courses, and 93.6% were willing to continue to teach online" (p. 105).

Regarding student satisfaction, Bolliger and Wasilik (2009) define it as "the student's perceived value of his or her educational experiences at an educational institution" (p. 104). Student assessment of their learning is essential in striving for and ensuring quality control. To that end, every semester at the institution, students are surveyed on their learning experience in the course. These results are reviewed by the instructor and the instructor's supervisor. Means for Introduction of Critical Pedagogy average 4.6 on a five-point Likert Scale (Institutional Review Board, n.d.; SUNY Empire State College, n.d.). Additionally, reflective assignments are embedded in the course as assessment tools, including students' experience participating in the Virtual Residency. Faculty and student input must be a constant recurrence in order to maintain high quality of the online teaching experience.

## Conclusion

Faculty may be hesitant to teach impactful, foundational courses such as Critical Pedagogy online due to the robust and demanding nature of dialogue required. The intention of this chapter was to demonstrate how proper online pedagogical techniques can make for an engaging experience for students and instructors. For example, the K-W-L chart students fill out as their first assignment is a particularly useful tool. At the end of the course, they are asked to revisit the chart and complete the "L" column to demonstrate what they have learned. Most responses inform the faculty that eyes have been opened to social inequities and the ways in which they can work towards social justice in their teaching practices.

A further indication of the impact of Introduction to Critical Pedagogy is when students reach the capstone stage. In their community-based or curricular capstone research-based project, the evaluation rubric includes categories mentioning topics students first learned in the ICP course, comprising critical thinking, community engagement, and context of student background. (See Appendix C for Capstone Rubric). The 2020 M.Ed. Annual Report revealed the capstone means for the three most recent terms were 92.9, 90.0 and 93.3 respectively (Wagle, 2020). This indicates students perform well on the capstone, including the critical pedagogy related sections, regardless of program format. Students retain and reuse the knowledge gained in the critical pedagogy course to inform their research-based action plans.

Teaching this particular course is exciting from the perspective of a faculty member, and students reveal that they find the course to be engaging and informative. Given the targeted population of adult learners, many of whom teaching in the P-12 community, online learning is a convenient way to learn and complete their degrees. While they need and appreciate the flexibility that the online format affords, they also need a quality experience to further their knowledge. The Master's in Education: Curriculum and Instruction Program supports these two requirements, and the Introduction to Critical Pedagogy course, in particular, provides a foundation in social justice which is needed today more than ever.

# Appendix A

## M.Ed. Curriculum Map

| | Intro to Critical Pedagogy | New Media and New Literacies | Leading in a Learning Environment | Contemporary Issues | Research Design | Capstone |
|---|---|---|---|---|---|---|
| Compare and contrast various perspectives and applications of critical pedagogy. | X | | | X | Depends on type of final project | Depends on type of final project |
| Collaborate in creating a process for reflection and action in a community of learners. | X | | | X | Depends on type of final project | Depends on type of final project |
| Generate ideas for programs and policies that develop effective learning communities. | | X | X | X | X | X |
| Create a learning reform model that takes into account developments in policies, research, technology, employment, and culture. | X | X | X | X | X | X |

|  | Intro to Critical Pedagogy | New Media and New Literacies | Leading in a Learning Environment | Contemporary Issues | Research Design | Capstone |
|---|---|---|---|---|---|---|
| Develop learning activities that utilize new media to foster the development of theories and methods that impact creative expression and communication across modalities and genres. |  | X |  |  |  |  |
| Develop strategies to effectively infuse social media into the work of communities of learning. |  | X |  |  |  |  |
| Adapt instructional strategies in response to institutional and systemic changes while developing students' capacity to become change agents toward a more just and democratic society. | X |  |  | X | X | X |

|  | Intro to Critical Pedagogy | New Media and New Literacies | Leading in a Learning Environment | Contemporary Issues | Research Design | Capstone |
| --- | --- | --- | --- | --- | --- | --- |
| Analyze and critique educational research studies including identifying components, methodologies, variables, theoretical frameworks, and ethical issues. | X | X | X |  | X | X |
| Design a curricular or community-based project based on researching best practices that can enhance P-20 learning. |  |  |  |  | X | X |
| Evaluate how the roles of educational researcher and reflective practitioner contribute to students' identities as educators. | X |  |  | X | X | X |

# Appendix B

### Course activities/syllabus

**Module 1: Introduction**
In this introductory module you will become acquainted with the course, as well as your classmates. You will also complete and initial KWL chart, identifying what you already know and what you want to learn.

**Module 2: Definitions and Perspectives of Critical Pedagogy**
In this module, we will explore what critical pedagogy is, and how it is conceptualized in the education field. You will view a video about paradigm shifts, and then develop and share your own viewpoints on this matter.

**Module 3: Diversity in Critical Pedagogy**
In this section, we will begin to look at issues of diversity and its relationship with critical pedagogy. You will also have your first written assignment.

**Module 4: Diversity in Critical Pedagogy Part II**
In this module we will explore how our views of others influence our interactions, as well as our social environment. In addition, we will examine the critical race theory more closely, including its relationship to critical pedagogy.

**Module 5: Critical Reading**
In this module, we will explore how critical literacy relates to K-12 education and the students you work with or will be working with. In addition, you will apply critical literacy skills to an annotated bibliography regarding Holocaust education and resources.

**Module 6: Critical Pedagogy Today: Is There New Knowledge?**
In this module we will explore teacher preparation and student motivation. These two items work together to facilitate successful learning experiences and quality education. We will also examine the difference between merely completing the basic school requirements, and actually gaining an education, and reflect on the roles that teachers can play in this.

**Module 7**
In this module we will explore teacher preparation and student motivation. These two items work together to facilitate successful learning experiences and quality education. We will also examine the difference between merely completing the basic school requirements, and actually gaining an education, and reflect on the roles that teachers can play in this.

*Course Schedule*

| Module | Readings | Due Date |
| --- | --- | --- |
| Introduction | KWL: What you know, and want to know, about critical pedagogy | KWL due: week 1 |
| Definitions of Critical Pedagogy | Critical Pedagogy Reader: p. 25–109<br>Critical Pedagogy Videos<br>Learning Guides<br>Discussion: Why Critical Pedagogy? | Discussion: Why Critical Pedagogy?<br>Response due: week 2<br>Discussion: Response to Critical Pedagogy Videos |
| Diversity in Critical Pedagogy | Critical Pedagogy Reader:<br>"Against Schooling: Education and Social Class" (Aronowitz), p. 118–134<br>"Social Class and the Hidden Curriculum of Work" (Anyon), p. 135–153<br>"Confronting Class in the Classroom" (Hooks), p. 181–187<br>Choose two of the four sections to read in "Part Four: Gender, Sexuality, and Schooling" (p. 267–360) | Written Assignment: Choose One due: week 3<br>Discussion: Share Your Assignment<br>Reading Response Paper due: week 4 |
| Diversity in Critical Pedagogy Part II | Critical Pedagogy Reader:<br>"Dancing with Bigotry: The Poisoning of Racial and Ethnic Identities" (Bartolome and Macedo), p. 196–215<br>"I won't Learn from You" (Kohl), p. 440–447<br>"A Feminist Reframing of Bullying and Harassment: Transforming Schools Through Critical Pedagogy" (Meyer), p. 448–460<br>"Power, Politics, and Critical Race Pedagogy" (Lynn and Jennings), p. 535–556<br>UCLA School of Public Affairs: What is Critical Race Theory? | Discussion: The Other<br>Written Assignment: Critical Race Theory due: week 6 |

| Module | Readings | Due Date |
|---|---|---|
| Critical Reading- Ethnographies | Read selections: Myths about Critical Literacy: What Teachers Need to Unlearn What do They Know? A Strategy for Assessing Critical Literacy Watch the Holocaust education video and choose 5 peer reviewed courses from the USHMM website. | Discussion: Critical Literacy Written Assignment: Annotated Bibliography due: week 9 |
| Critical Pedagogy today- Is there "new knowledge?" | Critical Pedagogy Reader "The Knowledge of Teacher Education: Developing a Critical Complex Epistemology" (Kincheloe), p. 503–517 "Broadening the Circle of Critical Pedagogy" (Ross), p. 608–617 Why I Hate School but Love Education (Video) Sir Ken Robinson (Video) | Written Assignment: Lesson Plan or Response paper due: week 12 Discussion: Today's Critical Lens |
| Reflection and Agency | Review assigned readings from the course Epstein framework (2018) | Revisit K-W_L Final Project due: Final week |

# Appendix C

**Final Project Rubric**
Student name: _____
Final Project Title: _____
Total Score: \_\_ /100

| | Excellent 90–100 | Satisfactory 80–89 | Needs Improvement 70–79 | Unsatisfactory Less than 70 | Category/ comments |
|---|---|---|---|---|---|
| Outcomes & Alignment with relevant Learning Standards or Community Engagement InTASC 4, 7, 10. NYS II, III, VII | The alignment with the relevant Learning Standards or Community Engagement is clear and explicit throughout the unit. The learning opportunities and assessments are directly related and clearly supportive of students' attainment of the standards. | The alignment with relevant Learning Standards or Community Engagement is clear and explicit but is not embedded in the learning opportunities for students. The learning opportunities and assessments are directly related to the standards. | The alignment with relevant Learning Standards or Community Engagement is not explicit but can be inferred. The learning opportunities and assessments are partially related to the standards. | The alignment with relevant Learning Standards or Community Engagement is contrived, superficial, or difficult to determine. The learning opportunities and assessments appear to be unrelated to the standards. | |
| Critical Thinking and Rigor InTASC 1, 3, 4, 5, 6, 8 NYS II, III, IV, V, VII | The design integrates the use of basic and higher levels of thinking through learning experiences that requires students to engage in a thorough exploration of a theme, problem, issue, or question by emulating professionals in the area in question. | The design addresses all levels of thinking in a sequential fashion, moving from basic to higher order thinking and enables students to develop an understanding and use of knowledge and skills acquired related to a theme, problem, or issue. | The design focuses primarily on recall, comprehension, basic understanding, and factual knowledge acquisition, although it includes one or more questions or activities that require higher order thinking. | The design focuses exclusively on recall, comprehension and basic application of knowledge and skills. The design lacks rigor. | |

| | Excellent 90–100 | Satisfactory 80–89 | Needs Improvement 70–79 | Unsatisfactory Less than 70 | Category/ comments |
|---|---|---|---|---|---|
| Consideration of context and student background InTASC 1, 2, 3, 6, 7, 8, 9 NYS I, III, IV, V, VI | Design demonstrates thorough knowledge of all students' backgrounds, skills, learning styles, and interests, and consistently uses this knowledge to address individual student learning. | The design uses knowledge of students' backgrounds, skills, learning styles, and interests to address groups of students. | The design builds in an acknowledgement of students' backgrounds, skills, learning styles, and interests, and uses this knowledge in the delivery of the unit. | The design shows no attempt to acquire knowledge of students' backgrounds, skills, learning styles, or interests. | |
| Connection between Theory and Practice InTASC 1–10 NYS I-VII. | The design demonstrates a strong alignment between theoretical and practical application of knowledge consistently. Sources are of the highest quality and are relevant to the chosen topic. | The design demonstrates alignment between theoretical and practical application of knowledge. Sources are acceptable. | The design shows some connection between theoretical and practical application of knowledge. Sources are a mix of appropriate and sources that are not acceptable. | The design shows little to no connection between theoretical and practical application of knowledge. Sources are not appropriate. | |
| Overall Clarity, Components and Mechanics InTASC 5, 6, 7, 9 NYS: I and VII | The project is organized using clear, relevant, and well-connected key components, including a detailed evaluation plan. Writing is clear, logical and free of grammatical errors. APA style is strictly adhered to. | The project is organized and key components were connected. An evaluation plan is included. Writing is generally clear, with a few grammatical errors. APA style is adhered to with a few errors. | The project has some level of organization but there are missing components. The writing is not always clear and there are numerous grammatical errors. APA style is used, but with many errors. | The project is minimally organized, and the writing is difficult to follow throughout. APA style is not adhered to. | |

## Notes

1. Learning contract is a long-used term at SUNY Empire State College depicting documentation that courses are shared experiences between faculty and student. Required components of the learning contract include a course description, learning activities, and criteria for evaluation including a separate section on formative assessment
2. SUNY Empire State College's mission is based on individualized learning. Thus, instructors have the freedom to tailor their courses to suit the needs of the students. It is not uncommon for instructors to add or modify assignments based on students' needs and interests.

## References

Bloom, B. S. L., Krathwohl, D. R. L., & Masia, B. B. (1969). *Taxonomy of educational objectives: The classification of educational goals; handbook*. MacKay.

Bolliger, D. U., & Wasilik, O. (2009). Factors influencing faculty satisfaction with online teaching and learning in higher education. *Distance Education*, *30*(1), 103–116. https://doi.org/10.1080/01587910902845949

Boud, D., & Cohen, R. (2013). *Peer learning in higher education: Learning from & with each other*. Routledge.

Breaks, S. (2012, Dec 2). *Why I Hate School but Love Education* [Video] YouTube. www.youtube.com/watch?v=y_ZmM7zPLyI

Breuing, M. (2011). Problematizing critical pedagogy. *The International Journal of Critical Pedagogy*, *3*(3), 2–23.

Burbules, N. C., & Berk, R. (1999). *Critical theories in education: Changing terrains of knowledge and politics: Critical thinking and critical pedagogy: Relations, differences, and limits*. Routeledge.

Conrad, D. (2005). Building and maintaining community in cohort-based online learning. *International Journal of E-Learning & Distance Education/Revue Internationale du E-Learning et la Formation à Distance*, *20*(1), 1–20.

Danielson, C. (2013). *The framework for teaching evaluation instrument, 2013 instructionally focused edition*. Danielson Group.

Dell, C. A., Low, C., & Wilker, J. F. (2010). Comparing student achievement in online and face-to-face class formats. *Journal of Online Learning and Teaching*, *6*(1), 30–42.

Darder, A., Baltodana, M., & Torres, R. (2017). *The critical pedagogy reader*. Routledge.

Diaz, V., Mitrano, T., & Christoph, K. (2009). *Copyright, fair use, and teaching and learning innovation in a Web 2.0 world*. EDUCAUSE Center for Applied Research.

Dolan, V. (2011). The isolation of online adjunct faculty and its impact on their performance. *International Review of Research in Open and Distributed Learning*, *12*(2), 62–77. https://doi.org/10.19173/irrodl.v12i2.793

Epstein, J. L. (2018). *School, family, and community partnerships: Preparing educators and improving schools.* Routledge.

Grant, M. R., & Thornton, H. R. (2007). Best practices in undergraduate adult-centered online learning: Mechanisms for course design and delivery. *Journal of Online Learning and Teaching, 3*(4), 346–356.

Gregory, G. H., & Kuzmich, L. (2014). *Data driven differentiation in the standards-based classroom.* Corwin Press.

Hoffman-Kipp, P., Artiles, A., & López-Torres, L. (2003). Beyond reflection: Teacher learning as praxis. *Theory into Practice, 42*(3), 248–254. https://doi.org/10.1207/s15430421tip4203_12

Marashi, H., & Azizi-Nassab, F. (2018). EFL teachers' language proficiency, classroom management, and self-efficacy. *International Journal of Foreign Language Teaching and Research, 6*(22), 89–102.

McDonald, B., Noakes, N., Stuckey, B., & Nyrop, S. (2005). *Breaking down learner isolation: How social network analysis informs design and facilitation for online learning. AERA.* https://citeseerx.ist.psu.edu/viewdoc/download?doi=10.1.1.451.9868&rep=rep1&type=pdf

National Education Association. (n.d.). Creating student empowerment through your garden-variety graphic organizer. https://www.nea.org/professional-excellence/student-engagement/tools-tips/creating-student

Office of Institutional Research. (n.d.). Student assessment of learning experiences. SUNY Empire State College.

Online Learning Consortium. (n. d.). *Quality Framework.* https://onlinelearningconsortium.org/about/quality-framework-five-pillars/

Robinson, K. (2010, January 7). *Do Schools Kill Creativity?* [Video] YouTube. https://www.youtube.com/watch?v=iG9CE55wbtYTileston, D. W. (2005). *Ten best teaching practices: How brain research, learning styles, and standards define teaching competencies.* Corwin Press.

Tileston, D. W. (2005). *Ten best teaching practices: How brain research, learning styles, and standards define teaching competencies.* Corwin Press.

Wagle, T. (2020). *Master in Education: Curriculum and Instruction Annual Report.* SUNY Empire State College.

Wiggins, G., & McTighe, J. (1998). What is backward design. *Understanding by Design, 1,* 7–19.

Wisker, G., Robinson, G., & Shacham, M. (2007). Postgraduate research success: Communities of practice involving cohorts, guardian supervisors and online communities. *Innovations in Education and Teaching International, 44*(3), 301–320. https://doi.org/10.1080/14703290701486720

Wong, H. K., Wong, R. T., & Seroyer, C. (2009). *The first days of school: How to be an effective teacher.* Harry K. Wong Publications.

CHAPTER FOUR

# (Digital) Media as Critical Pedagogy

MAXIMILLIAN ALVAREZ

"Within history, in concrete, objective contexts, both humanization and dehumanization are possibilities for a person as an uncompleted being conscious of their incompletion."
– PAULO FREIRE, PEDAGOGY OF THE OPPRESSED

"Since in reality there is nothing to which growth is relative save more growth, there is nothing to which education is subordinate save more education."
– JOHN DEWEY, DEMOCRACY AND EDUCATION

Over the past three decades, opining about the educational applications of digital technologies has become a cottage industry unto itself. "Indeed," Neil Selwyn writes, "most recently a fresh set of educational discourses has accompanied the emergence of 'new' technologies such as social media, wireless connectivity and cloud data storage, and not least the seemingly unassailable rise of personalized and portable computing devices such as smartphones and tablets" (2013, p. 3). From chalkboard sites to social media, from smartphones to Prezi, from in-class polling apps to interactive grading software, there is an almost suffocating overabundance of digital tools at our fingertips, many of which float into our classrooms on airy praise from university administrators, politicians, and corporate technicians alike who tout the incorporation of these technologies into our teaching as an undeniably positive step toward the "enhancement" of student learning (Ahalt &

Fecho, 2015). As a result, "Public debate, commercial marketing, education policy texts and academic research are now replete with sets of phrases and slogans such as 'twenty-first century skills', 'flipped classrooms', 'self-organised learning environments', 'unschooling', an 'iPad for every child', 'massively online open courses' [MOOCs] and so on" (Selwyn, 2017, p. 229). As our educational discourse continues to be pumped full of such slogans, the conclusion that the future of learning is – and must be – digital seems to have already been made for us.

That we and our students are living in a digitalized world is a blunt fact. And it seems futile, and perhaps even slightly irresponsible, not to actively engage students in the process of learning about (and learning on) the digital terrains that they have grown up navigating – and will continue to navigate once they leave our classrooms. And there is, indeed, much to be gained from doing so, for students and teachers alike. As Ernest Morrell, Rudy Dueñas, Veronica Garcia, and Jorge López note, "Today's youth spend the majority of their waking lives as consumers and producers of media [...] [They] blog, pin, post, comment, and share links with social networks on a scale that, a generation ago, would have been possible only for professional media personnel" (2013, p. 2). In their daily consumption and production of media, along with their flexible negotiation of ever-evolving media-worlds, students today are developing skills outside of the classroom that have tremendous capacities to inform what and how they learn *inside* the classroom. Moreover, on the flip side, what forms the learning process takes in the digitally connected classroom, and how students' own subjectivities are shaped and mediated through it, can have significant bearing on the kinds of "digital citizens" (Talib, 2018, p.56) students will become.

This is precisely why, even for those of us who try not to be total Luddites, there is something deeply unnerving in the spoken and unspoken presumptions that are being made about *students* and *learning* and *technology* throughout much of the professional, corporate, and governmental discourses of digital education. Such presumptions are routinely reinforced by the instrumentalist manner in which we deploy digital technologies in the classroom; that is, by the way we assume and accept our positions as users of tools whose uses themselves have been prescribed – and whose functionality has been programmed and hidden behind a black box (Goffey & Fuller, 2012) – by opaque commercial, governmental, and administrative forces beyond the classroom, *all* of which have their own incentives and agendas calibrated to the positions they occupy in our political economy. It is crucial to remember that there is nothing predestined about the sort of digital technologies we incorporate into our teaching, the specific shapes they take, the functions they perform, the skills they test, their methods for measuring success, the data they collect, the people they put out of work, etc. But there is nothing neutral about these things either. As Kristin Smith and Donna Jeffery write, "The widespread acceptance of online [and other digital] educational technologies is not simply the product of pure technological evolution. They are deeply embedded in the social, economic, and political contexts governed by neoliberal discourses and practices" (2013, p. 378). The top-down rush to "enhance" the learning process and "streamline" teaching duties through the adoption of new digital technologies has been part of an institutional realignment that is both "deeply embedded" in the historical contexts of neoliberalism and consonant with the aims of the generalized, but unevenly executed, neoliberalization of education as such (Bousquet, 2008; Giroux, 2014; Hall, 2016; Newfield, 2008; Schrecker, 2010).

Neoliberalism, as Wendy Brown writes:

> is most commonly understood as enacting an ensemble of economic policies in accord with its root principle of affirming free markets. These include deregulation of industries and capital flows; radical reduction in welfare state provisions and protections for the vulnerable; privatized and outsourced public goods, ranging from education, parks, postal services, roads, and social welfare to prisons and militaries; [...] the conversion of every human need or desire into a profitable enterprise, from college admissions preparation to human organ transplants, from baby adoptions to pollution rights, from avoiding lines to securing legroom on an airplane; and, most recently, the financialization of everything and the increasing dominance of finance capital over productive capital in the dynamics of the economy of everyday life (2015, p. 28).

Under the rank shadow of neoliberalism, more and more public goods and personal desires are broken down and rewired to accommodate the total and seamless penetration of market values into every facet of "the economy of everyday life." As critical sites for the accumulation of capital and the reproduction of neoliberal ideology, educational institutions are unmoored from the public good and restructured to ease the infiltration of money, personnel, and directives from the private sector (Cervone, 2018; Newfield, 2016; Weiner, 2004). This structural overhaul is accompanied by formal (and often strictly enforced) changes to curricula, teaching practices, learning outcomes, methods of assessment, etc. – changes designed to complement these retrofitted neoliberal prerogatives while (re)producing in students and teachers alike the sort of self-policing "responsible subjects" (Clarke, 2004, p. 33) neoliberalism requires. "As a result, educators are increasingly expected to enact cost containment measures, cooperate with the demands of efficiency-driven management styles, and work under expectations of labor flexibility and adaptability" (Smith & Jeffery, 2013, p. 375), all while being charged with the task of enacting and enforcing "an idea of education as content delivery and absorption, with students designated as recipients and clients rather than partners in an exploratory enterprise" (Mullen, 2002, p. 19).

These are the hard, practical contexts in which the push for integrating more digital technologies into the learning process is taking place. And it is precisely in this vein that we must critically appraise the ideological functions and subjective outcomes of said technological integration as well as the equally utopian and fatalistic narrative "that technology is inevitable, that technology is wrapped up in our notions of progress, and that somehow progress is inevitable itself and is positive" (Young & Watters, 2016). Because, at the same time that educational institutions have transformed into "administrative [apparatuses] whose morality is outsourced to the market" (Alvarez, 2017), the instrumentalist, techno-fetishist embrace of learning with and through digital tools is part and parcel of the essential reproduction of neoliberal market ideology. "Many elements of online education exemplify the core beliefs of the private, commercial sector in that they necessarily concern themselves with trying to measure and count narrow outcomes rather than with the complexities of learning […] challenging subject matter […]. If education is to be efficient, then it simply must be capable of being measured" (Jeffery & Smith, 2013, p. 377). That corporate, administrative, and governmental efforts to accelerate the incorporation of digital technologies into the learning process have surged in tandem with the thorough neoliberalization of education institutions is not a coincidence. These technologies are less designed and deployed to expand the horizons of critical student learning than to narrowly redefine the very shape and scope of formal learning in accordance with the prerogatives of the neoliberal power structure, which prizes, above all else, that which (and those who) can be standardized, quantified, managed, and monetized. Thus, as Jesse Stommel and Sean Michael Morris write in their open-access e-book, *An Urgency of Teachers*, "educators and students alike have found themselves more and more flummoxed by a system that values assessment over engagement, learning management over discovery, content over community, outcomes over epiphanies" (2018). And to uncritically approach the integration and use of digital technologies into the learning process is to make ourselves and our students vulnerable to being *used by* them – to being adjusted, programmed, and made comfortable with the very worldly conditions that we, as critical educators, are ostensibly trying to challenge. We must, therefore, be wary of the professional discourses that herald this process of technological integration as both inevitable and objectively positive.

In her contribution to the edited volume *Critical Learning in Digital Networks*, for instance, Sarah Hayes examines trends in these educational discourses from the U.S., E.U., and Australia, and picks up on a relatively recent and rather telling terminological shift. Hayes notes that the ubiquity of terms like "e-Learning" and "online learning," which, in more-or-less neutral ways, primarily served to describe the digital *context* in which learning (however it was defined) took place, has been largely usurped by the more explicitly value-judgment-laden discourse of "technology-enhanced learning." In this positivist discourse, it is not only taken as a given that to infuse education with newer technological elements is, by definition, to enhance the learning process; it is also presumed that the learning process itself is straightforward enough that its technology-induced "enhancement" can be so confidently assured. As Hayes writes, "The verb 'enhanced' is selected and placed in between 'technology' and 'learning' to imply (through a value judgment) that technology *has* now enhanced learning, and will continue to do so" (2015, p. 15). Ideologically, epistemologically, politically, the implicit value judgment that is buried in (and enforced by) the discourse of "technology-enhanced learning" is doing a lot of heavy lifting here. How the learning process will be defined, what will be learned, and to what ends – these and other vital questions are subsumed under the narrow purview of a formal education apparatus that, as mentioned above, is designed to clear the way for market forces to penetrate every level of daily life while also shaping and pumping out the kind of responsible subjects neoliberalism needs to reproduce and maintain its hegemony.

What must be noted here – especially given the theme of this issue of *Media Theory* – is that the positivist assertion embedded in the professional discourse of "technology-enhanced learning" explicitly (and even violently) forecloses the epistemological, subjective, and political possibilities that are otherwise expressed in the discourse of technological "affordance." "Technology-enhanced learning" bears out a self-affirming promise that the technology in question will not "afford" teachers and students the means to explore new learning possibilities so much as it will efficiently compel them to perform what the programmers of said technology have determined learning to be (and that said technology, with exacting precision, will evaluate teaching and learning on the strict basis of this performance). In fact, we could say that the political epistemology represented by the assertion of "technology-enhanced learning" is roundly antagonistic to the understanding of technology that is belied by the very notion of affordance. Because where there is affordance there is openness, uncertainty, a chance for thinking or doing something that is made possible – but is by no means guaranteed – by that which affords. Such openness is antithetical to the neoliberal prerogatives and parameters of "technology-enhanced learning."

Of course, as an analytical concept that can help us better understand the range and scope of technological functionality, "affordance" is equally a question of the possibilities that are opened up *and* foreclosed by the structural specificities of a particular tool, program, environment, etc. "Affordances are functional in the sense that they are enabling, as well as constraining, factors in a given organism's attempt to engage in some activity," Ian Hutchby notes (2001, p. 448). "Certain objects, environments or artefacts have affordances which enable the particular activity while others do not. But at the same time the affordances can shape the conditions of possibility associated with an action: it may be possible to do it one way, but not another" (2001, p. 448). Thus, while it is certainly true that the functional specificity of certain digital technologies can afford students and teachers the "conditions of possibility" for developing new forms of critical, collaborative, and exploratory learning, it is equally true that engaging with these – or any – technologies will inevitably limit the horizons of what is doable and thinkable to what their functional specificity allows (i.e. affords). For the purposes of this discussion, however, what is especially noteworthy is the fact that affordance names a *context* in which the horizon of possibilities is limited (and opened) by the relation between a human organism and the functional specificity of a distinct technology. The relation itself forms the generative matrix of possibility: "Affordances are thereby focused on the relationship between people and object, *their creative and adaptive interaction with the environment* rather than any compliant response to any designed features of that environment" (Conole & Dyke, 2004, p. 302, emphases added). Indeed, this is why the neoliberal instrumentality denoted by "technology-enhanced learning" steers clear of any serious reference to affordance. The former, which *does* seek to elicit (if not compel) a "compliant response to […] designed features," is not content with the relational limiting of possibilities named in the discourse of technological affordance; it is deliberately designed and deployed, rather, to foreclose (as much as possible) the contingency of possibility itself.

Rather than opening a learning space in which teachers, students and digital technologies can explore one another in a matrix of relational possibility, "technology-enhanced learning" inflates the neoliberal illusion of possibility with increasingly personalized, choice-adaptive programs and multi-modal functionalities that nevertheless reduce the user's say in what and how they learn to nil. "The embedding of the idea of 'enhancing learning through the use of technology,'" Hayes continues, "firmly structures educational technology within a framework of exchange value. It places emphasis on what technology is doing to yield a profit rather than how learning takes place as a human process" (2015, p. 16). There is no real acknowledgment of, let alone appreciation for, relational agency in the idea of "technology-enhanced learning" – at least not on the part of the learner. More than anything or anyone else, it is the technology itself that is granted a kind of coercive agency to convey learning subjects to their final destination; it alone maintains a sense of agential singularity that everyone else is denied. And, in so doing, it functions quite effectively as a medium for the reproduction of neoliberal subjecthood and authoritative social control shrouded in the illusion of personal choice. "If we discuss technology as detached from the humans who perform tasks with it, then it simply becomes an external force acting on our behalf. This objective approach disempowers the human subject to undertake any critique, as it effectively removes them from the equation, closing down possibilities for more varied conversations across diverse networks" (Hayes, 2015, p. 17).

As one illustrative example, we could look to the page on the U.S. Department of Education's website that is dedicated to "Use of Technology in Teaching and Learning." The opening passage on the website reads:

> Technology ushers in fundamental structural changes that can be integral to achieving significant improvements in productivity. Used to support both teaching and learning, technology infuses classrooms with digital learning tools, such as computers and hand held devices; expands course offerings, experiences, and learning materials; supports learning 24 hours a day, 7 days a week; builds 21$^{st}$ century skills; increases student engagement and motivation; and accelerates learning. Technology also has the power to transform teaching by ushering in a new model of connected teaching. This model links teachers to their students and to professional content, resources, and systems to help them improve their own instruction and personalize learning. Online learning opportunities and the use of open educational resources and other technologies can increase educational productivity by accelerating the rate of learning; reducing costs associated with instructional materials or program delivery; and better utilizing teacher time (U.S. Department of Education, 2019).

Notice that, unlike the examples analyzed by Hayes, this passage omits any specific mention of "technology-enhanced learning"; in fact, this particular page on the Department of Education website does not mention the words "enhance" or "enhancement" even once. Far from representing a deviation from the positivist fatalism embodied in the discourse of "technology-enhanced learning," however, we could argue that this passage represents its apotheosis. More than anything else, this description of educational technology reads like a company promo, a matter-of-fact discursive fusion of government and industry confidence that said technology *will* make good on these promises to "increase educational productivity by accelerating the rate of learning" while also forcing educators to adopt more of the qualities prized by the neoliberal model of (cheap) labor: hyper-productivity, 24–7 accessibility, flexibility, etc. Once again, that these are the given (and celebrated) parameters for "successful" teaching, and that learning as such is explicitly measured in terms of speed, quantity, and productivity, is not an accident. "The commodity form and its administrative simulacra are now able to penetrate hitherto protected zones," philosopher Andrew Feenberg notes, in conversation with Petar Jandrić (2015, p. 143). "This is the essence of neo-liberalism, the extension of commercial relations and criteria into every area of life […] Deskilling education and bringing it under central management is now on the agenda. Money would be saved and the 'product' standardized. Technology is hyped as the key to this neo-liberal transformation of education. Computer companies, governments, university administrations have formed an alliance around this utopian, or rather dystopian, promise" (2015, p. 143).

"The more our tools are naturalized, invisible, or inscrutable," as Morris and Stommel write, "the less likely we are to interrogate them" (2018). Likewise, the more intimately our professional responsibilities, and students' scholastic success, are bound to carrying out these instrumentalist directives, the more relentlessly the forces of neoliberal administration convert our learning environments into "dystopian" assemblages of "technology-enhanced learning," the harder it becomes to imagine a narrative of "new media encounter" whose arc has not already been determined for us. Because, as Alan Liu writes, "*Good accounts of new media encounter imagine affordances and configurations of potentiality.* We don't want a good story of new media with a punch line giving somebody the last word. We want a good world of new media that gives everyone at least one first word […] We want a way of imagining our encounter with new media that surprises us out of the 'us' we thought we knew" (2013, p. 16, emphases added). Under the market-calibrated aegis of "technology-enhanced learning," accounts of new media encountered in and outside the classroom have, for the most part, already been written for us – accounts that take it as a given that learning with and through digital technologies will be a process defined and measured by those technologies themselves. When it comes to imagining the "configurations of possibility" that may exist for us and our students in our potential encounter with new media, we are, once again, presented with the illusion of agency in a plot that has been scripted by the very authors of our own continued exploitation and domination. It is, thus, all the more incumbent upon us, as critical educators, to imagine – and engage our students in the vital process of imagining for themselves – a narrative of new media encounter in which "The future of learning will not be determined by tools but by the re-organization of power relationships and institutional protocols" (Scholz, 2011, p. IX).

Such an imperative necessarily involves engaging ourselves and our students in the critical pedagogical process of *learning to learn* in conversation with – not at the behest of – media. To do so gets to the very heart of critical pedagogy itself, because the project of critical pedagogy is ultimately a media project. And if we are to determine how to develop a sufficiently critical pedagogy in the age of digital media, critical pedagogy and/as media theory first enjoins us to re-examine (and intervene in) the sites where learning as such actually takes place. Because, I argue, the core political and ontological premises upon which critical pedagogy is based – and from which it maintains a sense of hope that we and our worlds can change – breathe life into an understanding of the learning process as a process of becoming in which we must explore, analyze, and praxically engage the open, dialectical circuits between human and world that mediate life itself.

Perhaps at no other point, then, has the need for a critical media pedagogy been so urgent at the same time that the institutional and technological conditions of formal learning have become so structurally hostile to the spirit of critical pedagogy itself. The more seamlessly digital technologies are integrated into the learning process, the more crucial it is for students and teachers alike to develop their capacities for critically analyzing – and intervening in – the broader, overlapping forces of social control that are mediated through them. It is imperative that we critically (re)examine our own pedagogies, and that we ask what it will mean to work with our students to hash out a vulnerable, critical, and creative learning praxis that not only resists the coercive interpellation of neoliberal subjectivation, but that also affirms and expands their humanity in the digitalized world while bolstering their capacities to interrogate, attack, and dismantle the conditions that dehumanize them by stifling their learning.

Critical pedagogy doesn't necessarily *start* with Paulo Freire, but it certainly doesn't exist without him. "To separate Paulo from critical pedagogy is not possible," Shirley Steinberg writes (2015, p. ix). "We know our own positionality within critical pedagogy by how we first came to know Paulo Freire" (2015, p. ix). A world-renowned educator and philosopher, Freire developed revolutionary and widely successful methods for teaching poor, illiterate populations in Brazil before the 1964 military coup (Golpe de 64), after which he was imprisoned for 70 days and forced to live in exile for fifteen years. It was during the first decade of his exile that Freire wrote and published his first book, *Education, the Practice of Freedom* (1967). This was followed by his most famous book, *Pedagogy of the Oppressed* (1970), which has served as the lodestar of critical pedagogues ever since. Half-a-century's worth of independent studies, internal debates, critical reappraisals, practical experimentations, and theoretical variations have unfolded in the wake of the publication of Freire's seminal work, but everything in the ever-exploding-and-rearranging field of critical pedagogy still orbits around the core, radical concept that is articulated in it. (By no means do I wish to suggest that practitioners have followed a singular, prescribed path in developing their own critical pedagogies, nor do I mean to imply that the "field" of critical pedagogy as such is not riven with necessary critiques and departures on practical and theoretical issues regarding, for instance, race, disability, the mind/body distinction, etc. (Brock & Orelus, 2015; Ellsworth, 1989; Erevelles, 2000; Shapiro, 1999). However, I argue that the coherence of critical pedagogy as an expressly political project rests on a set of ontological assumptions about the mediated relationship between human and world – assumptions that fundamentally challenge the reductive, dehumanizing treatment of student and teacher subjecthood that is materially reinforced by the neoliberal apparatus of "technology-enhanced learning.") At base, the project of critical pedagogy, as Henry Giroux puts it, remains fixated on "[drawing] attention to the ways in which knowledge, power, desire, and experience are produced under specific basic conditions of learning and [illuminating] the role that pedagogy plays as part of a struggle over assigned meanings, modes of expression, and directions of desire, particularly as these bear on the formation of the multiple and ever-contradictory versions of the 'self' and its relationship to the larger society" (2011, p. 4).

It was through Freire's distinct voice that the project of critical pedagogy as we understand it today found its first real articulation. That being said, Freire's was an articulation of something that has always been latent in the "struggle to be more fully human" (Freire, 2005, p. 47), a calling-forth of something that is always calling out, always reaching from somewhere just below the surface of *what is*, like fingers stretching the outer membrane of the possible in the endless, groping "struggle for a fuller humanity" (Freire, 2005, p. 47). It was an articulation that contained within it traces and echoes of those who came before Freire, and those who came after, those who sense, have sensed, or will sense – without Freire to hard boil their sensation into something tangible and familiar – that the reality roiling under the austere lid of what we call *education* is much more complex and consequential than we are compelled to think, that the process of *teaching* is neither straightforward nor unilateral, that the subjects and objects of *learning* are never set, self-contained things, and that the *contexts* for learning are never neutral.

Whether known to Freire or not, his work condensed and soldered together various insights that had manifested in bits and pieces across the scattered works of earlier critical thinkers and traditions – from Karl Marx and G.W.F. Hegel to John Dewey and Anísio Teixeira, from W.E.B. DuBois and Lev Vygotsky to the Frankfurt School and Franz Fanon.[1] What emerged in Freire's work, and has since taken shape in the radical project of critical pedagogy, has always been rooted in that nagging, discomfiting sense that the societal and individual stakes of education are incredibly high and that the means and ends of learning will vary significantly depending on how "education" is defined. Moreover, as discussed in relation to the neoliberal apparatus of "technology-enhanced learning," the types of subjects we are trained to become, and the ways we are compelled to fit and function inside the hegemonic power structure, are likewise made contingent upon decisions about who (and what) gets to define education as such and determine where it will take place, what its goals will be, how those goals will be set and measured, etc. Critical pedagogy "picks up on the idea that educational processes, practices, and modes of engagement play an active role in the production and reproduction of social relations and systems. [It] seeks to understand and is concerned with the ways that schools and the educational process sustain and reproduce systems and relations of oppression" (Porfilio & Ford, 2015, p. xvi).

Whether in public schools, private schools, charter schools, officially approved independent programs, etc., we spend the better part of (at least) our first two decades of life being formally "educated" in the customs of social life along with all the other "necessary" practices and forms of knowledge that will presumably equip us, as independent agents, to successfully navigate the world "out there" that we are preparing to enter. But the critical pedagogical project understands that educational institutions themselves are not worlds apart. At every step of the way, our formalized processes of education are thoroughly integrated into and reflective of the broader, given power arrangement in our society; they are a critical node in "the machinery by which […] power relations give rise to a possible corpus of knowledge [and by which said] knowledge extends and reinforces the effects of this power" (Foucault, 1995, p. 29). Thus, these processes of formal education serve as a vital technology of subjectivation, training students and teachers to become the kind of responsible subjects who are well-adjusted to – and who will go forth to reproduce – the conditions of their own domination. "A central tenet of [critical] pedagogy maintains that the classroom, curricular, and school structures teachers enter are not neutral sites waiting to be shaped by educational professionals," Joe Kincheloe writes (2004, p. 2). Thus, "proponents of critical pedagogy understand that every dimension of schooling and every form of educational practice are politically contested spaces" (2004, p. 2). That "every dimension of schooling and every form of educational practice" are political is a given; that they are "politically contested spaces," however, is not. The dimensions of formal learning are political inasmuch as they are imbricated in an educational apparatus that is built to, at worst, functionally replicate the historico-specific conditions that bolster the dominant power arrangement or, at best, leave those conditions uncontested. The naturalness of the conditions that maintain and enforce the given power arrangement in the world "out there" is inscribed in the minds and bodies (mind-bodies) of students and teachers. Thus, by the time students are ready to take what they've learned in school and "make their way" in the world, the world has already made its way through them.

Schools and official education systems are by no means the only sites where the political forces of social reproduction come to a head, but they do serve as critical conductors of possibility for what is, at base, Freire's primary concern: the oscillating movements, electrical currents, and stubborn blood clots of the macro- and micro-dialectics playing out in the mutual shaping of individual and world. "World and human beings do not exist apart from each other," Freire writes, "they exist in constant interaction" (2005, p. 50). The struggle for "humanization" unfolds in the dynamic and slowed-down spaces of life where this "constant interaction" mediates the flow, distribution, capture, and dispersion of energies that shape and re-shape the world ... which shapes and re-shapes the human ... who shapes and re-shapes the world ... which shapes and re-shapes the human ... who shapes and re-shapes ... *ad infinitum*. As a point of departure from any sort of vulgar economic or material determinism, it follows that the project of critical pedagogy is imbued with a sense of undying *hope* that things *can* change, and that pedagogy can play a vital role in that change. "Hope is a natural, possible, and necessary impetus in the context of our unfinishedness. Hope is an indispensable seasoning in our human, historical experience. Without it, instead of history we would have pure determinism" (Freire, 1998, p. 69). This hope derives from the essential belief in the multidirectionality of energy flows in the dialectical struggles of everyday life, in the mutually constitutive, back-and-forth circuit between the world that inscribes itself upon us and our subjective resistance to inscription (Garoian & Gaudelius, 2001, p. 334). It is a belief in the fundamental capacity for "always-unfinished" individuals to break far enough away from the grip of the material, cognitive, embodied contexts of their domination that they can *learn* and develop a critical consciousness (*conscientização*) of the fact that this isn't the only way things can or should be. On top of this, it is a belief that said individuals can and must turn around and direct their liveliness at attacking the structural supports behind these contexts. At the very core of critical pedagogy is an essential presumption of breakable worlds and unfinished people in motion:

> Reality which becomes oppressive results in the contradistinction of men as oppressors and oppressed. The latter, whose task it is to struggle for their liberation together with those who show true solidarity, must acquire a critical awareness of oppression through the praxis of this struggle. One of the gravest obstacles to the achievement of liberation is that oppressive reality absorbs those within it and thereby acts to submerge human beings' consciousness. Functionally, oppression is domesticating. To no longer be prey to its force, one must emerge from it and turn upon it. This can be done only by means of the praxis: reflection and action upon the world in order to transform it (Freire, 2005, p. 51).

What Freire brings to the surface here is a conceptualization of education as a contestable site of *vulnerable and volatile encounter*. Such encounters are strategically contained and policed within the contexts of schooling systems (but also in realms like popular culture, government, etc.) which, in turn, serve to reproduce the conditions of pacification (or "domestication") of the oppressed many and the corresponding conditions of societal domination by the oppressive few. Freire's conceptualization of education also positions it as an encounter that trembles, always, with the potential for something more, something radical, something *else*.

The critical pedagogue understands that education, more or less, names the formalized, teleologized containment of the humanizing processes of *learning*, the generative power of which is recognized by the oppressive few as an inherent threat to the preservation and maintenance of their domination. It is, thus, among the most vital charges of the project of critical pedagogy to locate and interrogate the ways that, materially, symbolically, and practically, a society's existing educational apparatus functions to sustain an "oppressive reality" that works the oppressed over, submerging human beings' consciousness of their oppression and of the *contingent, pliable,* and *breakable* nature of the worldly conditions that oppress and dehumanize them. Such a charge, moreover, carries with it a critically conscious recognition that *who one is* is also contingent, pliable, and dependent upon a world in motion that is as well. "It approaches individual growth as active, cooperative, and social process, because the self and society create each other" (Shor, 1992, p. 15). And one must take that recognition and follow through with praxis to break the world that subjugates them: "To no longer be prey to its force, one must emerge from it and turn upon it" (Freire, 2005, p. 51).

It is of insurmountable importance for Freire and for critical pedagogy writ large – as it is for media theorists – that concern for the mutual making, un-making, and remaking of *human and world* in the dialectical meatgrinder of history, holds fast an ontological understanding of the human as a fundamentally open-ended thing whose being is always, necessarily, a *being-in-process*, mediated by changing worlds in and through which it can become what it will be. "Education as the practice of freedom – as opposed to education as the practice of domination – denies that man is abstract, isolated, independent, and unattached to the world; it also denies that the world exists as a reality apart from people" (Freire, 2005, p. 81). The human, that is, figures as a kind of circuit between "inside" and "outside," between the biological organism and the world, without which it could not be(come) itself. Whether tacitly or explicitly, critical pedagogy, "as the practice of freedom," presupposes a process of being wherein life is mediated by "external" worlds that make the human what it is, and critical pedagogy itself names a consciously praxical intervention in this process, a harnessing of the fact that the human, consciously or not, *must* and *always does* have a hand in making, reproducing, and altering the worlds in which it can be(come) itself.

Perhaps nowhere else is this point made more clearly than in the oft-stated contempt Freire and other critical pedagogues have for the "banking" concept of learning in which students are understood as "'containers' to be 'filled' by the teacher" with demonstrably replicable forms of knowledge whose retention by student-receptacles can be easily tested. In a lengthy passage from *Pedagogy of the Oppressed*, Freire writes:

> Implicit in the banking concept is the assumption of a dichotomy between human beings and the world: a person is merely in the world, not with the world or with others; the individual is spectator, not re-creator. In this view, the person is not a conscious being (*corpo consciente*); he or she is rather the possessor of a consciousness: an empty "mind" passively open to the reception of deposits of reality from the world outside. For example, my desk, my books, my coffee cup, all the objects before me – as bits of the world which surround me – would be "inside" me, exactly as I am inside my study right now. This view makes no distinction between being accessible to consciousness and entering consciousness. The distinction, however, is essential: the objects which surround me are simply accessible to my consciousness, not located within it. I am aware of them, but they are not inside me. It follows logically from the banking notion of consciousness that the educator's role is to regulate the way the world "enters into" the students. The teacher's task is to organise a process which already occurs spontaneously, to "fill" the students by making deposits of information which he or she considers to constitute true knowledge. And since people "receive" the world as passive entities, education should make them more passive still, and adapt them to the world. The educated individual is the adapted person, because she or he is better "fit" for the world. Translated into practice, this concept is well suited to the purposes of the oppressors, whose tranquility rests on how well people fit the world the oppressors have created, and how little they question it (2005, pp. 75–76).

At issue here is nothing less than the ontological presumption of the human being as either a self-contained being in and of itself that merely exists *in* the world, or a being that cannot be itself "with[out] the world or with[out] others." The banking concept of education obviously rests on the former presumption, which further presumes that the process of learning is a matter of *representation*; that is, a matter of translating the world into a data stream that can be "poured" into and re-presented in the isolated consciousness of students. Such a process "already occurs spontaneously" in daily life as we, isolated receptacles that we are, absorb, process, and retain data from the world around us, but it is the teacher's job to "organize" this process as a functionary of an educational apparatus, which is itself a functionary of the oppressive power arrangement in our given world. Education's functional service to this power arrangement, as Freire notes, involves "[regulating] the way the world 'enters into' the students," deputizing teachers (but also other operators in the educational apparatus, from principals and superintendents to legislators and textbook makers) as authoritative arbiters of what sort of knowledge does and doesn't get passed on. However, from lessons and activities to course materials and evaluations, the specific *content* of this organized learning, while having much potential for exerting a "domesticating" influence on the (a) critical consciousness of students, is perhaps less consequential than the routinized form of the learning process itself as modeled on the banking concept. "Education can socialize students into critical thought or into dependence on authority, that is, into autonomous habits of mind or into passive habits of following authorities, waiting to be told what to do and what things mean" (Shor, 1992, p. 13). Day in, day out, this process continually fortifies and enforces the ontological fiction that people are static, self-contained, "passive entities" who "'receive' the world" in discrete representational forms, thus adapting them to a world that secures its existing power arrangement by ensuring the passivity of the oppressed and the accomplices of the oppressors.

In its varied iterations, and throughout its necessary critical reevaluations, the project of critical pedagogy has maintained a consistent and vital antagonism to this ontological fiction itself, which undergirds the banking concept of education. In the harried and high-stakes race to determine what learning will be in the digital age, however, this ontological fiction has found ever more sophisticated means of universalizing and enforcing itself. That the neoliberal apparatus of "technology-enhanced learning" has materialized a political epistemology that is founded upon this fiction is a case in point. And a critical pedagogy that is up to the task of contesting it must work to relocate the process of learning in the open spaces and soft tissue through which the dialectical negotiation of self and world is eternally mediated. To do so requires that, rather than eliciting a "compliant response to [specific] designed features" (Conole & Dyke, 2004, p. 302), the task of critically learning with and through (digital) media will necessarily entail exploring the contexts of our own "unfinishedness," and doing so within the generative matrix of possibility that is afforded by a relation to media that is not prescribed beforehand.

The goal here, of course, is not to give a complete and thorough accounting of the admittedly broad field of critical pedagogy and its many practical and theoretical variations, critiques, divergences, etc., but to tease out the underlying ontological assumptions (we might even say "ontological affordances") that make the radical project of critical pedagogy conceivable, let alone possible. Doing this work is especially crucial for critical pedagogues as we attempt to find and cultivate spaces where we and our students can develop a critical consciousness of – and the praxical means for intervening in – the diffuse operations of power in our twenty-first-century media-worlds. Because without interrogating the medial conditions that make us who we are, without feeling out and analyzing the dialectical circuits that open us and our world up to one another, and without grasping that the *hope* of liberatory learning is not inherent to the educational media we use but, rather, to the mediation of being as such, then we cannot hope to develop a sufficiently critical pedagogy for the digital age. Once again, Morris and Stommel's arguments in *An Urgency of Teachers* are instructive here:

> The tools we use for learning, the ones that have become so ubiquitous, each influence what, where, and how we learn – and, even more, how we think about learning. Books. Pixels. Trackpads. Keyboards. E-books. Databases. Digital archives. Learning management systems. New platforms and interfaces are developed every week, popping up like daisies (or wildfires). None of these tools have what we value most about education coded into them in advance. The best digital tools inspire us, often to use them in ways the designer couldn't anticipate. The worst digital tools attempt to dictate our pedagogies, determining what we can do with them and for whom. The digital pedagogue teaches her tools, doesn't let them teach her (2018).

This is why our focus has not necessarily been on the critical pedagogical affordances of specific digital learning technologies but, rather, on the critical pedagogical importance of openly exploring the matrix of possibility afforded by the very (and varying) ways we relate to technology. As noted earlier, the practical, epistemological, and even ontological violence of the cold neoliberal apparatus of "technology-enhanced learning" is enforced by the deployment of digital learning tools that leave as little room as possible for learning by way of exploring and expanding the potentialities of how we relate to media – and that, instead, dictate, limit, monitor, quantify, and monetize learning for us. And it would be a grave mistake to believe that these barriers to critical learning can be overcome through the incorporation of newer, "better" media into the learning process. It is incumbent upon us, rather, to develop and practice a critical pedagogy that directly challenges the ontological fiction embodied in such techno-fetishist instrumentality. "Digital pedagogy is not equivalent to teachers using digital tools. Rather, digital pedagogy demands that we think critically about our tools, demands that we reflect actively upon our own practice […] Good digital pedagogy is just good pedagogy" (Morris & Stommel, 2018).

In the increasingly digitalized classroom, how one practically develops their own critical pedagogy in conversation with students will, of course, vary widely depending on the institutional contexts, the life experiences and literacies collected in said classroom, and so on. But this does not mean that the introduction of digital technologies has somehow rewritten critical pedagogy's core concern for the "struggle to be more fully human" (Freire, 2005, p. 47) or its defining ontological assumptions about the mediation of being through the dialectical circuit between self and world. We must be wary if we start to believe otherwise, lest we submit to the same repressive logic by which the neoliberal apparatus of "technology-enhanced learning" reduces the scope of how we define ourselves, our media, and how they relate to one another. The more that our place in twenty-first-century media-worlds is dictated by such apparatuses, which boil our potential relations to new media down to a slate of prescribed uses, the more easily we are compelled to accept and abide by the ontological fiction by which they operate; that is, by the notion that we and the media through which we "learn" are discrete, closed-off, self-contained entities that do not need each other to be what they are. This is all the more reason to appreciate how necessary the project of critical pedagogy is for helping us and our students navigate the contemporary media-worlds we inhabit. Because the project of critical pedagogy is, at base, a media project: a struggle, that is, to find, feel, interrogate, attack, and rework the inextricable, mutually constituting medial connections between human and world. The ontological assumptions underwriting the very hope and possibility of critical pedagogy are nothing if not the essential coordinates for a media theory of being.

Before we can even begin to ask what digital media can do for the project of critical pedagogy, critical pedagogy enjoins us to confront the medial conditions of life itself. As a project of "humanization" that is, from the beginning, a technical praxis of negotiating the enlivened circuitry mediating human and world as they make, un-make, and re-make each other, critical pedagogy drills into the bedrock of media theory from its own distinct angle. The project of critical pedagogy is ultimately based on critically interrogating, working with, and challenging the medial conditions that give historical shape to the "transductive"[2] relationship between human and world. As such, critical pedagogy eschews the ontological conceptualization of the medium in the same instrumentalist register of a tool whose relation to the human upholds the chauvinistic fiction of a self-contained, isolated subject. Instead, it embraces a conceptualization of the medium, as Mark B. N. Hansen puts it, "as an *environment for life*" (2006, p. 299). The project of critical pedagogy, that is, strives for a process of humanization that unfolds through (not apart from) the circuitry of the world that mediate our lives, because it is that mediation of life through the "external" that makes us human in the first place.

"Before it becomes available to designate any given, technically-specific form of conversion or mediation," Hansen notes, "medium names an ontological condition of humanization – the constitutive dimension of exteriorization that is part and parcel of the transduction of technics and life" (2006, p. 300). Media theorists like Hansen and Bernard Stiegler take critical pedagogy's ontological assumptions to their roots; that is, to the "originary" constitution of the human, as such, as a technically mediated being, as a being (a distinct species) co-originated *with and through* technical mediation. Building on the work of paleontologist André Leroi-Gourhan, Stiegler asserts that human beings have evolved in ways that cannot be explained in purely zoological/biological terms. Our evolution inheres in the passing on of knowledge through externalized cultural worlds, the construction and maintenance of which is made possible through technics. The technical worlds we create, the worlds in which we can live and be, are the very medial support for a non-biological, "epiphylogenetic" memory; thus, the evolution that constitutes us *as* human is, from the beginning, *technical*:

> The problem arising here is that the evolution of this essentially technical being that the human is exceeds the biological, although this dimension is an essential part of the technical phenomenon itself, something like its enigma. The evolution of the "prosthesis," not itself living, by which the human is nonetheless defined as a living being, constitutes the reality of the human's evolution, as if, with it, the history of life were to continue by means other than life: this is the paradox of a living being characterized in its forms of life by the nonliving – or by the traces that its life leaves in the nonliving (Stiegler, 1998, p. 50).

Stiegler's description thus presents human evolution as irreducibly biological *and* technical, occurring as a process of what he terms "epiphylogenesis" (evolution of human life "by means other than life"). The human becomes itself through technical mediation, and human evolution is, necessarily, the "evolution of the 'prosthesis,'" which is, from the beginning, an exteriorization of the living organism in its pursuit of life by means other than life. "From this perspective," Hansen argues, "the medium is, from the very onset, a concept that is irrevocably implicated in life, in the epiphylogenesis of the human, and in the history to which it gives rise *qua* history of concrete effects" (2006, pp. 299–300). By the same token, human life is irrevocably implicated in the process of mediation:

> Thus, long before the appearance of the term 'medium' in the English language, and also long before the appearance of its root, the Latin term *medium* (meaning middle, center, midst, intermediate course, thus something implying mediation or an intermediary), the medium existed as an operation fundamentally bound up with the living, but also with the technical. *The medium, we might say, is implicated in the living as essentially technical, in what I elsewhere call 'technical life'; it is the operation of mediation – and perhaps also the support for the always concrete mediation – between a living being and the environment. In this sense, the medium perhaps names the very transduction between the organism and the environment that constitutes life as essentially technical*; thus it is nothing less than a medium for the exteriorization of the living, and correlatively, for the selective actualization of the environment, for the creation of what Francisco Varela calls a 'surplus significance', a demarcation of a world, of an existential domain, from the unmarked environment as such (Hansen, 2006, p. 300, emphases added).

From the vantage point of critical pedagogy, as noted previously, the human is necessarily understood as an open-ended *being-in-process*. It is, in fact, only upon such an understanding of the human that any sort of substance can be found in critical pedagogy's dialectical assertion that the oppressive historical *contexts* of students' lived experience and learning dig into and shape the *content* of their humanity. And it is only upon such an understanding that any sort of *hope* can be found in the promise that things can be different. From the vantage point of media theory, the processuality of our humanity is necessarily understood as *being-in-media*. Thus, mirroring Freire's assertion that critical pedagogy "denies that man is abstract, isolated, independent, and unattached to the world" and that "it also denies that the world exists as a reality apart from people" (2005, p. 81), Stiegler argues that "[t]he paradox [of *being-in-media*] is to have to speak of an exteriorization without a preceding interior: the interior is constituted in exteriorization … the appearance of the human is the appearance of the technical" (1998, p. 141). For Stiegler, the aporetic relationship between "inside" and "outside," "interior" and "exterior," "subject" and "object," can only be understood as *différance* – a movement of differing and deferral without origin, a transductive synthesis mutually constituting the *who* and the *what* while giving the illusion of their opposition.

Media are the passageways of being, the transductive circuitry by which human and world constitute each other as essentially inseparable in "technical life." Through technical mediation, we "selectively actualize" our environments that actualize us, creating worlds in and through which we become ourselves. "Making worlds is something humans do in order to be human. Our species came to define itself by our need to live in worlds we've had a hand in building" (Alvarez, 2018). Just as critical pedagogy posits the open-ended, mutual construction of human and world on its way to deconstructing the ontological fiction of the human as a passive, self-enclosed being underwriting the banking concept of education, so media theory posits life itself as technical mediation on its way to deconstructing the ontological fiction of the human as independent singularity whose humanity is not defined in communion with the world but by instrumental dominion over it. "Humans simply don't want to give up their self-assigned precious place in the modern cosmological hierarchy," Dominic Pettman writes (2006, p. 163). "Those definitions of technology which expel this phenomenon outside of the human sphere, quarantining it in 'objects' and 'machines' and 'artificial entities,' do so according to the logic of apartheid" (2006, p. 164). And there are consequences. Inasmuch as the banking concept of education traps us in pacified submission to oppressive power arrangements that anesthetize our critical capacities, "ignoring the function, genealogy, and history of those sociotechnical imbroglios […] that construct our political life and our fragile humanity" (Latour, 1994, p. 42), hubristically maintaining the illusion that we are always "in the driver's seat" – that we are always, only, beings *in* and not *with* and *through* the world – blinds us to the ways that the fragility of ourselves and our worlds is harnessed, exploited, and "enframed" in ways that point to the eventual destruction of both. "Quite simply, then, we are slaves to the notion that we are masters" (Pettman, 2006, p. 171).

As mentioned previously, the stakes here are quite high. Without closely and critically working through how the mediation of life itself operates as the ontological condition of possibility for the radical project of critical pedagogy as such, we run the perpetual risk of accepting and abiding by the ontological fictions of techno-political apparatuses that have an explicitly vested interest in foreclosing that possibility. "For the most part," as Paulo Blikstein writes, "schools have adopted computers as tools to empower extant curricular subtexts – i.e., as information devices or teaching machines" (2008, p. 209). And one can see how, nearly fifty years after Freire published his seminal work, the deployment of digital technologies in the classroom offers new opportunities for re-inscribing the conditions of students' subjective passivity that Freire linked to the banking concept:

> ... the traditional use of technology in schools contains its own hidden curriculum. It surreptitiously fosters students who are consumers of software and not constructors; adapt to the machine and not reinvent it; and accept the computer as a black box which only specialists can understand, program, or repair. For the most part, these passive uses of technologies include unidirectional access to information (the computer as an electronic library), communicate with other people (the computer as a telephone), and propagate information to others (the computer as a blackboard or newspaper). Not surprisingly, therefore, the new digital technologies are commonly called ICT (Information and Communication Technologies). In sum, a [critical digital pedagogy] – injecting into a critique of education a subversive political agenda – might position computers, for the most, as commonly recruited by "the system" to inculcate in future consumers the learned passivity that supports capitalism by perpetuating its inherent inequities. Yet, the most revolutionary aspect of the computer [...] is not to use it as an information machine, but as a universal construction environment (Blikstein, 2008, p. 209).

When it comes to learning as the vital process of humanization, digital technologies only "afford" as much as our critical pedagogical relation to them makes possible. As Blikstein notes, students' capacities to learn with and through these technologies depends on the contexts in which "learning" is defined as either "passive use" or as a matter of creativity and construction that enjoins students to directly engage and explore the medial points where their humanity can be felt in the circuital flow between "inside" and "outside," between self and world. From the analog to the digital, education without an active, critical, probing concern for the medial conditions of being-in-process, for the human as an open-ended thing whose being is mediated in and through the world, will further expose the vulnerable humanity of students and teachers to the oppressive forces that aim to pacify and subjugate them, which, in the age of global neoliberal dominance, is "part of [the] broader goal of creating new subjects wedded to the logic of privatization, efficiency, flexibility, the accumulation of capital, and the destruction of the social state" (Giroux, 2011, p. 910).

The techno-fetishist conceit that digital media will "enhance" learning on their own rests on the very same ontological assumptions that critical pedagogy and/as media theory aim(s) to deconstruct. In this context, then, to "think critically about our tools," as Morris and Stommel encourage us to do, is to eschew thinking that presumes tools to be simply "ours" to "use"; it is, rather, to embrace a praxical understanding of such tools, and ourselves, as being situated within the medial networks through which life and self and world become in – and as – flux. Likewise, it is to see that integrating digital media into the learning process ultimately serves to bolster our contemporary conditions of neoliberal domination insofar as they continue to sediment and enforce the ontological fiction of clear distinctions between subject and object, inside and outside, user and tool, human and world. However, as Mark Deuze writes, "If we let go of this deception – this dualistic fallacy of domination of man over machine (or vice versa) – it may be possible to come to terms with the world we are a part of in ways that are less about effects, things and what *happens*, more about process [and] practice" (2012, p. xiii). What might it look like, then, to practice a critical digital pedagogy that – as all critical pedagogy inevitably must – fosters and bears witness to learning as the struggle of *beings-in-process* to become "more fully human," to learning not as a matter of "banking," "using," "quantifying," or "testing," but as "a way of living that fuses life with material and mediated conditions of living in ways that bypass the real or perceived dichotomy between such constituent elements of human existence" (Deuze, 2012, p. 3)? This, again, is the core of critical pedagogy as such. In any of its multitudinous variations and iterations, the radical project of critical pedagogy is, at base, "a matter of studying reality that is alive, reality that we are living inside of, reality as history being made and also making us" (Freire, 1985, p. 18). As an extension of the actuated environment in which the technical mediation of life itself takes place, what might it mean *to learn to become human* in a digitally connected reality that is, itself, "alive"? What might it mean, and what practical forms might it take, if we approach the process of learning with digital technologies as a matter of aiding – of *midwifing*[3] – students' development of their own critical capacities to not only read the world as a concept or text, but to intervene in it as the vibrant contexts of their being – not just as an objective "outside" environment in which they live, but as the porous, moveable circuitry mediating life itself, shaping who they are at any given time as they struggle to shape it?

This article has been reprinted with permission from *Media Theory*.
Alvarez, M. (2019). (Digital) media as critical pedagogy. *Media Theory*, 3(1). https://mediatheoryjournal.org/maximillian-alvarez-digital-media-as-critical-pedagogy/

## Notes

1. For more on critical pedagogy's antecedents and on Freire's intellectual precursors and influences, see: Allen, R. L. (2013). Whiteness and critical pedagogy. *Educational Philosophy and Theory*, 36(2), 121–136; Deans, T. (1999). Service-learning in two keys: Paulo Freire's critical pedagogy in relation to John Dewey's Pragmatism. *Michigan Journal of Community Service Learning*, 6(1), 15–29; Fischman, G. E., & McLaren, P. (2005). Rethinking critical pedagogy and the Gramscian and Freirian legacies. *Cultural Studies ↔ Critical Methodologies*, 5(4), 425–447; Giroux, H. A. (2011). *On critical pedagogy*. New York: Continuum; Gottesman, I. (2010). Sitting in the waiting room: Paulo Freire and the critical turn in the field of education. *Educational Studies*, 46(4), 376–399; Kincheloe, J. L. (2004). *Critical pedagogy*. New York: Peter Lang; Kress, T., & Lake, R. (Eds.). (2013). *Paulo Freire's intellectual roots: Toward historicity in Praxis*. London: Bloomsbury
2. "Transduction, following Gilbert Simondon's conceptualization, is a relation in which the relation itself holds primacy over the terms related" (Hansen, 2005, p.299)
3. It is especially helpful to think of the teaching side of the vulnerable educational encounter, as I've described it here, in the terms laid out by Jacques Rancière in his (in)famous analysis of *The Ignorant Schoolmaster*. For Rancière, this encounter will only re-inscribe the inequalities and undemocratic hierarchies in the given aesthetic arrangement of our world if it begins from the presumption of inequality, with the teacher occupying the privileged position of *the one who knows more* than her pupils and who tries, however genuinely, to reach a state of equal knowledge between her and her pupils through teaching. The educational encounter, instead, must begin from the (democratic) presumption of *equality* in the capacity to learn with different forms of knowledge and expertise signaling different "manifestations" of common intelligence, which must be used by the teacher to pose questions and to try to help draw out ("midwife") and *bear witness to* students' exercise of their capacity to learn: "Here is everything that is in Calypso: The power of intelligence that is in any human manifestation. The same intelligence makes nouns and mathematical signs. What's more, it also makes signs and reasonings. There aren't two sorts of minds. There is inequality in the *manifestations* of intelligence, according to the greater or lesser energy communicated to the intelligence by the will for discovering and combining new relations; but there is no hierarchy of *intellectual capacity*" (1991, p.27)

## References

Ahalt, S., & Fecho, K. (2015). *Ten Emerging Technologies for Higher Education* [White Paper]. viewed 1 April 2019, from RENCI.org: <https://renci.org/wpcontent/uploads/2015/02/EmergingTechforHigherEd.pdf>

Alvarez, M. (2017). Administering Evil, *The Baffler*, 29 November, viewed 8 April 2019, <https://thebaffler.com/the-poverty-of-theory/administering-evil>

Alvarez, M. (2018). The Death of Media, *The Baffler*, 20 June 2018, viewed 10 September 2018, <https://thebaffler.com/the-poverty-of-theory/the-death-ofmedia>

Blikstein, P. (2008). Travels in Troy with Freire: Technology as an agent of Emancipation. In P. Noguera & C. Torres (Eds.), *Social justice education for teachers: Paulo Freire and the possible dream* (pp. 205–244). Rotterdam: Sense Publishers.

Bousquet, M. (2008). *How the university works: Higher education and the low-wage nation.* New York: NYU Press.

Brock, R., & Orelus, P. (Eds.). (2015). *Interrogating critical pedagogy: The voices of educators of color in the movement.* New York: Routledge.

Brown, W. (2015). *Undoing the demos: Neoliberalism's stealth revolution.* New York: ZONE Books.

Cervone, J. (2018). *Corporatizing rural education: Neoliberal globalization and reaction in the United States.* Cham: Palgrave Macmillan.

Clarke, J. (2004). Dissolving the public realm? The logics and limits of neoliberalism. *Journal of Social Policy*, *33*(1), 27–48.

Conole, G., & Dyke, M. (2004). Understanding and using technological affordances: A response to Boyle and Cook. *Research in Learning Technology*, *12*(3), 301–308.

Deuze, M. (2012). *Media life.* Cambridge, UK: Polity Press.

Ellsworth, E. (1989). Why doesn't this feel empowering? Working through the repressive myths of critical pedagogy. *Harvard Educational Review*, *59*(3), 297-324.

Erevelles, N. (2000). Educating unruly bodies: Critical pedagogy, disability studies, and the politics of schooling. *Educational Theory*, *50*(1), 25–47.

Feenberg, A., & Jandrić, P. (2015). The bursting boiler of digital education: Critical pedagogy and philosophy of technology. *Knowledge Cultures*, *3*(5), 132–148.

Foucault, M. (1995). *Discipline and punish* (A. Sheridan, Trans.). New York: Vintage Books.

Freire, P. (1985). Reading the world and reading the word: An interview with Paulo Freire. *Language Arts*, *62*(1), 15–21.

Freire, P. (1998). *Pedagogy of freedom: Ethics, democracy, & civic courage* (P. Clarke, Trans.). Lanham: Rowman & Littlefield.

Freire, P. (2005). *Pedagogy of the oppressed (30$^{th}$ Anniversary Edition)* (M. Ramos, Trans.). New York: Continuum.

Fuller, M., & Goffey, A. (2012). *Evil media.* Cambridge: The MIT Press.

Garoian, C.R. & Gaudelius, Y.M. (2001). Cyborg pedagogy: Performing resistance in the digital age. *Studies in Art Education*, *42*(4), 333–347.

Giroux, H. (2011). *On critical pedagogy.* New York: Continuum.

Giroux, H. (2014). *Neoliberalism's war on higher education.* Chicago: Haymarket Books.

Hall, G. (2016). *The uberfication of the university.* Minneapolis: University of Minnesota Press.

Hansen, M. B. N. (2006). Media theory. *Theory, Culture & Society*, *23*(2–3), 297–306.

Hayes, S. (2015). Counting on use of technology to enhance learning. In P. Jandrić & D. Boras (Eds.), *Critical learning in digital networks* (pp. 15–36). New York: Springer.

Hutchby, I. (2001). Technologies, texts and affordances. *Sociology, 35*(2), 441–456.

Jeffery, D., & Smith, K. (2013). Critical pedagogies in the neoliberal university: What happens when they go digital? *The Canadian Geographer/Le Géographe Canadien, 57*(3), 372–380.

Kincheloe, J. (2004). *Critical pedagogy.* New York: Peter Lang.

Latour, B. (1994). On technical mediation – Philosophy, sociology, genealogy. *Common Knowledge, 3*(2), 29–64.

Liu, A. (2013). Imagining the new media encounter. In R. Siemens & S. Schreibman (Eds.), *A companion to digital literary studies* (pp. 3–25). Malden: Wiley-Blackwell.

Morris, S., & Stommel, J. (2018). *An urgency of teachers: The work of critical digital pedagogy.* [Creative Commons ebook] Pressbooks, accessed 10 August 2018, <https://criticaldigitalpedagogy.pressbooks.com/>

Mullen, M. (2002). "If You're Not Mark Mullen, Click Here": Web-based courseware and the pedagogy of suspicion. *The Radical Teacher, 63*, 14–20.

Newfield, C. (2008). *Unmaking the public university: The forty-year assault on the middle class.* Cambridge: Harvard University Press.

Newfield, C. (2016). *The great mistake: How we wrecked public universities and how we can fix them.* Baltimore: Johns Hopkins University Press.

Pettman, D. (2006). *Love and other technologies: Retrofitting eros for the information age.* New York: Fordham University Press.

Porfilio, B., & Ford, D. (2015). Schools and/as barricades: An introduction. In B. Porfilio & D. Ford (Eds.), *Leaders in critical pedagogy: Narratives for understanding and solidarity* (pp. xv–xxv). Rotterdam: Sense Publishers.

Rancière, J. (1991). *The ignorant schoolmaster: Five lessons in intellectual emancipation* (K. Ross, Trans.). Stanford: Stanford University Press.

Scholz, T. (2011). Introduction: Learning through digital media. In T. Scholz (Ed.), *Learning through digital media: Experiments in technology and pedagogy* (pp. XIII–XIII). New York: Institute for Distributed Creativity.

Schrecker, E. (2010). *The lost soul of higher education: Corporatization, the assault on academic freedom, and the end of the American university.* New York: The New Press.

Selwyn, N. (2017). The discursive construction of education in the digital age. In R.H. Jones, A. Chik, & C. A. Hafner (Eds.), *Discourse and digital practices: Doing discourse analysis in the digital.* Routledge.

Shapiro, S. (1999). *Pedagogy and the politics of the body: A critical praxis.* New York: Garland.

Shor, I. (1992). *Empowering education: Critical teaching for social change.* Chicago: The University of Chicago Press.

Steinberg, S. (2015). Preface. In B. Porfilio & D. Ford (Eds.), *Leaders in critical pedagogy: Narratives for understanding and solidarity* (pp. ix–xi). Rotterdam: Sense Publishers.

Stiegler, B. (1998). *Technics and time, 1: The fault of epimetheus* (R. Beardsworth & G. Collins, Trans.). Stanford: Stanford University Press.

Talib, S. (2018). Social media pedagogy: Applying an interdisciplinary approach to teach multi-modal critical digital literacy. *E-Learning and Digital Media, 15*(2), 55–66.

U.S. Department of Education. (2019). Use of technology in teaching and learning. Viewed 1 April 2019, <https://www.ed.gov/oii-news/use-technology-teachingand-learning>

Watters, A., & Young, J. (2016). Why Audrey Watters thinks tech is a Trojan Horse set to "Dismantle" the academy. *The Chronicle of Higher Education*, 18 May, viewed 5 April 2019, <https://www.chronicle.com/article/Why-Audrey-Watters-ThinksTech/236525>

Weiner, E. (2004). *Private learning, public needs: The neoliberal assault on democratic education.* New York: Peter Lang.

CHAPTER FIVE

# Teaching and Learning in Hybrid Environments: Professor and Student Perspectives

DELORES D. LISTON AND HEATHER M. HULING

This chapter provides insight into the dynamics of two second-year doctoral-level hybrid courses addressing critical pedagogy. These courses are *Inquiry and Development into Educational Practice* (EDUC 9133) and *Advanced Critical Pedagogy* (EDUC 9233), both taught partially online and meeting in-person three times per semester. The hybrid format provides "the best of both worlds," online and in-person. Many of the challenges of teaching entirely online courses (e.g., explaining course requirements and expectations) are eliminated through the in-person meetings. Likewise, the challenges of synchronous learning required by exclusively in-person courses (e.g., commute time to the campus, setting class meeting times that do not match potential students' schedules) are greatly reduced from a minimum of sixteen to a maximum of four in-person meetings by the asynchronous online components. Both the in-person and online delivery formats temper critical pedagogy in different ways.

The courses are offered as part of the pedagogy component of an Ed.D. in Curriculum Studies program at a research-intensive comprehensive university in the Southeastern United States. This program has been offered using the hybrid model of delivery for nearly twenty years, and the student population matriculates from home counties across the state. Approximately 85% of doctoral students in the program are classroom teachers. Many intend to remain in the classroom as lead teachers, teacher coaches, or other leadership teaching roles. Others seek to move into college-level teaching, and our program successfully prepares students for both of these roles. Students in this program follow a cohort model which provides a ready-made support network of peers, with some flexibility for pursuing alternate pathways at second and third-year stages of the program. These courses in the pedagogy component are taken in the second year of study by a subset of each cohort interested in the pedagogical applications of the curriculum studies program. *Inquiry and Development into Educational Practice* is offered in the Fall, and *Advanced Critical Pedagogy* is offered in the Spring. Students generally take both of these courses in sequence. However, students may take one and not the other.

*Inquiry and Development into Educational Practice* (I&D) is designed to introduce second-year Ed.D. students to the theoretical perspectives of critical pedagogy and encourage them to begin seeing themselves as social justice educators. Doctoral candidates develop competencies in the research and design of grant and presentation proposals, as well as in the reflective analysis of teaching and professional growth. The class is comprised of students with an emphasis in K-12 or higher education. This class is taught using hybrid model with assignments and discussions submitted via Folio (Desire to Learn platform), as well as in-person classes three times per semester. Feedback on each assignment is provided online, and assignments are discussed in detail during in-person meetings.

*Advanced Critical Pedagogy* (ACP) is designed to provide the candidates with a deeper critical understanding, cementing their role as social justice educators practicing critical pedagogy. This course focuses on exploring the dimensions of inquiry as it supports, enhances, and strengthens the development of educational practice in a variety of settings. As with the I&D course, this class is also comprised of students with an emphasis in K-12 or higher education. It is taught using the hybrid model with assignments and discussions submitted via Folio (Desire to Learn platform), as well as in-person classes on campus three times during the semester. As with the I&D course, feedback on each assignment is provided online, and assignments are discussed in detail during campus meetings.

The first course in the sequence, I&D *introduces* students to critical pedagogy and requires students to explore themselves as critical pedagogues through autobiography, the primary assignment for this course, completed twice during the semester. The second course in the sequence, ACP *complexifies* critical pedagogy through bringing in international critical pedagogy discourse (see Appendix A for course requirements). Further, in this second course, students utilize a critical pedagogy lens to gain greater understanding of how and why one person's critical pedagogy may differ from another person's critical pedagogy. Ideally, students at the end of the second course should be able to discern how and why a critical pedagogy steeped in McLaren and Giroux (Darder et al., 2017; Giroux, 1983/

2017; McLaren, 1989/2017) is different from a one steeped in Freire and hooks (Darder, 2002/2017; Darder et al., 2016a; Freire, 1970/2005; hooks, 1994/2017) and is different still from critical pedagogy steeped in Fanon, Spivak and Said (Abu-Shomar, 2013/2016; Darder et al., 2016b; Dei, 2005/2016).

These hybrid courses further help students begin to see how the concepts of gender, race, social class, and sexual orientation directly influence who they are and how they conceptualize themselves as teachers. That is, the goal is to move students from memorizing definitions to redefining themselves as social justice educators.

The two authors, professor and student, explore each of these dynamics as experienced from their perspective as teacher or learner. Of particular importance, in keeping with the underlying theoretical framework of critical pedagogy (Freire, 1998, 1970/2005; Gay, 2010; hooks, 1994, 2003; Ladson-Billings, 1995, 2014), is the level of engagement with the assignments and readings, interaction with peers, interaction and support from the professor, as well as overall professional growth and knowledge acquisition in each model, especially in relation to critical pedagogy.

Exploring both the intention and design of instruction from the perspective of the professor while simultaneously exploring the experience of this design from the perspective of the student provides new insights on the teacher-learner relationship. Greater equanimity in the relation resonates with the goals and values of critical pedagogy (hooks, 2003). This exploration helps bridge the gap between what the professor teaches and what the student learns.

## Instructor's Perspective

In the first course, I&D, my objective as an instructor is for students to "get their feet wet" and consider how their own socio-economic status, gender identity, racial identity and sexual orientation, along with that of their family for three generations back, have had real-world influences on themselves as educators. To accomplish this, I assign students the writing of their own autobiography as bookends to the course.

When I inherited this course, the syllabus required three assignments: an autobiography, a grant proposal, and a literature review. From my previous experiences attempting to get students to write or even talk about how identity and social class influence their own lives, I knew they tended to avoid these topics. Therefore, I created a second, final, autobiography paper (see Appendix B). The hope was that after feedback on the first paper, and following class discussion, students would be better able to analyze their experiences from a critical pedagogy perspective.

True to form, in the first version students concentrated on telling their story and why they became educators, generally avoiding the influences of topics such as race, gender, class and sexual orientation on their experiences. The second version carried more weight in the grading segment of the class, and students provided deeper analysis of how these sociocultural aspects contributed to their identity and life.

In this first course, students also write and submit a proposal for a grant which they identify as providing support for their work as social justice educators. Thus, they take action in their professional lives to secure funds, for example, to bring new technologies to their Title I schools; or apply for STEM funding for their African American and Latino students; and similar projects.

Lastly, students submit a literature review (see Appendix C) which may contribute to their dissertation study. For most students in the class, this is their first introduction to writing a review of literature, and they struggle with differentiating a literature review from a typical research paper. The literature review is revisited in the ACP course.

My objective for the second course is for students to push that personal frame, which they developed through autobiographical investigation, in a more scholarly direction and gain insight into variations on the themes and perspectives of critical pedagogy. The ACP course encourages students to explore the strengths and weaknesses of a variety of critical pedagogy perspectives as they develop their own theoretical framework for their dissertation and continuing scholarship. The primary texts for this course are *The Critical Pedagogy Reader* (Darder et al., 2017) and *The International Critical Pedagogy Reader* (Darder et al., 2016a).

This course is conducted as a seminar wherein students read the material, write brief integrative papers, and then discuss the primary topics they identify as important. Prior to the second and third in-person meetings, students write integrative papers drawing from at least three different chapters in each text as well as at least three sources they have identified on their own as related to the topics discussed in the chapters from our course readings. In-person class meetings provide interactive opportunities for students to identify the variety of interpretations their peers brought to the readings.

The final assignment for this ACP course is to write a new literature review based on feedback they received from the professor on the previous version and incorporating critical pedagogy as a theoretical framework guiding the interpretation of the literature. Most students in this course will have identified at least a tentative dissertation topic.

Having taught doctoral-level hybrid classes for nearly twenty years, I have transitioned through a number of pedagogical strategies while waiting for technology to catch up with how I wanted to teach my online and in-person courses. Initially, I attempted synchronous chats and discovered that as an all or nothing proposition in which students either all respond at the same time and with an overwhelming level of redundancy; or, no one types anything until the professor types additional questions. I quickly abandoned synchronous chats for asynchronous discussion boards and was pleased with this format for a number of years. In this pedagogical vein, initially I would post questions based on the readings to the discussion board and students would have so many days to reply. Again, redundancy caused me to develop more staggered response rates where students were grouped together to either reply to me or further develop the discussion by replying to one or two peers.

One benefit of hybrid classes is the clarity gained by in-person communication. Therefore, class business questions are addressed in the first in-person meeting. Courses meet the first time very early on in the semester with one smaller assignment due just before the first meeting. The first 20 minutes of the campus meeting are spent clarifying assignments, and the rest of the class is spent deconstructing the initial assignment and using that discussion to present the class content. Assignments in my classes are very specific and are almost always posted on the discussion board for the whole class to see. Recently, I have also added a peer review of assignments (See Appendix D). This peer review ensures that students read the assignments of their classmates as well as providing them with an overview of the variety of ways their classmates interpreted the assignment. Additionally, this peer review introduces doctoral students to the gold standard peer review processes of scholarship, hopefully also developing a more scholarly relationship with published works as they progress through the doctoral program.

In her detailed narrative below, Huling describes thoughts and feelings as she evaluates her experiences in the two hybrid courses. Her voice is best to express the challenges she faced. She discusses the ways she learned and changed, from the difficulties related to learning critical pedagogy to the transformation that now allows the development of her own teaching praxis working with student teachers.

## A Student's Perspective

Taking classes in this doctoral program was a drastic change from my other graduate school experience. My mind was stretched and challenged in ways that I was not expecting while learning about critical pedagogy in a hybrid course format. Most graduate courses I took until then had been fully online. Upon entering the doctoral program, I was introduced to hybrid courses. This blended learning included both online and in-person components to maximize instruction (Dunbar & Melton, 2018; Ko & Rossen, 2017).

When taking the I&D course, I read several texts that I considered to be works from which our professors wanted to us learn content. I would read online and take notes to summarize the content without really stopping to think about what each author was discussing. I quickly learned from our professor that critical pedagogy is about questioning the views, not necessarily taking all of the content at face value. This skill of critiquing the work of other authors helped me start to see the real backbone of my understanding of critical pedagogy (Freire, 1998, 1970/2005; Gay, 2010; hooks, 1994, 2003; Ladson-Billings, 1995, 2014). Within both I&D and ACP, our professor had us engage in assignments and activities that taught us what critical pedagogy is and how it is applied to our professional and personal lives.

For these hybrid classes, we wrote two versions of one assignment during the semester—once at the beginning and again toward the end. Between these submissions, we received feedback from our peers and our professor. Feedback from the professor provided guidance on what direction to take when we wrote the next paper and what we would discuss in class. No two papers were ever the same and typically pushed us to think and reflect more on theory in our new work. These multistage assignments afforded us to truly experience growth as critical pedagogues. Completing an assignment, receiving feedback, and then applying that feedback immediately in the next iteration of the assignment pushed us to develop the concepts.

For the first course, I&D, the two-part assignment was an autobiography paper that explored our understanding of our place as a social justice educator. To do this, our professor challenged us to gather materials that placed us into a socio-historical context for *at least* three generations in our family. We had to consider multiple dimensions of identity, historical context of events, the intersection of both of those, and the impact these have had on who we are today. Learning about critical pedagogy can be a very uncomfortable situation at times as we are vulnerable and exposed. This assignment was a crucial point in our transition from learning *about* critical pedagogy to *seeing how* the theories we had studied are ingrained in our families and ourselves. Upon completion of the first assignment, we received feedback from our professor and conducted class discussions on everyone's submissions. After our discussions, we were assigned the second autobiography examining ourselves as social justice educators.

Opening up and exploring who you are and how you came to be this way is a very raw and vulnerable action, and it is extremely so when it is displayed for all in our class to see on an online platform and discussed in-person (Ko & Rossen,

2017). Talking about racism and sexism in the abstract is one thing, but this assignment brought these topics home. When one person writes about her mother as a White middle-class stay-at-home-mom, while another classmate writes about her mother as a White single-parent working two jobs, and still another classmate writes about her mother as a Black woman, domestic, cleaning houses and tending to White children, the impacts of racism and sexism take on new meaning. The acts of writing about our personal experiences, reading about the family experiences of our classmates, and then engaging in in-person conversations about our different experiences pushed us into uncomfortable dialogues with one another. These rich conversations about our autobiographies sparked personalized discussions about critical pedagogy and how *we* acknowledge our biases as educators (hooks, 1994; Wink, 2011).

Reading the autobiographies of my peers allowed me to see how different historical events and social aspects impacted their lives, which then made me reflect on similar experiences in my own life and how and why certain aspects were more important than others when I wrote my autobiography. By learning from each other's lives, we were able to further analyze our family histories to explore how the dynamics of race, gender, and social class impact us (hooks, 1994). For example, confronting the triple oppression of my classmate's Black mother working as a domestic in a White home, juxtaposed with my experience as a White middle-class child, provided new insights into the meaning of oppression. Hearing and understanding each other's experiences helped me to grow in my understanding of critical pedagogy and why others have different views of what it means. This assignment and our class discussions were vital in helping me to understand what critical pedagogy means to me and solidifying my understanding and interactions with multiple critical theories.

For both classes, we conducted peer reviews (see Appendix D) of classmates' papers for the courses. We completed peer reviews on both versions of the autobiography assignment and the literature review for the first course, I&D. For the second course, ACP, we completed peer review assignments the integrative papers and our literature review. In these reviews, we had to read all submissions to complete the review as directed (See Appendix D). The results were tallied and shared with the class so we could discuss them together in our next in-person meeting. The hybrid nature of the course and the use of the peer reviews required us to read everyone's work, which is usually an expectation but not a reality in online settings, and prepared us to discuss our own personal work with the class.

These peer review assignments were awkward at first because students feel bad about being critical of others' work, and they also have some reservations about how others perceive their work. However, these assignments have grown to be one of my favorite forms of feedback to receive because it allows me to practice reading and evaluating others' work to identify high quality pieces, while also practicing being accepting and reflective in my own writing. The peer review assignment allowed us to truly embrace what Freire's idea of critical pedagogy aims to do—teacher and student work together to challenge each other's thinking (Freire, 1970/2005). There was no definitive role of teacher and student during our peer review assignments and the corresponding class discussions, as the feedback from the peer reviews helped to guide our discussions rather than our professor. Without our hybrid environment, I do not think I would have had the same enactment of critical pedagogy in real-time because the in-person aspect increased our ability to converse and challenge each other in our knowledge.

For one of our final assignments in I&D, we had to write a grant or conference proposal. Our proposals had to address the issues of culturally relevant pedagogy, diversity, educational equity, democracy, and social justice. For my assignment, I completed a conference proposal that was accepted on the topic of reviewing teacher attrition and retention (Huling, 2019); I have since further developed by presenting at a second conference, while tying in the work of Freire (1970/2005) to highlight the need for equity and social justice (Reyes et al., 2019). This assignment was the most like what I expect in a fully online course because we completed the assignment and uploaded it into Folio, and we did not discuss it in class. Still this assignment really pushed me out of my comfort zone professionally, opening doors that allowed me to present my scholarship on critical pedagogy at multiple national conferences.

For both courses, we completed a literature review assignment. In I&D, this was our first attempt at a literature review, so our professor had us read and critique three literature review articles on critical pedagogy in varying content areas (Chakraborti-Ghosh et al., 2010; Choi & Chepyator-Thomson, 2011; Lehman, 2017; Machi & McEvoy, 2016). Engaging in this online critique of the three literature reviews helped us to practice independently reviewing articles for their quality, content, and positionality. In our I&D in-person class, we discussed our analysis of the literature reviews by reviewing key components of literature reviews prior to completing our assignment (Machi & McEvoy, 2016). While we learned the components and format of a traditional literature review, we struggled to fully grasp how to intertwine our theoretical framework within the assignment. In ACP, our struggle in the previous class became our new focus for the assignment. Our professor assigned our advanced class to write a new literature review utilizing a critical lens of our choosing related to our potential dissertation topics. This was an important assignment in my development as a critical pedagogue and scholar because I was able to understand how critical pedagogy is heavily embedded in common problems within education. Both of my literature reviews addressed teacher attrition. As I researched the numerous studies and articles, I began to see the issue through a critical lens developing my stance on the issue as a critical pedagogue. The feedback I received from my peers online through the peer review, the feedback from my professor online, and the feedback from our campus discussions helped me to be able to do this.

In the ACP course, we completed an assignment that required us to integrate works from our primary texts, recommended readings and outside sources to support our paper. This assignment furthered our identity within critical pedagogy and allowed us to select a theoretical framework within which to view and synthesize research cohesively, thus pushing us into scholarly work in critical pedagogy. This assignment was particularly challenging for our class because we wrote the first paper by trying to link the selected chapters and outside sources with one common idea or theme as we had done in the past. Our class quickly realized that this was not what our professor had intended our assignment be about, and during our next in-person meeting, she explained her expectations of the assignment and guided our class with her feedback for the second paper.

For our second paper, we strived to select a theoretical framework from which to analyze our chapters and outside sources on critical pedagogy. I really embraced embedding a theoretical framework in my paper and sources that supported my understanding of critical pedagogy through Freire (1970/2005, 1998). By reading my peers' second submissions, I practiced trying to identify their specific frameworks within critical pedagogy and key tenets they highlighted, as well as who they typically cited in their work. Being able to recognize others' stances on critical pedagogy was a huge take away for me from completing this assignment since I can now practice this in everything I read.

Through all of our coursework, both online and during our in-person meetings, our professor worked very hard to try to shift our mindsets from a conventional teacher and student relation to a more "mutual humanization" (Freire, 1970/2005, p. 75) stance, where we begin to collectively think critically. By engaging in activities that developed our skills as critical pedagogues, our professor was transitioning us out of the traditional concept of roles in education to the world of being critically conscious and moving towards an education of liberation from this order (Freire, 1970/2005). In theory, this is everything that we want it to be; in practice, we still struggled with letting go of the teacher-student dynamic in the classroom because it is so deeply embedded in our understanding of education.

These two courses have significantly shaped how I view curriculum and my pedagogical approaches in the classroom. The readings and assignments that we discussed in our in-person classes allowed me to explore my biases as an educator and showed me how to be cognizant of them in my teaching (Gay, 2010; hooks, 1994; Wink, 2011). I have begun to use a critical eye when evaluating the readings for class, the curriculum in the classroom, and the conversations I have with my students during the classes I teach. Applying critical pedagogy to my practice has allowed me to better serve my students by teaching them how to understand and question the world around them (Gay, 2010). The assignments in our hybrid I&D and ACP courses allowed me to experience this firsthand so that I can encourage and teach others how to do this as well.

Learning about critical pedagogy can be confusing for beginning students. In the traditional school setting, we are taught to believe that what the teacher and the textbooks say is factual and true. Freire (1970/2005) coined this as the banking concept of education. We grow up with the mindset that teachers, those with power in the classroom, will provide us with all the information we need to know. However, critical pedagogy has shown us that is not the true meaning of education. Education involves learning the skills necessary for critical thinking and questioning, which includes challenging both the text and the teacher within the classroom. Doing this allows students to overcome their confusion about power relations within their educational and social contexts (Freire, 1970/2005, 1998).

The autobiographies, literature reviews, integrative papers, and peer reviews aided greatly in my development as a critical pedagogue. The autobiographies helped me to understand how I view critical pedagogy and the life experiences that led me to that. The literature reviews and integrative papers taught me how important it is to be familiar with theoretical frameworks within critical pedagogy and how these are used to promote ideas in scholarly work. The peer reviews and discussions in class helped me to understand that critical pedagogy is a conversation with another rather than a lecture from another about issues in education.

The hybrid setting for this course was the perfect medium for learning about critical pedagogy for me. The online part frontloaded information and assignments prior to coming to class (Ko & Rossen, 2017), allowing me to form my own ideas and bring those to our discussions. It also allowed me to receive feedback from my professor and peers so I could identify my strengths and areas of growth in my development. The in-person meetings offered me the opportunity to receive clarification, not only on assignments, but also on my understandings as well. Some of the readings and frameworks were difficult to understand and follow; so, being able to ask questions and have misconceptions quickly corrected were crucial in a clear understanding of critical pedagogy.

My hybrid experiences in both courses have been a more blended experience because parts of the courses were completed online and others during our in-person classes (Ko & Rossen, 2017). According to Ko & Rossen (2017), online learning can be very distant and the people in your class do not really seem like people with past experiences and different social positions. The in-person components of our hybrid courses allowed us to put names with people who had stories to share and perspectives to discuss. The online component allowed us to continually review each other's work prior to coming to face-to-face class so that we could find connections or pose questions to help us better connect and understand each other's theoretical framework. This preparation enabled us to have authentic conversations about our work. These conversations also did not feel like a perfunctory requirement to be completed before midnight on Sunday, like many postings and responses do on discussion boards in fully online, asynchronous settings; rather, we were engaging in a critical dialogue that occurred in both virtual and in-person settings.

The hybrid environment forces an interrelation between the written word and the spoken word, creating a powerful conversation analyzing critical pedagogy. The hybrid classroom gives time to prepare and reflect prior to in-person classes. The asynchronous discussion board allows students to revisit discussions as often as desired. Meanwhile, the in-person meetings, when set-up by reflective writing assignments and peer review, provide space for solidifying and quickly correcting conceptualizations of critical pedagogy.

In addition to gaining an understanding of the basic tenets and theorists related to critical pedagogy, these courses demonstrate the general principles of critical pedagogy in practice. The third key objective is to help students come to understand themselves as critical social justice educators; the hoped-for "take away" from the course is that students, who are also teachers, will not only *understand* the theories of critical pedagogy, but will also *practice* critical pedagogy in their classes, thereby encouraging their students to move beyond the "banking method" (Freire, 1970/2005) of schooling toward claiming their education (hooks, 1994, 2003) and critiquing what they are told. I have had the opportunity to develop such practice as I currently am teaching and supervising elementary pre-service. I teach and supervise three of the four semesters that pre-service elementary teachers are required to complete in the teacher preparation program.

The knowledge about critical pedagogy that I have gained has been invaluable to my teaching, as well as the ideas I share with the preservice teachers about effective teaching. I have realized that part of my job is not only to help pre-service educators learn the skills to be great teachers, but to be teachers who have critical ethics and know that all students can succeed.

To enhance the values of critical pedagogy in my courses, I have used the work of Gay (2010) and Ladson-Billings (1995, 2014) to improve my module on culturally responsive pedagogy for my pre-service teachers. Doing so has helped my students move beyond the surface level understanding culturally responsive pedagogy to a level of understanding, appreciating, and encouraging diversity in the classroom (Gay, 2010; hooks, 1994; Ladson-Billings, 2014). After reading excerpts from Gay (2010) and Ladson-Billings (2014), my students reflect on effective strategies they observed and learned to use in elementary classrooms. Imparting my knowledge of pioneers in this area of critical pedagogy encourages the students in my classroom to take interest in advocating for the students in their future classrooms (Gay, 2010; Ladson-Billings, 1995, 2014).

When I first began teaching this course, I consolidated culturally relevant pedagogy into the class period that I taught differentiation strategies and taught it, regretfully, in the superficial manner that Ladson-Billings (2014) discussed in "Culturally Relevant Teaching 2.0 a.k.a the Remix." I was teaching about surface level connections with culture and not the level of individuality and appreciation that Ladson-Billings (1995, 2014) and Gay (2010) believe to be most effective for culturally responsive teaching. Since learning about critical pedagogy and taking these two classes, I now devote more class time exclusively to culturally responsive teaching. We read articles, search online for key examples, and students use standards to adapt lessons or instructional strategies to be culturally responsive. The skills practiced and gained during this class continue to impact pre-service teachers beyond this course as they incorporate the ideas of Ladson-Billings (1995, 2014) and Gay (2010) into their perspectives and activities as developing educators throughout the program and into their future classrooms.

I am moving beyond the surface and challenging students to dig deep when creating connections and appreciations with the diverse students they will be teaching. I have seen changes in my students when they reach student-teaching because they are not searching for some random link to culture. Rather, they have formed relationships within their classrooms that are meaningful and allow them to plan learning opportunities that are relevant to their diverse students. In a world that is striving to be more inclusive than ever before, these preservice teachers have the ability to empower their classrooms to be inclusive and equip the students they teach with the skills to develop a critical eye. Lessons emerging from the COVID-19 pandemic and concurrent Black Lives Matter movement have made clear that now is the time to engage in genuine critical pedagogy in which we listen, and *really hear*, one another in order to create lasting change leading toward social justice.

## Teaching and Learning Together in Hybrid Courses

As our instructor and student explorations have detailed, the hybrid classroom opened up additional opportunities for critical pedagogy. The hybrid classroom allowed for a blending of in-person and online experiences that brought to bear the best of both worlds, wherein students have additional time and space to reflect in asynchronous environments and follow-up with in-person discussions.

The in-person meetings gave faces to the names of students in the courses and permitted students and professor to recognize body language cues, intonation, and questioning facial expressions to help clarify any confusion about course requirements or content. Meeting together strengthened rapport among students and between students and professor.

Meanwhile, the online portions of the class helped deepen dialogue through text. Each student is held accountable through online discussions and assignments in a way that is not possible in an in-person classroom. This textual interaction necessitates that students read and think about that reading on their own. Without the online component, allowing for greater reflection through multiple readings and just simply more time for mulling over the content, the in-person meetings would not have been as productive.

To those who may be wondering how they might apply these insights to their own teaching of hybrid courses, perhaps the most important key is to identify ways to overcome the "student" vs. "teacher" dichotomy. As Huling describes her experiences, the peer review provided entry into a more fluid space where the students all became teachers of one another. This, in conjunction with developing theoretical understanding of critical pedagogy, permitted a new perspective whereby students learned that the authors they were reading had likewise generated scholarship for *peer review*. Then, what slips into place is an understanding that critical pedagogy is all about engaging in critical discourse *about* pedagogy with others who genuinely care about becoming educators for social justice.

Co-authoring this chapter has provided a new pedagogical space for both professor and student. As noted earlier in this chapter, the initial purpose was to write *about* critical pedagogy through the *pedagogical application of* critical pedagogy in doctoral-level courses in order to generate *social justice educators who promote* critical pedagogy in their own classrooms. However, this co-authorship has also yielded additional benefits and support to the praxis of critical pedagogy.

As we reflected on our diverse experiences in the two doctoral-level courses, we have deepened our understanding ways to advance the application of critical pedagogy in our classrooms. This opportunity to reflect as teachers, learners, and then co-authors has created a more leveled space in which the professor has learned as well as taught, and the student has taught as well as learned. Moving beyond the experiencing of critical pedagogy in the classroom has strengthened the dialogical dynamic promoted by critical pedagogy.

# Appendix A

### Inquiry and Development of Educational Practice

1. Autobiography/Multicultural Self-portrait: You will write a multicultural self-portrait that explores your understanding of your place as a "social justice educator." Late in the semester, you will write a second multicultural self-portrait exploring socio-cultural dynamics in greater depth.
2. Grant Proposal: Individually OR in small groups (of classmates or colleagues at your school), you will develop and submit ONE of the following: a proposal for a grant from a funding source, a proposal to present at a national or international conference, or manuscript for publication in a peer-reviewed journal. The proposal/manuscript should address the issues of culturally relevant pedagogy, diversity, educational equity, democracy and/or social justice. Full credit for grant proposal, partial credit for conference proposal (80%) or manuscript (90%).
3. Literature Review: You will complete a literature review on an educational trend/issue that is relevant to culturally responsive pedagogy, race-visible teaching, and teachers' conscientization. This literature review could be related to your dissertation topic.
4. Peer Review: Students will conduct peer reviews of classmate's papers for this course. Both Multicultural Self-Portraits and the Literature Review will be reviewed by classmates.
5. Final Exam: Students will participate in an oral cumulative final exam over course content during the final in-person class meeting.
6. Professional Dispositions: According to doctoral program policy, professional dispositions are evaluated in this course as a Key Assessment. You will submit a self-assessment of your professional dispositions, both within the context of this particular course and in your own professional setting. Your active participation in and commitment to the work of this course will be reflected in your evaluation. Your score on this assignment reflects the extent to which you accurately and honestly evaluate your own dispositions.

### Advanced Critical Pedagogy:

1. Integrative Papers: You will write three papers exploring literature related to Critical Pedagogy, drawing from at two selected chapters of each text, 3–5 recommended readings and your own research.

2. Literature Review: You will complete a literature review on an educational trend/ issue that is relevant to culturally responsive pedagogy, race-visible teaching, and teachers' conscientization. This literature review could be related to your dissertation topic.
3. Peer Review: Students will conduct peer reviews of classmate's literature review papers for this course.

# Appendix B

### Autobiography/Multicultural Self-Portrait

*Autobiography/Multicultural Self-portrait: You will write a multicultural self-portrait that explores your understanding of your place as a "social justice educator."*

Review the "Multicultural Self" assignment from the *Learning to Teach: A Critical Approach to Field Experiences* book (Adams et al., 2006). Use the questions in this material to help guide your approach to this assignment.

Gather materials placing yourself and *at least* three generations of your family into socio-historical context. Consider multiple dimensions of identity (gender, race, ethnicity, social class, first language, sexuality, religious beliefs, etc.) and how these dimensions have influenced the life trajectories and experiences of yourself and your family members. Consider how the intersections of these dimensions of identify have influenced these life trajectories and experiences. Consider how the historical context (internationally, nationally, regionally and locally) has influenced the life trajectories and experiences of yourself and your family members. Consider both involvement and lack of involvement in historical events. Reflect on your family culture and traditions. Reflect on the intersectionality of socio-cultural, economic and historical events on the life trajectories and experiences of you and your family.

Then, write an autobiography utilizing these reflections. At the end of the semester, students will write a new autobiography exploring sociocultural influences on their own autobiography more closely.

# Appendix C

### Literature Review Assignment

*Literature Review: You will complete a literature review on an educational trend/ issue that is relevant to culturally responsive pedagogy, race-visible teaching, and teachers' conscientization. This literature review could be related to your dissertation topic.*

Recommended resources:

> Machi, L. A., & McEvoy, B. T. (2016). *The literature review: Six steps to success* (3rd ed.). Corwin Press. Review the journal articles below prior to our first class meeting:
> Chakraborti-Ghosh, S., Mofield, E., & Orellana, K. (2010). Cross-cultural comparisons and implications for students with EBD: A decade of understanding. *International Journal of Special Education, 25*(2), 162–170.
> Choi, W., & Chepyator-Thomson, R. (2011). Multiculturalism Ain teaching physical education: A review of U.S. based literature. *ICHPER-SD Journal of Research, 6*(2), 14–20.
> Lehman, C. L. (2017). Multicultural competence: A literature review supporting focused training for preservice teachers teaching diverse students. *Journal of Education and Practice, 8*(10), 109–116.

**Guidelines for writing literature review**

The purpose of a literature review is to provide a *comprehensive* overview of "what's been done already by others." Identify the research related to your topic. Conduct a thorough and comprehensive search for research related to your topic. Identify the primary discourses related to your topic and gather primary and secondary sources as needed to explicate these discourses. Develop a thesis synthesizing your conclusions based on your review of literature.

# Appendix D

**Peer Review Assignments**

*Peer Review: Students will conduct peer reviews of classmate's papers for this course. Both Multicultural Self-Portraits and the Literature Review will be reviewed by classmates.*

Genuine peer review is a gold standard mode of evaluation in the academy. By reviewing the papers of your classmates, you will be able to improve your own writing abilities. The goal is for you to learn to recognize good writing when you see it. Reading and evaluating the quality of the papers of your peers is helpful to you in learning to apply greater skill in analysis. By learning to identify good thesis statements, good analyses, correct grammar and APA format, and good reference lists, you will grow in your ability to employ these skills in your own writing.

**Part 1. Identify the top 3 papers in the class.**

Following careful review of the class papers, make a list identifying the top three papers according to your analysis/evaluation. Briefly justify your list using examples from the papers.

**Part 2. Identify the "best" parts.**

From your review of your classmates' papers, identify the one that you feel is the best for each category listed here: Best thesis statement, Best analysis, Most interesting or creative, Best grammar, Best APA format, Best reference list or bibliography. **Justify** your selection.

**Part 3. Change.**

From your review of your classmates' papers identify the weakest part/s of the papers overall. What aspects of these papers need the most skill development? Then, consider **your own paper**. Identify the weakest part/s of your paper and how you will address this/these aspects in your subsequent papers.

# References

Abu-Shomar, A. (2016). Critical pedagogy and postcolonial education. In A. Darder, P. Mayo, & J. Paraskeva (Eds.), *International critical pedagogy reader* (pp. 17–26). Routledge. (Work originally published in 2013).

Adams, N. G., Shea, C., Liston, D. D., & Deever, B. (2006). *Learning to teach: A critical approach to field experiences*. Lawrence Erlbaum Associates.

Chakraborti-Ghosh, S., Mofield, E., & Orellana, K. (2010). Cross-cultural comparisons and implications for students with EBD: A decade of understanding. *International Journal of Special Education, 25*(2), 162–170.

Choi, W., & Chepyator-Thomson, R. (2011). Multiculturalism Ain teaching physical education: A review of U.S. based literature. *ICHPER-SD Journal of Research, 6*(2), 14–20.

Darder, A. (2017). Pedagogy of love: Embodying our humanity. In A. Darder, R. D. Torres, & M. P. Baltodano (Eds.), *The critical pedagogy reader* (3rd ed., pp. 494–502). Routledge. (Work originally published in 2002).

Darder, A., Baltodano, M. P., & Torres, R. D. (2017). *The critical pedagogy reader* (3rd ed.). Routledge.

Darder, A., Mayo, P., & Paraskeva, J. (2016a). *International critical pedagogy reader*. Routledge.

Darder, A., Mayo, P., & Paraskeva, J. (2016b). The internationalization of critical pedagogy: An introduction. In A. Darder, P. Mayo, & J. Paraskeva (Eds.), *International critical pedagogy reader* (pp. 1–14). Routledge.

Dei, G. J. S. (2016). The challenge of inclusive schooling in Africa. In A. Darder, P. Mayo, & J. Paraskeva (Eds.), *International critical pedagogy reader* (pp. 69–76). Routledge. (Work originally published in 2005).

Dunbar, M., & Melton, T. (2018). Self-efficacy and training of faculty who teach online. In C. Hodges (Ed.), *Self-efficacy in instructional technology contexts* (pp. 15–34). Springer.

Freire, P. (1998). *Pedagogy of freedom: Ethics, democracy and civic courage*. Rowman & Littlefield.

Freire, P. (2005). *Pedagogy of the oppressed*. Continuum Press. (Original work published 1970).

Gay, G. (2010). *Culturally responsive teaching* (2nd ed.). Teachers College Press.

Giroux, H. A. (2017). Critical theory and educational practice. In A. Darder, R. D. Torres, & M. P. Baltodano (Eds.), *The critical pedagogy reader* (3rd ed., pp. 31–55). Routledge. (Work originally published in 1983).

hooks, b. (1994). *Teaching to transgress: Education as the practice of freedom*. Routledge.

hooks, b. (2003). *Teaching community: A pedagogy of hope*. Routledge.

hooks, b. (2017). Confronting class in the classroom. In A. Darder, R. D. Torres, & M. P. Baltodano (Eds.), *The critical pedagogy reader* (3rd ed., pp. 181–187). Routledge. (Work originally published in 1994).

Huling, H. (2019, March 4–6). *Teach like your hair's on fire: But how do we light the flame to make teacher's passionate again?* [Conference Session]. Critical Questions in Education Conference, Savannah, GA.

Ko, S., & Rossen, S. (2017). *Teaching online: A practical guide* (4th ed.). Routledge.

Ladson-Billings, G. (1995). Toward a theory of culturally relevant pedagogy. *American Educational Research Journal, 32*(3), 465–491.

Ladson-Billings, G. (2014). Culturally relevant teaching 2.0 a.k.a the remix. *Harvard Educational Review, 84*, 74–84. https://doi.org/10.17763/haer.84.1.p2rj131485484751

Lehman, C. L. (2017). Multicultural competence: A literature review supporting focused training for preservice teachers teaching diverse students. *Journal of Education and Practice, 8*(10), 109–116.

Machi, L. A., & McEvoy, B. T. (2016). *The literature review: Six steps to success* (3rd ed.). Corwin Press.

McLaren, P. (2017). Critical pedagogy: A look at the major concepts. In A. Darder, R. D. Torres, & M. P. Baltodano (Eds.), *The critical pedagogy reader* (3rd ed., pp. 56–78). Routledge. (Work originally published in 1989).

Reyes, A. J., Jensen, L. J., Toledo, C. A., & Huling, H. M. (2019, June 12–14). *How can we become what we cannot see? Imagining possible selves in underresourced spaces* [Conference session]. Curriculum Studies Summer Collaborate, Savannah, GA.

Wink, J. (2011). *Critical pedagogy: Notes from the real world* (4th ed.). Pearson.

CHAPTER SIX

# Promoting Transformative Learning Using Critical Pedagogy and Moore's Theory of Transactional Distance

SARA DONALDSON, HEATHER YUHANIAK, CAREY BORKOSKI, AND YOLANDA ABEL

The racial divide between U.S. students and their teachers is large and widening. Today's student body is more culturally and linguistically diverse than ever, while the teaching force remains primarily White (National Center for Education Statistics, 2017). The single multicultural teacher education (MTE) course included in most teacher preparation programs (Ladson-Billings, 2000; Little & Bartlett, 2010; Weisman & Garza, 2002) has the potential to function as a transformative environment in which participants question, analyze, and critique their implicit beliefs about themselves and students (Pohan & Aguilar, 2001). In the context of an online Doctor of Education (Ed.D.) program which prepares scholar-practitioners to address educational challenges in multicultural settings, a careful blend of critical pedagogy and social learning theories has the potential to create such a transformative online learning environment.

## Review of the Literature

Transformative Learning Theory

Transformative Learning (TL) theory is especially salient for scholar-practitioners seeking to make sense of their daily lives in ever-shifting national and international education contexts. TL enables adult learners to critically examine the world around them while negotiating the collision of pre-existing beliefs with the new learning, ideas, and experiences that surface when designing research-based solutions to complex problems in diverse contexts (Mezirow, 1996). Part of this work for adults, such as the students in this online Ed.D. program, requires developing a more inclusive and less discriminatory world view by reflecting upon and revising existing frames of reference, including tacit points of view, beliefs, and feelings based on prior experience (Mezirow, 1996; Taylor, 2017).

Adults have often uncritically amassed frames of reference through acculturation and socialization during childhood, mostly through experiences with significant adults in their lives (Mezirow, 2000). Individuals' frames of reference likely represent the dominant culture into which they have been socialized and are often comprised of cultural assumptions (Taylor, 2017), which may be problematic for educators tasked with improving outcomes for increasingly diverse students. Unexamined frames of reference may distort their perceptions of racial and cultural others, including the students they serve.

The end goal of the transformative learning process is "a more fully developed (more functional) frame of reference ... that is more (a) inclusive, (b) differentiating, (c) permeable, (d) critically reflective, and (e) integrative of experience" (Mezirow, 1996, p. 163). This transformation can be prompted by what Mezirow (2000) calls *disorienting dilemmas*. Though usually triggered by life events or transitions, disorienting dilemmas can also be purposely built into adult learning experiences to challenge existing frames of reference. Course content and processes which prompt student dissonance can trigger the critical scrutiny required to make one's frame of reference more nuanced and encompassing (Taylor, 2017). The next section explores how facilitators of adult learning can leverage critical pedagogy to facilitate transformational learning in online settings.

## Critical Pedagogy

A social emancipatory view of transformative learning considers the role of context and social change in TL and not just the individual (Taylor, 2017). The scholar-practitioners in this program are tasked with implementing policies, practices, and organizational change processes that are inclusive and socially just. Creation of meaningful policy and practice hinges on having well-informed frames of reference about the individuals and social groups they are designed to impact. Rooted in the work of Paulo Freire, the social emancipatory view of TL views individuals as capable of constant reflection and action designed to transform their world into a more equitable and just place (Taylor, 2017). Freire viewed the goal of education as social transformation and critical consciousness development through critical pedagogy (CP), a "radical pedagogy that makes concrete the values of solidarity, social responsibility, creativity, and discipline in the service of the common good and critical spirit" (Freire & Macedo, 1995, p. 108). Learners' critical consciousness is developed through engagement with CP, which unearths and examines the complexities of teaching and learning for individuals striving to create a more just world. CP interrogates the relationships between classroom teaching, knowledge production, and schooling as an institution situated in the broader milieu of society (McLaren, 1998). Engaging in CP requires educators question their long-held assumptions and examine the critical context of both teaching and learning to transform the world for the better through education (Wink, 2011).

The first step toward developing critical consciousness and engaging in CP is critical reflection. Critical reflection is seen as the conscious and explicit reassessment of the consequence and origin of an individual's meaning structures, including examining personal assumptions and the differing viewpoints of others (Mezirow & Welton, 1995). Critical reflection enables those who engage in it to critique existing societal power structures and how they impact education, a process which may be wholly unfamiliar to some educators who have benefited from being members of social groups who hold institutional and structural power.

Critical reflection can help educators, as lifelong learners, discover a sense of both awareness and agency to transform their educational spheres of influence (Taylor, 2017) to better serve those who lack power. Engagement in "problem-posing" (Freire & Macedo, 1995, p. 70) rather than more traditional transmission-style learning (Wink, 2011) allows learners to critically examine educational problems and allows them the time and practice needed to develop new frames of reference based on more than just their own lived experiences. Carefully structured learning, relearning, and unlearning (Wink, 2011) is crucial for critical reflection and can occur through collaborative dialogue, critical questioning, and reflective journaling (Taylor, 2017).

Critical reflection is not merely an individual endeavor and is often spurred by interaction with others. Course structures should be designed in recognition of the importance of relationships when fostering transformative learning through critical reflection. Both happen "through trustful relationships that allow individuals to have questioning discussions, share information openly and achieve mutual and consensual understanding" (Taylor, 2017, p. 179). Through these structures, educators test out their theories about educational problems of practice, related factors, and potential solutions. Engagement with others through dialogue and questioning can expand educators' current frames of reference and lead to more meaningful and socially-just interventions.

## Transactional Distance

Although it is clear that a safe environment promotes dialogue involving personal disclosure, meaningful discourse, and social negotiation, research is unclear as to exactly which characteristics of online instructional design promote transformative learning and critical reflection (Gilbert & Dabbagh, 2005; Hill et al., 2009; Lambert & Fisher, 2013). Moore's (1997) concept of transactional distance (TD), or the degree of interaction in terms of program and instructional structures, learner-instructor interactions, and the degree of learner self-directedness, is one lens for evaluating characteristics of learning environments and instructional design Instead of viewing distance as a physical characteristic, TD refers to the degree of psychological distance between learner and instructor that includes both the learners' sense of the instructor's availability for support and their connectedness to the instructor, peers, and the institution itself (Moore, 1997; Shin, 2003; Weidlich & Bastiaens, 2018).

In online learning contexts, TD is influenced by factors associated with learners' perceptions of (a) the ratio, frequency, and directionality of communication; (b) the rigidity or responsiveness of course structures; and (c) their degree of autonomy or control over learning processes (Hill et al., 2009; Moore, 1997; Weidlich & Bastiaens, 2018). When structures are more flexible and two-way dialogue is promoted, such as in courses utilizing frequent synchronous discussions, TD is smaller as learners perceive interactions with peers and instructors as more responsive. On the other hand, when structures are rigid and dialogue is primarily unilateral, such as courses consisting primarily of recorded presentations and asynchronous discussions, TD tends to be larger (Moore, 1997). Greater TD promotes agency as learners have more control over how they engage with course materials to meet personal learning goals; however, it also increases the potential for misunderstandings and misinterpretations of key ideas and a feeling of disconnection with course content, peers, and instructors (Moore, 1997; Shedletsky & Aitken, 2010).

In MTE courses, this potential is even greater as students are being asked to not just learn new information but to also *unlearn* ideas stemming from past experiences (Wink, 2011). For example, conceptualizations of culturally responsive teaching commonly require unlearning for educators, many of whom presume instructional strategies alone can transcend racial and cultural mismatches between educators and students. As each educator brings a unique background and perspective to the classroom, they need spaces to interrogate the impact of their own experiences on how they perceive students who are culturally and linguistically diverse. Educators also need self-reflection strategies that penetrate beyond content and pedagogy and into their hearts and minds (Boyd & Glazier, 2017). Creating online learning environments that support social construction of knowledge, including the sharing of transformational experiences, discursive dialogue, and knowledge distribution, requires attention to both cognitive and social dimensions of interactions (Hill et al., 2009). Overall, determining the appropriate degree of TD for transformative learning in online MTE courses requires consideration of necessary levels of support, interaction, and individual agency to allow adult learners to feel control over their learning while also stimulating the collaborative discourse needed for critical reflection (Bondy et al., 2015; Moore, 1997; Shedletsky & Aitken, 2010; Taylor, 2017).

## Influence of Instructional Design on Critical Reflection

Transformative learning in online spaces occurs through interactions between students and the instructional core: teachers (S-T), other students (S-S), and the content (S-C; Hill et al., 2009; MacLeod et al., 2019). Effective instructional design for MTE courses supports asynchronous and synchronous interactivity and collaborative discourse by leveraging available technologies to facilitate self-reflection and social negotiation as learners move beyond knowledge acquisition in reconciling existing beliefs, new ideas, and divergent perspectives (Bondy et al., 2015; Caruthers & Friend, 2014; Gilbert & Dabbagh, 2005; Grant & Lee, 2014). Strong modeling and guidance from skilled instructors promote high-quality reflective dialogue and critical self-analysis, especially when students are afforded a variety of types of interactions and supports within a safe and engaging environment (Bondy et al., 2015; Hill et al., 2009; Shedletsky & Aitken, 2010). Therefore, MTE instructors must balance the need to validate and support individuals' feelings while also ensuring opportunities for students to confront common assumptions about themselves and diverse others (Grant & Lee, 2014) through a combination of individual reflection and critical discourse with others.

Meaningful discourse with both peers and knowledgeable others is a key component of critical reflection as it supports learners' ability to connect, interpret, analyze, synthesize, and evaluate ideas, practice-based issues, and personal experiences (Boyd & Glazier, 2017; Gilbert & Dabbagh, 2005). In online learning environments, meaningful S-S and S-T discourse can occur in both virtual synchronous and text-based asynchronous contexts. Asynchronous dialogue provides time for reflection and development of carefully crafted comments (Bondy et al., 2015), but it is also less spontaneous and responsive, as participants may have to wait days for responses to questions and comments and may struggle to gauge reactions without facial expressions or body language. As a result, asynchronous discussions are associated with greater TD as they require a higher degree of autonomy. On the other hand, synchronous media creates a "more intensive, personal, and dynamic dialogue" (Moore, 1997, p. 25) that promotes inter-learner dialogue and inter-dependence and allows for less structure, a combination that results in a smaller TD (Bondy et al., 2015). Mayer's cognitive theory of multimedia proposes that learners process verbal and written information differently; thus, deep learning depends on active processing through multiple modalities, such as text-based asynchronous discussion forums and verbal synchronous discussions (Lajoie, 2014).

Regardless of potential, neither asynchronous nor synchronous media will necessarily promote the type of high-quality dialogue needed for transformative learning. Moore (1997) proposes that effective discussions are:

> "controlled by the teachers who might for good reasons or bad, decide not to take advantage of its interactivity, and it is used by learners who might not be able or willing to enter into dialogue with their teachers [and/or peers]." (p. 25)

For this reason, the instructor's ability to effectively facilitate "cognitive and social processes for the purpose of realizing personally meaningful and educationally worthwhile learning outcomes" (Anderson et al., 2001, p. 5) strongly influences students' satisfaction, perceived learning, and sense of engagement and autonomy (Bondy et al., 2015; Goldingay & Land, 2014). Students' perceptions of their instructor's ability to design and direct these potentially transformative learning experiences, as reported through formal and informal course feedback, are influenced by instructional decisions that impact:

- S-C interactions (e.g.; the choice, sequence, and relevancy of assigned readings and discussion topics),
- S-T interactions (e.g.; the timing and level of feedback provided and attention to learners' affect, emotions, and self-efficacy); and
- S-S interactions (e.g.; formation and facilitation of student discussion groups, structures, and platforms; Bondy et al., 2015; Hill et al., 2009).

In online contexts, the ability to project one's identity and to see peers and instructors as real people is a necessary prequel to the collaborative, critical discourse, questioning, and reflection associated with transformative learning (Goldingay & Land, 2014; Maddrell et al., 2017; Taylor, 2017). Video conferencing promotes a sense of instructor and peer availability and connectedness as it humanizes individuals and conveys both presence and immediacy, elements often absent in text-based, asynchronous formats that promote a sense of the learning space as a safe, accepting, and supportive environment (Bondy et al., 2015; Goldingay & Land, 2014; Maddrell et al., 2017). As a result, increased opportunities for S-S and S-T interactivity may promote critical dialogue and lessen TD; however, they may also interfere with an individual's needs for the autonomy and flexibility in asynchronous, online learning environments (Shin, 2003). Although individual interactivity needs vary, it is clear that design and facilitation of S-S and S-T interactions and discussions influence levels of reflective practice when (a) clear models and feedback are provided, (b) collaborative learning occurs around activities and questions that require critical thinking, (c) independent learning opportunities exist, and (d) space is provided for reflective application of new ideas (Grant & Lee, 2014; Lambert & Fisher, 2013).

## Research Purpose

Using course artifacts obtained with IRB approval, this chapter examines the intersection of two discrete phenomena: critical reflection and transactional distance within one section of a doctoral level MTE course. Participants ($N$ = 14) included students from two different program cohorts, who were taking the course at the end of either their third ($n$ = 7) or sixth ($n$ = 7) semester of the nine-semester program. Approximately 64% of the participants identified as female and 50% identified as being a member of a marginalized group based on race, sexuality, and/or cultural affiliation (see Table 6.1).

Table 6.1: Participant Characteristics (N = 14)

| | | n (%) |
|---|---|---|
| Program Cohort | 3rd semester | 7 (50) |
| | 6th semester | 7 (50) |
| Gender | Female | 9 (64) |
| | Male | 5 (36) |
| Marginalized Group Membership | Yes | 7 (50) |
| | No | 7 (50) |
| Professional Role | Classroom Teacher | 1 (<1) |
| | Specialist/Administrator | 11 (79) |
| | Other | 3 (21) |

Source: Author

As part of ongoing programmatic improvement efforts, the authors jointly reflected on implementation of this required MTE course prior to the beginning of the semester with a goal of designing course structures that would maximize the potential of S-C, S-S and S-T interactivity for promoting transformative learning. Based on principles of transformative learning and critical pedagogy, it was hypothesized that planned changes to the course structures would decrease TD and result in a subsequent increase in critical reflection for course participants (see Figure 6.1). As described in detail below, course structures were redesigned to include more synchronous video-based discussion in addition to traditional asynchronous discussion boards in hopes of decreasing TD and increasing opportunities for critical reflection through real-time dialogue.

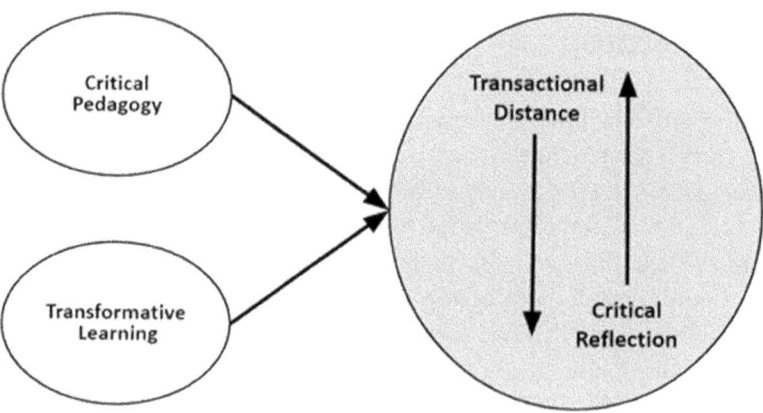

Figure 6.1: Hypothesized Conceptual Framework. Source: Author

Course Redesign

This Ed.D. program and the MTE course, in particular, seek to prepare individuals to participate in and contribute to public discourse around improving education for diverse communities. This work involves supporting an individual's ability to identify and critically reflect on the multiple social, cultural, and economic factors that have influenced their own cultural identity development and that of others in their community. In its original design, this MTE course sought to provide opportunities for critical reflection through student-to-content (S-C), student-to-teacher (S-T), and student-to-student (S-S) interactions. S-C interactions occurred as individuals read empirical literature, viewed media presentations including both recorded lectures and relevant videos, and responded to prompts connected to key ideas within asynchronous discussion forums. S-C interactions also occurred as individuals completed three reflections throughout the course asking students to connect course content to their own cultural identity development and work within their professional contexts. S-T interactions occurred through weekly announcements highlighting key ideas from previous discussions upcoming readings and media, teacher-led synchronous sessions explaining assignments, feedback in discussion forums and on written assignments, and personal correspondence through email and phone conversations. S-S interactions occurred within the text-based discussion forum as individuals responded to each other's weekly posts connected to teacher provided prompts (see Appendix).

## Impetus for Change

Having graduated from the program, three of the researchers agreed that their experiences involved less-than-optimal engagement with peers and instructors. Asynchronous discussion participation (threaded discussion of a prompt requiring citation) felt *formulaic*, student engagement in the transmission model synchronous sessions (lecture with slides) was minimal, and as instructors, they worried that a limited amount of S-S and S-T connectedness was impeding the positive interdependence and promotive interactions needed for transformative learning in online contexts (Abrami et al., 2011; Donaldson et al., 2018). With this problem in mind, the redesign of this MTE course built from work happening in other courses in the Ed.D. program where Zoom Video Communications had been introduced to shift synchronous sessions from teacher-centered to student-centered discussions and promote a sense of teacher and student presence in small group discussions (see Table 6.2).

Feedback from other program courses indicated that students felt synchronous videoconferencing discussions were an appropriate addition to this primarily asynchronous program because they "provided opportunities to interact face-to-face with peers and instructors, to think about and verbally articulate their ideas 'on the spot,' to get immediate feedback and clarification on emerging ideas, and to make connections and bridges from theory to practice" (Donaldson et al., 2018, p. 11). Additionally, students reported the synchronous video sessions supported their sense of S-T and S-S connectedness as it allowed them to see individuals' reactions to comments and questions through their facial features and body language, as well as to simply put a face to a name (Donaldson et al., 2018). In other words, engaging with peers and teachers in videoconferencing dialogue helped convey presence, immediacy, and connectedness as it humanized individuals and decreased TD (Maddrell et al., 2017), factors associated with an improved sense of engagement, autonomy, and perceived learning that are often absent in text-based, asynchronous discussions (Bondy et al., 2015; Goldingay & Land, 2014).

## Redesign Elements

Prior to this course redesign work, instructors in all program courses held synchronous sessions to introduce students to key assignments; however, these sessions were typically teacher-centered with a goal of transferring information about assignment components, expectations, and structures. In these sessions, students took a passive role, taking notes and occasionally asking clarifying questions. As a result, S-S interactions throughout the course were limited to asynchronous discussion forums with students processing information through written text, thus providing limited opportunities for the critical dialogue or multi-modal, active processing needed for transformative learning (LaJoie, 2014; Mezirow, 1997). To shift this dynamic, synchronous sessions were restructured to create student-centered opportunities for critical dialogue and increased interactivity.

Table 6.2: Overview of Course Design Changes in Terms of Opportunities for Course Interactions

| Type of Interaction | Original Design | Revised Design |
| --- | --- | --- |
| student-to-content (S-C) | · empirical literature<br>· recorded lectures<br>· related media<br>· discussion posts<br>· reflection papers | · empirical literature<br>· recorded lectures<br>· related media<br>· discussion posts<br>· *preparation for synchronous discussions*<br>· reflection papers |
| student-to-teacher (S-T) | · weekly announcements<br>· teacher led synchronous sessions for assignments<br>· discussion forum participation and feedback<br>· feedback on reflection papers<br>· personal email and phone conversations | · weekly announcements<br>· *interactive synchronous discussions around shared media presentations*<br>· discussion forum participation and feedback<br>· feedback on reflection papers<br>· personal email, phone, and *videoconferencing conversations* |
| student-to-student (S-S) | · asynchronous discussion forum dialogue | · asynchronous discussion forum dialogue<br>· *synchronous videoconferencing dialogue* |

Source: Author

*Note.* Design revisions are italicized. See Appendix for more detailed examples.

Using student and faculty feedback from other course redesign work (Donaldson et al., 2018), two new synchronous video sessions were added to the course using the following design elements:

- no more than five students attended at a time to ensure adequate speaking time for all participants,
- all participants were encouraged to use both Zoom's audio and video functions to ensure they were *seen* and *heard* by all,
- guiding questions were provided ahead of time so students felt confident in their ability to contribute to the conversations,
- explicit facilitation ensured equitable participation and maintained a focus on key ideas without overly structuring the conversation (Moore, 1997), and
- conversations were structured around media that provided a shared real-world context representing a meaningful and safe reference point for critical discourse and improved social construction of knowledge (LaJoie, 2014; Males et al., 2010; van Es, 2012).

With these changes in place, the two lead authors, as the course instructor and teaching assistant, carefully monitored student participation in both synchronous and asynchronous discussions throughout the semester. They provided questions and comments designed to probe participant worldviews, noting levels and quality of participation for different individuals, and personal and professional characteristics that appeared to influence individual's levels of interactivity and self-reflection. They paid special attention to the quality of written self-reflections and whether these reflections became more discriminating and nuanced as the course progressed and students participated in the newly-added synchronous sessions. The course instructor and teaching assistant shared these observations regularly throughout the semester as they worked to support individual learning needs.

## Analysis of Student Response to Course Participation

Several patterns emerged in terms of participants' level of transformation, which are discussed below using Bondy et al.'s (2015) categories of course experiences. Their three level continuum examines whether participants found course participation to be (a) simply informative, in that they learned but did not change their perspective; (b) intensifying, in that understandings gained a sharper focus through increased knowledge of precise terminology and theoretical frameworks; or (c) transforming, in that interactions led to deep reflection and a process of *conscientization* as personal blind spots and assumptions were examined. A revised hypothesis of the interaction between TD and TL is then presented.

### Simply Informative Experiences

Some participants ($n = 2$) in the course had what Bondy et al. (2015) deem *simply informative* experiences. They took advantage of the autonomy and flexibility provided by the asynchronous, online learning environment and participated adequately in posted discussion threads (S-S and S-T interaction). In both their asynchronous posts and written self-reflections, they regurgitated course content but demonstrated little responsibility for applying multicultural education principles in their own contexts. The first course reflection asked participants to complete a survey about their own attitudes and practices, to reflect on how they align to the ideals of multiculturalism, and to set goals for their growth throughout the semester. Both of these participants rated themselves highly at the course onset and articulated goals that were either vague (not well-connected to their research or professional context) or self-congratulatory. At times they outright rejected course theories (e.g. arguing that models of racial identity development did not apply to them or their lived experiences) or claimed that their professional organizations already embodied multicultural education and should be championed as models for others seeking to improve in that dimension. Their participation in the synchronous sessions, implemented to decrease TD and increase TL, was either minimal, contributing comments disconnected from personal experience, or non-existent, claiming scheduling conflicts prevented their attendance. These participants demonstrated through written posts and reflections that they had indeed learned course content but that it did not change their overall worldviews or frames of reference. In other words, their participation in the course was informative but not transformative.

### Intensifying Experiences

Several participants ($n = 3$) experienced *intensifying experiences* (Bondy et al., 2015) as they increased their knowledge of theories and terminology and were able to apply these new learnings to analyses of their organizations. They applied frameworks presented in the course (Banks, 2015; Banks et al., 2001; Nieto, 2008) to critique the chasm between their organizations' stated goals around diversity, equity and inclusion, and lack of aligned policy and practice. Over the course of three written reflections, they struggled, though, to define precise actions to take in challenging organizational disconnects between multicultural theory and practice. Their written posts and reflections also lacked an analysis of their own personal role in moving their workplaces into greater alignment with the principles of multicultural education. Transactional distance was generally low for these participants as they actively participated in both synchronous and asynchronous discussions and engaged in personal email communication with the instructor. Unfortunately, this lack of TD did not promote transformative learning experiences for these participants as they were unable to fully and critically reflect on their responsibility to make the world more just through education as a result of various personal and contextual factors.

## Transformative Experiences

The majority of participants ($n = 9$) had transformative experiences as demonstrated through their engagement in discussion and personal reflections. Two different types of transformative experiences emerged throughout the course: revisions to frames of reference for those who (a) had experienced oppression as members of marginalized social groups and (b) those who had not.

## Transformative Experiences for the Oppressed

Participants ($n = 5$) who had these types of transformations described themselves as members of oppressed racial, cultural, and/or sexual-orientation groups. These individuals held a variety of roles in both K-12 and higher-education contexts. Their initial written reflections could be characterized as both informative and intensifying as they described the tensions between the theories they learned in the course and their lack of implementation in their settings. As the course progressed, they began to reflect deeply on these disconnects and how their own intersectional identities affected how they conceptualize multicultural education and their experiences as members of marginalized groups within their organizations.

For example, participants who worked in small private schools with specific cultural agendas experienced immediate dissonance with the concept of "cultural encapsulation" (Pedersen, 2000; Wrenn, 1962, 1985), which Pedersen (2000) argues is often the opposite of multiculturalism. The authors argue that culturally encapsulated counselors often use self-reference criteria to evaluate others, as they (a) leverage a single set of stereotypes and assumptions to define reality, (b) demonstrate insensitivity to other cultural viewpoints, (c) protect their unreasoned assumptions despite evidence to the contrary, and (d) judge their own and others' behavior from naïve, self-referenced criteria (Pedersen, 2000). These participants named a goal of their schools as cultural encapsulation of students as members of an oppressed cultural group that feared assimilation as a threat to the survival of the group. They noted the tension between the perceived need for encapsulation and the desire to prepare students for life in a multicultural society. Their written reflections became more nuanced throughout the course as they re-examined past assumptions (e.g. that some organizational conflicts had arisen from cultural differences among staff members rather than insubordination; questioning how accepting their organization was to issues of gender identity and sexual orientation) and created more refined and inclusive frames of reference. Their written reflections dove progressively deeper into analysis of past behaviors and beliefs and used course theories to guide this analysis and reflection. They named and problematized their previously-amassed frames of reference (Mezirow, 2000) and questioned the cultural assumptions into which they had been socialized (Taylor, 2017). For example, they named experiencing tension between previous beliefs about religion, sexuality, and personal identity and their new learning about the value of multicultural education. They championed the need for multiculturalism in their organizations but noted that lived experiences had not prepared them to lead this work. They rejected concepts they had previously embraced such as assimilation, acculturation, homogeneity, heteronormativity, monoculturalism, and tolerance. Their final reflections ended with strong personal commitments to eliminate cultural encapsulation in their organization in order to promote authentic multicultural education.

### Transformative Experiences for Members of Dominant Culture

Participants ($n$ = 4) in this category identified as members of the dominant White racial group and held a variety of roles ranging from classroom instructor to district content specialist in both K-12 and higher education settings. They were mostly independent learners who primarily interacted autonomously with course content and had varying levels of asynchronous interaction with peers and their instructor (Andersen, 2003). Each of these individuals engaged meaningfully with both the content and their peers during synchronous sessions fielding probing questions from others and appearing to reflect deeply and authentically on challenges to their existing frames of reference. They were able to identify potential blind spots arising from their membership in a racially dominant group and seemed to benefit greatly from challenges to their worldviews in the context of a safe instructional space (synchronous sessions).

In one such session, a participant fielded a question about his organization's stance on sexuality and how its seeming lack of tolerance may impede his work toward implementing multicultural education. His next several written reflections explicitly critiqued the monocultural and assimilationist culture of his workplace, demonstrating a greater depth of examination than he had previously displayed. Another participant progressed from blaming her peers for having racially-differential expectations for students in her first written reflection, to accepting responsibility for her own potentially problematic expectations in her final reflection: "I know that I have made assumptions about diverse individuals' abilities, and it is likely that teachers in my district do as well." Her initial course goal was to research cooperative learning strategies that better aligned to students' collectivist cultures (a strategy-focused view of culturally responsive teaching). By her final reflection, she had abandoned a focus on instructional strategies in favor of researching "systems and practices such as tracking, grouping, and testing processes [that] contribute to inequities in the educational system." She planned to conduct an analysis of mathematics course composition to uncover existing racial disproportionality and to leverage her district-level leadership role to alter existing course recommendation practices.

Like these participants, the transformation of others in this category could likely be attributed to a blend of (a) permanent asynchronous text-based discussions in which they had more time to carefully craft their responses and (b) synchronous discussions which pushed participants to think *on their feet* to respond to peers and instructor comments and queries and which were not recorded to promote a sense of safety among participants.

Since the *autonomous* nature of course structures likely contributed to the transformation of individuals in this category, their experiences are more disparate than those in other categories. A common thread in their written reflections, though, was an increasingly deepened sense of personal responsibility for addressing inequities in their contexts. In many cases they reflected on their roles in maintaining a status quo that further oppressed students from marginalized groups, and they expressed strong desires to change their organizational cultures to remedy this. They spoke about the need to shift other's frames of reference as their own had been enlarged based on what they learned in this course. They accepted responsibility for impacting their total school environments (Banks, 2015) through addressing cultural stagnation, discriminatory behaviors, racially disproportionate discipline, academic tracking, and other hindrances to multicultural education at the classroom, school, district, and organizational levels.

## Discussion

The four trends described above appear to somewhat disprove the hypothesis that decreased transactional distance is associated with increased levels of critical reflection (see Figure 6.1). Instead, the relationship between TD and critical reflection may be more nuanced (see Figure 6.2). The informal analysis of formative assessment data described in the section above indicates that conditions leading to transformative learning differ based on individuals' backgrounds. For those individuals entering MTE courses having experienced personal oppression, connectivity and interactivity did not seem necessary as they independently worked to apply new theoretical knowledge to their lived experience. In contrast, for individuals coming from places of greater cultural dominance, smaller TD and high levels of meaningful interaction allowed them to make sense of evolving theoretical knowledge as well as envision how they can take meaningful action to apply that knowledge to their own professional and personal contexts.

## Next Steps and Future Research

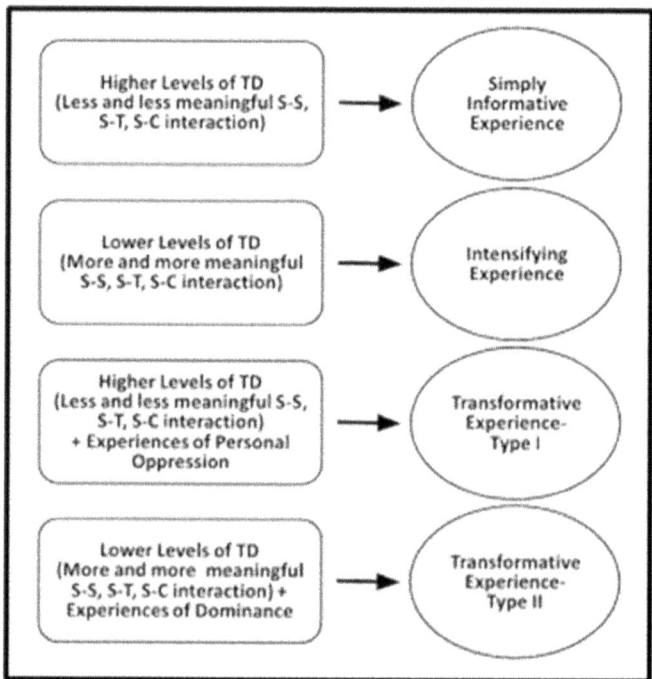

Figure 6.2: Study Outcomes: Trends in Participants' Course Experiences. Source: Author

Note. Highlights correlation between levels of transactional distance (TD) and participants' overall degree of transformative learning based on Bondy et al.'s (2015) levels.

These observations provide further support for calls for more research into what kind and how much interactivity influences learning outcomes in online MTE courses (Grant & Lee, 2014; Hill et al., 2009), as well as how course activities, content, and facilitation influence the *conscientization* process for individuals with unique backgrounds and learning profiles (Bondy et al., 2015). The current iteration of this MTE course now begins with explicit framing about the goal of fostering transformative learning through engagement in critical pedagogy. Discussion and written reflection prompts have been revised to reflect this focus on TL and CP. Initial reflection on students' participation in both synchronous and asynchronous communication (S-T, S-S, S-C) indicates that this reframing has helped students reflect more deeply and explicitly about revisions to their existing frames of reference.

Additionally, work has been done to further refine asynchronous discussion procedures. Noting the convenience of asynchronous communication but the potential feelings of isolation due to increased TD (Hara et al., 2000; Jiang, 2017), specifically-designed protocols for participation in traditional discussion threads have been implemented. One example is the starter-wrapper with roles technique (Hara et al., 2000; Olesova et al., 2016; Zhu, 1996), where students assume assigned roles including discussion starter, moderator, and wrapper. The starter begins a thread in response to the posted discussion question(s), the moderator ensures participation in the thread throughout the session, and the wrapper summarizes the discussion at the end of the session. Role assignment is thought to help students take greater responsibility for their own learning and to engage in more thoughtful interaction with peers (Jiang, 2017), both of which are required to engage in TL.

Teaching online in this manner can be time-consuming, but building the types of practices outlined in this chapter into existing course frameworks can mitigate this issue. For instance,

1. the instructor and TA schedule dedicated time to meet and reflect on the processes of the course and whether course goals are being met,
2. the sessions that have the potential to generate the most cognitive dissonance among students are scheduled for the synchronous sessions, and
3. time allotted to traditional office hours is redistributed to support small group synchronous sessions (when class size allows).

Although preliminary data seems to indicate these course design elements support TL, structured, mixed-methods analysis of student participation in asynchronous structures (discussion posts using roles) and synchronous video-conference sessions is needed to determine their level of impact on the critical nature of individuals' written self-reflections, as well as students' perceptions of transactional distance and the role of different types of interactivity on their learning experience throughout the duration of the course. It is critically important that we as teacher educators develop concrete, data-informed, and sustainable processes to help other educators examine their frames of reference and ensure we are all operating in ways that provide equitable learning experiences for all learners.

# Appendix

## Types of Learning Interaction

| Type of Interaction | Key Features | Examples |
|---|---|---|
| student-to-content (S-C): degree of cognitive presence in terms of students' ability to construct meaning through engagement with and connection to new ideas and diverse perspectives (Garrison et al., 2000) | • individual, small group, and/or whole class interactions<br>• reading, listening, and/or viewing<br>• writing, presenting, and/or oral discussion<br>• access, synthesis, and application | • reading empirical literature<br>• listening to recorded lectures<br>• viewing related media<br>• participating in asynchronous forum discussions<br>• preparing for synchronous discussions<br>• writing reflection papers |
| student-to-teacher (S-T): degree of teaching presence in terms of course design and organization, discourse facilitation, direct instruction, feedback, and assessment (Garrison et al., 2000) | • synchronous and/or asynchronous<br>• one-on-one, small group, or whole class<br>• teacher or student centered<br>• academic and/or social focus | • reading weekly announcements<br>• participating in synchronous interactive discussions<br>• examining feedback on assignments, discussion posts, and course participation<br>• conversing through personal email, phone calls, and videoconferencing |
| student-to-student (S-S): degree of social presence in terms of students' ability to project their identity and develop relationships in the learning environment (Garrison et al., 2000) | • synchronous and/or asynchronous<br>• small group and/or whole class<br>• academic and/or social focus<br>• facilitated or not facilitated | • interacting through asynchronous discussion forum dialogue<br>• interacting through synchronous videoconferencing dialogue<br>• interacting through small group assignments |

Source: Author

# References

Abrami, P. C., Bernard, R. M., Bures, E. M., Borokhovski, E., & Tamim, R. M. (2011). Interaction in distance education and online learning using evidence and theory to improve practice. *Journal of Computing in Higher Education, 23*, 82–103. http://dx.doi.org/10.1007/s12528-011-9043-x

Andersen, M. L. (2003). Whitewashing race: A critical perspective on whiteness. In A. W. Doane & E. Bonilla-Silva (Eds.), *White out: The continuing significance of racism* (pp. 21–34). Psychology Press.

Anderson, T., Rourke, L., Garrison, D. R., & Archer, W. (2001). Assessing teaching presence in a computer conference context. *Journal of Asynchronous Learning Networks, 5*(2), 1–17. http://dx.doi.org/10.24059/olj.v5i2.1875

Banks, J. A. (2015). *Cultural diversity and education: Foundations, curriculum, and teaching* (5th ed.). Pearson.

Banks, J. A., Cookson, P., Gay, G., Hawley, W. D., Irvine, J. J., Nieto, S., Schofield, J. W., & Stephan, W. G. (2001). Diversity within unity: Essential principles for teaching and learning in a multicultural society. *Phi Delta Kappan, 83*(3), 196–203. https://doi.org/10.1177/003172170108300309

Bondy, E., Hambacher, E., Murphy, A. S., Wolkenhauer, R., & Krell, D. (2015). Developing critical social justice literacy in an online seminar. *Equity & Excellence in Education, 48*(2), 227–248. http://dx.doi.org/10.1080/10665684.2015.1025652

Boyd, A. S., & Glazier, J. A. (2017). The choreography of conversation: An exploration of collaboration and difficult discussions in cross disciplinary teacher discourse communities. *The High School Journal, 100*(2), 130–145. https://www.jstor.org/stable/90000752

Caruthers, L., & Friend, J. (2014). Critical pedagogy in online environments as thirdspace: A narrative analysis of voices of candidates in educational preparatory programs. *American Educational Studies Association, 50*(1), 8–35. http://dx.doi.org/10.1080/00131946.2013.866953

Donaldson, S., Caldwell, K., & Borkoski, C. (2018). Connected: Building meaningful relationships for online learning. *NEFDC Exchange, 31*, 9–12. https://nefdc.org/wp-content/uploads/2019/01/NEFDC-Fall2018Exchange.pdf

Freire, P., & Macedo, D. (1995). A dialogue: Culture, language, and race. *Harvard Educational Review, 65*(3), 377–403. https://doi.org/10.17763/haer.65.3.12g1923330p1xhj8

Garrison, R., Anderson, T., & Archer, W. (2000). Critical inquiry in a text-based environment: Computer conferencing in higher education. *The Internet and Higher Education, 2*(2–3), 87–105. http://dx.doi.org/10.1016/j.iheduc.2009.10.003

Gilbert, P. K., & Dabbagh, N. (2005). How to structure online discussions for meaningful discourse: A case study. *British Journal of Educational Technology, 36*(1), 5–18. http://dx.doi.org/10.1111/j.1467-8535.2005.00434.x

Goldingay, S., & Land, C. (2014). Emotion: The 'e' in engagement in online distance education in social work. *Journal of Open, Flexible, and Distance Learning, 18*(1), 58–72. https://files.eric.ed.gov/fulltext/EJ1079840.pdf

Grant, K. S. L., & Lee, V. J. (2014). Wrestling with issues of diversity in online courses. *The Qualitative Report, 19*, 1–25. https://files.eric.ed.gov/fulltext/EJ1043563.pdf

Hara, N., Bonk, C. J., & Angeli, C. (2000). Content analysis of online discussion in an applied educational psychology course. *Instructional Science, 28*(2), 115–152. https://www.jstor.org/stable/23371529

Hill, J. R., Song, L., & West, R. E. (2009). Social learning theory and web-based learning environments: A review of research and discussion of implications. *The American Journal of Distance Education, 23*(2), 88–103. http://dx.doi.org/10.1080/08923640902857713

Jiang, W. (2017). Interdependence of roles, role rotation, and sense of community in an online course. *Distance Education, 38*(1), 84–105, http://dx.doi.org/10.1080/01587919.2017.1299564

Ladson-Billings, G. (2000). Fighting for our lives: Preparing teachers to teach African American students. *Journal of Teacher Education, 51*(3), 206–214. http://dx.doi.org/10.1177/0022487100051003008

Lajoie, S. P. (2014). Multimedia learning of cognitive processes. In R. Mayer (Ed.), *The Cambridge handbook of multimedia learning* (pp. 623–646). Cambridge University Press.

Lambert, J. L., & Fisher, J. L. (2013). Community of inquiry framework: Establishing community in an online course. *Journal of Interactive Online Learning, 12*(1), 1–16. http://www.ncolr.org/jiol/issues/pdf/12.1.1.pdf

Little, J. W., & Bartlett, L. (2010). The teacher workforce and problems of educational equity. *Review of Research in Education, 34*, 285–328. http://dx.doi.org/10.3102/0091732X09356099

MacLeod, K. R., Swart, W. W., & Paul, R. C. (2019). Continual improvement of online and blended teaching using relative proximity theory. *Decision Sciences Journal of Innovative Education, 17*(1), 53–75. http://dx.doi.org/10.1111/dsji.12169

Maddrell, J. A., Morrison, G. R., & Watson, G. S. (2017). Presence and learning in a community of inquiry. *Distance Education, 38*(2), 245–258. https://doi.org/10.1080/01587919.2017.1322062

Males, L. M., Otten, S., & Herbel-Eisenmann, B. A. (2010). Challenges of critical colleagueship: Examining and reflecting on mathematics teacher study group interactions. *Journal of Mathematics Teacher Education, 13*, 459–471. http://dx.doi.org/10.1007/s10857-010-9156-6

McLaren, P. (1998). Revolutionary pedagogy in post-revolutionary times: Rethinking the political economy of critical education. *Educational Theory, 48*(4), 431–462.

Mezirow, J. (1996). Contemporary paradigms of learning. *Adult Education Quarterly, 46*(3), 158–172. https://doi.org/10.1177%2F074171369604600303

Mezirow, J. (1997). Transformative learning: Theory to practice. *New Directions for Adult and Continuing Education*, *5*(12). http://dx.doi.org/10.1002/ace.7401

Mezirow, J. (2000): *Learning as transformation. Critical Perspectives on a theory in progress.* Jossey-Bass.

Mezirow, J., & Welton, M. (1995). *In defense of the lifeworld*. State University of New York Press.

Moore, M. (1997). Theory of transactional distance. In D. Keegan (Ed.), *Theoretical principles of distance education* (pp. 22–38). Routledge.

National Center for Education Statistics. (2017). *Characteristics of public elementary and secondary school teachers in the United States: Results from the 2015–16 National Teacher and Principal Survey.* https://nces.ed.gov/pubs2017/2017071.pdf

Nieto, S. (2008). Affirmation, solidarity and critique: Moving beyond tolerance in education. In E. Lee, D. Menkart, & M. Okazawa-Rey (Eds.), *Beyond heroes and holidays* (pp. 18–29). Teaching for Change.

Olesova, L., Slavin, M., & Lim, J. (2016). Exploring the effect of scripted roles on cognitive presence in asynchronous online discussions. *Online Learning*, *20*(4), 34–53. http://dx.doi.org/10.24059/olj.v20i4.1058

Pedersen, P. (2000). *A handbook for developing multicultural awareness* (3rd ed.). American Counseling Association.

Pohan, C. A., & Aguilar, T. E. (2001). Measuring educators' beliefs about diversity in personal and professional contexts. *American Educational Research Journal*, *38*(1), 159–182. http://dx.doi.org/10.3102/00028312038001159

Shedletsky, L., & Aitken, J. E. (2010). *Cases on online discussion and interaction: Experiences and outcomes.* Information Science Reference.

Shin, N. (2003). Transactional presence as a critical predictor of success in distance learning. *Distance Learning, Distance Education*, *24*(1), 69–86. http://dx.doi.org/10.1080/01587910303048

Taylor, E. W. (2017). Transformative learning theory. In A. Laros, T. Fuhr, & E. W. Taylor (Eds.), *Transformative learning meets bildung: An international exchange* (pp. 17–29). Sense Publishers.

van Es, E. (2012). Examining the development of a teacher learning community: The case of a video club. *Teaching and Teacher Education*, *28*(2), 182–192. https://doi.org/10.1016/j.tate.2011.09.005

Weidlich, J., & Bastiaens, T. J. (2018). Technology matters – The impact of transactional distance on satisfaction in online distance learning. *International Review of Research in Open and Distributed Learning*, *19*(3), 222–242. http://dx.doi.org/10.19173/irrodl.v19i3.3417

Weisman, E., & Garza, S. (2002). Preservice teacher attitudes toward diversity: Can one class make a difference? *Equity & Excellence in Education*, *35*(1), 28–34. https://doi.org/10.1080/713845246

Wink, J. (2011). *Critical pedagogy: Notes from the real world*. Pearson.

Wrenn, C. G. (1962). The culturally encapsulated counselor. *Harvard Educational Review, 32*(4), 444–449.

Wrenn, C. G. (1985). Afterword: The culturally encapsulated counselor revisited. In P. Pedersen (Ed.), *Handbook of cross-cultural counseling and therapy* (pp. 323–329). Greenwood Press.

Zhu, E. (1996). Meaning negotiation, knowledge construction, and mentoring in a distance learning course. In *Proceedings of selected research and development presentations at the 1996 National Convention of the Association for Educational Communications and Technology* (pp. 821–844). Indianapolis, IN. Retrieved July 1, 2008, from http://eric.ed.gov/ERICWebPortal/recordDetail?accno=ED397849

CHAPTER SEVEN

# Creating Community Through Meaningful Interactions: A Framework to Support Critical Pedagogy and Social Justice[1]

BRIANNE MORETTINI

Most people in U.S. society would likely say we live in an increasingly virtual world, as methods of communication, learning, and information gathering are more accessible in online platforms than ever before. Consequently, faculty in higher education settings find themselves constantly confronted with the benefits and challenges of living, learning, and teaching in this increasingly online world. I situate this chapter as a faculty member at an increasingly research-focused institution but with roots as a normal school focused on teacher preparation. More specifically, our institution is known for a focus on teaching; yet faculty feel there is much greater emphasis now placed on scholarly productivity than on teaching quality.

I share this context because conversations with colleagues across the country reveal this is a common theme—teaching is still a significant part of our workload, but there is a growing emphasis placed on research. In addition, the nature of our teaching is changing from traditional face-to-face to more hybrid and online formats. To borrow from van Manen's (2002) term, many of us now feel as though we are teaching "in the dark" (p. 2) and figuring out instructional strategies in a trial-by-error process we thought we had pedagogically overcome some years ago. We are expected to provide our online students with the same learning outcomes as students in face-to-face classes without being given any significant support to move along the learning curve associated with online teaching. Indeed, the "ease of simplicity is deceptive" (van Manen, 2002, p. 2).

Moreover, I struggle with finding ways to engage online learners with aspects of social justice because doing so requires trust and vulnerability—both of which can be difficult to create in asynchronous online classes. Over the past several semesters, I have found that with online courses focused on social justice, giving students access to both the professor and to one another allows for meaningful interactions and a sense of belonging.

My goal in this chapter, therefore, is to illustrate the pedagogical tools and methods that I have developed as a way to establish rapport and foster meaningful interactions with my students and among students. To situate my specific pedagogical tools and methods, I sketch the larger landscape of my approach to online teaching by first describing the overall context of the particular online course on which I focus in this chapter and then drawing connections to larger learning theories in an effort to maintain scholarly discourse around the ever-evolving practices of educator preparation and online teaching and learning. After sketching this landscape, I go on to describe the pedagogical tools and assignments I employ to structure an online community of practice in this particular course.

## Course Introduction and Overview

I currently serve as the professor for a course called *Foundations and Philosophies of Education*[2], which is a required course in an undergraduate inclusive education program leading to dual certification in PK-6 general and special education. Students are required to take the course in their freshman year as a way to build their knowledge base about the theoretical underpinnings of educational philosophies, particularly as they pertain to the sociocultural and sociopolitical influences that shape today's educational system. Specifically, the course description in the undergraduate course catalog for the university reads:

> This course examines educational philosophies, psychological influences on education, and the development of the Standards Movement as these ideas pertain to current educational practices. Through seminal readings and course assignments, students will explore how various philosophies as well as socio-cultural, socio-political, and psychological influences shape today's schools and the teaching profession.

That course description relates to the following course objectives, as listed in the course syllabus:

1. To describe how historical influences impact current educational practice;
2. To explore the Standards Movement to consider how it shapes state and national assessment and accountability in schools;
3. To discuss implications of accountability, diversity, and marginalized populations in schools;
4. To demonstrate knowledge of educational philosophies and psychological influences on classroom practice;
5. To develop a personal educational philosophy grounded in research;
6. To investigate the socio-historical, socio-political, and socio-economic trends of poverty and the effects and influences in U.S. Schools;
7. To explore the intersection of the teaching profession with the socio-economic, cultural, and political issues that shape our society.

To fulfill these course objectives and to foster rapport and establish meaningful scholarly interactions among students and with students, I build in certain pedagogical methods and assignments, which have been revised over time. I discuss these specific pedagogical methods and assignments later in this chapter. For now, I want to continue to sketch the larger landscape of my pedagogical approach by describing how I situate myself as the instructor in a community of practice given the goals and focus of this particular course.

## Situating the Role of Instructor

Instructors of online courses focused on social justice and critical pedagogy often examine and reflect upon their role and how they enact their responsibilities to students. As a former classroom teacher, I value getting to know my students and building relationships with them. On my university's learning management system (LMS), learning is approached as decontextualized, ahistorical, and linear in order to accommodate the wide range and variance of content in courses offered across the university. My pedagogical approach tries to deconstruct this didactic approach by giving students access to an online community of learners, where each learner's personal experience and positionality is valued.

In my role as course instructor, I view myself as a critical mentor and facilitator of learning and growth. I include the following quote by Connelly and Clandinin (1988) in the course syllabus: "There is no better way to study curriculum than to study ourselves ... It is possible to reconstruct, to build a narrative that 'remakes' the taken-for-granted, habitual ways we all have of responding to our curriculum situations" (p. 31). The reason I include this quote in the course syllabus is because it captures how I view my role as a teacher educator with a focus on social justice and advocacy.

In order for teachers to be effective, to build positive relationships with students, and to advocate for students with disabilities, we need to take stock of who we are as individuals and what we bring to bear in any teaching context. To that end, I discuss with my candidates the struggles and challenges I faced as a teacher as part of my Learner Autobiography—discussed in the Pedagogical Methods section—at the beginning of the semester. In sharing my struggles and challenges as a former teacher, I model vulnerability and trust building for students. I also place a significant sense of importance on my students' abilities to work with young learners who bring cultural, linguistic, and/or cognitive differences into the classroom. Being a critical mentor means that while I maintain high expectations for my students, I make sure to provide my students with the support necessary to achieve those expectations.

## Related Theoretical Considerations

In our contemporary world, learners encounter a complex web of ideas and information on a daily basis. Consequently, the challenge for thoughtful educators is deciding what knowledge counts as worthy of study, how best to present this knowledge, and how to teach learners to be able to make complex decisions for themselves. The fact that all of this takes place within schooling environments dedicated to advancing the dispositions of a multicultural democratic citizenry only adds to this complexity.

Education, therefore, is an on-going, goal-oriented collaborative process based on sound principles and methods that maximize academic learning and advance the social and emotional development of all children. In a course that examines the broad social foundations of education, this becomes particularly poignant. In fact, education involves preparing learners for a rapidly changing world that we cannot even begin to imagine, and as a result, teachers are charged with cultivating a sense of resiliency and resolve in students within the context of equitable classrooms.

It is widely agreed that teaching and learning are sociocultural processes, that teachers and students bring their own cultural experiences, customs, backgrounds, and perceptions to the teaching and learning processes (Freire, 1998; Hollins, 1996; Nieto, 2002; Vygotsky, 1978). Nieto (2002) explained that social relationships are at the heart of teaching and learning. As a result, I place primacy on creating a community of practice so as to enhance the experiences of my students and to demonstrate progressive pedagogical practice that affirms and respects students' own social and cultural worlds.

Demonstrating an authentic respect for students' social and cultural worlds requires a degree of cultural competence that is broadly defined as the attitudes, behaviors, knowledge, skills, and abilities that enable a teacher to work and respond effectively in cross-cultural settings (Ladson-Billings, 2001; Williams, 2001). I agree with Ukpokodu (2011) that cultural competence is exemplified by a "commitment to serving diverse students well, to ensure their educational equity justice, and to systematically assess the effectiveness of that commitment and service" (p. 437). Such commitment is reflected in a teacher's ability to demonstrate genuine care for students.

Related to that notion, in a multicultural society, it is paramount to create learning environments in which *all students* realize their inherent value as human beings. Differences among students should be situated as assets to the teaching and learning environment, an environment in which every student necessarily deserves to feel valued and dignified. My pedagogical approach reflects the complex nature of teachers' work and my own humility in engaging in such a "gnostic" act (Freire, 2000, p. 67) with my students.

Grounded in a sociocultural theoretical framework (Vygotsky, 1978), I believe that learning occurs when educational opportunities attend to context, including learners' specific needs. Specifically, educational opportunities ought to meet individuals where they currently are and challenge them appropriately to create incremental learning. Effective teaching engages students in meaningful, relevant, and challenging work within a safe and secure environment.

Building on a sociocultural theoretical approach to learning, I also believe communities of practice (Wenger, 1998) are fundamental to the learning experience. To that end, Wenger (1998) writes, "Practice is, first and foremost, a process by which we can experience the world and our engagement with it as meaningful" (p. 51). As individuals, we mine and cultivate meaning from experiences based on various aspects of context, including social relations, language, and history, interpretation, and action (Wenger, 1998). In this way, "Meaning exists neither in us, nor in the world, but in the dynamic relation of living in the world" (Wenger, 1998, p. 54). My felt obligations, then, as an instructor in an asynchronous online learning space, are to foster meaningful interactions *with* students and *among* students so they can begin to cultivate meaning and participate in a community of practice.

Together, action and reflection on that action—what Freire (1972) terms praxis—allow me to think about creating spaces for dialogue with students and among students. In prepackaged asynchronous online learning environments, my belief is that educators need to demonstrate for students the importance of thinking and reflecting on our thinking both within oneself and with peers through shared discourse and dialogue. In this way, my online teaching attends to reflection-in-action and reflection-on-action (Schön, 1983), yielding new insights for learners about themselves and their burgeoning teacher practice.

## Enacting a Framework for Online Social Participation

My own theoretical framework as an instructor is related to the overall philosophical framework that undergirds the Inclusive Education program, in which the *Foundations and Philosophies of Education* course is embedded. That philosophical framework states:

> A commitment to inclusive education requires active efforts to identify and remove all barriers to learning for all children. This means that educators must attend to increasing participation not just for students with disabilities but for all those students experiencing disadvantage, whether this results from poverty, sexuality, minority ethnic status, or other characteristics assigned significance by the dominant culture in their society. (Baglieri et al., 2011)

With a commitment to a sociocultural theoretical framework (Vygotsky, 1978), Wenger's (1998) *communities of practice* and Freire's (1972) notion of *praxis* to guide my pedagogical approach, I maintain that learners work best when learning experiences acknowledge one's *being* in the world and how one's social action can shape and change the world. My online course, therefore, is designed to: (1) acknowledge the situatedness of online learners in an increasingly complex global structure; and, (2) provide opportunities for students to have meaningful dialogic interactions with each other and with me as the course instructor.

## Pedagogical Methods

Faculty focused on pedagogical modeling live the tension between online teaching and the enactment of critical pedagogy and social justice in our teaching practice. I have tinkered with different pedagogical methods to help create the sense of community necessary to support the social justice-oriented conversations that stem from a focus on critical pedagogy. The methods discussed here have been implemented in the *Foundations and Philosophies of Education* course for prospective inclusive education teachers; however, they are generalizable to other education courses with an emphasis on social justice and critical pedagogy.

Just as young children need to learn in a caring and safe environment, so do teacher candidates at the collegiate level. Consistent with a sociocultural theoretical framework, I believe that *how* one learns influences *what* one learns. Specifically, I believe that teacher candidates will learn more and develop deeper connections with ideas if they feel they are able to take risks, ask questions, and view their peers as valuable resources. For this to occur, learners need to feel a sense of community and belonging. The following figure (Figure 7.1) shows the various pedagogical methods I use to create an online community of practice and a sense of belonging by fostering meaningful interactions, building rapport, and enabling social participation in an online class.

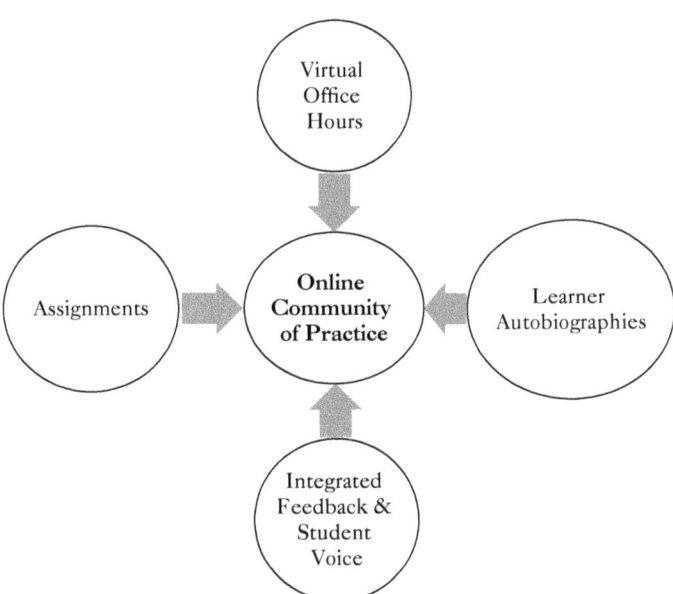

Figure 7.1. Pedagogical Methods to Structure an Online Community of Practice. Source: Author

Together these pedagogical methods give students *access* to an online community of practice (Wenger, 1998) through structured social participation. They create a sense of belonging and community, both of which enable students to confront their own and each other's biases in order to begin to understand and develop social justice as a stance and as a pedagogical commitment. Moving along the figure clockwise, each pedagogical method is now described in greater detail.

### Virtual Office Hours

Similar to other institutions of higher education, many of the students enrolled in the college where I work maintain part-time employment and commute during their time with us. As a result—and because we live in a digital age marked by the pervasiveness of email communication accessible through smart phones—most of my students do not take advantage of traditional office hours. Instead, whenever students have a question or concern, they send me an email. In an online class with as many as thirty students, keeping on top of my email responses to students in a timely manner proves difficult, especially when trying to meet the other demands my job presents (e.g., research and service).

As a way to implement a structure that works both for students and for me as an instructor, I establish virtual office hours each semester, which are different for each online class I teach. Specifically, in the beginning of this course I survey students asking when they can meet virtually in a chat room. Then, I make myself available to students during the most popular times and keep flex hours dedicated to students each week.

### Learner Autobiographies

The students need to see the course instructor as a human being in this learning effort alongside them; in addition, students need to see that the instructor is willing to demonstrate the same vulnerability expected of students. The Learner Autobiography task provides a space for such vulnerability. For this ungraded task, I upload a brief video to our online platform of myself and my educational journey. Then, students are asked to upload a short video introduction of themselves as learners and prospective teachers. Among other things in my video, I tell students:

> I am a former kindergarten teacher who had a lot of students with different needs in my classes. While in many ways I did not feel prepared to meet the range of needs my students presented, I did have a strong commitment to each of my student's individual growth and sense of belonging and security in my classroom. I believe that students cannot learn and develop to the best of their abilities unless they feel safe, secure, and perceive they are part of a community of learners. Through this class, and the assignments I am asking you to complete, I hope you will begin to also see the importance of building community in your classroom as a way to help students feel safe and to help them learn and grow. Please remember throughout this class that I, too, am a learner alongside you in our journey toward creating more equitable and accessible learning spaces for students.

The act of doing a task *alongside* students signals its importance as well as the importance of who we are as learners in an online community of practice.

## Integrated Feedback & Student Voice

Through the enactment of a sociocultural theoretical framework, I believe that teacher candidates will learn more and develop deeper connections with ideas if they feel they are able to take risks, ask questions, and view their peers as valuable resources. In order for this to occur in my own college classes, certain conditions need to be put into place in the classroom. For example, I work to put students' ideas in conversation with each other so that students receive feedback not just from me as the course instructor, but from each other as peers. Students need to hear each other's voices, and students need to know that their own voices, ideas, and questions are heard not just by the instructor, but also by their peers who are learning alongside them.

More specifically, each week students are given discussion questions based on key ideas from assigned readings. Students answer the questions on a discussion board and then respond to 3–4 peers' responses. After reading the entire corpus of responses, I choose several representative words and create a word cloud to illustrate *my* interpretation of students' thinking around the week's key ideas. Below is an example of a word cloud I created based on students' responses to how controversy can be used to influence learning, since I want students to be equipped for the controversial and sometimes heated discussions surrounding critical pedagogy and social justice.

Figure 7.2. Integrated Feedback and Student Voice Represented by a Word Cloud

After creating and sharing the word cloud on our course site, I invite students' responses to my interpretation of their thinking related to the weekly readings and discussion questions. I think that for students, seeing that the course instructor is reflecting on their ideas validates their thinking, and they are encouraged to continue to engage with the weekly readings and discussion questions in thoughtful ways.

## Assignments

In addition to virtual office hours, learner autobiographies at the beginning of the semester, and integrated feedback and student voice, I use three main assignments to further create and structure an online community of practice: A Critical Friends assignment, a Community Engagement activity, and a Personal Educational Philosophy. For the purposes of exposition, each assignment is described in detail along with a redacted student example.

## Critical Friends Assignment

For this assignment, I create randomized pairs of students at the beginning of the semester whose progress and learning they are instructed to follow through close readings of discussion posts and assignments. At the end of the course, each student answers the following questions about his/her critical friend and shares them with me and with each other: What did I learn about my critical friend relative to the focus of our course? What questions do I have for my critical friend? And what do I see as the next steps in my critical friend's social justice journey? Below are some redacted examples of the Critical Friends assignment from students. One student wrote,

> Something that I learned about from my critical friend was about the responsive system. The responsive system in the classroom is also about understanding that all students are different and because of that each student has different strengths. That in the classroom students will respond if there is a nourishing and safe environment for the students.

Another student wrote,

> My critical friend mentioned that schools should provide a safe place for students to learn and be with other people of their age in order to gain social skills. She also takes a stand against test scores to reflect the student and teacher. She mentions that students have little say within the classroom and does not appreciate such little authority they have. I would like to ask my critical friend, "Are you happy with the way curriculum is taught within schools today?" I really enjoyed reading her assignments. If there's one thing I can recommend to her, it is to provide her own preferences to certain issues pertaining to certain discussion questions. I would have loved to read about what she had thought about a certain situation rather than pulling things straight from the textbook. Information from the textbook is great and answers the questions perfectly, but a student's input allows the reader to understand that they are knowledgeable on the topic. Over the course, she has become stronger within her assignments although her assignments were very strong off the bat. I encourage her to keep up the great work and to always give each assignment her all.

The Critical Friends assignment prompts students to begin to look at learning through the lens of a teacher rather than solely through their own lens as students; it prompts students to engage with someone else's ideas, take stock of a peer's learning, and I hope, serves as a way to thoughtfully reflect on how their peers might perceive *their* learning journey relative to social justice. Overall, this assignment helps create a community of practice by structuring students' meaningful interactions with each other.

## Community Engagement Activity

For this assignment, students go out into their surrounding community as participant observers and complete an observation of an informal learning experience (e.g. Board of Education meeting, community recreation center events, etc.). Based on Freire's notion of praxis (Freire, 1972), this assignment encourages students to reflect on the world and the intersection of theory and action. After their observation, students are instructed to submit a written analysis of how critical pedagogies and learning theories are/not enacted in the learning experience they observe. Students are also invited to offer some critique of the experience related to critical pedagogy. Below is a redacted excerpt from a student's Community Engagement Activity assignment.

> As part of my assignment, I had the pleasure of attending a Special Olympics practice. This organization gathers children with intellectual and physical disabilities from around the local neighborhood to learn the basics of basketball in preparation for upcoming tournaments. The coaches encourage the children to work together as a team, and they use interactive skills to help them understand the sport. Combining a simple objective with elements of Vygotsky and Piaget's learning theories, this practice showed me that children with disabilities can have an impact in the sports world just like anyone else.

The way the coaches instructed the players reminded me of two learning theories that focus on cognitive growth. At certain points, I noticed that some athletes were doing the drills on their own, but a few were struggling to grasp simple concepts. When I saw the coaches assisting them, I immediately thought of Vygotsky's theory, specifically the zone of proximal development. This idea is the "range of tasks that are too difficult for the child to master alone but can be learned with guidance and assistance from adults or more-skilled children" (Santrock, 2018, p. 50). As a result of their cognitive impairments, some athletes had trouble mastering skills like shooting and dribbling. The coaches helped them retain the information by shadowing them and demonstrating the skills face-to-face. The hand-over-hand technique was used to help with shooting forms, and they tried to break the athletes' habits of one-handed dribbling by doing the proper form in front of them. They made sure that the athletes were coached based on where they lied in this zone, but the usage of learning theories did not stop there.

The coaches also used the concepts of assimilation and accommodation, a part of Piaget's Theory. This is when a child puts new data into a pre-made schema and then modifies "their schemas to fit new information and experiences" (Santrock, 2018, p. 40). In this practice, the coaches enforced new ideas for drills that the athletes haven't attempted yet. This strategy was done to help encourage the athletes to create new ways to approach situations that they would possibly encounter during a tournament run. For example, the coaches said that the team kept shooting the ball after making one pass during the offensive scrimmages. It took some time, but the children assimilated this new approach into their minds and adjusted their routine to meet the accommodations. Even if the coaches didn't know it, they were using prominent learning theories in their teachings and it was intriguing to observe.

In conclusion, I thought the practice was a good learning experience for everyone involved. The athletes were willing to participate, as they memorized drills successfully and looked like they were having fun in the process. The coaches were great at leading their players, but they excelled at showing strong patience and maintaining teamwork over individuality. At times they were hard on the athletes, but it was done to make them focus. The environment was also very professional in that the drills were put together in an organized matter. If I were the head coach, I would be good at interacting with the athletes but I wouldn't be able to put together a practice this organized. This team is an inspiration, and I wish them the best of luck in all they do in the future.

### Personal Educational Philosophy

The culminating assignment in this class is for students to synthesize their learning and the assignments and readings they have previously completed to develop and write a personal educational philosophy. Students are instructed to document how the course readings have shaped their philosophy, write about their fundamental understanding of the process of learning and the forces that influence it, and write a rationale that supports their philosophy. An excerpt from a student's Personal Educational Philosophy, drawing on *The Challenge to Care in Schools* by Nel Noddings (1992), appears below.

> In her book, *The Challenge to Care in Schools*, Nel Noddings explains that the act of caring and really relating to students is more important in the context of learning than concepts from their textbooks. This is a concept I fully agree with. Noddings notes

throughout her book that teachers who make students feel like they care are more effective and trusted teachers than those who are simply experts on the curriculum. I also believe that if more teachers implemented care into their philosophy of education like Noddings suggests, children would genuinely love going to school and associate school with positive feelings. Too often I have noticed the dread that can accompany school and schoolwork, oftentimes because students are afraid of teachers and/or administration or because they just do not believe their teachers care about them.

It is these critical viewpoints that need to be the main focus in schools. Focusing on the individual needs of each student and focusing first on care will lead to students who not only understand the core curriculum but also who are well informed of current social and political issues. The philosophy that shapes the way we teach affects every aspect of our students and the way they learn and grow, and we owe them the very best efforts to help them find their paths. By implementing these philosophies in and outside of the classroom I believe we can make a lasting difference.

Online courses cannot be isolated exchanges between the professor and individual students. The pedagogical methods outlined here enable students to explore the course with and through their peers, thereby structuring the process of social participation (Lave & Wenger, 1991) that creates a community of practice and embeds opportunities for students to learn about each other, to meaningfully communicate with each other, and to build rapport with one another *and* with the instructor. This is the only way social-justice-oriented conversations—which grow from a focus on critical pedagogy—can occur.

Feedback from Students

I have spent several semesters revising and refining my approach to this online course. From its inception five years ago, I have pushed colleagues to consider this course not just as a didactic and linear online course, but as a way to build our students' competencies with digital technologies and with the various lenses through which social justice is viewed. In sum, I did not want this course to become yet another course in my institution's bank of prepackaged online courses. I wanted this course to be a model for our teacher candidates of ways to engage learners in an increasingly digital world.

Feedback from students suggests they are satisfied with the approach to online learning described in this chapter. In the anonymous student evaluation of the course for the most recent semester, which is administered by the online learning management system after the course ends, students responded positively to survey items related to me as an instructor specifically and to the format of the class in general. For example, 88% of the class replied "always" when asked, "Did the instructor teach the class in a way that helped students make connections to their personal and professional lives?" In response to the question, "Was the instructor open to student feedback about the course and instructional methods?" 75% of students replied "always." Further, 81% of students replied "always" when asked if the instructor communicated course and lesson goals. In addition, 94% of students "strongly agreed" with whether or not they would recommend this online course to another student.

On this course evaluation survey, students have the opportunity to write open-ended, unprompted comments about the course in general or about the instructor specifically. Some of the open-ended comments students wrote were, "I truly enjoyed this class. The readings were truly enlightening and I feel more prepared for my future as a teacher." Another student wrote, "The instructor is very helpful. This class is very interesting and I have learned a lot." Another student's comment was,

> Professor Morettini is great. She is very responsive and her comments on my work are always encouraging as well as informative. The lay out of this class is very easy to use and understand. I wish other online classes could be as flexible and informational as this one. Very refreshing.

### Related Challenges and Obstacles

Research on social justice points to the importance of knowing students' gender and social class. In particular, James (2008) discusses some of the challenges of online teaching wherein students' identities are not clear. In a course focused on building capacity for social justice and critical pedagogy, there is an emphasis on acknowledging and appreciating the complexity of students' identities. However, doing so remains more obscure in online courses because students' identities themselves are unclear. This chapter discussed ways to break down the challenge of getting to know students in asynchronous online learning environments by describing the pedagogical methods and assignments that help to foster meaningful interaction with and among students as a way to structure an online community of practice.

Since students are becoming accustomed to more transactional and didactic approaches to online courses, enacting this approach to online pedagogy is not always met with enthusiasm from students. Students are simply not used to answering questions from each other in addition to answering questions from the instructor. Further, students are not used to having to follow the learning journey of a peer through the Critical Friends assignment or to having an instructor provide integrated feedback and try to dialogue with them about their work. As a result, not *all* students are completely satisfied with their learning experience in this course. For example, on the course evaluation, one student wrote, "I didn't like her. Try picking another professor." The closed-ended responses from students about this course are overwhelmingly positive, so this student's experience does appear to be an outlier. Still, each student's experience is important, and seeing that one student was dissatisfied enough to write an optional open-ended comment about his/her dissatisfaction leaves me feeling as though I failed this student in some way.

## Conclusion

Because of the growing available offerings of online courses as prepackaged modules at my institution, it is difficult for students when they realize that this particular online course is different. This course is different because, among other things, my personal teaching philosophy and related approach to instruction—online or face-to-face—is such that I want students to get to know me, I want to get to know them, and I want them to get to know each other. In any learning environment, this requires a considerable investment of time and care.

In the end, it is important to remember that the pervasiveness of prepackaged, didactic instruction through asynchronous online learning experiences influences students' expectations of online teaching and learning. When compared with more traditional face-to-face courses, students might not expect to have to devote as much time to engaging in dialogue with peers and with the instructor. However, such engagement helps build a sense of community and belonging, and such a sense of community and belonging allows students to demonstrate vulnerability and to trust each other enough to open up and discuss their thinking and attitudes toward social justice and critical pedagogy. Indeed, students cannot develop and take up a social justice stance and critical pedagogy without first feeling a sense of belonging and experiencing the vulnerability associated with growth and learning in those areas. In sum, online learning environments need to bring students into contact with each other and with the instructor in meaningful ways to create safe spaces for the courageous and challenging conversations that enable students to take up social justice and critical pedagogy.

My own experiences as a teacher of both young learners and of prospective teachers have shaped my understanding of the relationship between teaching and learning in online environments. As Freire (2000) wrote, "The reciprocal learning between teachers and students is what gives educational practice its gnostic character" (p. 67). I believe there is no teaching without learning. As an educator, I believe in establishing a community of practice through a culture of mutual respect because relationships are as significant and impressive upon students as the knowledge and skills we cultivate in them. In establishing such a community of practice, students learn from the teacher in much the same ways as a teacher learns from students. I have learned to be open to feedback from students, to devote *even more time* for my online classes than is necessary for my face-to-face classes, and to show students that I am a learner right alongside them in our increasingly digital age.

## Notes

1. This chapter addresses the topic *Establishing rapport/Fostering meaningful interactions.*
2. The name of the course used here is a pseudonym to protect the confidentiality of future, former, and current students.

## References

Baglieri, S., Bejoian, L., Broderick, A., Connor, D., & Valle, J. (2011). [Re]claiming "inclusive education" toward cohesion in educational reform: Disability studies unravels the myth of the normal child. *Teachers College Record, 113*(10), 2122–2154.

Connelly, F. M., & Clandinin, D. J. (1988). *Teachers as curriculum planners: Narratives of experience.* Teachers College Press.

Freire, P. (1972). *Pedagogy of the oppressed.* Penguin Books.

Freire, P. (1998). *Teachers as cultural workers: Letters to those who dare to teach.* Westview Press.

Freire, P. (2000). *Pedagogy of freedom: Ethics, democracy, and civic courage.* Rowman & Littlefield.

Hollins, E. (1996). *Culture in school learning: Revealing the deep meaning.* Erlbaum Associates.

James, E. A. (2008). Studying and improving connection and inclusion in online professorship dealing with the dark side. In M. L. Heston, D. L. Tidwell, K. K. East, & L. M. Fitzgerald (Eds.), *Pathways to change in teacher education: Dialogue, diversity and self-study. Proceedings for the 7th international conference on self-study of teacher education practices* (pp. 182–186). University of Northern Iowa.

Ladson-Billings, G. (2001). *Crossing over to Canaan: The journey of new teachers in diverse classrooms.* Jossey-Bass.

Lave, J., & Wenger, E. (1991). *Situated learning: Legitimate peripheral participation.* Cambridge University Press.

Nieto, S. (2002). *Language, culture, and teaching: Critical perspectives for a new century.* Erlbaum Associates.

Noddings, N. (1992). *The challenge to care in schools: An alternative approach to education.* Teachers College Press.

Santrock, J. W. (2018). *Educational psychology* (6th ed.). McGraw-Hill.

Schön, D. (1983). *The reflective practitioner: How professionals think in action.* Basic Books.

Ukpokodu, O. (2011). Developing teachers' cultural competence. *Teacher Education Yearbook XX: Action in Teacher Education Special Issue, 33*(5–6), 432–454. https://doi.org/10.1080/01626620.2011.627033

van Manen, M. (2002). Writing phenomenology. In M. van Manen (Ed.), *Writing in the dark: Phenomenological studies in interpretive inquiry* (pp. 1–8). Althouse Press.

Vygotsky, L. S. (1978). *Mind in society: The development of higher psychological processes.* Harvard University Press.

Wenger, E. (1998). *Communities of practice: Learning, meaning, and identity.* Cambridge University Press.

Williams, B. (2001). Accomplishing cross cultural competence in youth development programs. *Journal of Extension, 39*(6), 1–5.

CHAPTER EIGHT

# COVID-19 and the Exacerbation of Educational Inequalities in New Zealand

CAROL A. MUTCH

On 25 March 2020, in response to the arrival of the COVID-19 virus in New Zealand, the Prime Minister, Jacinda Ardern, put the entire country into strict lockdown. Schooling was suspended so that the Ministry of Education could assess readiness for converting educational delivery to online teaching and teachers could have time to prepare and upload teaching programmes. The Ministry of Education's assessment revealed that only half the country's approximately 750 000 students in the compulsory schooling sector would be able to easily access their learning through electronic means (New Zealand Government, 2020).

Since adopting neo-liberal economic policies in the 1980s, the gap between rich and poor in New Zealand has widened (Mutch, 2012). Increasing economic disparity has led to higher levels of poverty, food insecurity, poor housing, domestic violence, child mortality and youth suicide (Ministry of Health, 2019; Statistics New Zealand, 2020). In the education sector, the divide manifests itself in what is colloquially known as "the long tail of underachievement" (Snook et al., 2013). It appears that those most affected by poverty, poor housing and lower educational attainment are New Zealand's indigenous people, Māori, and migrants from the various Pacific Islands (Haig, 2018). Pacific people are often referred to by the term Pasifika to denote New Zealand residents or citizens of Pacific descent (Samu, 2006)

The news that half of New Zealand's school students would be disadvantaged by a digital divide was tempered with the recognition that students in lower-socio-economic areas, such as Māori in rural locations, or Pasifika in high density urban suburbs would be most negatively affected. In this article I will outline how the educational and digital divide manifested itself during the pandemic and what attempts were made to alleviate it. I will discuss what we have learnt about how successful those attempts were and what lessons we can take from the lockdown experiences into the future. First, I will outline the chronology of the pandemic's arrival and impact on New Zealand, then report the steps taken to support students' online learning during the lockdowns. Next, I will review the recent studies, mostly surveys, that have been undertaken in New Zealand to gauge the impact of the lockdowns on students' achievement and wellbeing, supplementing this with some preliminary insights from my own qualitative study. In the conclusion, I will argue that while the pandemic and consequent lockdowns threw the economic, social and educational disparities into sharp relief (Cook et al., 2020), the return of a Labour government by an outright majority in the 2020 October elections, provides the opportunity to take up the challenge to address the disparities that are prevalent in our education system.

## The Arrival of COVID-19 in New Zealand

When news of a novel coronavirus first reached New Zealand in January, it was initially considered to be another flu epidemic that would be under control before it reached our shores. As death rates overseas began to climb and cases started arriving in New Zealand, it soon became clear the country would need to take the virus seriously. Health systems in other countries were struggling to contain the virus and concerns were being raised here that, with decades of chronic underfunding of our health system, public health authorities and hospitals might not cope. One analyst said: "The key message was, if things gets out of control, our health system will be overwhelmed and very quickly, and it will be disastrous" (Cameron, 2020, p. 4).

Contrary to the response in many other countries, the New Zealand government acted quickly. The Prime Minister began gathering expert advice and weighing the options. Table 8.1 provides a timeline of just how quickly the virus arrived and infections spread. Several large gatherings, now known as superspreader events – an international conference, a wedding and a St Patrick's Day celebration – bringing people together from different parts of New Zealand, were responsible for the virus spreading quickly around the country, even to the isolated West Coast of the South Island, which recorded the country's first death on March 29.

Table 8.1: COVID-19 in New Zealand from First Infections to First Lockdown

| | |
|---|---|
| January 2020 | • A new strain of the coronavirus, named later in short form, as COVID-19, is reported in Wuhan, China |
| | • 27–28 January 2020, the New Zealand government activates the National Security System and the Ministry of Health activates the National Health Co-ordination Centre in case the virus arrives in New Zealand |
| February | • Travellers from or through China are barred from entering New Zealand |
| | • A repatriation flight brings New Zealanders trapped in Wuhan home |
| | • The Department of the Prime Minister and Cabinet organises a team of analysts to lead a government response strategy |
| | • Despite pleas from universities, foreign students from China are not granted exemptions to return to or begin their studies in New Zealand in the new academic year |
| | • Public health modellers and biomedical experts are called in to support policy development and decision making |
| March | • Cases arrive in New Zealand from Italy and Iran where the virus is spreading quickly |
| | • Further restrictions are placed on incoming travellers who are now required to self-isolate for two weeks on arrival |
| | • An attendee at a large international conference in the South Island tests positive for COVID-19 and other linked cases begin appearing around the country |
| | • Gatherings of more than 500 people are banned and, several weeks later, no more than 100 people are allowed to meet together |
| | • Epidemiologists and other experts contribute to the growing pool of expertise informing the Director General of Health's response plan |
| | • Cases in New Zealand continue to rise |
| | • Severe concerns are raised about the under-preparedness of the country's health system and its inability to cope |
| | • The Prime Minister creates an *ad hoc* cross-party committee to manage the pandemic response |
| | • New Zealanders overseas are told to make plans to return home as quickly as possible |
| | • Debates begin about the best approach to take – lockdown (as per Wuhan) or herd immunity (an approach championed by Sweden) |
| | • A scientific paper from Imperial College London paints a stark warning of the possible consequences of the virus and swings the debate in favour of a "stamp it out" approach |

(*Continued*)

Table 8.1: Continued

|  |
|---|
| • The Prime Minister requests the creation of an alert level system, such as the familiar geological hazard system, Geonet |
| • Alongside the level system, a communication plan is devised with a simple message: "Unite against Covid-19," with four recommended actions: "wash your hands; cough or sneeze into your elbow; stay home if you are sick; and be kind" |
| • On 20 March 2020, the four-level alert system is presented to the government: Level 1 – prepare; Level 2 – reduce; Level 3 – restrict; and Level 4 – eliminate |
| • One day later the country is put into Level 2 |
| • On 23 March 2020 the country moves to Level 3 |
| • On 25 March 2020, the country goes into full lockdown at Level 4, where it is announced it will stay for at least four weeks |
| • The Prime Minister, Jacinda Ardern, and the Director General of Health, Dr. Ashley Bloomfield, begin the first of their regular daily televised 1pm briefings to inform the country of the latest numbers (infections, hospitalisations, recoveries and, from late March, deaths) |
| • School holidays, due to begin on 9 April 2020, are brought forward several weeks to allow the Ministry of Education and schools to prepare for online learning |

Sources: Cameron (2020), Ministry of Education (2020), Ministry of Health (2020), New Zealand Doctor (2020), New Zealand Government (2020), and Radio New Zealand (2020).
Source: Author

In Level 4 lockdown, people were restricted to interacting only with those living in their immediate household. The analogy of a bubble was used. People were to seal themselves in their bubble, not to burst someone else's bubble by mixing with people from a different bubble and not to allow others into their bubble. While an effective metaphor, it instantly separated families, friends and neighbours, adding to social anxiety and dislocation. Elderly people aged 70 and over, and others at risk were to stay indoors. In my own extended family, for example, an elderly aunt passed away early in lockdown. My sister who works at the local hospital was in a different bubble than my mother. She relayed the sad news through an open door and they stood and cried unable to offer physical comfort to each other. In my aunt's family, no one could go and see their mother before she was hurriedly buried.

Social distancing and masks became a reality. Families were to choose a designated shopper who would be their contact with the outside world for exempted activities such as getting medical supplies or going to the supermarket. Bubble groups were allowed out to take exercise as long as they stayed local and maintained a safe distance.

Looking back, it was a time that felt as if a black cloud hung over the country. Each day we tuned in to the televised one o'clock COVID-19 briefing to watch the national and international numbers steadily rise. In retrospect, we can see that the "go hard and go fast" approach, along with the exhortations to "be kind," seemed to work. New Zealanders were mostly compliant and the virus was contained. After eight weeks, the country's restrictions began to lift and we re-emerged from our small bubbles into a nationwide bubble with closed borders. Since then, a community case of unknown origin put the Auckland region into a local lockdown for several weeks in August. In general, however, the lockdowns, public health measures, border closures, two-week quarantines for returnees, regular community testing, and tracking and tracing procedures have seemingly worked. We are in relative freedom compared to much of the rest of the world where they are still dealing with rising case numbers or second waves of infections.

## The Impact of COVID-19 on Schools

To coincide with the March Level 4 lockdown, the Ministry of Education brought forward the April school holidays by two weeks. Students went into lockdown in their family bubbles. It was not a holiday for principals and teachers, however, as they used the break to quickly plan and prepare for online teaching and learning. Table 8.2 below outlines the chronology for school closures and re-openings.

Table 8.2: Timeline Outlining the Impact of COVID-19 on the Education System

| | |
|---|---|
| March 2020 | • 17 March 2020 a Dunedin high school closes temporarily as a student tests positive for COVID-19<br>• Calls increase for the closure of schools<br>• The Ministry of Education announces the decision to bring the April school holidays forward by two weeks<br>• 23 March 2020 schools are warned to get ready to close<br>• 25 March 2020 schools are closed as Level 4 comes into force<br>• The Ministry of Education contacts schools to assess their readiness for remote learning |
| April | • 8 April a government press release notes that with only 50% schools able to provide online learning, the Ministry will roll out a four-pronged support programme to increase capacity across the sector<br>• Most schools phase into online learning after Easter, beginning on 15 April 2020<br>• Level 4 lockdown is extended until after Anzac Day (27 April), then the country moves to Level 3<br>• 13 May 2020 the country moves to Level 2 |
| May | • From 18 May 2020 schools could begin a phased approach for students to return to school sites with the necessary precautions: students staying in designated bubbles, maintaining social distance and continuing strict hygiene routines<br>• 8 June 2020 the country moves to Level 1 |
| June | • The border is still closed with only returning New Zealanders, or others with exemptions, admitted. Returnees must spend 14 days in government-mandated quarantine facilities<br>• Over 100 days pass without new cases in the community |
| August | • 12 August 2020 a community outbreak puts the city of Auckland into Level 3 lockdown and the rest of the country on Level 2<br>• Schools in the greater Auckland area return to online learning<br>• 30 August 2020 Auckland comes out of Level 3 lockdown and schools reopen at the newly created Level 2.5 (more restrictive than Level 2 but not as restrictive as Level 3) |
| September | • 23 September 2020 Auckland moves down to Level 2 and the rest of the country to Level 1 |
| October | • 5 October 2020 the entire country moves back to Alert Level 1 |

Sources: Cameron (2020), Education Review Office (2020a), Greater Christchurch Schools Network (2020), Ministry of Education (2020), New Zealand Government (2020), Te (2020), and Wade (2020).
Source: Author

Bringing the school holidays forward enabled the Ministry of Education and schools to buy some time. As already noted, the Ministry contacted every school to ascertain their readiness for online learning. What they found was that only half the country's schools thought that it was possible for teachers to deliver and students to access online learning appropriately. Lack of access to the internet and suitable devices were the major problems. In a press release on 8 April 2020 the Minister of Education, the Honourable Chris Hipkins, states:

> We know that tens of thousands of households either lack an internet connection or an education device at home. We're working with telecommunications companies and internet service providers to connect as many of these households as we can as quickly as possible (New Zealand Government, 2020).

Minister Hipkins explains that he wants all families to have at least one education delivery option available when Term 2 starts. He outlines a rolling four-pronged delivery strategy that would (a) increase access to the internet and provide devices to homes; (b) deliver hard copy learning packs to families in hard-to-access areas; (c) present learning via two television channels, one in English and one in *te reo Māori* and (d) make a variety of web resources available for teachers and parents.

Minister Hipkins also notes that principals and teachers are getting ready for the start of the new term to help students continue their learning. His brief comment belies the huge effort that principals and teachers were to put in, foregoing their usual break at the end of the first school term to become familiar with different virtual platforms, re-plan their programmes, revise their lessons, find suitable materials and make arrangements for their own families so that they could keep their students engaged in learning. Derek Wenmoth, an expert in educational technology, highlights some of the challenges they were to face:

> For most teachers the sudden shift to remote learning, without any time for preparation posed significant challenges and exposed the need for a range of skills and knowledge required to operate effectively in these new environments and with these new tools (Wenmoth, 2020).

In Hood's study, one teacher, for example, needed to become familiar with fifteen different platforms and applications that would be used by the school (Hood, 2020a). New tools were only one of the concerns raised by Moore and Andersen (2020, p. 6):

> Distance learning brought to the fore considerations of pedagogy, content, and being fully conversant in a digital world. Social media was filled with stories of challenge and concern by teachers. For many, the intricacies of distance learning saw extensive disruption to their normal ways of teaching and thinking about teaching. Additionally, some parents were anxious that they were thrust into a more intense role of supporting their child's learning, while for many continuing to be busy with their own work and home demands.

Despite the quick turnaround time, online, remote or home schooling in some form was underway for most students by 15 April 2020. Students settled into their new routines with varying levels of success. The following section discusses findings from formal and informal studies undertaken during or following the nationwide lockdown to provide insights into the experience of lockdown teaching and learning.

## A Synthesis of Recent New Zealand-Based Lockdown Learning Studies

Hood notes (2020a, p. 6), "[t]he lockdown period brought substantial changes to the day-to-day realities of educators, students and their families." In order to understand what these changes were, a few organisations undertook quick-turnaround studies to gain real-time snapshots of learning during the lockdown. Two of the studies reported here have larger representative samples, while others use convenience or self-selected samples, but they all, in some way, provide insights into students' varied experiences. Table 8.3 provides the details of the studies to be discussed.

Table 8.3: Summary of Studies Conducted During or After the National Lockdown

| Authors and date | Study type | Sample details |
| --- | --- | --- |
| Education Review Office (government evaluation agency) published in two reports (2020a, b) | Online survey Qualitative Interviews | 10,000 students; 700 teachers 95 Early Childhood Centres; 110 schools |
| Nina Hood, The Education Hub, published in two reports (2020a, b) | Online qualitative narrative responses | 251 responses from teachers and school leaders; 64 from parents; 47 from students |
| Heidi Leeson, Sue Duignan, Desiree Wehrle & James Beavis, The Springboard Trust (2020) | Phone questionnaire | 65 principals all former participants in Springboard Trust's programmes |
| Wendy Moore & Irene Andersen, Evaluation Associates (2020) | An analysis of students' written or video commentaries | 31 students who responded to an invitation to comment on their experiences |
| Melanie Riwai-Couch et al., Evaluation Associates (2020) | Online survey of Māori and Pasifika parents | 134 participants (102 Māori; 32 Pasifika) |
| Greater Christchurch Schools Network (2020) | Online survey (Canterbury region only) | 3 105 responses from school staff, students, parents and wider family from 150 schools |

Source: Author

The studies mostly asked generic questions around matters such as what worked well, what could have been done better and what we can learn from the experience. A central feature that emerged was the widely varying experiences students encountered. While anxiety around the nature of COVID-19 and loss of social interaction were common concerns, some students benefitted from supportive home environments and were able to engage in deep and meaningful learning, whereas others struggled to find focus and became disengaged from their learning.

While synthesising the findings, I created a continuum of experiences from positive to negative (see Table 8.4). Some of the variation is explained by the different ways that schools and teachers approached lockdown teaching and learning or in terms of the ways students engaged with and experienced what was provided for them (Hood, 2020a, b). Overall, however, the studies highlight that prior economic and social disadvantage led to a digital divide that exacerbated existing educational inequity (Education Review Office, 2020a, b; Greater Christchurch Schools Network, 2020; Hood, 2020a, b; Leeson et al., 2020; Moore & Andersen, 2020; Riwai-Couch et al., 2020).

a) Accessible internet and device ⟷ Limited access
b) Sufficient skills for online study ⟷ Limited skills and training
c) Quiet or suitable study space ⟷ Crowded or noisy home situation
d) Relevant materials ⟷ Inappropriate or insufficient materials
e) Quality curriculum ⟷ Busy work rather than deep learning
f) Flexibility, choice or tailored activities ⟷ One-size-fits-all activities
g) Clear communication between school and family ⟷ Difficult access or unclear messages
h) Clear instructions and expectations ⟷ Confusing or vague instructions or expectations
i) Regular contact and feedback from teacher ⟷ Irregular contact and limited feedback
j) Learning support from family ⟷ Families lacking knowledge, skill, time or energy
k) Self-regulation and time management ⟷ Students struggle with managing time and focus
l) Autonomy and independence ⟷ Students lack confidence and are dependent on others
m) Less distraction ⟷ More distraction, loss of focus
n) Improved concentration ⟷ Inability to concentrate
o) Regular engagement ⟷ Intermittent or no engagement
p) Enjoyment in learning ⟷ Loss of enjoyment in learning
q) Visible progress ⟷ Lack of progress, slipping back
r) Enhanced wellbeing ⟷ Loss of wellbeing, anxiety, stress, mental health concerns

Table 8.4: Continuum of Lockdown Learning in New Zealand Continuum of Lockdown Learning Experiences

Source: Author

The first six factors (a–f) focus more on the learning provisions, such as digital access and devices, the home study environment and materials or content for learning. The next six factors (g–l) are more about what happened during the learning process, including what students brought to their learning and how this was fostered by their teachers and/or family. The final six factors (m–r) highlight the learning outcomes, including how the learning provisions, context and process enhanced their learning; what they gained from the experience. What the continuum highlights is that, at each step, those in advantageous situations were able to continue their learning and those already disadvantaged by the system were primed to fall further behind. Each of the three steps will be discussed in turn in relation to the studies listed in Table 8.3.

### Learning Provisions: Starting at Different Places

The studies highlight successes and challenges. Moore and Andersen (2020) report on a self-selected group of students who were willing to share their learning experiences in writing or by video. This study tended to attract students who found themselves on the positive side of the continuum, but it provides a valuable insight into what lockdown was like for this more successful group of students. On the positive side, students reported that they enjoyed the freedom and flexibility to choose the materials they wanted to engage with and to structure their day to suit their needs and interests. These students often found being at home less stressful, "due to being able to work in their own spaces, enjoy music and generally work more comfortably" (Moore & Anderson, 2020, p. 12). Another positive aspect was having their parents more closely involved with their learning. On the other hand, not having a teacher easily available sometimes led to lack of clarity, loss of motivation and anxiety. Moore and Andersen (2020, p. 3) explain, "No longer could learners physically work alongside their peers and their teacher, the virtual world of Zoom, Google Meets and other platforms became the new portal for communication." Engaging with these new technologies, however, while disruptive at first, was something that these students quickly gained familiarity with and felt could be integrated more into their learning once they returned to school.

Students who found themselves on the negative side of the ledger were impacted by inequities already present in the system. Leeson et al. (2020, p. 9) state, "Many students, despite best efforts, remained cut off from the same learning opportunities as others due to a technological divide stemming from structural inequality. In this, Covid-19 has not created new problems but highlighted longstanding ones." In contrast to Moore and Andersen's study (2020), findings from the other studies highlight poor internet connectivity, lack of devices and limited digital literacy as the first set of barriers that disadvantaged students were to face (Education Review Office, 2020a, b; Greater Christchurch Schools Network, 2020; Hood, 2020a, b; Leeson et al., 2020; Riwai-Couch et al., 2020). As Hood (2020a, p. 4) notes, "The most immediately apparent embodiment of this inequality was those students who did not have access to a device or internet connection at home." The Education Review Office reports (2020a, b) highlight that Māori, Pasifika and students in low socio-economic communities were the groups most likely to have limited access to devices and connectivity or would have to share a device between siblings. While the Ministry of Education worked hard to improve access and deliver devices or provide hard-copy materials, given the urgency of the need and the difficulty in obtaining and delivering materials, these did not always arrive in a timely manner – and in some cases not all (Leeson et al., 2020). One of my teacher education students, who is also a parent living in an isolated rural community, told the story of bundling her family into the car, driving 20 minutes to the top of a hill to get a signal, then each taking turns to copy down their learning instructions from a single cell phone.

The second immediate barrier that students in disadvantaged communities faced was the lack of a conducive environment in which to study (Education Review Office, 2020b; Greater Christchurch Schools Network, 2020; Hood, 2020a, b; Leeson et al., 2020; Riwai-Couch et al., 2020). In crowded homes, often there was not a suitable space to study or the space, along with any learning devices, was shared with other siblings. Again, the same groups of students were most affected (Education Review Office, 2020b; Riwai-Couch et al., 2020), although some secondary Pasifika students in low socio-economic families reported feeling more comfortable at home than at school (Education Review Office, 2020a). In general, secondary students, especially boys, found it harder to study at home (Education Review Office, 2020a). Difficulty with learning from home increased with each year level (Education Review Office, 2020a). Parents in low socio-economic families were often juggling multiple priorities or working long hours in low-paid employment as essential workers and struggled to help their children with their studies. They did not always have the language, knowledge, skill, time or energy to support their children's learning (Hood, 2020a; Riwai-Couch et al., 2020). Older students often became responsible for looking after their younger siblings and helping them with their learning to the detriment of their own studies (Education Review Office, 2020a Riwai-Couch et al., 2020). Sometimes, older students needed to abandon their studies altogether to gain employment to help their families survive (Education Review Office, 2020b).

## Learning Processes: Facing Different Stressors

Digging deeper into why some students engaged with home learning better than others, Hood (2020b) notes that teachers explained variation as access to devices or the internet and the nature of home environment. In Hood's study, parents gave wider explanations including students' age, motivation, time management and interest. Parents also commented that the quantity or nature of the work set, the lack of clear expectations or feedback from teachers and the opportunities for student agency also contributed to the variation in engagement. Students reported being unable to cope with the workload or not receiving sufficient support or feedback to move forward as contributing to their lack of engagement or enjoyment (Education Review Office, 2020a).

Teachers in Hood's study (2020a) also indicated that there were individual student-level factors contributing to students' ability to engage with online learning. They cited foundational content knowledge, learning skills, social and emotional competencies and student self-regulation or self-management. Students also noted that they missed their teacher's regular presence as a motivator (Education Review Office, 2020a; Greater Christchurch Schools Network, 2020; Hood, 2020a).

For students in lower socio-economic areas, there were added stressors. Hood notes, "While access to a device and the internet is a very tangible (and real) representation of the inequalities that exist within education and society more broadly, it belies a deeper set of issues affecting equity in educational achievement" (2020a, p. 14). Schools quickly became aware that some of their students' families were financially hurt by the lockdown. Not only were they struggling prior to the pandemic but, given their precarious employment, these parents were often the first to lose their jobs as business began to close. Up to 38 percent of parents lost a third or more of their income because of COVID-19 (Greater Christchurch Schools Network, 2020).

The Education Review Office (2020b) reports that one quarter of schools throughout the country needed to deliver care packages to their families. They provided food, clothing, face masks and sanitiser, often in conjunction with the local *marae* (Māori community centres) or the charity KidsCan. One principal in the Lesson et al. (2020) study reported providing around 400 lunches for struggling families. Teachers and principals reported that many Māori students attending *kura* (Māori immersion schools) or regular schools, along with Pasifika students and their families, needed ongoing support to combat hardship (Education Review Office, 2020b; Leeson et al., 2020). Some families ceased contact because of high levels of stress or moved because they could no longer afford to remain in their present location.

## Learning Outcomes: Exacerbated Inequities

While the lockdown provided "silver linings" for some individuals and families (Foon, 2020) including more time spent together as a family and living in a quieter, less busy environment, this was not the reality for all. Those already at a disadvantage rarely caught up with their more advantaged peers. For example, students without devices prior to lockdown, even when they gained access, progressed at a lower rate than those who already had access (Greater Christchurch Schools Network, 2020).

Two-thirds of parents needed to continue working inside or outside the home during lockdown (Greater Christchurch Schools Network, 2020). Stressors built up as time went on to the point that some families took the step of opting out of home schooling altogether (Hood, 2020a). Levels of psychological distress, family violence and suicidality increased (Foon, 2020). The Education Review Office (2020b) report notes that one third of principals had concerns about the safety and wellbeing of particular students. Distressing family situations or violent incidents were referred to Oranga Tamariki (the relevant government agency) or to the police to follow up. At risk students were also slower to return to schools when they reopened. These students had lower attendance rates, were difficult to contact, displayed high levels of trauma and had more unsettled or challenging behaviours (Education Review Office, 2020b). Sometimes families had separation anxieties post-lockdown or worries about their children mixing with other students because of the impact it might have on the vulnerable members of their extended family (Education Review Office, 2020b).

A further lockdown in August closed schools in the greater Auckland region for several weeks. Anecdotally, teachers reported to me that their students found this lockdown harder than the first because it brought home the reality that regular lockdowns might become the "new normal." Auckland is home to some of the more disadvantaged communities in the country and this was to put the students in these schools even further at risk. As Hood (2020a, p. 4) notes, "The lockdown period shone a light on the range of inequities, disparities and divides within New Zealand's educational system, as well as potentially exacerbating them."

## The Voices of Disadvantaged Students During COVID-19 Lockdowns

In order to give voice to the young people whose educational experiences were further negatively affected by COVID-19, I provide excerpts from a qualitative research project I am currently conducting on young people's responses to learning in lockdown. While the data collection and analysis are still ongoing, I have selected examples from interviews with students in one Auckland, low socio-economic, urban, multi-cultural high school with a high proportion of Pasifika students. Their stories resonate with the findings relating to economic and structural inequities and exemplify the way in which students in this demographic experienced their learning during the lockdowns.

Access to the internet or learning devices often hindered the students' engagement or progress. This student was working on a joint project with another student, making a documentary for one of her classes while in lockdown:

> Um, sometimes we, we couldn't communicate with each other, 'cos one or the other, like, didn't have internet or didn't have a device to communicate with each other. So that … that also, like, disrupted our work of continuing to finish our documentary. … a lot of effort was put into, into the documentary and there's a lot of times where I wanted to give up. But now it's finished … yeah, I guess I'm pretty proud of it … of me and my partners' effort to finish it. Yeah …

Students missed the social aspects of their school day. One student explains how the loss of routine and social contact was difficult for her, combined with her anxiety about the pandemic and its possible effects on her family:

> Yeah. I think really, during lockdown, it's just the whole thing, like, changed, in the way that my days used to run. I mean, I'd just come to school, see my friends, you know, do my schoolwork. It was really just a routine almost every day. I mean, we're so used to having contact and, you know, physically, seeing our family and friends and connecting with each other. And then all of a sudden, that just got cut off and, like, we had to stay at home. And I guess a lot of us were really scared for ways that our families or ourselves could be affected by the virus, especially since my mum works at the airport. So, she was on the front line and welcoming people. And up until last week, she was still working at the airport, all through the lockdown and stuff. Yeah, so, it was real scary.

Many students from this community live in extended family groups in crowded housing. One student shares her experience:

> Yeah, it was quite stressful. Because at my dad's house, we have, like, a big family. So, we've two younger siblings. And, like, I'm trying to help them with their schoolwork because my dad's an essential worker. And then there's my stepmother who lives there. My great grandmother, my cousin. So, it's, like, really hard just trying to do everything as well as my schoolwork because your parents they're telling you to do all this stuff, but you have this huge load of schoolwork to do, so it was really stressful.

The families of students from disadvantaged communities often work in precarious low-paid employment and were the first to be laid off. One student says:

> In the beginning, I really liked the idea of lockdown, no school. Yeah. And then a couple weeks, and, um, my dad couldn't go to work because it was level 4 and he's, like, a trainee, so he couldn't work. And then I started seeing the financial effects that started kicking in and things aren't the best at home. Yeah, so yeah, it was really hard trying to, like, keep doing schoolwork and then trying to enjoy things at the same time and keep a focus on mental health and everything.

Alongside attending school, some students work after school to help support their families. Another student discusses having to continue working as an essential worker while trying to keep her family safe and do schoolwork:

> From my family, even I am … we're working as essential workers. So, we continued to work during lockdown. And the added precautions of being at home and taking care of your family as well. And thinking of their safety along with yours is kind of nerve-wracking at times. So, like, when we get home, we're hand sanitising and taking our clothes off and going straight for a shower and all that. And the same goes for most of my friends in Year 13. They have to do the same.

Another student talks about the lack of support from home because of the added stress in her family:

> … it was just so hard to just do my schoolwork at home because, like, I don't know, my household just then … I live in a really small house. So, it was really hard to get work done with my family there. Yeah, 'cos, I didn't have much support at home. So, it was really hard to do my schoolwork. Yeah. Because my mum and my sister were essential workers. But when they came home, they'll just get angry at me for like no reason, and it was really hard to just, you know, be there …

In the end, some students struggled to focus, became overwhelmed and even gave up. This student explains how it affected her:

> … I was one of those people that just tried to pass or when teachers would email me work, I would just, just do it when I could. Not when they asked for, I just, sometimes, I'd be doing work at, like, one in the morning for, like, no reason, because I had nothing else to do. But the work was there. But I just never did it. I just felt like I couldn't do it. Like, I didn't know what I was doing. Even though the teacher was telling me what I was doing. I still was confused and it was just stressful.

The voices of these students clearly resonate with the findings shared earlier. In early 2021, the Education Review Office (the government agency that evaluates the quality of education in all schools in New Zealand) stated that over half of the schools they surveyed reported that lockdowns had affected student progress and achievement. Schools suggested that some students would begin the new year up to 10 weeks behind, with students in low socioeconomic communities being most affected (Gerritson, 2021). Meanwhile, the New Zealand Qualifications Authority, (the agency that monitors secondary school examinations and qualifications) has instigated a system of "learning recognition credits" to acknowledge the disruption to students' learning during 2020.

Given that research findings to date confirm the extent of educational disparity, Hood exhorts us to make good use of this knowledge:

> The lockdown as a whole, plus the experiences of teachers, students and parents, present an opportunity. However, it is easy to fall back into business as usual and not to follow up on the questions the experiences raised, the opportunities it presented or the challenges it uncovered or exacerbated" (Hood, 2020a, p. 9).

## Conclusion: Where to from Here?

The leadership of the Prime Minister through the COVID-19 pandemic in New Zealand garnered much international acclaim. In the October elections, her party received a majority of the votes and the mandate to govern alone without the need for a coalition partner. Three years earlier, Ardern had promised a transformational government. The mosque massacre of 2019 and pandemic of 2020 took the focus away from this goal. With COVID-19 vaccines on the horizon, there is an opportunity to use the COVID-19 economic recovery to tackle the chronic housing shortage, increase employment outcomes, reduce poverty, improve the health system and address educational disparities. Several of the studies reported on in this article ended with sets of recommendations for policy and practice that are worthy of serious consideration. As political commentator, Rod Oram highlights, if New Zealand can pull together as a country to overcome COVID-19, we can do the same to create a more socially just nation for all our citizens, in particular, for the children and young people who are our future. Oram (2020) concludes:

> Indeed, these are no ordinary times. Covid-19 is teaching us we have to respond decisively, collectively and comprehensively. To do so, we have to prioritise, communicate and support each other. Then we can learn as we go in this fast, all-encompassing crisis. These things we have done well as a society, showing great purpose, innovation and resilience during the pandemic. Now we have to apply those lessons to solving our pre-existing and interdependent social, economic and ecological challenges.

*Kia kaha, kia maia, kia manawaui.*
(Māori proverb: Be strong, be brave, be steadfast)

**Ethical clearance**: The author's study was approved by the University of Auckland Human Participants Ethics Committee on 6 October, 2020, Protocol number UAHPEC3078.

## Postscript

New Zealand entered 2021 with cautious optimism. The measures put in place appeared to have kept the worst of COVID-19 at bay. In February, there were two developments. An outbreak in the community in Auckland put the country's largest city into a short sharp lockdown that was able to contain the outbreak. At the same time, the government began the rollout of the Pfizer-BioNTech vaccine, with frontline workers being prioritised. Over the next few months, a few freedoms followed, including reciprocal travel bubbles with Australia and the Cook Islands, until Australian case numbers began to rise again. In June, the Delta variant was discovered in Wellington, leading to a short sharp lockdown for that city. The vaccination rollout continued including border workers, the elderly and others with severe health risks. The government continued its eradication strategy using a three-pronged approach: (a) the alert level system with its gradations of lockdowns and social restrictions; (b) continued vaccination rollouts descending through the age ranges; and (c) the use of various scanning, tracking and tracing strategies. In mid-August, however, these measures were not enough to stop the Delta variant quickly spreading throughout Auckland. On August 17, Auckland went into another lockdown, where it has remained until the time of writing this piece in late October, and with a predicted extension to late November and beyond.

What the current outbreak has shown is that at various levels of decision making, from the government down, and across different sectors, especially health, education and social services, we did not learn from the lessons of 2020. Two of the most disadvantaged regions in the country, South Auckland and Northland again bear the brunt of the impact. Overcrowded housing, poor health statistics, economic vulnerability and food insecurity have meant that the residents of these communities are at higher risk. While local community, cultural and religious groups have provided food parcels, social support and encouragement to get vaccinated, vulnerable and minority communities, Māori and Pasifika in particular, have the highest case numbers and lowest vaccination rates. Educationally, it has been hard to keep the students in these communities focused on their learning as access to devices or Internet has not improved, their family circumstances have become more precarious, levels of anxiety have increased, and engagement has decreased. As a teacher in one of our most recent studies said:

> It was a different experience for the students who had difficulties at home or whose parents lost jobs and they were really suffering and struggling for food and things. They didn't bother about learning because learning was the last thing.

This time, however, the disparities were harder to hide, especially given the statistics around the vaccination rates highlighted regularly in the media. Because the vaccination rollout was conceived through a Eurocentric-lens, where it was delivered in age cohorts from over 70, to over 60 and so on down, it privileged the majority Pākehā (European) population, whose life expectancy and health projections exceed those of their less privileged Māori and Pasifika communities, whose health status is 10–20 years behind. Community leaders became more vocal. They chastised the government for not working with and though local community organisations. Rather than providing vaccination advice in English through formal media channels, such as mainstream newspapers or television channels and expecting vulnerable community members to travel to vaccination centres, where they feel alienated and unsure what to do, they asked for alternative means of reaching their communities. These calls have resulted in some innovative responses, such as vaccination buses that travel to disadvantaged and isolated communities, with names such as "Shot Bro," "Shot Cuz" or "Busifika," as a nod to local idiom. There have been more local vaccination events, with music, food and community language vaccinators, vaccination clinics open at night for shift workers and a national "Super Saturday" vaccination drive with entertainment and prizes, which drew in 130,000 more people for vaccinations.

Yet, when the government recently announced their roadmap for New Zealand in a post-COVID future, they continued to use blanket categories that are not adjusted for the cultural disparities that have been clearly obvious to social commentators and researchers, not to mention the communities themselves. The government has agreed to provide $120 million dollars to Māori health providers to bring up vaccination rates, but when New Zealand's vulnerable populations reach the government's ambitious 90 percent fully vaccinated target, what then? Will their lives materially change? Or will they continue to lag behind in any post-COVID economic boom and social readjustment that continues to be blind to longstanding inequality and disparity?

This has been updated and reprinted with permission from *Educational Perspectives*.

Mutch, C. A. (2021). Covid-19 and the exacerbation of educational inequalities in New Zealand. *Educational Perspectives, 39*(1), 242–256.

# References

Cameron, B. (2020). Captaining a team of 5 million: New Zealand beats back Covid-19, March-June 2020. Innovations for Successful Societies, Princeton University. [Online]. Available at https://successfulsocieties.princeton.edu/publications/captaining-team-5-million-new-zealand-beats-back-covid-19-march-%E2%80%93-june-2020. Accessed 2 November 2020.

Cook, D., Evans, P., Ihaka-McLeod, H., Nepe-Apatu, K., Tavita, J., & Huges, T. (2020). *He Kāhui Waiora: Living Standards Framework. COVID-19: Impacts on wellbeing*. Wellington: New Zealand Treasury.

Education Review Office. (2020a). Covid-19: Learning in Lockdown. [Online]. Available at https://www.ero.govt.nz/publications/covid-19-learning-in-lockdown/. Accessed 11 November 2020.

Education Review Office. (2020b). Covid-19: Impact on schools and early childhood services. Interim Report. [Online]. Available at https://www.ero.govt.nz/publications/covid-19-impact-on-schools-and-early-childhood-services-interim-report/. Accessed 11 November 2020.

Foon, E. (2020). Lockdown distressing for almost half of young people, study finds. Radio New Zealand. [Online]. Available at: https://www.rnz.co.nz/news/national/429893/lockdown-distressing-for-almost-half-of-young-people-study-finds. Accessed 19 November 2020.

Gerritson, J. (2021). Schools will feel impact of 2020 lockdowns in 2021, Education Review Office warns. Available at https://www.rnz.co.nz/news/national/434741/schools-will-feel-impact-of-2020-lockdowns-in-2021-education-review-office-warns. Accessed 26 January 2021.

Greater Christchurch Schools Network. (2020). *Closing the digital divide: Student, whānau [family] and staff perspectives*. Christchurch: Greater Christchurch Schools Network.

Haigh, D. (2018). Poverty in New Zealand. *Whanake: The Pacific Journal of Community Development, 4*(2), 102–115.

Hood, N. (2020a). Learning from lockdown: What the experience of teachers, students and parents can tell us about what happened and where to next for New Zealand school system. [Online]. Available at: https://theeducationhub.org.nz/learning-from-lockdown/. Accessed 11 November 2020.

Hood, N. (2020b). Learning from lockdown: Trying to understand variations in student engagement. [Online]. Available at https://theeducationhub.org.nz/learning-from-lockdown-trying-to-understand-the-variations-in-student-engagement/. Accessed 11 November 2020.

Leeson, H., Duignan, S., Wehrle, D., & Beavis, J. (2020). *Connecting with principals. New Zealand principal perspectives on education through Covid-19*. Auckland: Springboard Trust.

Ministry of Education. (2020). COVID-19 [Online]. Available: https://www.education.govt.nz/covid-19/. Accessed 11 November 2020.

Ministry of Health. (2019). *Every Life Matters – He Tapu te Oranga o ia Tangata: Suicide Prevention Strategy 2019–2029 and Suicide Prevention Action Plan 2019–2024 for Aotearoa New Zealand*. Wellington: Ministry of Health.

Ministry of Health. (2020). Sadly, first death from COVID-19 in New Zealand [Online]. Available: https://www.health.govt.nz/news-media/media-releases/sadly-first-death-covid-19-new-zealand

Moore, W., & Andersen, I. (2020). *Insights from learners in lockdown*. Auckland, Evaluation Associates Ltd.

Mutch, C. (2012). New Zealand. In C. L. Glenn & J. De Groof (Eds.), *Balancing freedom, autonomy and accountability in education, volume 3*. Oisterwijk, Netherlands: Wolf Legal Publishers.

New Zealand Doctor. (2020). Timeline – Coronavirus – Covid-19. [Online]. Available at https://www.nzdoctor.co.nz/timeline-coronavirus. Accessed 15 November 2020.

New Zealand Government. (2020). Covid-19: Government moving quickly to roll out learning from home. [Online]. Available at https://www.beehive.govt.nz/release/covid19-government-moving-quickly-roll-out-learning-home. Accessed: 12 November 2020.

New Zealand Qualifications Authority. (2021). Clarifications on learning recognition credits. [Online]. Available at https://www.nzqa.govt.nz/about-us/publications/newsletters-and-circulars/covid-19-updates/teacher-resources-for-assessing-during-covid-19/clarifications-on-learning-recognition-credits/. Accessed 26 January 2021.

Oram, R. (2020). Brave politics for a better future. Newsroom.pro. Available at: https://www.newsroom.co.nz/pro/rod-oram-brave-politics-for-a-better-future?utm_source=Friends+of+the+Newsroom&utm_campaign=fed072be14-Daily+Briefing+23.10.20&utm_medium=email&utm_term=0_71de5c4b35-fed072be14-97847331. Accessed 15 November 2020.

Radio New Zealand. (2020). Covid-19 pandemic timeline. [Online]. Available at https://shorthand.radionz.co.nz/coronavirus-timeline/. Accessed 12 November 2020.

Riwai-Couch, M., Bull, A., Ellis, B., Hall, K., Nicholls, J., Taleni, T., & Watkinson, R. (2020). *School-led learning at home: Voices of parents of Māori and Pasifika students*. Auckland: Evaluation Associates Ltd.

Samu, T. (2006). The 'Pasifika Umbrella' and quality teaching: Understanding and responding to the diverse realities within. *Waikato Journal of Education*, *12*, 35–49.

Snook, I., O'Neill, J., Birks, K., Stuart, J., Church, J., & Rawlins, P. (2013). *The assessment of teacher quality: An investigation into current issues in evaluating and rewarding teachers.* Hamilton: Education Policy Response Group, Institute of Education, Massey University.

Statistics New Zealand. (2020). Child poverty statistics year ended June 2019. Stats NZ. [Online]. Available at https://www.stats.govt.nz/information-releases/child-poverty-statistics-year-ended-june-2019. Accessed 19 November 2020.

Te, M. (2020). Coronavirus; Thousands of students expected to head back to school next week. Stuff. Available at: https://www.stuff.co.nz/national/education/121472915/coronavirus-thousands-of-students-expected-to-head-back-to-school-next-week. Accessed 15 November 2020.

Wade, A. (2020). Coronavirus lockdown: What it means for schools, universities and other education facilities. New Zealand Herald. Available at: https://www.nzherald.co.nz/nz/coronavirus-lockdown-what-it-means-for-schools-universities-and-other-education-facilities/P7CSW25T7QRWG3PH2SICIBCDVI/. Accessed 15 November 2020.

Wenmoth, D. (2020). Lessons from lockdown. [Online blog]. Available at https://wenmoth.net/2020/08/20/lessons-from-lockdown/. Accessed 15 November 2020.

CHAPTER NINE

# Teaching for Social Justice: Online Classes at Historically Black College and Universities

JOHN BANNISTER, ANITA BLEDSOE-GARDNER, AND MARY HOLIMAN

The notion of all courses having an online footprint will be used as a framework to discuss the social justice-focused course offerings at Historically Black Colleges and Universities (HBCUs), offering a vision of future directions. HBCUs have long been at the forefront of social justice issues in the communities they service. From being the leading voices during the Civil Rights Movement of the 1960s, to organizing peaceful protest and voter registration drives during the recent presidential 2020 election cycle, HBCUs have always been a beacon for rights in our communities.

Academically, these institutions often educate students to lead the charge in understanding the landscape of social obstacles and passageways, especially for African American students. Courses offered in many degree programs focus on cultural competence, human behavior, understanding political systems and navigating challenging environments to ensure career success. Regardless of academic discipline, HBCUs tend to infuse social justice issues into the framework of all their course offerings. By providing a multi-layered perspective to students, HBCUs provide knowledge and insights on the history and development of fields of study, while offering a roadmap to success as a practitioner. Additionally, the ability of HBCUs to develop a strong sense of family both on individual campuses and throughout their networks of schools is driven by the shared sense of struggle by the communities we attract and serve.

HBCUs have an undeniable positive track record of developing students that hold the functional knowledge of their field of study and the ability to navigate its social political waters. This is in part due to HBCUs standing at ground zero of the social changes taking place over the last century, leading to access to unique sources of information to impart to their students.

For example, when the Civil Rights Movement is taught in predominantly white schools, students likely hear about Martin Luther King Jr. and Rosa Parks. According to Hubbard and Swain (2016), this mutes the movement's pluralist and participatory elements by focusing solely on select individuals. In fact, in 2010, 36 out of 50 states had minimal to no requirements for teaching the Civil Rights Movement as a part of the curriculum.

Hale (2016), the author, dissects the importance of student activists in the Civil Rights Movement, crediting them as one of the factors that led it to its success. The Student Nonviolent Coordinating Committee (SNCC) emerged in the 1960s after a conference at Shaw University, the oldest historically Black college and university in the Southern United States. Its development led to several sit-ins, including the ones led by our own Johnson C. Smith University students, which has been credited with desegregating Charlotte, NC. According to the author, Black students quickly became a force for social change, despite the fact that many of them were not old enough to vote. Despite political turmoil being scattered across the country, the young activists were able to stay up to date through the use of mass media ranging from television to newspapers, and radio:

> What the American public did not see on television or read in the newspaper was how the dialectical relationship between locally sophisticated civil rights networks and the larger national movement influenced the political socialization of young people across the state of Mississippi. There is a much longer history of locally organized black resistance than is usually supposed ... Understanding how the movement educated young people as students of the civil rights movement leads to comprehensive understanding that places young people in the center of the struggle (Hale, 2016, p. 38).

Undoubtably, HBCUs have provided grounds for diverse movement networks to develop on campuses and in surrounding communities; that is, they provide space for the construction of knowledge and action to implement personal and social change. Such critical pedagogical practice through social justice-focused education more recently has journeyed from face-to-face to online classrooms, with constraints and contributions.

## HBCUs and Online Learning

From the onset, colleges and universities questioned the traction, or lack thereof, regarding the impact of online education (Cejda, 2010). According to Mbuva (2015), it was not until the early adopters of distance learning begin to garner attention in the educational market. Only through fashioning an environment to reach those aspiring to attend colleges and universities did most institutions begin to take notice and institute change in their respective educational delivery modalities and pedagogical instructional strategies.

Although these standards of online teaching coincided with rapid change in the academy, and student needs, HBCUs have had a limited presence in the online community. Notwithstanding, they constitute approximately 20% of online course delivery, while granting 25% of bachelor's degrees to African American students (Jones & Davenport, 2018).

Although the number of course offerings has consistently been increasing over the years, they are at best protracted, resulting from insufficient funding, and a shortage of resources. These administrative challenges have presented themselves at these institutions through lagging course enrollment and doubts of long-term course viability (Jones & Davenport, 2018) in comparison to college and university counterparts. Further, data indicate that in 2015, only 51% of African American students had access to high-speed internet in their home compared to 70% of white students (Jones & Davenport, p. 60). Theoretically and practically, this disparity could also facilitate explaining the cultural shifts, or lack thereof, in understanding the gradual institutionalization of online learning at HBCUs. Many have learning labs and computer centers; however, because access to the tools and technologies needed to be effective online may be restricted, their academic communities may be reluctant to depend on them (Buzzetto-More, 2008).

The advancement of online course offerings has been spurred in part by the advancements in learning management systems, sometimes called LMSs. These systems are designed to allow students and faculty to work in a centralized space, normally managed on a per class basis. The cost of acquiring and maintaining a LMS has plagued many HBCUs with limited resources.

Research indicates that one of the most widely utilized learning management systems employed by HBCUs is Canvas. The Canvas product have become a preferred tool due to its ease of use and functionalities for testing (Wilcox et al., 2016). Specifically, the survey indicated that 60% of the respondents use Canvas as an online learning management system while the other 40% employ Blackboard.

According to Wilcox et al. (2016), there are distinct differences in the way faculty and students use technology. Specifically, this presents a challenge for its intended purposes for faculty and student engagement and content delivery. This disconnect presents several challenges: (1) faculty design their courses for delivery on laptops, but students use smartphones to access course content, (2) Canvas has limited ability when utilizing smartphone devices, although to date improvements have been rendered, and (3) this issue creates a conspicuous challenge for faculty who lack knowledge of the concerns this presents for 21$^{st}$ century students who rely primarily on their smart devices for their academic and personal communications. Wilcox et al. (2016) further assert that Canvas is designed to be used within Canvas mobile applications. Specifically, the authors argue that Canvas pages within a mobile browser are only supported when an action in the app links directly to the browser, such as when a student takes certain types of quizzes. As such, support is not extended to pages that cannot currently be used in the app, such as conferences or collaborations. It is worthy to note that periodically functionalities are added, changed, or removed from the Canvas learning management system to enhance its usability. These changes are typically instituted multiple times throughout a calendar year.

Amid these challenges, there is an ongoing effort to afford students who attend Historically Black Colleges and Universities access to a variety of online course offerings mirrored by their counterparts (Burnsed, 2010). In addition to the fiscal benefit of expanding to online, HBCUs see these offerings as a way to engage in new discussions in the teaching and learning space. These offerings include courses that are culturally and universally impacting the lives of marginalized individuals, specifically within the African American population, such as Black Women's Studies, African Politics, Counseling, Historical Sociology, Criminology, Environmental Sociology and Crisis Management, and Public Administration/Safety (Cole-Martin, 2017).

The evolving nature of higher education has yet to grasp that all courses offered at an institution are now essentially online courses. While the division of online and traditional course offerings are common at many institutions and are viewed as separate entities on many campuses, regardless of modality, every course is at least supported by some sort of online infrastructure.

## Social Justice Within the Framework of Online Pedagogy

One of the goals of higher education is to prepare students to address social problems on a local and global level (Guthrie & McCracken, 2010). Professors are not only challenged to manifest a diverse context of pedagogical delivery but to create a space for students from different backgrounds to feel safe and welcome to discuss their experiences related to social justice issues, while sharing a sense of connectedness and collaboration (Guthrie & McCracken, 2010). Specifically, it is important that the instructor is committed to being inclusive and creating a learning environment that is culturally responsive. Woodley et al. (2017) note that culturally responsive teaching allows for the characteristics, experiences, and perspectives of ethnically diverse student to serve as conduits for learning.

Social justice pedagogy can be situated in varying theoretical frameworks, including critical race theory (Yosso, 2005) and socialization (Harro, 2000). Moreover, understanding an educator's role in social justice-focused teaching expands beyond the notion of personal awareness, experiential learning, and motivation. Rather, as Kincheloe (2008) asserts, it is converged on clarifying the relationships between culture, power, and domination. More specifically, Kincheloe argues that while learning requires choice and action from students, teaching demands relationships that embark on a trajectory of individual and personal development within the context to discover new information and theoretical paradigms. Teaching for social justice has the potential to enliven and employ students in acknowledging and reacting to obstacles to full humanity (Ayers, 1998; Greene, 1998).

Online, as well as in a traditional environment, social justice-focused teaching affords professors the opportunity to educate scholars beyond the boundaries that are situated in micro-level injustices by providing tools for students to work towards the goal of action on both local and global levels. In addition, such courses seek to empower students in creating collaborative relationships with communities that extend beyond the academic setting.

Classes that have a focus on social justice tend to increase cognitive development. By allowing the use of social media in these academic settings to enhance the learning experience, universities grant students the opportunity to become more aware of issues through a portable, handheld device. In fact, traditional methods of learning have been criticized for being outdated and ostracizing to the main group of people typically on the receiving end of society's oppression (Ashworth & Bourelle, 2014). With mandatory volunteerism such as community service as a graduation requirement, students are required to devote a certain amount of time outside of their regular academic coursework to volunteering.

By utilizing online platforms to inhabit social justice, universities make critical parts of learning more accessible to students who are low-income or first generation who cannot dedicate physical time to service-learning projects. In 2020, as technology continues to advance, learning will continue to drift further and further away from the classrooms and onto our phones. In fact, inspired by social media movements, some teachers have already adapted their teaching to help students actively and self-consciously participate in their communities through innovative praxis (Cumberbatch & Trujillo-Pagan, 2016).

For example, according to Cooper and Lindsey (2018), #BlackLivesMatter has emerged as of the most influential social movements of the post-civil rights era a mere five years after it was created. Born in the wake of widespread police brutality by three queer Black women activists, it has forged a movement that is far more inclusive and democratic than either the Black Panther Party or civil rights activists ever imagined (Joseph, 2017). He credits the movement with embracing the full complexity of Black identity as its most active leaders are members of the LGBTQ+ community and feminists. By placing the lives of trans and queer individuals, Black women, young people, and the poor at the center of its agenda, #BlackLivesMatter has become a movement that fully embraces the intersectionality of Black identity and challenges people to understand the broad spectrum of what it means to be Black in this society (Joseph, 2017). #BlackLivesMatter has organized local chapters, including those located on HBCUs campuses, and has actively used of social media to share and advance its agenda. In fact, #BlackLivesMatter is a prominent example of how social media has become a platform for activists to champion for immigration rights, a higher minimum wage, workers' rights, better gun laws, and more.

Dubbed "Hashtag Activism," thanks to the use of social media's hashtag format that allows users to show their support for a cause, these platforms have been praised for meeting people where they are (Woodley et al., 2017). Simultaneously, it has also become a tool in academic settings to not only develop relationships but also spread awareness. In these interactive, online realms, topics that were once taboo, such as feminism and police brutality, now have a strong presence. Since social media grants people access to a plethora of individuals, it allows users to challenge politicians, media personalities, and corporations to make change (Hentges, 2016); the wrong stance or comment has been known to cost said individuals their jobs and even funding. #Black Lives Matter, for example, has become such a powerful movement that scientists started analyzing the emotions behind the nearly 30 million tweets in 2014 and 2015 that led to nationwide protests (Safdar, 2016). According to theses scientists, social media provided a sense of solidarity—users began using "we" and "us" to express frustration towards the criminal justice system and less isolating words such as "I" while also allowing organizers and activists to communicate with each other across geographic lines (Safdar, 2016).

For Cumberbatch and Trujillo-Pagan (2016), this "Hashtag Activism" amplifies voices that are often overlooked and ignored, giving marginalized communities an opportunity to express their frustration and address issues that are critical to them. They make the claim that "A critical part of this discursive struggle involves social media, which creates a virtual space to challenge, reframe, and reinscribe representations of who is victimize" (Cumberbatch & Trujillo-Pagan, 2016, p. 2). Beyond raising awareness, it has been used to organize protests such as die-ins against police brutality and gun violence (Cumberbatch & Trujillo-Pagan, 2016).

While their Civil Rights era predecessors relied on the likes of newspaper and television to transmit their message, the youth of today are using social media to join their voices and challenge what is tradition and mainstream (Cumberbatch & Trujillo-Pagan, 2016). They also make the claim that social media allows for humanization of the movement through the representation of its leaders and victims. Much like Mamie Till's public display of Emmett Till's mutilated body, images of Trayvon Martin in a hoodie and looking like a teenager instills a sense of vulnerability that is often not allotted to certain populations (Cumberbatch & Trujillo-Pagan, 2016).

Furthermore, in reference to the impact of social media, data compiled by Fatal Encounters (Zuckerman et al., 2019), an organization that tracks police-involved deaths, shows that before Michael Brown's death in August 2014, a Black man killed by police in a city with the median population had a 39.34% chance of having at least one article published about him. After Brown's death, this percentage surged to 64.25% due to public awareness spread through social media (Ethanz, 2019). Their data also revealed that after his death, which sparked the Ferguson riots, stories involving police-related shooting victims began to mention other victims, showing the impact of Black Lives Matter activists protesting against police brutality as an ongoing pattern instead of individual, isolated incidents.

Online movements, such as Black Lives Matter, have offered unique settings for reflection and participation in the context of critical pedagogy and social justice-oriented online courses that HBCUs and others offer to their students.

## Online Teaching Practices in Social Justice Courses

Professors have to navigate the challenges associated with distance learning while developing their classroom setting. These challenges are similar to those faced with developing courses for in-person modalities; however, the relative newness of teaching online for many HBCU faculty often creates additional discomfort. Faculty have started to embrace the value of online classrooms. Garrison et al. (2000) posit that virtual classrooms provide environments in which reflective discourse is fostered and critical inquiry is cultivated as a means to broaden concerted educational transactions. Professors can formulate meaningful partnerships with students that facilitate a continuing narrative, foster insight, as well as document individual and collective learning outcomes. Additionally, as online course enrollment continues to grow it is increasingly important to develop strategies to support being both culturally responsive and inclusive both in terms of content being converted and the delivery of that content.

One of the main ways to be culturally responsive is to form a sense of community. According to Hentges (2016), community can be developed through sharing stories, finding common experiences, and learning about oppression. Several methods can be employed in online classes to develop community. For example, discussion boards allow students and teachers to interact with each other similarly to a face-to-face experience. Some critics argue that students in an online environment are not actively involving themselves in issues, as one would with mandatory volunteerism (Ashworth & Bourelle, 2014). However, the use of discussion boards and forums does allow for the two-way communication vital for developing community.

A drawback of discussions in virtual classrooms is that in many cases students can only get the perspectives of those participating in the class. These viewpoints may often be narrow and play out as they do in traditional class setting with the professor being the primary voice being heard. Fortunately, with the rise in activism and social networking through platforms such as Twitter, Facebook, Instagram, and Tumblr, social media has emerged as an outlet to not only foster community but to educate on social justice as well, as Black Lives Matter exemplifies. Used correctly, these platforms can equip students with the tools to critically evaluate and analyze social scenarios that are anchored in scientific and theoretical inquiry. The classroom community can be expanded through social media by connecting with thought leaders on social- justice topics, using these platforms to discuss conflicting opinions on topics covered in courses. This level of discourse can be impactful as it will allow the community to be exposed to a much wider basket of knowledge.

Social media can serve as an educational platform that can be both constraining and enabling. Professors can use these platforms to validate and strengthen the understanding of issues and topics, but they are also used to dispel falsehoods. This does present a challenge; however, the learning that can be experienced using this practice will mirror what HBCU students will face in their post college careers and life.

## Towards the Future of HBCUs Online Course Offerings

Online social justice courses at HBCUs have the opportunity to greatly influence teaching and student learning on and off campuses. In merging strategies used at these institutions with the technologies commonly used in online education, these institutions can provide robust course offerings, while connecting their students to diverse communities. The role of instructional designers is central in this process. Instruction designers are often charged with providing insight to faculty members on ways they can improve their course delivery. It is vital that HBCUs employ people with teaching, project management, and communication skills that can partner with academics to improve classes. Viewing instructional design offers the possibility of maximum impact for social justice-oriented courses.

Furthermore, HBCUs should consider partnering together to create large format courses that build on the principles of collaboration and sharing. There are many ways in which online technologies and offerings can be expanded to become even more beneficial, particularly in courses and programs with social justice focuses. Specifically, MOOC (Massive Open Online Courses) styled offerings practically and theoretically increase collaborations among students and faculty, thereby creating a learning environment that is conducive to include numerous entry points for learning and multiple pathways for practice and ongoing investigation (Ayers, 1998).

MOOCs were initially touted as a means to disrupt the delivery of education at institutions such as MIT and Harvard, which offered large-scale courses to anyone having an interest in the topic being covered. As their popularity started to grow, institutions such as the Georgia Institute of Technology developed MOOC offerings and models in which students could receive credit for work accomplished (Wulf et al., 2014).

Almost concurrently, companies such as EdX and Coursera created platforms and worked both on their own and in partnership with colleges and universities to develop credentialed programs. It was at this point that the research on the MOOCs being offered started to uncover challenges in using this framework. These included low levels of engagement and learner interaction, and difficulty identifying assessment methods that adequately measured students' progress (Eriksson et al., 2017; Zheng et al., 2015).

Combined with an undercurrent of distrust by faculty that saw MOOCs as a potential tool for administrators to justify larger student loads or cuts in staffing, institutions started to scale back or abandon MOOC projects. On many college campuses today, the mention of MOOCs is almost taboo and receive support only from progressive faculty and staff members who still believe in the framework's potential.

Notwithstanding, the MOOC framework could prove extremely valuable as a tool for use in social justice related courses. For example, courses could use their online presence to set up MOOC-styled courses that allow larger groups of students to gain insights, share perspectives, and collaborate in learning activities.

These activities already take place in many courses regardless of delivery modality. However, the widening of this forum across multiple institutions and spaces could bring immense value to any classroom setting. Social justice-focused material is primed for this type of engagement as much of this material covered often lends itself to a wide range of perspectives for faculty and students alike.

As an example of these possibilities, imagine students from a HBCU and a predominantly white institution (PWI) covering topics based on race relations in a MOOC-framed course. Well-crafted assignments that require interactions between the two student groups could provide engagement and transmission of knowledge in ways a facilitator working independently could only hope. Even those who choose to limit their participation, defined by the use of the term lurking in MOOC research, could get value out of monitoring the interactions between participants in these courses.

Many learning management systems allow for large courses; however, the collaboration required to develop such courses make their development challenging. Some would argue that the mechanics of running a course in this way could bring to many administrative challenges between institutions in terms of enrolling, billing and grading students; however, these courses should not be viewed different than study abroad or other experiential learning programs in which the students' home institutions would manage. The creative use of MOOCs could increase the presence and value of social justice courses offered at any institution.

Online technologies can be used to further expand collaboration, develop resource sharing networks between HBCUs, and provide a greater level of access. This access is vital to a community that desperately needs to understand how social issues have been handled in the past in order to form strategies for dealing with the challenges of today. If done correctly, the online environment offers the opportunity to show what much of the HBCU community already knows: our schools will always remain relevant as no one can emulate what it is like to be a part of a HBCU family.

## References

Ashworth, E., & Bourelle, T. (2014). Utilizing critical service-learning pedagogy in the online classroom: Promoting social justice and effecting change? *Currents in Teaching & Learning*, 7(1), 64–79.

Ayers, W. (1998). Popular education: Teaching for social justice. In W. Ayers, J. A. Hunt, & T. Quinn (Eds.), *Teaching for social justice* (pp. xvii–xxv). New Press.

Burnsed, B. (2010). More HBCUs offer online degrees: Historically black colleges and universities are going online, but some top schools aren't plugging in. US News.

Buzzetto-More, N. (2008). Student perceptions of various e-learning components. *Interdisciplinary Journal of E-Learning and Learning Objects, 4*(1), 113–135.

Cejda, B. (2010). Online education in community colleges. *New Directions for Community Colleges, 2010*(150), 7–16. https://doi.org/10.1002/cc.400

Cole-Martin, L. (2017). Going online: An examination of online learning at historically black colleges and universities (Doctoral dissertation). http://hdl.handle.net/2346/73212

Cooper, B., & Lindsey, T. B. (2018). Introduction: M4BL and the Critical Matter of Black Lives. *Biography, 41*(4), 731–740.

Cumberbatch, P., & Trujillo-Pagán, N. (2016). Hashtag Activism and Why #BlackLivesMatter In (and To) the Classroom. *Radical Teacher, 106*, 78–86. https://doi.org/10.5195/rt.2016.302

Eriksson, T., Adawi, T., & Stöhr, C. (2017). "Time is the bottleneck": A qualitative study exploring why learners drop out of MOOCs. *Journal of Computing in Higher Education, 29*(1), 133–146. https://doi.org/10.1007/s12528-016-9127-8

Ethanz. (2019, October 2). *Whose deaths matter? New research on Black Lives Matters and media attention.* Civic Media: Creating Technology for Social Change. https://civic.mit.edu/2019/10/02/whose-deaths-matter-new-research-on-black-lives-matter-and-media-attention/

Garrison, D. R., Anderson, T., & Archer, W. (2000). Critical Inquiry in a text-based environment: Computer conferencing in higher education. *The Internet and Higher Education, 2*(2–3), 87–105. https://doi.org/10.1016/S1096-7516(00)00016-6

Greene, M. (1998). Teaching for social justice. In W. Ayers, J. A. Hunt, & T. Quinn (Eds.), *Teaching for social justice* (pp. xxvii–Xlvi). New Press.

Guthrie, K. L., & McCracken, H. (2010). Teaching and learning social justice through online service-learning courses. *The International Review of Research in Open and Distributed Learning, 11*(3), 78–94. https://doi.org/10.19173/irrodl.v11i3.894

Hale, J. N. (2016). *The freedom schools: Student activists in the Mississippi civil rights movement.* Columbia University Press.

Harro, B. (2000). The cycle of socialization. In M. Adams, W. J. Blumenfeld, R. Castaneda, H. W. Hackman, M. L. Peters, & X. Zuniga (Eds.), *Readings for diversity and social justice* (pp. 15–21). Routledge.

Hentges, S. (2016). Toward #SocialJustice: Creating social media community in live and online classrooms. *Transformations: The Journal of Inclusive Scholarship and Pedagogy, 26*(2), 230–238. https://doi.org/10.1353/tnf.2016.0026

Hubbard, J., & Swain, H. (2016). Using the U.S. Civil Rights Movement to explore social justice education with K-6 pre-service teachers. *The Journal of Social Studies Research, 41*(3). https://doi.org/10.1016/j.jssr.2016.09.002

Jones, P. W., & Davenport, E. K. (2018). Resistance to change: HBCUs and online learning. *Thought and Action, 34*(1), 59–80. https://www.learntechlib.org/p/191795/

Joseph, P. E. (2017). Why black lives matter still matters. *New Republic, 248*(5), 16–19.

Kincheloe, J. (2008). *Critical pedagogy primer.* Peter Lang Publishing.

Maynes, N., & Hatt, B. (2014). Threading the discussion: A model to examine the quality of posts in an online learning environment. *Teaching and Learning, 8*(1). https://doi.org/10.26522/tl.v8i1.427

Mbuva, J. M. (2015). Examining the effectiveness of online educational technological tools for teaching and learning and the challenges ahead. *Journal of Higher Education Theory and Practice, 15*(2), 115–127.

Safdar, A. (2016, August 3). *The social media patterns behind Black Lives Matter*. Al Jazeera. https://www.aljazeera.com/news/2016/8/3/black-lives-matter-the-social-media-behind-a-movement.

Wilcox, D., Thall, J., & Griffin, O. (2016). One canvas, two Audiences: How faculty and students use a newly adopted learning management system. In G. Chamblee & L. Langub (Eds.), *Proceedings of society for information technology & teacher education international conference* (pp. 1163–1168). Association for the Advancement of Computing in Education.

Woodley, X., Hernandez, C., Parra, J., & Negash, B. (2017). Celebrating difference: Best practices in culturally responsive teaching online. *TechTrends, 61*(5), 470–478. https://doi.org/10.1007/s11528-017-0207-z

Wulf, J., Blohm, I., Leimeister, J. M., & Brenner, W. (2014). Massive open online courses. *Business and Information Systems Engineering, 6*, 111–114. https://doi.org/10.1007/s12599-014-0313-9

Yosso, T. J. (2005). Whose culture has capital. A critical race theory discussion of community cultural wealth. *Race Ethnicity and Education, 8*(1), 69–91. https://doi.org/10.1080/1361332052000341006

Zheng, S., Rosson, M. B., Shih, P. C., & Carroll, J. M. (2015). Understanding student motivation, behaviors and perceptions in MOOCs. In *Proceedings of the 18th ACM conference on computer supported cooperative work & social computing* (pp. 1882–1895). ACM.

Zuckerman, E., Matias, N., Bhargava, R., Bermejo, F., & Ko, A. (2019). Whose death matters? A quantitative analysis of media attention to deaths of black Americans in police confrontations, 2013–2016. *The International Journal of Communication, 13*, 4751–4777.

CHAPTER TEN

# Knowledge Production and Power in an Online Critical Multicultural Teacher Education Course

RAMONA MAILE CUTRI, ERIN FEINAUER WHITING, AND ERIC RUIZ BYBEE

A growing number of universities already offer, or are planning to offer, online teacher certification and endorsements (AACTE, 2013; Bull et al., 2012; Dell, Hobbs, & Miller, 2008; Keengwe & Kang, 2012;). Often, the impetus of transitioning to online courses has not been quality instruction, but rather keeping up with administrative pressures and with student demand for online learning (DiRienzo & Lilly, 2014).

Accompanying the surge in online teacher education is the preponderance of the consumption and production of social media (online videos, memes, etc.) that creates unprecedented opportunities for students to co-construct knowledge in online spaces. Students today bring a knowledge of online spaces and experiences outside of class learning that can be relevant to teaching them online. In addition to funny memes and cat videos, online spaces have also been fruitful for the dissemination of equity perspectives on issues of race (#blacklivesmatter), gender (#metoo), and other topics relevant to critical multicultural education. However, much work remains to be done to fully understand the complexities of teaching critical multicultural education online with an attention to students as knowledge producers.

Critical pedagogy is foundational to critical multicultural teacher education, and an emergent body of research has begun to examine how critical pedagogy can be implemented online. Schneider and Smith (2014) remind us that it is not the technology, itself, that must be critically examined, but rather how technology integration contributes to the control of the production of knowledge, the commodification of learning, and how it normalizes surveillance of students. It is not clear what designing opportunities to use technology to extend ownership of knowledge production looks like in a critical multicultural education course. Work is needed that examines actual classroom practices.

This reflection on social foundations piece explored online teacher education through the lens of reflexivity in the context of critical pedagogy online. The question explored in this reflexive inquiry was

> What are the motivations, experiences, and insights of a teacher educator designing an online course with the intention of sharing the production of knowledge with her students?

A reflexivity orientation strives to inquire into present moments of practice in a way that allows the inquirers to become responsible and accountable for their choices, actions, and contributions to a relational system, such as a classroom (Oliver, 2004). Reflexive questions are questions that aim to leave the inquirer changed as a result of engaging in them and that call for the inquirer to have a meta-awareness of the process of learning from the reflexive inquiry (Elliott-Johns & Thomas, 2019). Indeed, reflexive inquiries into classrooms allow teacher educators to change and improve their classroom practice.

The course in this reflexive inquiry aimed to relationally engage students intellectually and emotionally to promote systematic self- and societal-critique regarding issues of equity and social justice (Cutri & Whiting, 2015; Gay & Kirkland, 2003; Gorski, 2010; Hill-Jackson, 2007). Sociocultural theory influenced the design of the online course to draw forward students' own experiences as a basis for building on and developing their knowledge, skills, and dispositions and generating knowledge in preparation to be teachers (Vygotsky, 1978).

Boler (1999) asserts that educators who endeavor to get students to think about their own complicities in systems of social inequalities and institutionalized oppression must employ "a pedagogy of discomfort" (p. 119). Students can be challenged by critical multicultural teacher education's call for attention to overlapping structural inequalities in society and school and dispositional learning outcomes regarding working to dismantle educational inequalities (Artiles, 2011; Gorski, 2009; Payne & Smith, 2012; Vaurus, 2009; Walker, Shafer, & Iiams, 2004). Much work is needed that examines how an online version of a critical multicultural teacher education course impacts this type of inquiry intentionally involving a pedagogy of discomfort.

Researchers call for acknowledgment of the risks and intimacies experienced by students and instructors in online spaces and for research into the potential of online environments to foster critical pedagogy (Caruthers & Friend, 2014; Schneider & Smith, 2014). Meabon Bartow (2014) describes the unmooring of the tyrannies of geography, schedule, subject, age, and expertise that rule traditional teaching and inquires into opportunities for critical pedagogy online to create new practices of shared knowledge construction, expertise, and authority. Empirical research is needed to explore the nuances of this type of teacher preparation.

## Methods

### Context

Two years ago, Ramona, the first author of this article, was tasked with transitioning her blended multicultural teacher education course entirely online. Working collaboratively with the second author, she designed the course to address inequitable distributions of power and access to educational opportunities, and to attend to an underlying discussion of social privileges. The course also addressed social inequalities at the individual and institutional levels. It sought to attend to national standards for teacher education accreditation that mandate the development of core dispositions and professional attitudes, values, and beliefs about diverse students, families, and communities (Council for the Accreditation of Educator Preparation Standards, 2013). The course qualifies for what Gorski (2009) characterizes as "Teaching in Sociopolitical Context," which includes: "(1) a focus on critical analysis of educational policy and practice at an institutional level, (2) consideration of this analysis in a larger sociopolitical context, and (3) the engagement of critical theories" (p. 14).

The semester-length course consisted of 14 course sessions. Ten course sessions were held synchronously via Adobe Connect (a video conferencing platform) and four course sessions were conducted asynchronously via Canvas (a course management system). Enrollment numbers were kept intentionally low as the course was in the early implementation stage. After approval from the institutional review board (IRB), all eight of the students in the class gave consent to be interviewed for this reflexive inquiry into their class.

The majority of students in the course were women from dominant-culture backgrounds, including being White, middle-class, English-speaking, Christian, and heterosexual. Although the religious context of the university influences the teacher candidates in this reflexive inquiry, their demographic characteristics actually are remarkably similar to teacher candidates in secular institutions, and thus the particulars uncovered in this research can inform others.

Ramona, the first author and professor of the course, shared some commonalities with the students such as being cisgender, but her own background—having grown up in poverty and as a woman of mixed ethnicities—differs from the majority of the teacher candidates. As the professor of the course, Ramona was in a position of power, determining content and enforcing the requirements and assigning grades. She acknowledged her own schooling background in the traditional banking model that relied heavily on traditional texts, the disembodiment of knowledge, and did not include students in the production of knowledge. Transitioning her course to an entirely online format prompted her to confront and explore ways the affordances of teaching online could move beyond the circumstances of traditional education.

### Data Analysis

An initial critical reflection by Ramona (Jaeger, 2013; Koonce, 2018) on her design process served as the data source for accessing her motivation to design an online course to encourage students to co-construct content for the course using their social media knowledge and skills. The second data source was a structured interview focused on course design choices and implementation experiences and insights gained over multiple iterations of teaching and modifying the course. In an effort to provide additional insights into the implementation experience, student data was collected during the third-semester iteration of the course and provided the third data source. To avoid undue pressure on the students, the open-ended written prompt on the survey was administered by the third author who was not involved in the design or teaching of the course. The prompt explored students' experiences of (a) the pedagogy of discomfort implemented online and (b) course design modifications. The fourth data source was a final critical reflection by Ramona. Jaegar (2013), drawing on Schon (1983), asserts that the ability to reflect-inaction "should be our ultimate goal in teacher education" (p. 96). With this goal in mind, Ramona specifically reviewed and reflected on her design modifications across multiple semesters. This included documented changes in assignments, course organization, and curriculum content across the different iterations of the course.

Ramona used open coding to identify patterns and themes in her initial and final critical reflections. The second author used open coding to identify patterns and themes in the student data. The third author used open coding to identify patterns and themes in Ramona's interview. All results of these open coding passes on the data were shared amongst the authors and validated as trustworthy (Saldaña, 2009). Finally, these four data sources were then brought into conversation with one another to pursue the research question.

Findings

This section reports on the motivation, experiences, and insights of a teacher educator designing opportunities for students to use their knowledge of social media to contribute content to their online critical multicultural education course. The findings coalesce around themes of contradictions, risks, and tensions.

Motivations Grounded in Contradictions

When reflecting on the design process, Ramona recalled:

> Students would email me links to videos, memes, etc. that they found on social media that related to what we are learning that week. I love it and wrote them back about how wonderful the connections were that they were making. However, I didn't make time in class for discussing the things that they found because I spent class time discussing the readings and lecture slides I already had prepared. Sometimes it felt like the students' good finds were being wasted.
> (initial reflection)

The students conveyed excitement in their emails to Ramona about what they found on social media that related to class. She, in turn, expressed excitement about their ability to apply critical multicultural education concepts to things and events in their daily lives. Such excitement is in contrast to the disappointment Ramona conveys about the fact that she didn't capture this learning momentum and bring it into class.

The initial critical reflection on the design process (initial reflection) evidences a pattern of instances in which Ramona recognized that she was controlling all of the content in the course. This approach was in contradiction to the goals of critical pedagogy regarding a shared and equitable production of knowledge between teachers and students. Additionally, the data show Ramona coming to recognize that the online format encouraged students to use their social media skills to contribute knowledge to the course, but that she was not taking advantage of that affordance. This contradiction led Ramona to an exploration of research (such as Caruthers & Friend, 2014; Meabon Bartow, 2014) to inform and reform her practice. She committed to opening up spaces for learning activities and assignments that prompted students to engage in the content as knowers, not just consumers of carefully packaged ideas in the form of readings and lecture slides.

The initial reflection documents the experiences leading Ramona to come to consider the students as producers of knowledge in an online critical multicultural education class. Identifying the contradictions in her practice became the foundation for Ramona's willingness to take pedagogical risks designed to prompt students to use their knowledge of social media to contribute content to the course. The next section further explores the risks and tensions that emerged throughout Ramona's experiences.

## Experiences Grounded in Risks

As a middle-aged woman, Ramona was never schooled in an online environment nor formally taught how to teach online. In this regard, Ramona was positioned to learn about the educational potential of social media from students. Meabon Bartow (2014) describes this shift in teacher/learner roles:

> Using social media often puts teachers in a learner's role. Learning a key attribute of using social media, these teachers variously recognize that social media proffer a different way to learn than the learning that has been impressed upon, and previously experienced by, these teachers. Learning directly from students, they use what students are doing to improve their teaching and class learning. (p. 52)

Ramona put herself in a learner's role as she intentionally departed from traditional sources for disseminating knowledge in class, such as professor-generated reading packets and lecture presentations. In an effort to make room for student-generated content in the course, Ramona decided to stop using a reading packet of foundational multicultural education and sociology articles, although she retained the main textbook. She noted: "It took me a few semesters to get up the courage to actually throw the reader out. When I finally did it, I didn't have any concrete plan on how to replace that content. It felt risky" (final reflection).

Giving up the course reading packet allowed Ramona to formalize the inclusion of student-generated content in the course. Ramona proceeded to spend class time with students analyzing and discussing student-generated content. This pedagogical change felt risky to Ramona because it departed from more traditional learning objects in higher education courses.

Ramona could recognize that student-generated course content synched well with the critical pedagogy ideal of students exercising ownership of knowledge production. Additionally, the student-generated content brilliantly helped to teach the course content. Ramona told the following story:

KNOWLEDGE PRODUCTION AND POWER | 199

Without structuring our course discussions around articles from the reading packet, both the students and I were learning and interacting in a different way because there was so much more time and energy. For example, in the session on gender, sexual identity, and body image, I shared with them Beyonce's video "Pretty Hurts" and did an activity around it. Then, I actually remember the surprise in on the students' faces and the tentativeness in their voices as they asked me during class if they could also share a video. I said sure, and one student came up and Googled the Colbie Caillat video "Try." We all watched it together, and then the students just took over a whole analysis of it using the sociological and multicultural concepts we had learned in class. We would have never had time for such student contributions if we had still been using the reader. (Ramona interview)

The students' tentativeness when asking Ramona if they could share a relevant video in class reveals the risk they experienced when first asserting that they had knowledge to contribute to the curriculum. Such experiences confirmed to Ramona the value of the pedagogical risks she was taking.

Student data corroborate the value of the course design changes that Ramona was making in an effort to share the production of knowledge with her students. One student commented, "It works well because we can use the Internet and other resources to help our understanding" (student survey). Another student stated:

> I loved the different inquiry assignments we had to do and feel like we learned a lot! It really helped us to take the course into our own hands and we had to be willing and motivated to learn a lot on our own before we came to class so that we could be prepared. (student survey)

However, learning online presented challenges, too, for students. A student articulated an idea that many others shared when she commented:

> We do a lot of discussion, which is exactly what this class is about (getting us to think and see from another perspective). Discussion is hard, because it is much harder to make connections with those you are discussing with through a webcam and a live square on the screen. Also, when we discuss, we have to be very careful as to not overlap each other when talking, otherwise no one will get heard; whereas with in-person discussion, you can still hear people when others are talking. (student survey)

The format of the course influenced how students saw their participation with each other, and they often compared the online discussions with those they experienced in more traditional courses. This added some challenges as in having to be very careful taking turns, yet some students also acknowledged that this format facilitated their participation more than in their face-to-face classes. Yet, another student stated, "I actually think the uncomfortable things we learned were easier in an online setting." Student experiences document both challenges and affordances of learning critical multicultural education in the online setting.

Ramona's and her students' experiences document risk taking around designing opportunities for sharing the production of knowledge in an online critical multicultural course. Their experiences echo Meabon Bartow's following description: "Teachers take risks and try projects, activities, and tools they do not know. Using social media with students alters the way teachers think about content as massive new arenas open for students' separate pursuit" (2014, p. 54).

Insights Grounded in Tensions

Ramona's experiences taking risks to design opportunities for students to use their knowledge of social media to contribute content to their online critical multicultural education course contrasts with traditional professor roles. Professors are socialized and expected to be experts in charge of delivering content to enrich students' knowledge and even influence their opinions and dispositions. Yet, as the data in this article have shown, critical pedagogy and online instruction can challenge the tyranny of professor expertise (Meabon Bartow, 2014).

With the highly contentious national political environment after the US presidential elections of 2016, Ramona noticed an uptick in the number of students who would email her links to various articles, memes, vines, etc. that they thought related to course issues. The students' consumption and distribution of such materials far outpaced her own and encouraged Ramona to create an assignment that would further formalize the incorporation of student-generated content into the course. The media inquiry assignment asked students to connect current events to course concepts (ideology, hegemony, internalized dominance, and internalized oppression) across a range of media sources representing various (conservative, liberal, etc.) perspectives.

Though excited about the potential of this assignment, Ramona also had concerns. She explained:

> Students couldn't just have free reign to just express their personal opinions when producing content for the course with current events. There had to be some boundaries that helped them elevate their discussion from the level of personal opinion to critical analysis of media coverage. (Ramona interview)

This pedagogical concern was in response to scholarly recognition that "opinion discourse" can be used to circumvent engagement with uncomfortable issues in critical multicultural education (DiAngelo & Sensoy, 2009, p. 443).

Ramona consciously created boundaries for students' analysis of the current events by requiring explicit attention to critical multicultural education concerns such as ideology, hegemony, internalized dominance, and internalized oppression.

Students' expertise in identifying learning objects from social media also sparked Ramona to create another new assignment utilizing asynchronous online discussion groups. The assignment required students to engage in student-led online discussion groups that were intended to, "encourage freedom of expression, disrupt the power balance between professor and students, and give you the feeling that you own these discussions" (bold included in original). Once again, though excited about the potential of a new assignment, Ramona simultaneously had concerns:

> So much of [student] online discussions can seem as if they are written to "please the professor." I didn't want this, so I didn't even want to read them, but rather have my TA [teaching assistant] grade them for participation, not content. BUT, I still had my moral and professional responsibility to monitor for potential inappropriate and hurtful comments and to not allow opinion statements to go unexamined and uncritiqued. I didn't know how to balance these two desires. (Ramona interview)

The dilemma that Ramona experienced highlights the complexities involved in attempting to reduce the surveillance of students' dispositions and opinions while simultaneously maintaining the professional responsibilities of a critical multicultural teacher educator. Sensoy and DiAngelo (2014) write about the complications involved in establishing discussion guidelines in social justice education in traditional classrooms, "We design controlled opportunities for students to practice articulating a social justice framework (vocabulary and concepts) that moves them into humility, openness, and analysis rather than certainty, rebuttal, or refusal" (p. 8). Ramona had the task of designing such controlled opportunities for students in an online format where she intentionally eliminated her presence in the online discussion.

Ramona instructed her TA to notify her of any disturbing comments and to identify trends in students' comments. However, she recognized such responsibilities exceeded usual TA responsibilities and, perhaps, even capacities. She recalled, "I had to sit in the tension of balancing my desire for students to have authentic, unsupervised discussions and my feelings of professional responsibilities" (Ramona interview). Designing opportunities for students to generate course content in a largely unsupervised asynchronous online discussion setting pushed Ramona to face the tensions between her responsibilities to guide learning and to encourage student production of knowledge in the course.

Another source of tension for Ramona was how to accomplish the critical multicultural education learning objective to develop teacher candidates' dispositions toward social justice and diverse students, families, and communities. Ramona approached this dispositional learning by implementing a pedagogy of discomfort (Boler, 1999) and an ethic of discomfort (Zembylas, 2010). This type of critical multicultural teacher education involves instigating, managing, and reconciling discomfort in teacher candidates. Ramona had previously researched the inherent emotional work on the part of teacher candidates and teacher educators involved in a pedagogy and ethic of discomfort in traditional face-to-face settings (Cutri & Whiting, 2015). However, she struggled to enact this approach online:

> So, the emotional work for the kids, for the students, um, yeah, like I said, online I haven't figured it out yet. I feel like I'm much better at doing the emotional work and helping them with their emotional work when I'm face-to-face. I don't know how to do it in this format, yet. I don't feel like I … um … I feel like I connect with them, but not in the same way.
> (Ramona interview)

Fostering and supporting students' emotional work in an online format necessitated that Ramona attend to how the online format and content interacted in an effort to honor the moral imperatives and professional commitments of critical multicultural teacher education.

Students also acknowledged the discomfort of grappling with challenging content essential to critical multicultural education. Although the online environment did not alter the fundamental challenges of the course, participants expressed varied responses to a pedagogy of discomfort in this online environment. Students reported that one of the hardest things to learn from the course was the identification of their own biases. However, most of the students agreed that acknowledging that they were biased and critiquing those biases would have been equally challenging for them in an online or a face-to-face class setting. One student explained it this way, "I think it was hardest to realize that we all have set and automatic judgments that we make about people and situations. I don't think this would have changed if the course were in person." The concept of hegemony and the topic of race were also cited by students as being hard to learn. However, students were quick to acknowledge that these concepts would have been hard to learn in any format. Ramona's experiences suggest that enacting a pedagogy of discomfort was more difficult for her online, but the students' experience of the pedagogy of discomfort did not appear to be related to the course format, learning the content of critical multicultural education is challenging.

## Challenges and Implications

This reflexive inquiry has explored the contradictions, risks, and tensions experienced by a teacher educator designing and implementing an online critical multicultural teacher education course with the explicit goal of sharing knowledge production with her students. The insights revealed address the call for research into the potential of online environments to foster critical pedagogy (Caruthers & Friend, 2014; Meabon Bartow, 2014; Schneider & Smith, 2014).

Findings from this reflexive inquiry identify steps critical multicultural education pedagogues can take to enact the critical pedagogy ideal of sharing knowledge production with their students. These steps include (a) identify contradictions in your practice; (b) take pedagogical risks; and (c) be willing to live in tension. These steps represent opportunities for critical pedagogy online to create new practices of shared knowledge construction, expertise, and authority. However, not all teacher educators may be ready to pursue these ideals in an online setting.

Teacher educator e-readiness to develop online courses and implement their pedagogical commitments online is fraught with many challenges. Teacher educator e-readiness, in this context, is operationalized as a pre-assessment of faculty's preparedness to develop and implement a course online (Cutri & Whiting, 2015). This reflexive inquiry highlights three prominent challenges in teaching and learning in online spaces.

The findings of this reflection on social foundations piece document the productive process of identifying contradictions in one's practice. This inherently involves affective efforts. Similar challenges have been documented in research on the affective dispositions involved in creating online versions of existing courses. These affective dispositions include individual teacher educators' responses to risk taking, responses to change, identity disruption, and stress (Johnson, Ehrlich, Watts-Taffe, & Williams, 2014; Redmond, 2015; Salmon, 2011; Sockman & Sharma, 2008).

In this reflexive inquiry, the power relations in the course shifted away from the teacher educator as the sole expert in the classroom. This resulted in opportunities for both teacher educator and students to enact their areas of expertise and have their collective expertises coalesce in joint learning experiences in the relational system of the class. However, such efforts to share power with students can be experienced as quite risky by teacher educators and requires them to have a meta-cognitive awareness of their practice. This finding highlights a second challenge that research has documented related to teacher educators developing and implementing online courses. Pedagogical challenges related to such efforts include sharing power with students, lack of sensory input, conveying personality online, and avoiding monologues (Garrison, Anderson, & Archer, 2004; McQuiggan, 2007; Salmon, 2011).

In this reflexive inquiry, the benefits of the teacher educator examining the online format for contradictions became clear. The teacher educator was willing to remain in tension with emerging contradictions in her practices to reflexively learn from them. However, the challenges involved in this process are complex. These challenges involve the tensions between the two agendas of (a) extending to students opportunities to produce curricular content and (b) establishing and maintaining guidelines for online discussions of critical multicultural education issues where the teacher educator was intentionally not present. Negotiating this tension pushed the teacher educator to face the complexities inherent in her desire both to encourage student production of knowledge and monitor for and address any microaggressions and not allow opinion statements to go unexamined and uncritiqued. This raises questions that need to be further explored through research. As the movement for online courses in teacher education marches forward, more inquiry is needed into the ways that critical pedagogy can be accomplished online.

This article has been reprinted with permission from *Educational Studies: Journal of the Americal Educational Studies Association*

Cutri, R.M., Whiting, E.F., & Bybee, E.R. (2020). Knowledge production and power in an online critical multicultural teacher education course. *Educational Studies: Journal of the Americal Educational Studies Association, 56*(1), 54-65.

# References

American Association of Colleges for Teacher Education (AACTE). (2013). Online teaching preparation is widespread (AACTE). Retrieved from ///Users/rmb45/Downloads/AACTE%202013%20PEDS%20Report.pdf

Artiles, A. J. (2011). Toward an interdisciplinary understanding of educational equity and difference: The case of the racialization of ability. *Educational Researcher, 40*(9), 431–445.

Boler, M. (1999). *Feeling power: Emotions and education*. New York, NY: Routledge.

Bull, G., George, M., Shoffner, M., Bolick, C., Lee, J., Anderson, J., … West, E. (2012). Editorial: Implementing the teacher education initiative. *Contemporary Issues in Technology and Teacher Education, 12*(2), 115–121.

Caruthers, L., & Friend, J. (2014). Critical pedagogy in online environments as thirdspace: A narrative analysis of voices of candidates in educational preparatory programs. *Educational Studies, 50*(1), 8–35. https://doi.org/10.1080/ 00131946.2013.866953

Council for the Accreditation of Educator Preparation Standards. (2013). Standards for accreditation of educator preparation. Retrieved from http://caepnet.org/standards/standards/

Cutri, R. M., & Whiting, E. F. (2015). The emotional work of discomfort and vulnerability in multicultural teacher education. *Teachers and Teaching*, *21*(8), 1010–1025. https://doi.org/10.1080/13540602.2015.1005869

Dell, C. A., Hobbs, S. F., & Miller, K. (2008). Effective online teacher preparation: Lessons learned. *MERLOT Journal of Online Learning and Teaching*, *4*(4), 602–610.

DiAngelo, R., & Sensoy, O. (2009). "We don't want your opinion": Knowledge construction and the discourse of opinion in the equity classroom. *Equity & Excellence in Education*, *42*(4), 443–455.

DiRienzo, C., & Lilly, G. (2014). Online versus face-to-face: Does delivery method matter for undergraduate business school learning? *Business Education & Accreditation*, *6*(1), 1–11.

Elliott-Johns, S. E., & Thomas, M. (2019). The design and enactment of reflexive self-study. In *Workshop presented at the annual meeting of the American Educational Research Association*, New York, NY.

Garrison, D. R., Anderson, T., & Archer, W. (2004). Critical thinking, cognitive presence, and computer conferencing in distance education. *The American Journal of Distance Education*, *13*(1), 57–75. https://doi.org/10.1080/ 08923640109527071

Gay, G., & Kirkland, K. (2003). Developing cultural critical consciousness and self-reflection in preservice teacher education. *Theory into Practice*, *42*(3), 181–187. https://doi.org/10.1207/s15430421tip4203_3

Gorski, P. C. (2009). What we're teaching teachers: An analysis of multicultural teacher education coursework syllabi. *Teaching and Teacher Education*, *25*(2), 309–318. https://doi.org/10.1016/j.tate.2008.07.008

Gorski, P. C. (2010). The scholarship informing the practice: Multicultural teacher education philosophy and practice in the US. *International Journal of Multicultural Education*, *12*(2). https://doi.org/10.18251/ijme.v12i2.352

Hill-Jackson, V. (2007). Wrestling whiteness: Three stages of shifting multicultural perspectives among White preservice teachers. *Multicultural Perspectives*, *9*(2), 29–35. https://doi.org/10.1080/15210960701386285

Jaeger, E. L. (2013). Teacher reflection: Supports, barriers, and results. *Issues in Teacher Education*, *22*(1), 89–104.

Johnson, H., Ehrlich, S., Watts-Taffe, S., & Williams, C. (2014). Who am I here? Disrupted identities and gentle shifts when teaching in cyberspace. *Journal of Instructional Research*, *3*, 43–54.

Keengwe, J., & Kang, J. J. (2012). Blended learning in teacher preparation programs: A literature review. *International Journal of Information and Communication Technology Education*, *8*(2), 81–93. https://doi.org/10.4018/jicte. 2012040107

Koonce, J. B. (2018). Critical race theory and caring as channels for transcending borders between an African American Professor and her Latina/o students. *International Journal of Multicultural Education, 20*(2), 101–116.

McQuiggan, C. A. (2007). The role of faculty development in online teaching's potential to question teaching beliefs and assumptions. *Online Journal of Distance Learning Administration, 10*(3), 1–13.

Meabon Bartow, S. (2014). Teaching with social media: Disrupting present day public education. *Educational Studies, 50*(1), 36–64. https://doi.org/10.1080/00131946.2013.866954

Oliver, C. (2004). Reflexive inquiry and the strange loop tool. *Human Systems: The Journal of Systemic Consultation and Management, 15*(2), 127–140.

Payne, E., & Smith, M. (2012). Rethinking safe schools approaches for LGBTQ students: Changing the questions we ask. *Multicultural Perspectives, 14*(4), 187–193. https://doi.org/10.1080/15210960.2012.725293

Redmond, P. (2015). A pedagogical continuum: The journey from face-to-face to online teaching. In P. Redmond, J. Lock, & P. A. Danaher (Eds.), *Educational innovations and contemporary technologies* (pp. 107–132). London, UK: Palgrave Macmillan.

Saldaña, J. (2009). *The coding manual for qualitative researchers.* London, UK: Sage Publications Ltd.

Salmon, G. (2011). *E-moder@ting: The key to teaching and learning online* (3rd ed.). New York, NY: Routledge.

Schneider, S. B., & Smith, D. (2014). Constructing and reconstructing a critical discourse and pedagogy of technoknowledge. *Educational Studies, 50*(1), 3–7. https://doi.org/10.1080/00131946.2014.867218

Schon, D. A. (1983). *The reflective practitioner: How professionals think in action.* New York, NY: Basic Books, Inc.

Sensoy, O., & DiAngelo, R. (2014). Respect differences? Challenging the common guidelines in social justice education. *Democracy and Education, 22*(2), 1.

Sockman, B. R., & Sharma, P. (2008). Struggling toward a transformative model of instruction: It's not so easy! *Teaching and Teacher Education, 24*(4), 1070–1082. https://doi.org/10.1016/j.tate.2007.11.008

Vavrus, M. (2009). Sexuality, schooling, and teacher identity formation: A critical pedagogy for teacher education. *Teaching and Teacher Education, 25*(3), 383–390. https://doi.org/10.1016/j.tate.2008.09.002

Vygotsky, L. S. (1978). *Mind in society: The development of higher psychological processes.* Cambridge, MA: Harvard University Press.

Walker, A., Shafer, J., & Iiams, M. (2004). "Not in my classroom": Teacher attitudes towards English language learners in the mainstream classroom. *NABE Journal of Research and Practice, 2*(1), 130–160.

Zembylas, M. (2010). Teachers' emotional experiences of growing diversity and multiculturalism in schools and the prospects of an ethic of discomfort. *Teachers and Teaching: Theory and Practice, 16*(6), 703–716. https://doi.org/10.1080/13540602.2010.517687

CHAPTER ELEVEN

# Critical Pedagogy and Online Discussions in a Multicultural Education Teacher Preparation Course

JESSAMAY T. PESEK

My formal teaching career began as a secondary (grades 5–12) social studies educator. Discussion, inquiry, social justice, and global-mindedness were primary elements of my classroom praxis. I aimed to have my students be engaged with each other in rich, deep dialogue where they encountered opportunities to question the status quo and discuss ways to push for social, economic, and political change. I encouraged classroom participants to take control of their own learning and critically evaluate their preexisting opinions and biases to create new ways of viewing and acting within our local, state, and international contexts. I also maintained strong relationships with my students and, in turn, worked to have our classroom curriculum reflect their lived experiences and cultures. My social studies classroom teaching philosophy was influenced by critical pedagogues and researchers such as Paulo Freire, bell hooks, Howard Zinn, Ira Shor, and Michael Apple. These scholars encouraged me to trudge through resistance and to act in the classroom to nurture a space that was safe and engaging for all students. I was determined to carry this teaching philosophy, knowing I would adapt and evolve as an educator, as I began my graduate work and post-secondary level teaching.

My first professorship was with a hybrid teacher education program. My course load included a multicultural education course, a cornerstone in teacher education programs across the United States. I was eager for the opportunity but unclear on how I would create space for a rich and authentic social justice-focused classroom experience within an online setting that evoked critical pedagogy. Furthermore, I was uncertain on how to create opportunity for active dialogue where all participants would be able to engage in meaningful conversations, a vital practice for multicultural education-based courses. Through communication with others, I realized I was not alone in this quest. My journey started to explore ways to apply critical pedagogy within digital classroom spaces and also to demonstrate critical pedagogy in action for my K-12 preservice teachers to replicate in their current and future teaching praxis.

## Online Classrooms and Critical Pedagogy

As online education continues to gain popularity (Seaman et al., 2018), it is important for instructors dedicated to critical pedagogy to consider: *How best to teach critically within an online environment?* An online critical instructor must recognize that it takes time, integrity, reflection, and deep understanding of the teaching philosophy of critical pedagogy. The purpose of this chapter is not to argue if online or traditional (in-person) is better suited for critical pedagogy as both settings have their benefits and drawbacks (Nguyen, 2015; Stark, 2019; Stern, 2004). Rather, the purpose of this chapter is to focus on applying critical pedagogy within online learning spaces while considering the online setting's unique characteristics. For instance, a key characteristic is the freedom of time and openness of online courses. Online instructors have flexible parameters to implement critical-based pedagogies attending to students' needs, goals, and time restraints. Other attributes of online learning include opportunities to implement interactive technologies, encourage multiple student-to-student interactions, and foster prolonged periods of discussion and reflection.

One of the first steps to apply critical pedagogy in an online classroom is to consider how to structure the course to center and empower students. The course structure matters (Tibi, 2018) and should offer opportunities to increase the potential for learners to take charge of their own learning and to facilitate the development of a sense of community (Palloff & Pratt, 2013). The structure of the course ought to include the student's involvement and engagement in what is taught and how it is taught within the introduction part of the course. Furthermore, empowerment includes trust, respect, and the building of relationships. The online classroom has great potential to foster relationships between the teacher and students and among the students, which may have significant positive contributions to the learning environment (Dalelio, 2013; Palloff & Pratt, 2013; Wegmann & McCauley, 2014). These relationships may provide opportunity to set the foundation to empower students to feel their voice is respected and heard and that they truly have a voice to recommend course preferences and share observations.

Within the structure of an online course, there are many strategies that may be applied to practice critical pedagogy. This chapter focuses on the utilization of the online discussion board tool, available in most Learning Management System (LMS) course platforms (e.g., D2L Brightspace, Blackboard). Online discussion boards are asynchronous communication platforms that allow participants to electronically post messages in a common line area for everyone to read and respond (Huang, 2000). The discussion board is a place to exchange ideas, creatively express thoughts, and respectively challenge the content, instructor, and other students. The online discussion board, if used thoughtfully and with clear intent, is a place where online learning and critical pedagogy may intersect.

## Online Learning and Fostering Meaningful Discussion

Discussion in all course settings is important. The comparison between the traditional (in-person) discussions and online discussions in the development of critical thinking and meaningful learning is a continued discussion among educational researchers (e.g., Ernst, 2008; Gilbert & Dabbagh, 2005; Palloff & Pratt, 2013). A benefit of in-person discussion is that it allows opportunity for verbal cues and non-verbal communication to supplement the spoken word. Second, it is in the present, thus, the moment of dialogue is shared among the participants, and the instructor may promptly facilitate the conversation if it becomes emotionally charged. Third, a traditional synchronous discussion allows opportunity for the negotiation of ideas and dialogue, which may promote understanding in the moment. On the other hand, online discussion has benefits. Online discussion may offer more opportunity for all students to participate rather than having a few students dominant the conversation. Second, online discussion may allow additional time for reflection and synthesis before a response is written and shared (Chadha, 2017). Third, the discussion may encourage all to participate in a more collaborative environment. Zhou (2015) conducted a meta-analysis of studies of online discussion over the past 15 years and discussed trends about online discussion and participation. Zhou (2015) found: (1) all students talk more in an online discussion than in a face-to-face environment, and (2) the majority of online classroom discussions are collaborative and constructive. It is important to acknowledge that online discussions are worthwhile, meaningful, and present multiple opportunities for participants to discuss varied topics. For this to occur, the instructor must be dedicated to the process of discussion and be skilled in structuring space for effective discussion, which is important for creating a space for a meaningful online multicultural education course.

## The Role of the Instructor

Regardless of setting, the instructor must carefully consider how best to incorporate and nurture meaningful, inclusive discussion. The organization of the course and course instruction matter. Means et al. (2009) suggest that student performance of online versus in-person courses, including differences in grades and learning advantages, is dependent not so much on the delivery method, but more so on the course structure and instructor. For discussion to successfully occur, the instructor must be dedicated to the aim of supporting meaningful discussion. The course instructor must also have awareness of power structures and inequalities and the societal challenges related to oppression, particularly of minoritized groups, and acknowledge what hooks (1994) claims, "Racism, sexism, and class elitism shape the structure of classrooms, creating a lived reality of insider versus outsider that is predetermined, often in place before any class discussion begins" (p. 83). In all course discussions, including asynchronous discussions, the instructor must consider the dynamics of power in place. In a discussion, a student may make a statement that upsets others, or a student from a minoritized background may not feel comfortable sharing about their experiences. hooks continues to argue that it is up to the teacher to determine the classroom dynamics. In these moments, the teacher has work to do to support effective, inclusive discussions.

Furthermore, the discussion in an online class should not be used for simply the sake of having students show their work or having individuals post to measure participation and frequency of participation; rather, the discussion tool should be used to apply concepts of critical pedagogy. The discussion should reflect a holistic process that engages students and builds off their experiences, truths, and knowledge, as "knowledge (truth) is socially constructed, culturally mediated, and historically situated" (McLaren, 2007, p. 210). Furthermore, the discussion in an online class should set the stage to acknowledge the "habits of thought, reading, writing, and speaking which go beneath surface meaning, first impressions, dominant myths, official pronouncements, traditional clichés, received wisdom, and mere opinions" (Shor, 1992, p. 129). The aim is for students to participate in meaningful and profound discussions that reflect their experiences and empower their knowledge and contributions.

In the end, regardless of the medium in which the course is taught, an effective educator provides opportunities for all learners to recognize that their voices, perspectives, and livelihoods matter and that learners are cognizant that they can be a source of change to benefit society. The instructor must also create and maintain a space that works against oppression and structures in society that are damaging to students. In an online classroom, this takes on a different approach, but it is possible with deliberate action and continuous reflection. In this chapter, discussion is examined as a tool for critical teaching and as a medium to exchange ideas, listen to others, and participate in active inquiry. Students are encouraged to engage in collective action that incorporates deliberation, social justice, equality, and empowerment (McLaren, 2009). Scholarly work has examined critical pedagogy in the classroom (e.g., Freire, 1970; Giroux, 1981; McLaren, 2009; Young, 1997). This chapter builds off this research to focus on how online classrooms absorb critical pedagogy practices through online discussions.

## Why Discussion?

Freire (1970) claims, "Only through communication can human life hold meaning" (p. 63). Discussion reveals that, "questions of democracy and justice cannot be separated from the most fundamental features of teaching and learning" (Kincheloe, 2008). A strong citizenship rationale for applying discussion as a teaching method is that discussion has a central role in most forms of deliberative democracy, a concept that focuses on multiple points of view, talking with others to think critically about societal options, and expanding their perspectives (Gutmann & Thompson, 2004). It is a worthwhile endeavor to teach young people to have conversations with each other where actual listening and the quest of understanding another viewpoint occur versus conversations that are combative. The well-being of our society depends on our ability to engage others' perspectives and seek understanding through dialogue (Parker & Hess, 2001).

In an online classroom, discussion is also good for student learning and discovery. It grants opportunities for students to critically investigate numerous ways of thinking and acting, and it helps students actively process information rather than simply passively receive it, allowing for opportunity of higher-order learning experiences (Levine, 2007). Students may thoroughly explore their own ideas and experiences and the ideas and experiences of others. Online discussions provide students opportunities to learn from their peers by reading posts and responses (Xie, 2013); and reading peers' responses can provide additional opportunities to improve their self-efficacy (Huang, 2017). It is also a way for students to feel connected to classroom learning as the online discussion board may be a space where students share experiences, histories, and resources, and they also feel part of an inclusive online learning community (Levine, 2007). There is also evidence that students may feel more comfortable to post and respond more thoroughly in an online discussion versus an in-person discussion (Kemp & Grieve, 2014). In addition, during asynchronous online discussions, students may respond at their own pace without the constraint of time and place, allowing additional time for reflection and investigation before immediately responding (Thompson, 2006). In sum, online discussions are good for students.

A well-planned, quality discussion can encourage and stimulate student learning, but good discussion does not spontaneously appear. In an online classroom, due to the parameters of time and space, the guidelines often are different than in traditional classroom spaces. Educators must carefully consider how to foster and support effective discussion among the members of the classroom and also gather student preferences regarding how to structure the discussion. Online critical instructors must adapt their teaching practices, which include a shift in power relations between instructor and students, to provide opportunities for the instructor and students to co-create the discussion experiences. Creating opportunities for productive discussion reflective of critical pedagogy takes continuous consideration and action. There is not a one-size fits all procedural guideline to create critically focused discussion opportunities in an online classroom. This depends on the students in the classroom. Thus, the instructor must continue to reflect and adapt instruction based on the needs of the students.

## Discussion and Multicultural Education

The following sections will review discussion strategies I have implemented in my online multicultural education course to encourage effective use of critical pedagogy applicable to online teaching. The multicultural education course is offered at the undergraduate and graduate levels for 25–35 students per semester. All students aim to be licensed teachers across varied teacher licensures (e.g., elementary, special education, math, social studies). The demographics vary at the undergraduate and graduate levels, but most students are non-traditional, aged 25-years or older, who aim to enter teaching later in their lives. They live in different communities across the state of Minnesota.

## Discussion Strategies

The following sections focus on the work I do as a critical online instructor to organize and facilitate the online discussion board in my multicultural education course. Each section reviews an adoptable strategy to assist instructors with the discussion components of their courses. Practices include:

- Teaching *with* and *for* critical pedagogy
- Setting the stage: Creating a safe and inclusive environment for discussion
- Decentering the knowledge
- Decentering assessment
- Remaining flexible

These strategies are important because discussion tools are available in most Learning Management Systems (LMS) used in higher education (Dahlstrom et al., 2014). However, it is important to keep in mind that the above practices must be implemented based on the needs of the students, the course content, and overall course expectations.

### Teaching *With* and *For* Critical Pedagogy

Walter Parker and Diana Hess, in the article Teaching With and For Discussion (2001), explain the need to teach content through discussion as a method and also as a curriculum objective. We can apply this understanding to the online setting and critical pedagogy. Teacher educators must practice utilizing critical pedagogy-based practices while teaching about critical pedagogy as a curriculum goal. Through this, the teacher educator must apply and model critical pedagogy but also intentionally teach students about critical pedagogy and its many multidimensional facets. Thus, teacher educators have a major role to play; they ought to prepare their students, who will be future K-12 classroom teachers, to effectively teach while continuing to model how to teach utilizing critical pedagogical strategies. The aim being to teach *with* and *for* critical pedagogy.

In my multicultural education course, to teach with and for critical pedagogy, I offer opportunities for students to consider the societal injustices present in schools and communities and how these affect their role and responsibilities as a teacher. This involves a challenging journey of reflection and critique. I offer flexibility of work and options for assessment. For example, I provide a variety of options for a summative (final) assessment project, allowing each student to select how they wish to demonstrate what they learn. Their project may be in a form of an essay, artwork, presentation, or video that expresses a key message they took away from the course, which is eventually shared in our course discussions. These options of assessments are not be limited to the confines of the course outcomes, but rather extend beyond to societal and political issues (Boyd, 2016). To teach with and for critical pedagogy, I make transparent the process and the pedagogical intent of offering a variety of options, and in turn, provide assessment choice examples that the students may utilize in their future K-12 classrooms. Thus, the learner is able to experience choice, feel empowered, and have a critical-based tool they may employ in their future classrooms.

For a second example, I focus on the course content, multicultural education in K-12 settings. We examine culturally responsive pedagogy (Gay, 2010; Ladson-Billings, 1994), also identified as culturally sustaining pedagogy (Paris & Alim, 2017). Culturally responsive pedagogy (CRP) recognizes the importance of including students' cultural references in all aspects of learning (Ladson-Billings, 1994) to provide support to marginalized students. CRP focuses on increasing the learning capacity of each individual student and demands the need for the teachers to know their students in order to be able to employ effective teaching strategies (Gay, 2010; Ladson-Billings,1994); additionally, CRP-focused teachers firmly believe that all students can succeed, maintain a supportive student–teacher relationship, and consider student diversity and individual differences (Paris & Alim, 2017). Through teaching about CRP, I also draw from critical pedagogy and the aim to empower the students that too often have been silenced and been representatives of marginalized and oppressed groups. While teaching, I model culturally responsive teaching that is also in line with critical teaching. Here is a list of CRP techniques, compiled by Zeichner (1992), that I consider and model while communicating with students in course discussions and also provide examples for use in K-12 teaching:

- Teachers reflect and seek to understand their own ethnic and cultural identities.
- Teachers communicate high expectations for all students and believe all students can succeed.
- Teachers aspire to make a difference in their students' learning.
- Teachers develop meaningful relationships with their students.
- Teachers cease seeing students as "the other."
- Teacher's curricula reflect the contributions and perspectives of the different ethnocultural groups.
- Teachers are involved in political struggles outside the classroom that are aimed at achieving a more just and humane society.

To add to this list, I also focus on my teacher presence, working not to dominate course discussions. These strategies are in line with both culturally responsive and critical pedagogies. Although focused on teaching diverse students, these elements may be applied to all students regardless of language and background. Although the suggestions do not directly apply to leading effective discussions in an online classroom, the critical online instructor can teach with and for critical pedagogy and apply these examples to begin the process of setting the stage to successfully use discussion as a method while teaching with and for critical pedagogy. It is not possible to have a healthy, effective, inclusive discussion if the course instructor creates an environment in which students feel silenced.

To teach with and for critical pedagogy takes intentionality and a strong effort to be transparent and open about one's teaching practices. The instructor needs to be dedicated to creating a classroom space that genuinely provides equal opportunity for all their students and explains ways in which their students—future educators—may provide opportunities for their K-12 students.

## Setting the Stage: Creating a Safe and Inclusive Environment for Discussion

For a critical pedagogy-based online course, much work must happen at the forefront to ensure there is a framework in place to provide support for participation, student discovery and reflection (Major, 2016; Palloff & Pratt, 2007). This includes providing a discussion board forum organized to promote student engagement and critical thought, with the "capacity to facilitate meaningful dialogue" (Boyd, 2016, p. 177). The discussion board is often the core of an online course as far as providing opportunities for student dynamics, establishing a space for conducting the weekly activities, and offering a venue for collaboration, personal exchanges, interactions, and critical inquiry. Thus, to nurture a positive discussion board design, it is essential for the instructor to set the stage and establish a clear framework for how students should organize and participate in the discussion.

To set the stage for my multicultural education course, I make clear the purpose of the discussion board as a way to discuss our discoveries and to practice reflection. I also offer examples of positive, effective online discussions (Meyers, 2008) and clarify course expectations by using video, audio, and written documents. To encourage student agency, I collaborate with students on guidelines for course discussion, and we reflect on what is good discussion (Brookfield & Preskill, 2005). I also indicate the purpose of the discussions is not to showcase what is learned; rather, it is to dig deeper, present new questions, and examine related ideas.

It is also important to be clear about weekly participation expectations, to discuss them with students, and to share research on online discussion to help them determine their expectations throughout the semester. For example, when discussing participation expectations, I share research by Palloff and Pratt (2001) who recommend that students log into the course five times per week. They suggest that the students do not need to post each time they log in but that they should check-in on the discussions to read and reflect about the posts. Draves (2007) and Palloff and Pratt (2001) state that the optimal posting requirement for mandatory discussions should include 2–3 posts per week. Teachers should also be present in the course and continue to frequently log in, although it should be students, not the teachers, that are more active in the course discussions. Given this information, the students can select their posting guidelines with the agreement that participation and work is required for all of us to dig deeper into the content.

Overall, for a course to be productive, logistics matter. Logistics depend on your course expectations and goals, your individual students and student learning needs, and overall course design, but these are all important questions to ponder as the course is designed. For example, instructors do not want learners to spend hours trying to locate the discussion board's prompt instructions. We want them to spend time on content and reflection. Learners will continuously get frustrated within an online course if it is challenging to navigate or unorganized. We want to ensure that they have as much time possible to reflect on the content and participate in meaningful discussions with their peers. An instructor may have the best content, but if the content is difficult to navigate or is challenging to access, it simply is not as powerful. Many universities and colleges have resources and support for instructors that teach online to achieve this goal.

The next component to setting the stage focuses on creating a collaborative, safe, and inclusive classroom space. Building relationships and establishing and maintaining a safe, inclusive classroom space is important for online learning environments. Strong relationships strengthen instructor-student (I-S) and student-student interactions (S-S), connection to course content (CC), and sense of belonging. This helps to encourage a shift to normative power structures and empowers students to co-construct their learning experience along with guidance from the instructor (Cornejo, 2017).

To build relationships among teachers and students, students may introduce themselves via video or written response with an attached picture to the group in an initial discussion assignment. They may participate in "get-to-know-you" activities at the start of and throughout the course. They may also share their areas of expertise and professional and personal goals. Furthermore, it is also important to continue to encourage students to access the instructor and connect with their peers throughout the course session. The instructor should facilitate an environment that encompasses the phrase, "we are all in this together," a concept reflected in Freire's work that we, students and instructors, learn collectively. The instructor should continue to practice the use of "we" when explaining course goals and activities to demonstrate participation in the learning experience.

In addition, it is important that instructors get to know their students in ways that extend outside of the classroom. Instructors may investigate socioeconomic status, cultural backgrounds, religious affiliations, communities, and experiences of their students (hooks, 1994). As an online instructor, through exhibiting respect and care, I believe I provide safe spaces where all students feel valued and are also willing to share experiences in an effort to decenter the knowledge.

## Decentering Knowledge

The critical educator shares authority with their students, and all participants in the classroom space have power to teach and to learn. This takes work and continuous reflection for the instructor, as the curriculum, instruction, and assessment (which each could be discussed at length) must be adapted to align with this aim. Here we discuss how the discussion board may respect and honor the authority and knowledge of the students.

The instructor must clearly explain the intent of the critical learning classroom experience with the participants and recognize that for some students this may be their first encounter with critical pedagogical practices. These transformative ideals related to critical pedagogy, such as questioning the status quo and being critical of the political structures of schools and other social organizations, may take time for the students to consider and understand. However, the primary takeaway for the student is to be granted permission to share knowledge, consider multiple perspectives, question authority and the status quo, and accept multiple ways of being and doing. Furthermore, critical educators,

> Maintain that students should study the world around them, in the process of learning who they are and what has shaped them. In this context students as odd as it may sound become epistemologically informed scholars. As such, they are challenged to analyze and interpret data, conduct research, and develop a love for scholarship that studies things that matter to the well-being of the people of the world. (Kincheloe, 2008, p. 11)

For my multicultural education course, I aim to engage students in inquiry and exploration, while being transparent about the course outcomes and allowing students to contribute to the content, processes, and discussions. I work with the students to create discussion prompts that allow us to examine course content, lived experiences, alternative perspectives and positions, and articulate understandings. Here are my general guidelines for considering how to model writing effective prompts for an online setting.

- The prompts should be open-ended to elicit more than one answer and not always have a single correct answer. The focus should be on higher order thinking questions.

- The prompts ought to encourage classroom participants to share their opinion, perspective, and experience.
- The prompts should excite or encourage participants to engage in conversation.
- The prompts should connect the course content to societal issues and present opportunities to discuss possibilities for action to elicit change.

I also share these guidelines with my students to encourage participants to create prompts and assist in facilitating the discussion. Allowing students to generate their own prompts and facilitate the discussion decenters the knowledge and provides a strategy to make the course interactive (Durrington et al., 2006). This is particularly important in a multicultural education course as all members continue to learn more about everyone's personal experience. This practice allows you as the instructor to admit that you do not know everything and provide evidence that you are continuing to learn. In these discussions, the instructor should not be the directive voice, but rather a facilitator of the discussion to encourage students to share knowledge and experience. Facilitation is an important skill for online instructors given the sensitive nature of the topics discussed in the online multicultural education course. The instructor must be prepared to facilitate online conversations. This means that as instructors, we must be aware of our identities and how we position ourselves and are perceived by students. We should consider when we should step back, listen, or jump in. However, we must keep in mind that, like us, when students as K-12 teachers witness negative racial comments or inappropriate actions, they must know that staying silent is not option. We also must remember that learning occurs across contexts. Instructors ought to be aware of and sensitive to the fact that, for some students, accepting the existence of oppression and racial privilege may mean potential conflict with their family and friends, and this may affect the course discussion. Below, there are three suggestions of strategies I utilize in my multicultural education to create a collaborative discussion board that welcomes critical dialogue and empowers participants.

### Dilemmas, Case Studies, and Scenarios: Real-World Application

Dilemmas, case studies, and scenarios are all examples of how learners may grapple with course content and real-world application. Mezirow (1991) posits that students experience personal and intellectual growth when they examine complex, real-world dilemmas which create opportunities to check their assumptions and explore contradictory information and multiple perspectives. These real-world application prompts foster opportunity to not just search for the correct answer, but rather they deepen our level of understanding and developing additional questions.

Participants may also share their own dilemmas or scenarios to discuss with the group. For pre-service teachers starting their work in the classroom, there are infinite numbers of topics based on their experiences that are important to discuss. Examples of real-world, critical case studies are provided in a book by Gorski and Pothini (2018), *Case Studies on Diversity and Social Justice Education*. Course participants may also provide their own dilemmas for class discussion.

## Moving Beyond the Written Prompt

Critical pedagogues share a goal of academic success for each learner and the course instructor may have to think beyond written text to improve the learning experience. Online discussions are rather writing and reading intensive. Many times, my students have shared that the weekly discussions were becoming mundane as there were always writing prompts, and they have voiced that they appreciate when they can share their experiences in other ways such as concept maps, artistic expression, or video or oral recordings. For example, during a unit in which we explored the challenges K-12 students from low-income groups' experience, one student wrote and recorded a song about acceptance and respect and shared it with our class through YouTube. Rather than being forced to draft a written response, the student explored the content through song and allowed the other classmates to explore another viewpoint.

## Offer Choice

It is important not to force students each week to respond to a similar set of prompts as this may discourage participation and critical thought. To keep the course interesting, the instructor may set up choice for learners in how they wish to engage with the course content. Choice may include creating opportunities for students to design prompts, allowing students to select from a set of questions, to post a video response, or to submit an image to add to a response. Furthermore, some students in a course may prefer to do live discussions as a small or larger group and may work together to find a time that works for everyone. Overall, the purpose of offering choice is to have multiple, flexible ways in which participants may examine the content and share their observations, insights, and knowledge.

Other methods to decenter the knowledge include being flexible with the time requirements of posting, allowing students to take a prompt or question in another direction, granting options for students to co-write posts with other students, and supporting ways other than the course formal discussion board for students to discuss the course content. Overall, there is a responsibility on the part of the teacher to implement critical pedagogical methods that are appropriate for their learners and classroom context (Keesing-Styles, 2003). There is not one specific guide on how to decenter the knowledge in the online classroom. Thus, the teacher has work to do as they consider their audience and ways best to respect and honor the experiences and wisdom of all participants.

Decentering Assessment

The traditional expectations of grades are disrupted when one applies critical pedagogy to classroom assessment, including online discussion. The instructor and students must reconceptualize "traditional" power relations (Shor, 1996) and not rely on the instructor to simply independently offer the grade without student input. This is a shift from traditional classroom where students rely on the expert teacher to share information and students are assessed on this given knowledge.

To achieve a critical approach to assessment of the online discussion board, it must be centered on dialogic interactions between the teacher and learner to ensure all perspectives are respected and validated. One practice to achieve this goal is self-assessment. Self-assessment of one's own work, along with instructor guidance, encourages independence, responsibility for one's own learning, motivation, and self-reflection (Andrade & Valtcheva, 2009). Self-assessment allows opportunity for students to examine their own learning and participation and to collaborate and continually dialogue with the teacher regarding the progress. This action of dialogue requires a relationship between the learner and teacher where one "knowing subject [is] face to face with other knowing subjects" (Freire, 1989, p. 49, as explained by Keesing-Styles, 2003). Education thus becomes a pedagogy of knowing (Freire, 1989). Thus, students, through self-assessment, enhance their opportunities to become knowing subjects (Keesing-Styles, 2003). This critical stance to assessment highlights the importance of having learners actively engaged in their leaning process and being able to develop their opinions and positions of their own understanding of the course content.

Therefore, for assessment of the discussion board, online instructors must consider:

Have we engaged students in some way not measurable by clicks, hits, and quantity of discussion posts and replies? Are we reviewing the discussion board in ways in which examine depth of discovery rather than counting to measure participation? To assess, instructors should share this task with students to determine the grade or participation of their work. This action may occur at the start of the course when the teacher and learners co-write the discussion board expectations and co-design a rubric and then continue throughout the semester as the students self-assess and dialogue with the instructor to examine their discussion board participation.

As online instructors, we must reflect on the purpose of grading and contemplate what is being graded. The discussion board is a place for students to grapple with the content, not necessarily to showcase their learning and knowledge gained. Hence, the instructor may consider not offering a formal grade on discussion board activities. Rather, participation and learning may be evaluated by student-to-teacher dialogue through the term, relying on opportunities for students to do continual self-assessment as the core of this goal. Considering the goals of critical pedagogy, this is one process of many that allows the power of learning into the hands of the students.

Remaining Flexible

Critical pedagogy changes depending on the context. As an online instructor, my work remains fluid, and my teaching methods adapt based on students' needs, knowledge, and experiences. To be able to adapt, I continuously work to build positive relationships among all classroom participants, practice critical listening and critical thought, and remain sensitive to students' needs within the learning environments. I believe a teacher must also be flexible with student power and voice. Having students question authority (in some cases the teacher) and challenge the status quo (in sometimes the classroom or institution) allows students to take control of their own learning and critically evaluate their pre-existing knowledge, opinions, and biases they may have been taught to have. These thought transformations by the students often takes extra nurturing on behalf of the teacher. The biggest takeaway of critical pedagogy is that being a critical teacher takes time and continuous effort. It takes honesty, humbleness, and a realization that teaching is a craft. A critical teacher must remain flexible to empower and respect their students. Being a critical teacher is difficult, but important, as its efforts present opportunities to liberate individuals and change society (Freire, 1970).

Reflection Activity

I present questions that invite the readers to reflect upon their own practice as critical instructors in an online environment, specifically in reference to the online discussion board. Review your course discussion expectations and consider the following:

- Have you created opportunities for the students and the instructor to interact and get to know each other?
- Do you encourage multiple perspectives and signal to students those diverse perspectives are welcomed?

- Have you offered opportunities for students to create discussion board prompts and activities?
- Have you offered a variety of ways in which students may respond to discussion board questions?
- How will students be able to deepen their understanding of the course content?
- How may you as the instructor continue to learn from your students' discussion board posts?
- Overall, as a critical instructor, what challenges and/or successes have you experienced on facilitating the online discussion board?

Through reflection, we may better recognize that teaching is elastic and ever changing as our societies and students' needs change. Viewing pedagogy from a critical perspective allows educators to question assumed practices. As a result, instructors may integrate strategies that promote a holistic view of education.

## Conclusion

Paulo Freire's philosophy and dedication to transformative education continues to be a source of inspiration for critical educators. He has demonstrated that the classroom is a possibility for social and political change. The classroom has its imperfections, but dedicated teachers have the power to create a place where change may happen. The power of the classroom is also voiced by bell hooks (1994),

> The academy is not paradise. But learning is a place where paradise can be created. The classroom, with all its limitations, remains a location of possibility. In that field of possibility, we have the opportunity to labor for freedom, to demand of ourselves and our comrades, an openness of mind and heart that allows us to face reality even as we collectively imagine ways to move beyond boundaries, to transgress. This is education as the practice of freedom. (p. 207)

Online discussions are places of possibilities in which meaningful, authentic conversations occur. They allow all students to share their experiences, critically engage with the classroom participants, honestly reflect on the course content, question norms, and consider other options to address relevant issues. It is important that the instructor embraces discussion, teaches with and for critical pedagogy, sets the stage, decenters knowledge, decenters assessment, and remains flexible.

# References

Andrade, H., & Valtcheva, A. (2009). Promoting learning and achievement through self-assessment. *Theory into Practice*, *48*(1), 12–19. https://doi.org/10.1080/00405840802577544

Boyd, D. (2016). What would Paulo Freire think of Blackboard: Critical pedagogy in an age of online learning. *International Journal of Critical Pedagogy*, *7*, 165–186.

Brookfield, S. D., & Preskill, S. (2005). *Discussion as a way of teaching: Tools and techniques for democratic classrooms* (2nd ed.). Jossey-Bass.

Chadha, A. (2017). Comparing student reflectiveness in online discussion forums across modes of instruction and levels of courses. *Journal of Educators Online*, *14*(2). https://doi.org/10.9743/jeo.2017.14.2.8

Cornejo, M. N. (2017). *Critical pedagogy: Building strong learning communities*. UNLV Best Teaching Practices Expo 39. https://digitalscholarship.unlv.edu/btp_expo/39

Dalelio, C. (2013). Student participation in online discussion boards in a higher education setting. *International Journal on E-Learning*, *12*(3), 249–271. https://www.learntechlib.org/primary/p/37555/

Dahlstrom, E., Brooks, D. C., & Bichsel, J. (2014). *The current ecosystem of learning management systems in higher education: Student faculty, and IT perspectives*. Research Report. ECAR. https://www.digitallernen.ch/wp-content/uploads/2016/02/ers1414.pdf

Draves, W. A. (2007). *Advanced Teaching Online* (3rd ed.). LERN Books.

Durrington, V., Berryhill, A., & Swafford, J. (2006). Strategies for enhancing student interactivity in an online environment. *College Teaching*, *54*(1), 190–193. https://doi.org/10.3200/CTCH.54.1.190-193

Ernst, J. V. (2008). A comparison of traditional and hybrid online instructional presentation in communication technology. *Journal of Technology Education*, *19*(2), 40–49. https://www.learntechlib.org/p/54855/

Freire, P. (1970). *Pedagogy of the oppressed*. Continuum Publishing Corporation.

Freire, P. (1989). The politics of education. In P. Murphy & B. Moon (Eds.), *Developments in learning and assessment* (pp. 48–54). Hodder & Stoughton.

Gay, G. (2010). *Culturally responsive teaching: Theory, research, and practice* (2nd ed.). Teachers College Press.

Gilbert, P. K., & Dabbagh, N. (2005). How to structure online discussions for meaningful discourse: A case study. *British Journal of Educational Technology*, *36*(1), 5–18. https://psycnet.apa.org/doi/10.1111/j.1467-8535.2005.00434.x

Giroux, H. A. (1981). *Ideology culture and the process of schooling*. Temple University Press.

Gorski, P. C., & Pothini, S. G. (2018). *Case studies on diversity and social justice education* (2nd ed.). Routledge.

Gutmann, A., & Thompson, D. (2004). *Why deliberative democracy?* Princeton University Press.

hooks, b. (1994). *Teaching to transgress: Education as the practice of freedom*. Routledge.

Huang, H. (2000). Instructional technologies facilitating online courses. *Educational Technology, 40*(4), 41–46.

Huang, X. (2017). Example-based learning: Effects of different types of examples on student performance, cognitive load and self-efficacy in a statistical learning task. *Interactive Learning Environments, 25*(3), 283–294. https://doi.org/10.1080/10494820.2015.1121154

Keesing-Styles, L. (2003). The relationship between critical pedagogy and assessment in teacher education. *Radical Pedagogy, 5*(1). https://hdl.handle.net/10652/1931

Kemp, N., & Grieve, R. (2014). Face-to-face or face-to-screen? Undergraduates' opinions and test performance in classroom vs. online learning. *Frontiers in Psychology, 5*(1278). https://doi.org/10.3389/fpsyg.2014.01278

Kincheloe, J. L. (2008). *Knowledge and critical pedagogy: An introduction.* Springer.

Ladson-Billings, G. (1994). *The dreamkeepers.* Jossey-Bass Publishing Co.

Levine, S. J. (2007). The online discussion board. *New Directions for Adult & Continuing Education, 113,* 67–74. https://doi.org/10.1002/ace.248

Major, C. H. (2016). *Teaching online: A guide to theory, research, and practice.* John Hopkins University Press.

McLaren, P. (2007). *Life in schools: An introduction to critical pedagogy in the foundations of education* (5th ed.). Pearson.

McLaren, P. (2009). Critical pedagogy: A look at major concepts. In A. Darder, M. P. Baltodano, & R. D. Torres. (Eds.), *The critical pedagogy reader* (pp. 61–83). Routledge.

Means, B., Toyama, Y., Murphy, R., Bakia, M., & Jones, K. (2009). *Evaluation of evidence-based practices in online learning: A meta-analysis and review of online learning studies.* US Department of Education. https://files.eric.ed.gov/fulltext/ED505824.pdf

Meyers, S. A. (2008). Using transformative pedagogy when teaching online. *College Teaching, 56*(4), 219–224. https://doi.org/10.3200/CTCH.56.4.219-224

Mezirow, J. (1991). *Transformative dimensions of adult learning.* Jossey-Bass.

Nguyen, T. (2015). The effectiveness of online learning: Beyond no significant difference and future horizons. *MERLOT Journal of Online Learning and Teaching, 11*(2), 309–319.

Palloff, R., & Pratt, K. (2001). *Lessons from the cyberspace classroom: The realities of online teaching.* Jossey-Bass.

Palloff, R. M., & Pratt, K. (2007). *Building online learning communities: Effective strategies for the virtual classroom* (2nd ed.). Jossey-Bass.

Palloff, R. M., & Pratt, K. (2013). *Lessons from the virtual classroom* (2nd ed.). Jossey-Bass.

Paris, D., & Alim, H. S. (2017). *Culturally sustaining pedagogies: Teaching and learning for justice in a changing world.* Teachers College Press.

Parker, W. C., & Hess, D. (2001). Teaching with and for discussion. *Teaching and Teacher Education, 17*(3), 273–289. https://doi.org/10.1016/S0742-051X(00)00057-3

Seaman, J. E., Allen, I. E., & Seaman, J. (2018). *Grade increase: Tracking distance education in the United States.* The Babson Survey Research Group.

Shor, I. (1992). *Empowering education: Critical teaching for social change.* University of Chicago Press.

Shor, I. (1996). *When students have power: Negotiating authority in a critical pedagogy.* University of Chicago Press.

Stark, E. (2019). Examining the role of motivation and learning strategies in student success in online versus face-to-face courses. *Online Learning, 23*(3), 234–251. http://dx.doi.org/10.24059/olj.v23i3.1556

Stern, B. S. (2004). A comparison of online and face-to-face instruction in an undergraduate foundations of American education course. *Contemporary Issues in Technology and Teacher Education, 4*(2), 196–213.

Thompson, J. T. (2006). Best practices in asynchronous online course discussions. *Journal of College Teaching and Learning, 3*(7), 19–30. http://doi.org/10.19030/tlc.v3i7.1698

Tibi, M. H. (2018). Computer science students' attitudes towards the use of structured and unstructured discussion forums in online courses. *Online Learning, 22*(1), 93–106. http://dx.doi.org/10.24059/olj.v22i1.995

Wegmann, S. J., & McCauley, J. K. (2014). Investigating asynchronous online communication: A connected stance revealed. *Journal of Asynchronous Learning Networks, 18*(1). http://dx.doi.org/10.24059/olj.v18i1.351

Xie, K. (2013). What do the numbers say? The influence of motivation and peer feedback on students' behaviour in online discussions. *British Journal of Educational Technology, 44*(2), 288–301. https://doi.org/10.1111/j.1467-8535.2012.01291.x

Young, R. (1997). A critical-pragmatic theory of classroom talk. In B. Davies & D. Corson (Eds.), *Encyclopedia of language and education: Oral discourse and education* (pp. 11–20). Kluwer.

Zeichner, K. M. (1992). *Educating teachers for cultural diversity.* National Center for Research on Teacher Learning.

Zhou, H. (2015). A systematic review of empirical studies on participants' interactions in internet- mediated discussion boards as a course component in formal higher education settings. *Online Learning Journal, 19*(3). http://dx.doi.org/10.24059/olj.v19i3.495

# CHAPTER TWELVE

# Evolving Toward Critical Social Justice Online: A Rogerian-Based Theoretical Model

JENNIFER L. MARTIN AND DENISE K. BOCKMIER-SOMMERS

There has been much debate among higher education professionals about how to engage Generation Z students—those who are tech savvy and purport to learn best by "doing" (Banaji & Greenwald, 2013). The need for heightened student engagement is particularly salient with content considered to be "unsafe" or troubling, i.e., content pertaining to social justice issues involving race, class, gender, sexuality, ableism, and other non-dominant identities. In this chapter, we ask, "How can we best deliver 'unsafe content' in online environments?"

We argue that this question is crucial in our fast-paced, politically contentious, and tech-heavy world. Expectations for students preparing to be working professionals in the fields of education and human services include compassion and empathy for their students and clients, a sense of caring, and, most importantly, a commitment to social justice. The latter is the underpinning sentiment of the desire to correct social ills in the interest of the public good. We acknowledge the importance for educators and human service professionals to recognize social injustice and understand the intersectionality of oppressions.

To successfully accomplish these goals, we examine pedagogy and content. Our online content involves dismantling stereotypes through counter-story. Our pedagogy is based upon a theoretical model—Evolving Toward Critical Social Justice—we developed based on the person-centered work of Carl Rogers, using his three conditions—empathy, genuineness, and unconditional positive regard—to facilitate meaningful life-changing dialogue in classrooms, live and online. Our model creates the safety necessary for the depth of dialogue required to reduce student biases and to engage students in critical social justice work (CSJ), which we define as actively engaging the classroom as a site for social change. We aim to prepare our students to do CSJ work in their future classrooms or working environments.

## The Importance of Social Justice in Education and Human Services Fields

The K-12 teaching force is currently more than 80% white (Bureau of Labor Statistics, 2019), a vast majority. In human service occupations, women comprise 67% of these professionals. Of the total number of human services professionals, 72% are white, 20% are Black or African American, 4% are Asian, and 12% are Hispanic or Latino (Bureau of Labor Statistics, 2019). At the same time, student populations and individuals being served by social service agencies are becoming more diverse. We must better prepare educators and human service professionals to engage in CSJ in order to "provide equal educational opportunities to all [people] regardless of race, ethnicity, gender, socioeconomic status, language, religion, and country of origin" (Akiba, 2011, p. 659).

Critical social justice work seeks to challenge and confront the dominant social order (Bolotin Joseph et al., 2000). But this work is difficult, and students tend to resist it (Martin, 2015; Milner, 2013). According to Leonardo (2016), "When confronted by challenges to their unearned advantages, Whites become possessively invested in identity politics based on race, and cling to the idea of meritocracy, even as they claim that Whites have deserved their disproportionate share of advantages in social life" (p. xiii). To acknowledge various -isms exist, is to acknowledge that those in the majority have benefitted from them. Many dominant students are unwilling to accept this, for then they are a part of a system that has benefitted from the exclusion, destruction, and dehumanization of other human beings.

In our experience doing CSJ work in online learning environments, we often utilize race as an exemplar—as race/racism is one of the most difficult areas for white students to face. The suggestions we postulate in our theoretical model (Evolving Toward Critical Social Justice) applies to other -isms within our educational milieu. Gay (2000) reminds us that students can feel ashamed, embarrassed, and angry when their ethnic or racial group is either portrayed only negatively through the curriculum or not at all.

Students studying to be working professionals in the fields of education and human services must be authentically prepared to work with individuals different from themselves (Colina et al., 2019), and become aware of historical societal and educational injustices, the price of which is being paid by our current and future children. For example, in our current educational milieu, we face:

- An overrepresentation of students of color in special education,
- An overrepresentation of students of color referred for disciplinary actions,
- An overwhelming number of students of color expelled or suspended,
- An underrepresentation of students of color in schoolwide clubs and organizations, and in other prestigious arenas, such as the school's homecoming court and student government,
- An underrepresentation of students of color in gifted education (Milner, 2012, pp. 871–872, and see DiAngelo, 2018; Goff et al., 2014; Matias, 2016).

Teacher training or other programs that do not provide culturally responsive instruction serve to exacerbate this problem (Milner, 2013). Cheryl Matias, a critical teacher educator, has done much work to analyze white student resistance to anti-racist and social justice work. She has found that her mainly white female students mask their racialized animus as paternalistic "caring." That is, despite the fact that pre-service teachers claim to care about all students, they often lack an *authentic* sense of caring for their students because of racial and cultural bias (Matias, 2016). Matias (2016) argues these students continually position themselves and their experiences at the center of all conversations, while they communicate the need to *save* students of color:

> If the sensibilities of teacher candidates are such that they do not even want to learn about racism or white supremacy because it is emotionally discomforting to them, and/or refuse to be corrected about racial assumptions, then how can teacher educators expect teacher candidates to muster the emotional investment needed to engage in prolonged projects of anti-racist teaching beyond a mere utterance of self-professing that they are? (p. 34)

This assertion that white pre-service teachers think they know enough to *save* anyone is presumptuous. It presupposes a belief in the superiority of their cultures and worldviews over those of their future students to whom they have had yet no exposure to and currently know nothing about.

If teachers and social service professionals are not trained to acknowledge, support, and convey empathy to people from diverse backgrounds, they do people of color as well as of other disenfranchised groups a disservice. They also run the risk of doing significant harm.

# Evolving Toward Critical Social Justice Theoretical Model

Our theoretical Evolving Toward Critical Social Justice Model for online teaching is based on Carl Roger's person-centered model. Carl Rogers, an American humanistic psychologist, believed that all human beings deserve dignity in the teaching and learning environments, and this can only result from three conditions: offering each student empathy, genuineness, and unconditional positive regard (Aspy & Roebuck, 1988; Rogers, 1969; Rogers et al., 2014). According to Motschnig-Pitrik (2005), "Person-centered significant or experiential learning as developed by Carl Rogers addresses the learner at three levels: intellect, social skills, and feelings or intuitions" (p. 503).

Learning is facilitated when students feel safe, trusted, creative, and knowledgeable. Rogers's theory encourages teachers to view students as co-learners as opposed to teachers being considered the "sole experts" in the classroom. He posited that the three conditions are necessary to establish a safe relationship between instructor and student. Empathy is defined as "the emotional and cognitive ability to feel the problems or distress of another person combined with the desire to help or to relieve his/her distress" (Tausch & Huls, 2014, p. 136). Genuineness is communicated from the professor being authentic and transparent. Unconditional positive regard is derived from the professor's acceptance of the student—regardless of circumstances.

Tausch and Huls (2014) found that 60% of university students believed they received no empathy from their professors. Similarly, Rogers et al. (2014) found that student feelings are rarely addressed in the classroom and that students tend to be distrustful of instructors who are not aware of students' feelings. However, if an instructor is genuine when interacting, students are more likely to trust them and feel valued and free to discuss course content when instructors demonstrate high regard for them.

Integrated into online environments, this learner-centered approach is apt to support students in feeling more comfortable and likely to utilize similar strategies as they interact with the instructor and with other students. As the instructor models and uses empathy, genuineness, and high regard in their interactions, students feel emotional safety, freedom, engagement, and curiosity, which become the pillars of support needed to move to deeper levels of learning (Rogers et al., 2014).

Rogerian theories about person or learner-centered teaching and learning are foundational to creating a more interpersonal presence within all learning environments (Rogers, 1969; 1983). As noted in Figure 12.1, once the instructor has displayed Rogers's three conditions, opportunities will arise to move toward culturally responsive practices. This involves, first, instructors exposing their own vulnerability, or their own transformation with regard to implicit bias and their relationship with "the other"; second, an open/dynamic classroom, including responsive online contact, engaging dialogue, and critical reflection on the part of all participants; and third, direct teaching of content that uses counter-stereotypical counter-stories to reduce stereotypical thinking of "the other" in white students, with an analysis of society and systemic causes of injustice (Mayhew & Deluca Fernandez, 2007). These practices will lead to the following outcomes: 1. safety, 2. student self-disclosure, and 3. an increased commitment to CSJ for students (Martin & Beese, 2020), which will eventually facilitate student critical understanding regarding their relationship to ideas about "the other."[1]

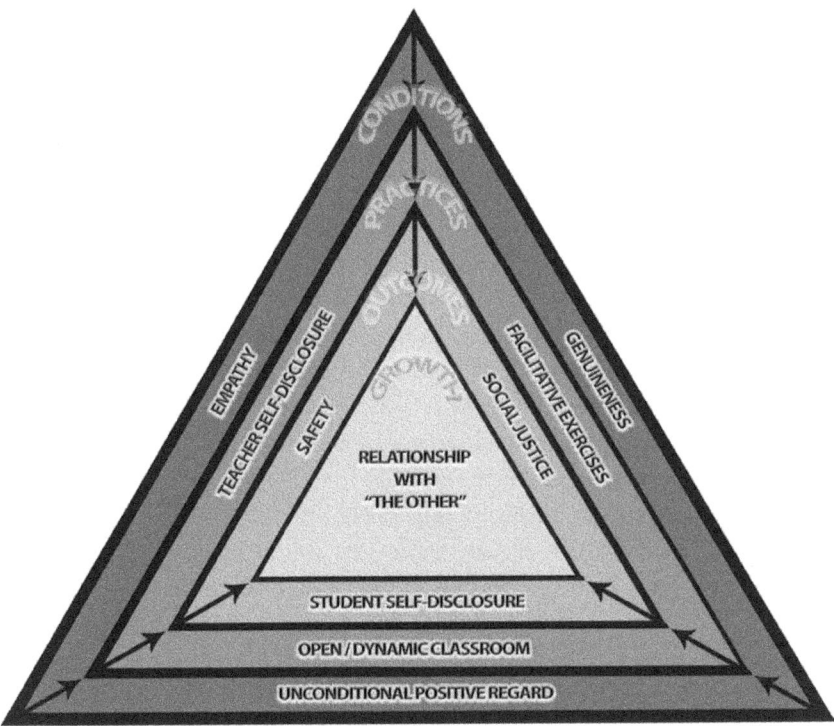

Figure 12.1: Evolving Toward Critical Social Justice: A Theoretical Model. Figure design assistance provided by Jeffrey Sudduth, IT Technical Associate, Information Technology Services, University of Illinois Springfield.

Source: Author

Person-centered learning as illustrated in our model above should be versatile, nonrepetitive, flexible, and individualized (Motschnig-Pitrik, 2005; Whiteside et al., 2017). These aims can be accomplished through the crafting of a community of inquiry (CoI), as discussed next, which also constitutes an integral part of our online pedagogy.

## Creating a Community of Inquiry (CoI) Online

O'Sullivan et al. (2004) argue that when a facilitative exchange between student and instructor is maintained, students are more motivated and engaged. The community of inquiry (CoI) approach meets this criterion, as it describes the interaction between social, teaching, and cognitive presences when designing and teaching online courses. Swan et al. (2008) and Cleveland-Innes and Campbell (2012) clearly express person-centeredness when they discuss these three types of online.

*Social presence* refers to the extent to which learners feel socially and emotionally connected with their online peers. It is indicated by "affective expression, open communication, and group cohesion" (Cleveland-Innes & Campbell, 2012, p. 281). *Teaching presence* refers to the design, facilitation, and direction of cognitive and social processes for the realization of personally meaningful and educationally worthwhile learning outcomes. Teaching presence is indicated by 1. Design and organization, 2. Facilitation of discourse, and 3. Direct instruction. According to Cleveland-Innes and Campbell (2012), "Cognitive presence is identified by four subcategories: triggering events, exploration, integration, and resolution" (p. 281). *Cognitive presence* describes the extent to which learners are able to construct and confirm meaning through sustained reflection and discourse. A CoI also requires online students to take personal responsibility for their engagement in learning as well as some degree of shared control with the content and structure of the course.

Paulsen and McCormick (2020) argue that the key elements of online student engagement include: active learning, peer collaboration, and interaction with faculty. Despite the fact that some online courses have less peer-to-peer engagement than traditional face-to-face courses, the authors found higher order learning and reflective and integrative learning to be higher in online environments. This may be because online modalities, by their very nature, challenge students to engage in more challenging cognitive activities. It crucial for online learning to involve "meaningful interactions with peers. …. and opportunities for collaborative learning" (p. 27). It is also important for online students to be able to interact with the instructor. In general, for successful online learning to occur, there must be meaningful peer-to-peer and student-to-professor interactions. Instructors thus must build a strong community of learners who feel safe enough to make themselves vulnerable in order to move from their comfort zones and discuss societal problems and confront their own biases that perpetuate unjust social arrangements.

According to Swan (2003), there are six best practices when designing and teaching online:

1. Create clear goals and instructions.
2. Devise varied presentation of course content.
3. Develop active and engaging learning exercises.
4. Provide students with feedback and clarity.
5. Be flexible as students are achieving their learning goals.
6. Provide students with mentoring and support.

The six principles also coincide with the person-centered approach to learning.

Brooks and Young (2015) found that timely responses to student questions and overall professor availability are critical to more facilitative relationships. Prompt responses to each student helps them feel important, highly regarded, and understood. There are many phone apps that facilitate this quick communication, and students can use these to share relevant news stories and experiences that relate to course content, further building personal connections, peer-to-peer, and professor-to-student (e.g., Bonfire, GroupMe). Demonstrating empathy, genuineness, and positive regard in course design and facilitation can be instrumental in developing student motivation and learning. It follows that when motivation increases, online students become more interactive with each other and with the professor, which may have a circular effect of further increasing motivation and engagement. Moreover, when an emotionally safe environment is present online, students have the potential to be more engaging and feel more challenged and motivated to engage in CSJ pedagogy.

In general, emotions can both help and hinder learning, are a crucial part of the learning process, and are a great influence on student learning experiences (Cleveland-Innes & Campbell, 2012). Professors who teach online should attempt to maximize positive emotions regarding the flexibility of online learning (e.g., joy, excitement, enthusiasm) and minimize negative emotions (e.g., fear, anxiety, guilt):

> Key to online environments is to acknowledge and discuss emotional tenor as much communicative information is lost without tone of voice and facial expression—emotions excepted. The exploration of emotional states that are *not* present—hidden yet influential—needs attention" (Cleveland-Innes & Campbell, 2012, p. 285).

It is crucial that professors teaching online create conditions for their students to feel secure and self-confident and to challenge them without being threatening.

Ultimately, building an online learning community begins with the individual. If a student does not feel inherently safe in an online classroom environment, they will be less likely to engage and connect with others. In order to create this sense of safety and connection, professors can embrace shared decision making and student choice, elicit student feedback throughout the course, allow for occasional confusion, and have an understanding for students who dislike a particular delivery method or expectation (Brooks & Young, 2015). In addition, instructors should create the conditions for students to evaluate themselves, determine some aspects of the course content, allow students to solve authentic problems, and share in power. Students are often neither accustomed to taking responsibility for their learning nor taking an active role in their learning (Motschnig-Pitrik, 2005).

Instructors may face some resistance because of this as students often fear the unknown or what they are not used to being asked to do. According to Reese (2015), collaboration, freedom to create knowledge, and critical thinking skills, along with an interactive instructor, are necessary in increasing engagement and participation online.

## Critical Social Justice Content: Difficult Online Conversations and Counter-Narratives

In this section, we discuss some aspects of our anti-racism educational approach. We depart from the fact that many white Americans believe that we are already living in a post-racial society—with former President Barack Obama as the norm—as opposed to a counter-story masking the real oppressions that still exist for many people of color. These perceptions equate to colorblindness. Samuels (2014) defines colorblindness, "also known as oppression-blindness. …. or identity-blindness. …. [as a situation where] [m]any white Americans believe that if they pretend not to see a person's race, then they cannot be racist" (p. 12). Colorblindness also carries the added benefit of metaphorically absolving white people of their white guilt and/or privilege, and it reinforces the validity of the meritocracy; for to acknowledge inequities, means that success is unearned.

According to Milner (2012), "Teachers cannot afford to embrace color blindness in their practices with students because teachers and their students' identities, experiences, worldviews, and consequently behaviors are intricately shaped by race" (p. 868). In other words, if teachers ignore their students' racial and other identities, they are effectively communicating to them that their life experiences, and who they are, do not matter. Rather, we need to center students' racial, cultural, and identity experiences into the classroom in order for all of our students to connect to the curriculum (DiAngelo, 2018; Gay, 2000).

Instead of an uncritical acceptance of colorblindness, we engage our students to work for anti-racism and CSJ. According to Singleton and Linton (2006), "Anti-racism can be defined as conscious and deliberate efforts to challenge the impact and perpetuation of institutions White racial power, presence, and privilege. . . . . . . . To be anti-racist is to be active" (p. 45). Likewise, anti-racist pedagogues do not ignore the history of oppressed peoples, as do so many of our schools (Loewen, 2010).

To be an anti-racist pedagogue means not only to address the difficult and complicated conversations of race and other forms of prejudice in our society but also to be mindful of the differences between minoritized and non-minoritized students sitting within the same classroom. As stated previously, these critical conversations can be more difficult online, especially if a community of learners is not first created. Students must struggle with the idea of colorblindness, and professors must create the conditions for dominant students to see how color and identity blindness can damage all students, but particularly students of color.

## Using Counter-Narratives to Motivate Students

Teaching multicultural competencies can provide students with a venue to discuss issues of race, gender, sexuality, and other -isms, and likely, the only time many dominant students are asked to do this work, but conversations about white privilege are often met with resistance and denial. From engaging in this work for many years, respectively, we have learned that most of our students feel that their predominantly white institutions are, in fact, diverse.

Adopting colorblind and "other-blind" ideologies makes it difficult to recognize systemic and institutional policies and practices; instead, our dominant students may blame their eventual students or clients for their failure to conform to dominant ideologies. For Milner (2013), for individuals from dominant groups to work in diverse settings, they must be well-versed in the following areas: cultural and racial awareness, critical reflection, and the merging of theory and practice. Milner (2013) calls attention to the possibility that "by adopting color-blind ideologies, practices, and mind-sets that ignore the importance of race, educators can contribute to and actually exacerbate the persistence of opportunity gaps" (p. 23). In essence, it is not uncommon for white college students to engage in the aforementioned denials of inequality and a general questioning of the need for multicultural education, both in their own educations and in their future classrooms or workspaces (Matias, 2016); in a pre-service diversity course, many white students have not had the opportunity to think about issues of diversity, particularly issues of race, prior to the course. Without such courses, students from dominant groups will often be oblivious to many issues faced by their eventual students or clients. In asynchronous online environments, there is much that can slip through the cracks; students can miss problematic comments that are made, and so can instructors.

Colina Neri et al. (2019) conceptualize resistance to social justice as a problem of learning; if instructors redress this resistance "through the engagement of participative decision-making rather than top-down imposition of change" (p. 201), then resistance can be reduced. Additionally, they argue that there exists a profound mismatch between professors and students in terms of their frames of reference, which reveal large gaps in racial and cultural knowledge. These mismatches can cause educators and human service professionals to misconstrue behaviors of those who differ from them.

This development becomes particularly challenging in online environments because, again, instructors are not able to gauge facial expressions, non-verbal communication, and in-the-moment reactions to critical course content. In online environments, students can pause before reacting—"hiding" behind the anonymity of online instruction, editing their responses, and masking their true feelings (Cleveland-Innes & Campbell, 2012; Colina Neri et al., 2019). Thus, teaching for CSJ online requires the mutual revelation of vulnerability.

CSJ professors can do much to better prepare their students to serve non-dominant individuals. For example, they can provide readings that include non-stereotyped, high-achieving, culturally diverse people. Racial stereotypes, including racist ideas about intelligence, combined with ideas about the underachievement of Students of Color, impact urban students' relationship to their school and overall intellectual identities (Milner, 2013). Contact theory—that is, the more contact we have with others who are different from us, the more likely relationships will form—is also relevant to these issues (Banaji & Greenwald, 2013). Providing this contact through story is the first step in dismantling the status quo, which compartmentalizes non-dominant individuals through stereotyping.

The psychology of racism and "otherism" (Gallese, 2009) has much to do with mirror neurons, areas of the brain that contribute to in-group bias, or the bias that inspires people to immediately trust those who are like them, and to distrust those unlike them. When we ask students to change their behaviors and their beliefs in order to foster the goals of CSJ, we are literally asking them to change their brains. The key to inspiring CSJ is to allow the story of the more vulnerable person to override the stereotypes held by the more hegemonic reader. But this type of racial literacy must be taught, for white people will read whiteness unless they are taught to read against whiteness (DiAngelo, 2018). According to Gallese (2009):

> Anytime we meet someone, we are implicitly aware of his or her similarity to us, because we literally embody it. The very same neural substrate is activated when actions are executed or emotions and sensations are subjectively experienced, is also activated when the same actions, emotions, and sensations are executed or experienced by others. A common underlying functional mechanism—embodied simulation—mediates our capacity to share the meaning of actions, intentions, feelings, and emotions with others, thus grounding our identification with and connectedness to others. (para. 23)

The good news is that planned interventions can in fact alter racial attitudes (Okoye-Johnson, 2011).

## Conclusion

Education and human services students are entering professions that have the potential to do harm or do good to the vulnerable people they serve. Before these students can work in the field, they must have opportunities to discuss their concerns, fears, misgivings, and biases. Our theoretical model can optimize the possibility of these conversations occurring online. We have found that utilizing the Evolving Toward Critical Social Justice: A Theoretical Model can be instrumental in dismantling stereotypes that students hold. In fact, utilizing this model can lead to increases in students' feelings of safety within the classroom. In turn, students' safety can lead to heightened levels of self-disclosure. Heightened self-disclosure may lead to a more critical examination of one's own biases and societal and institutional barriers based on various -isms. The end result in this logical chain of progression is an increased commitment to CSJ for students.

## References

Akiba, M. (2011). Identifying program characteristics for preparing pre-service teachers for diversity. *Teachers College Record, 113*(3), 658–697.

Aspy, D. N., & Roebuck, F. N. (1988). Carl Roger's contributions to education. *Person-Centered Review, 3*(1), 10–18.

Banaji, M. R., & Greenwald, A. G. (2013). *Blindspot: Hidden biases of good people.* Delacorte Press.

Bolotin Joseph, P., Luster Bravmann, S., Windschitl, M. A., Mikel, E. R., & Stewart Green, N. (2000). *Cultures of curriculum.* Lawrence Erlbaum Associates, Publishers.

Brooks, C. F., & Young, S. L. (2015). Emotion in online college classrooms: Examining the influence of perceived teacher communication behavior on students' emotional experiences. *Technology, Pedagogy and Education, 24*(4), 515–527. https://doi.org/10.1080/1475939X.2014.995215

Bureau of Labor Statistics. (2019). *Employed persons by detailed occupation, sex, race, and Hispanic or Latino ethnicity.* https://www.bls.gov/cps/cpsaat11.htm

Cleveland-Innes, M., & Campbell, P. (2012). Emotional presence, learning, and the online learning environment. *The International Review of Research in Open in Distance Learning, 13*(4), 269–292. https://doi.org/10.19173/irrodl.v13i4.1234

Colina Neri, R., Lozano, M., & Gomez, L. M. (2019). (Re)framing resistance to culturally relevant education as a multilevel learning problem. *Review of Research in Education, 43*, 197–226. https://doi.org/10.3102%2F0091732X18821120

DiAngelo, R. (2018). *White fragility: Why it's so hard for white people to talk about racism.* Beacon Press.

Gallese, V. (2009). Mirror neurons, embodied simulation, and the neural basis of social identification. *Psychoanalytic Dialogues, 19*(5), 519–536.

Gay, G. (2000). *Culturally responsive teaching: Theory, research and practice.* Teachers College Press.

Goff, P. A., Jackson, M. C., Di Leone, B. A., L., Culotta, C. M., & DiTomasso, N. A. (2014). The essence of innocence: Consequences of dehumanizing black children. *Journal of Personality and Social Psychology, 106*(4), 526–545.

Leonardo, Z. (2016). Foreword. In C. Matias (Ed.), *Feeling white: Whiteness, emotionality, and education.* Sense Publishers.

Loewen, J. W. (2010). *Teaching what really happened: How to avoid the tyranny of textbooks and get students excited about doing history.* Teachers College Press.

Martin, J. L. (Ed.). (2015). *Racial battle fatigue: Insights from the front lines of social justice advocacy.* Praeger.

Martin, J. L., & Beese, J. A. (2020). Moving beyond the lecture: Inspiring social justice engagement through counter-story using case study pedagogy. *The Educational Forum, 84*(3), 210–215. https://doi.org/10.1080/00131725.2020.1730531

Matias, C. (2016). *Feeling white: Whiteness, emotionality, and education.* Sense Publishers.

Mayhew, M. J., & Deluca Fernandez, S. (2007). Pedagogical practices that contribute to social justice outcomes. *The Review of Higher Education, 31*(1), 55–80.

Milner, H. R. (2012). Losing the color-blind mind in the urban classroom. *Urban Education, 47*(5), 868–875.

Milner, H. R. (2013). *Start where you are, but don't stay there: Understanding diversity, opportunity gaps, and teaching in today's classrooms.* Harvard Education Press.

Motschnig-Pitrik, R. (2005). Person-centered e-learning in action: Can technology help to manifest person-centered values in academic environments. *Journal of Humanistic Psychology, 45*(4), 503–530. https://doi.org/10.1177%2F0022167805279816

Okoye-Johnson, O. (2011). Does multicultural education improve students' racial attitudes? Implications for closing the achievement gap. *Journal of Black Studies, 42*(8), 1252–1274. https://doi.org/10.1177%2F0021934711408901

O'Sullivan, P. B., Hunt, S. R., & Lippert, L. R. (2004). Mediated immediacy: A language of affiliation in a technological age. *Journal of Language and Social Psychology, 23*(4), 464–490.

Paulsen, J., & McCormick, A. C. (2020). Reassessing disparities in online learner student engagement in higher education. *Educational Researcher, 49*(1), 20–29. https://doi.org/10.3102%2F0013189X19898690

Reese, S. A. (2015). Online learning environments in higher education: Connectivism vs. dissociation. *Education Information Technology, 20*(3), 579–588. https://doi.org/10.1007/s10639-013-9303-7

Rogers, C. R. (1969). *Freedom to learn.* Charles E. Merrill Publishing Company.

Rogers, C. R. (1983). *Freedom to learn for the 80s.* Charles E. Merrill Publishing Company.

Rogers, C. R., Lyon, H. C., & Tausch, R. (2014). *On becoming an effective teacher: Person-centered teaching, psychology, philosophy, and dialogues with Carl R. Rogers and Harold C. Lyon, Jr.* Routledge.

Samuels, D. R. (2014). *The culturally inclusive educator: Preparing for a multicultural world.* New York, NY: Teachers College Press.

Singleton, G. E., & Linton, C. (2006). *Courageous conversations about race: A field guide for achieving equity in schools.* Thousand Oaks, CA: Corwin Press.

Swan, K. (2003). Learning effectiveness: What the research tells us. In J. Bourne & J. C. Moore (Eds.), *Elements of quality online education: Practice and direction* (pp. 13–45). Sloan-C.

Swan, K. P., Richardson, J. C., Ice, P., Garrison, D. R., Cleveland-Innes, M., & Arbaugh, J. B. (2008). Validating a measurement tool of presence in online communities of inquiry. *e-mentor, 2*(24). http://www.e-mentor.edu.pl/artykul/index/numer/24/id/543

Tausch, R., & Huls, R. (2014). Students, patients, and employees cry out for empathy. In C. R. Rogers, H. C. Lyon, & R. Tausch Jr. (Eds.), *On becoming an effective: Person-centered teaching, psychology, philosophy, and dialogues with Carl R. Rogers and Harold Lyon.* Routledge.

Whiteside, A. L., Garrett Dikkers, A., & Swan, K. (Eds.). (2017). *Social presence in online learning.* Online Learning Consortium.

CHAPTER THIRTEEN

# Ignatian Pedagogy Online[1]

MARGARET DEBELIUS, KIMBERLY HUISMAN LUBRESKI, MINDY MCWILLIAMS, JAMES OLSEN, LEE SKALLERUP BESSETTE, AND YIANNA VOVIDES

As universities around the world face the aftermath of a pandemic that forced them to teach virtually, the need to design online courses that teach to the whole person has never been more urgent. Electronic connections matter, but human connections matter more. This chapter explores how Ignatian pedagogy, a teaching and learning approach central to a Jesuit education, can inform the design of online courses. We begin with a comparison of critical pedagogy and Ignatian pedagogy, noting the points of intersection as well as important differences between the approaches. Through the example of two courses being taught at Georgetown University in Washington, DC, this chapter will show how the elements and principles of Ignatian pedagogy and critical pedagogy were used as a framework to guide the design of two undergraduate courses: an online Introduction to Ethics course and a hybrid Gender, Immigration and Social Justice course. We conclude with some considerations about the future of critical and Ignatian digital pedagogy.

The term "critical pedagogy" has undergone many transformations, as definitions and taxonomies have evolved out of different social, historical, and disciplinary contexts. Thus, while there is no universally agreed upon definition of critical pedagogy, there are several core principles that underlie critical pedagogies, including an emphasis on social justice; raising students' self-awareness and critical consciousness around issues of equity and inclusivity; meaningful dialogue and reflection; the importance of praxis; and empowering students as agents in their own learning.

Many of these same principles underlie Ignatian pedagogy, a method of teaching and learning promoted at Jesuit colleges and universities, which has its roots in the 16th century spiritual exercises of St. Ignatius of Loyola, the founder of the Society of Jesus (Jesuits). Ignatian pedagogy was formalized in a 1993 document written by the International Commission on the Apostolate of Jesuit Education (ICAJE) to extend Ignatian values and constructs into a practical pedagogy for teachers and their students (ICAJE, 1993). According to Sharon Korth:

> The Ignatian pedagogical paradigm is a practical teaching framework that is consistent with and effective in communicating the Ignatian values and worldview. Faculty, regardless of discipline, can utilize this approach so that their teaching is academically sound and at the same time formative of persons for others. (Korth, 2008, p. 280)

Ignatian pedagogy, also called the Ignatian pedagogical paradigm, involves an interplay between the following five elements: context, experience, reflection, action, and evaluation. These elements are intended to guide the design of learning experiences, inclusive of teacher-student, peer-to-peer, and student-content engagements, and, we argue, can provide a robust framework for designing online learning experiences that stay true to many of the ideals and aspirations of transformational learning—another commonality between critical and Ignatian pedagogies.

Previous authors (see Merys, 2016 and Pace and Merys, 2016) have identified the complementarity and similarity between Ignatian and critical pedagogy in much the same ways that feminist, queer, postcolonial, and inclusive pedagogies have been identified or compared to critical pedagogy. For example, a number of Jesuit institutions of higher education with schools of education have worked with preservice teachers to help them see the connections between critical and Ignatian pedagogy in order to strive for socially just teaching (Chubbuck, 2007) and to "challenge students' preconceived notions about people who are culturally, linguistically, and socioeconomically different from them by forcing students to rethink their long-held conceptions of the world" (Foster, 2012, pp. 134–135). In their essay on contemporary Ignatian Pedagogy, Mountin and Nowacek (2012) link Ignatian and critical pedagogy through their shared focus on student experience and link Ignatian with feminist pedagogy through the shared concept of knowledge-in-action (p. 137).

Pace and Merys (2016) point out the commonalities between critical and Ignatian elements of context, praxis, transformation, and the cyclical nature of each:

> When analyzed carefully, it can be seen that the learning cycle Freire sets up in his theories includes similar complex elements [to Ignatian pedagogy], beginning with a sharp and intentional awareness of context and moving to the core of his theories, *praxis* (action + reflection), and ending with a transformational experience that interpellates us to continue the cycle, going ever deeper into knowledge and naming (*word*) of the world. (pp. 244–245)

The same authors identify Paulo Freire's Catholic upbringing and Jesuit education as influences on his eventual development of the critical pedagogy cycle; not surprisingly, perhaps, as Paulo Freire interacted significantly with Jesuit educators, who were themselves influenced by liberation theology and the concept of striving to move toward greater freedom. Despite this similarity, Jesuit emphasis on liberation was typically in the context of moving closer to God, rather than the political or emancipatory meaning common in critical theory. Pace and Merys (2016) also give a much more thorough examination of the philosophical similarities between Ignatian pedagogy and critical pedagogy than there is space for here.

In Table 13.1, we set the five elements of Ignatian pedagogy next to Freire's critical pedagogy cycle in order to illuminate some of the parallels, as well as areas of divergence, between the two models. Note that the elements of Ignatian pedagogy are typically presented in the order of context, experience, reflection, action and evaluation, but they are re-ordered here to more closely parallel the critical pedagogy cycle. In critical pedagogy, the focus of the first step, conscientization, is on the coming to consciousness of the learner of their own contextual situation, while in Ignatian pedagogy, the first step focuses on the teacher and their coming to understand the context of the learner. While both are grounded in the teacher-learner relationship, critical pedagogy is more learner-centered in this first step and Ignatian pedagogy more teacher-centered. Theory (in critical pedagogy) and experience (in Ignatian pedagogy) tend to indicate similar aspects of the cycle, where students begin to critically assess and understand their own experiences. Similarly, application and action both emphasize a practical doing as necessary for, and the natural result of, transformational learning.

Table 13.1: Comparing the Critical Pedagogy and Ignatian Pedagogy Cycles

| Critical Pedagogy | Ignatian Pedagogy |
|---|---|
| Conscientization | Context |
| Theory | Experience |
| Application | Action |
| Evaluation | Evaluation |
| Reflection | Reflection |

Source: Author

As Table 13.1 demonstrates, these two pedagogical approaches align, with Freire clearly having been influenced by his own experiences with Jesuit education. But despite the parallelism and similarly named components such as reflection and evaluation, there are some important differences between the Ignatian and Freirean models of learning. One key difference to note between critical and Ignatian pedagogy concerns power. Critical pedagogy is concerned with how relationships of power are produced and can be challenged in educational contexts, while Ignatian pedagogy has its roots in an inherently patriarchal system, the priesthood. There also could be a difference between an understanding of who or what is being transformed through this process: the individual or society? It appears Ignatian pedagogy is more explicitly concerned with individual formation and growth, especially that which brings one closer to God, whereas critical pedagogy focuses more on radical societal change.[2] The Ignatian-Jesuit concept of *cura personalis*, or care of the person, and the traditional mentor-student spiritual and educational pairings illustrates this focus on the individual rather than on the larger society. While both pedagogies clearly hold the values of social justice at their cores, the explicit religious and spiritual components of Ignatian pedagogy understandably make some critical pedagogues uncomfortable. According to Chubbuck (2007), "Both critical pedagogy and Ignatian pedagogy have conceptual roots in Christian faith, though Ignatian pedagogy remains closely aligned to faith while critical pedagogy only slightly references those origins in favor of postmodernism's resistance to any meta-narrative of belief" (p. 260).

Figure 13.1, which we developed for the purposes of this study, illustrates the intersection between critical and Ignatian pedagogies. It takes the connections between critical and Ignatian pedagogies highlighted in Table 13.1 and visualizes the intersections as concentric circles stemming from the core circle that is focused on action or application. These circles are not static but rather always in motion; in this visual, the movement is in a clockwise direction. Evaluation and reflection are part of the outer circle of the image as they envelop and inform context and conscientization, experience and theory leading to action and application. As the arrows show, evaluation influences reflection, and reflection influences evaluation creating a continuous flow of inputs to inform context and deepen our conscientization of the context itself. Note that the arrows cut across all layers of the model as both evaluation and reflection are also informed by action and application, by experience and theory, and context and conscientization.

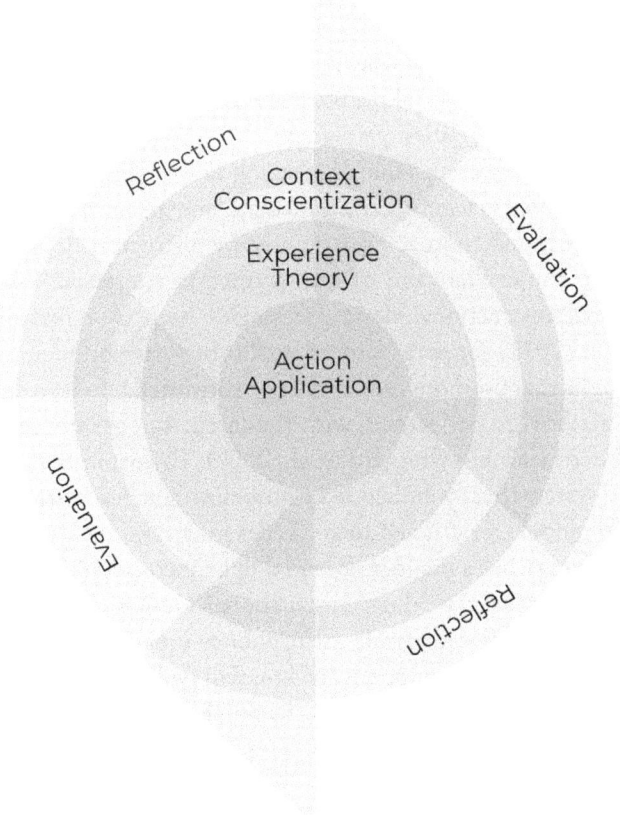

Figure 13.1: Intersections of Critical Pedagogy and Ignatian Pedagogy. Source: Author

Several Jesuit institutions have begun to explore what Ignatian pedagogy looks like when it moves online, including Fordham, Boston College, The University of San Francisco, Gonzaga, University of Loyola Chicago, Regis, and others. The common thrust has been to apply individual values or characteristics of Jesuit education to online learning, such as *cura personalis* or *eloquentia perfecta*.

However, few have applied the Ignatian pedagogical paradigm with its five distinct elements directly to an online course as a framework for the course and learning experience design. An exception to this is Kreimeyer and Huntington's (2018) paper which describes the infusion of the five elements of Ignatian pedagogy to the online certificate in Counseling Military Families offered at Regis University. And although not addressing Jesuit or Ignatian teaching or values, Boyd (2016) argues that critical pedagogy has a lot to offer online course designers and instructors in terms of countering the banking-oriented approach to learning, creating constructivist, democratic classrooms, creating creative approaches to embodied learning in a disembodied context, and creating community and connections. So, we ask here, what might it look like to design an online course that attempts to take advantage of the possibilities and alignment of critical pedagogy and Ignatian pedagogy?

At first glance, the Ignatian value of teaching to the whole person may seem at odds with an online course where screens mediate human contact, but the Ignatian pedagogical elements and approach can be used by instructors designing their online courses, with the explicit aim of transformation and social justice (Rogers, 2019). Intentional instructional design strategies such as reflection amplifiers (Verpoorten et al., 2011) support learners' intellectual development toward transformation. Designs that promote such higher quality interactions in online courses, be it with the material to be learned, with the instructor, or between peers, positively affect student learning (Bernard et al., 2009). To ensure that these types of interactions are systematically embedded into online courses, instructional design frameworks and models are utilized to guide designers and instructors.

Ignatian pedagogy has a distinct potential to be incorporated into such design frameworks. For example, the Magis Instructional Design (ID) Model (Rogers, 2019) for online courses systematically incorporates Ignatian pedagogy in the design process, where the five components of Ignatian pedagogy noted in Table 13.1 are integrated in the following eight steps in order to teach to the whole person online:

1. Analyze human learning experience online/offline
2. Establish relationships of mutual respect online/offline
3. Tap into learner's prior knowledge & experience
4. Design optimal learning experience for whole person
5. Assimilate new information
6. Transfer learning into lifeworld
7. Encourage lifelong learning & reflections beyond self-interest
8. Learners become contemplatives in action

Designing with an instructional model in mind allows instructors or designers to deepen their reflective practice by surfacing their design choices and making them visible to their students. Below we lay out two case studies that illustrate how an Ignatian-critical approach can be used in designing hybrid and online courses. The cases are two undergraduate courses at Georgetown University: (1) an online Introduction to Ethics course, and (2) a hybrid Gender, Immigration and Social Justice course. These case studies speak to both the learner and the instructor experience. Our intent is to highlight the holistic potential and benefit of the Ignatian-critical approach in the online space.

## Case Study 1: Introduction to Ethics Online

Iteration is a key element of Jesuit practice and online course design. Professor James Olsen's experience teaching Introduction to Ethics at Georgetown is a case in point, one where the key elements of Ignatian pedagogy were intentionally leveraged not only to improve the course as a whole, but specifically to think through how to transform a traditional course for an online iteration. With yearly revisions, multiple sections of the course have now run for four years.

The original face-to-face iteration was heavily influenced by critical theory and pedagogy to focus not merely on conveying to students the content of normative ethical theory (or the theory of ethical action), but to utilize normative ethics as a means to personally explore and engage issues of injustice, the systems that contribute to injustice, and issues of personal and collective responsibility with regard to that injustice. Each unit of the course focused on a different normative ethical theory and ended with readings applying that theory to the topics of global poverty and treatment of non-human animals. The final unit wove together themes of responsibility, hope, and pursuing a meaningful life in an intentional effort to merge Freire's pedagogies of freedom and of hope.

While redesigning the course to run online, Olsen attended a lecture on Ignatian pedagogy. Recognizing the resonance between critical and Ignatian pedagogies, he saw the latter as a means to more fully instantiate the original "critical" goals of the course in a specifically online context. In particular, he sensed an opportunity to work through what he took to be his main challenge: How does one focus on local issues of oppression among a dispersed group of students in an entirely asynchronous online course? The online course is offered only in the summer session to undergraduates spending the term either at home or traveling to other locations for job or internship opportunities.

Attempting to maintain a critical-inspired course by leveraging Ignatian pedagogy, Olsen's overall goal was for his online class to serve as a site where students were compelled to grapple with three unavoidable variables of their lives: their identities as individuals, how these identities and their individual experiences relate to universal moral norms, and how this relation specifically plays out (or ought to play out) in their lives as members of Georgetown University. In earlier face-to-face versions of the class, Olsen used the large issues of poverty and animal ethics to cap off each unit and would occasionally bring in articles and issues happening at Georgetown to punctuate the discussion; however, the online version built each module around a specific issue of social justice currently animating students at Georgetown. In this way, students dispersed across the globe were able to focus on a shared and local context that became their case study for ethical analysis, and this analysis was explicitly oriented around the practical moral upshot for each individual student in their lives as members of a shared community.

Another key change was to double down on writing activities and assignments as a means of implementing the Ignatian concept of *eloquentia perfecta*: the use of "language and rhetoric to be informed, ethical, sympathetic, and articulate writers and speakers, willing and committed to engage with their larger communities through the careful use of words" (Pace & Merys, 2016, p. 234). Reading quizzes became content retention tools rather than graded assessments, and students tacked back and forth between personal reflection and formal essays in each module. This assessment structure served as an invitation to students to continually articulate their self-understanding and rational positions as a means of self-transformation oriented explicitly around local issues of justice.

Ignatian pedagogy is holistic in nature—emphasizing "educating the whole person" rather than more narrow goals like increasing critical thinking skills—and in practice its elements are dynamic and overlapping. This was certainly true for Olsen's online course, with various assignments and activities serving more than one purpose. As a means of analysis, however, we find it suggestive and helpful to structure the remainder of this section around the cornerstone elements of Ignatian pedagogy: context, experience, reflection, action, and evaluation. Each subsection is structured by a look at course goals, course structure, activities, and assessment, and a reflection on particular affordances of the online format. We hope that this analysis offers readers an opportunity for practical reflection on harnessing critical and Ignatian pedagogy online.

## Context

"Teachers … …. should take account of … …. the institutional environment of the school or learning centre, i.e. the complex and often subtle network of norms, expectations and especially relationships that create the atmosphere of school life" (ICAJE, 1993, p. 11).

*Goals*: Georgetown University—as a shared context for a diverse and distributed set of students—was itself a critical design element, manifest in the structure of the course. Among the higher-order course goals and more narrow learning objectives, context was prominent. For example, the fifth course goal focused on students as embedded community members, asking them to reflect seriously on:

- What it means to be authentic and to flourish as a Georgetown University student;
- The concrete practices in which you're currently engaged in order to promote your overall well-being, both in your individual life and as a member of our Georgetown community; and
- Changes you would like to make in order to further promote your own and our community's flourishing.

In addition to the embedded Georgetown context, course goals included a focus on the inescapably philosophical and ethical context of their historically embedded lives (e.g., noting that "you are always already doing philosophy" and inviting students to intentionally "participate in a moral dialogue several millennia old").

*Structure, Activities, Assessment*: The course structure itself was a major component of the redesign that highlighted the Georgetown context. Following an introduction to major normative theories, subsequent modules explored philosophical issues in a local Georgetown context, including:

- Relativism & Authenticity
- Slavery, Memory, and Reconciliation
- Climate Change
- Responsibility & Solidarity
- Capabilities & Flourishing
- Conclusions: (Y) Our Life at Georgetown

As a list, all but the last of these is recognizable as topics in ethics, broadly applicable on most campuses. Anyone who has been a member of Georgetown's campus community for the last several years, however, will also recognize each of these as major topics of local discussion and concern. Intermingled with scholarly articles on these topics, each module introduced class members to related student activist groups on campus, articles and editorials in local and campus newspapers, and campus bodies such as the Working Group on Slavery, Memory and Reconciliation, which studies how the university can best address its legacy of slavery on campus. This intermingling was reinforced by writing assignments that explicitly took Georgetown as a case study.

*Online Affordances*: A similar focus on local context and mode of engagement is possible (and worthwhile!) in a traditional course. There were, however, specific affordances of the online environment that lent emphasis to and helped to promote these aspects relating to context. The online platform (in this case, the Canvas learning management system) allowed the home page to visually display the course structure and narrative and so reinforce student understanding of this narrative each time they logged in. Second is the ease of technological integration. Of particular note for this class was the use of mobile polling, offering students an engaging way to respond to course content in real time as they consumed course materials. Polling data made the views of others immediately visible, which helped to establish relationships of understanding and respect in the online space, as described in the Magis ID model.

## Experience

"….. any activity in which in addition to a cognitive grasp of the matter being considered, some sensation of an affective nature is registered by the student" (ICAJE, 1993, p. 12).

*Goals*: In addition to promulgating key concepts and principles, the course was structured to continuously ask students: What do you bring to this discussion? What does this discussion mean to you personally? While several course goals aimed not only for students to cognitively grasp the course material but for this material to register on a personal level; one, unabashedly so: "Come to either 'give a damn' or 'give more of a damn'."

*Structure, Activities, Assessment*: The course's main strategy on this end was to continually show the students that the elements of life about which they already cared deeply were unavoidably ethical in nature and thus directly related to the course content. To use words from the Magis ID Model (Rogers, 2019), students were asked to "transfer learning into lifeworld." In addition to using Georgetown as a case study as described above, an important way in which this was accomplished was by focusing on personal authenticity as a moral value and on the nature of moral responsibility. In the wake of philosophical readings on authenticity, each student wrote a letter to a fictional stranger analyzing whether and to what degree the student considered her or himself to be authentic and what that meant vis-à-vis the student's sense of identity. Having articulated this self-conception, students grappled in readings, reflections, online polls, and writing assignments with the implications of their identity and especially how it relates to issues of responsibility.

*Online Affordances*: The online platform allowed students to continually be solicited concerning their topics of concern. This was done via polls, discussion boards, and asynchronous but collective projects. These allowed for an immediate as well as a slower, more deliberate and polished kind of discourse. Such activities are also available within a traditional class, but they are typically made available (or practicable) only via online technologies.

Reflection

"..... a thoughtful reconsideration of some subject matter, experience, idea, purpose or spontaneous reaction, in order to grasp its significance more fully" (ICAJE, 1993, p. 14).

*Goals*: As made clear in the *context* section, goals and objectives related to reflection were prominent. The fourth course goal—related to empathy—included the learning objective to "Reflect on your own positionality and how this positionality grants you certain privileges and carries certain constraints." This objective is an example of the way that critical and Ignatian pedagogy were brought together in the online iteration of the course.

*Structure, Activities, Assessment*: The most significant way in which reflection was instantiated in the course was by means of specific reflection papers assigned to each module. This was a significant change from the course's earlier iteration and one of its more conspicuous Ignatian features. These reflections were placed at the end of each module and tasked students with synthesizing that module's content with experiences from their life. While acknowledging the less formal nature of these assignments and the "intention that it be enjoyable," students were nevertheless exhorted to take the task seriously and given a rubric and specific criteria to follow, such as the need to be concrete and utilize specific passages of text in their reflection.

*Online Affordances*: As with *experience*, the specific tools available for reflectively engaging students are available for the traditional classroom. Importantly, however, online technologies facilitate and make practicable students' ability to read and respond to one another's reflections. For example, the "authenticity letters" mentioned earlier were anonymized and randomly distributed, with every student offering a candid response to the letter they received. These responses were in turn anonymized and returned to each letter's author. (Both letters and responses were read by the instructor prior to their distributions so interventions could be made when needed.) Although first implemented in the course's traditional iteration, the anonymization, random distribution, and returns were a laborious, time-intensive process. Embedding the activity online dramatically simplified the process.

## Action

"..... internal human growth based upon experience that has been reflected upon as well as its manifestation externally" (ICAJE, 1993, p. 16).

*Goals*: One objective was to "Reflect on changes you would like to make in order to further promote your own and our community's flourishing." The focus on topics of student concern within the students' shared local context was intended as a catalyst for action.

*Structure, Activities, Assessment*: As part of an assignment, students were tasked with entering the community and engaging with its activists. "Engagement Points" assignments in each module contained multiple options, but all students were tasked at least once with going into their current community (wherever that might be), identifying, and attending an activist event of some kind. Specifically, students were instructed to:

- **Attend any local event** that fits the criterion (i.e., an explicit activist event)
- Your attendance **must last at least one hour**; you are welcome to participate or merely spectate as you feel appropriate
- You **must talk to someone who is participating**; ask the participant **questions** that will help you better understand the moral values or assumptions that motivate their work

Students then wrote a reflection on the experience wherein the activist's animating moral values were articulated and related to course readings. The intent was to provide an internal and external experience related to the course content that students otherwise would not gain.

*Online Affordances*: The key online affordance for this activity was the way that it allowed for variability of location. An earlier variation ran in a traditional class yielded a fairly small range of events and issues. The online version yielded significantly greater diversity, showcasing "local community activism" from all over the globe. Additionally, it exposed many students to community activism in their hometowns. The online platform allowed for this diversity and the multiplication of *local*.

## Evaluation

"..... aims at formation which includes but goes beyond academic mastery. Here we are concerned about students' well-rounded growth as persons for others" (ICAJE, 1993, p. 17).

*Goals*: In addition to the reflection-related goals discussed above, one learning objective in particular took its cue directly from the Ignatian concept of *evaluation*: "Recognize your interdependence with others and identify ways in which your actions impact (positively and negatively) others, both locally and globally."

*Structure, Activities, Assessment*: Again, the reflection papers offered unique access to the ways in which students were personally and affectively responding to course content. The course also incorporated more traditional pre-, mid-, and post-surveys. Perhaps most importantly, each module ended with a "Muddiest Point" prompt that allowed students to share whatever was least clear or most difficult about that module. Responses ranged from noting particularly dense material, to difficulties digesting certain troubling topics, to requests for changes in course design. This was a particularly helpful form of assessment, allowing the professor to respond collectively or in a personal way to students as needed.

*Online Affordances*: Meeting with students individually is a key element of Ignatian evaluation. This can be trickier in an online class without informal opportunities for questions and conversations and where students are not able to physically attend office hours. This fact is exacerbated in an asynchronous course where students and instructor do not even share a time zone. This context necessitates a more individualized approach. Embedded videoconferencing within Canvas allows for live, face-to-face appointments. It also raises the possibility of unreasonable demands being made on faculty time and availability. If addressed explicitly with students, however, this challenge is relatively easy to meet, making online office hours potentially more flexible and personalized for students.

Shifting this Introduction to Ethics course from a traditional course to one completely online allowed for the infusion of additional elements of Ignatian and critical pedagogy compared to the face-to-face version. Drawing on thoughtful instructional design principles and affordances of technology, the redesigned course enabled students to reflect and act even more deeply than in previous versions of the course. Giving up regular face-to-face contact did not mean giving up care for the context and perspectives of individual students. The online version of the course shows great promise in developing learners who are contemplatives in action, which will be an area of further study.

## Case Study 2: Gender, Immigration, and Social Justice: A Hybrid Model

Over the past nineteen years, Professor Kim Huisman Lubreski has taught multiple versions of an undergraduate course on gender and immigration—at three different institutions, using three different learning management systems, and under four different presidential administrations. While the readings and political landscape have varied considerably over these years, the one constant has been the semester-long project where students interview someone who immigrated to the U.S. This assignment grew directly out of Huisman Lubreski's dissertation experience and commitment to the tenets of critical pedagogy, feminist ethnographic research, and Jesuit humanism. This section describes the background of the course and explains how it evolved from a face-to-face course focused on service-learning and reciprocity to a technology-enhanced course focused on service-learning, reciprocity, and the Jesuit concept of *cura personalis*, to a hybrid course that is deeply rooted in the five multilayered tenets of Ignatian pedagogy—context, experience, reflection, action, and evaluation—as well as the Jesuit ideals of *eloquentia perfecta* and *cura personalis*. Her experience shows how the Ignatian-critical approach can be transformative not only for students but instructors as well.

Back in 2000, Huisman Lubreski was deeply immersed in her dissertation fieldwork, an ethnographic study exploring the ways in which gender relations and identities were changing among Bosnian Muslim refugees who had resettled in Vermont. While doing this research, it became obvious that although gender relations and identities were indeed undergoing considerable changes in this new context, given the tremendous loss and upheaval Bosnians had experienced through war and relocation, gender was generally not a key concern of the refugees. Additionally, Huisman Lubreski could not shake the nagging feeling that she was gaining far more than her research participants and decided to address this asymmetry. In the interest of reciprocity, she obtained funding for twenty garden plots for families to grow their own food, an idea that came about after hearing repeatedly from participants that one of the things they missed most about their homes was having a yard where they could grow fresh vegetables.

Huisman Lubreski was teaching sociology at the University of Vermont at the time, which allowed her to apply her fieldwork to a course she was designing on gender and immigration. This face-to-face course was grounded in feminist reciprocal principles, where students engaged in a semester-long project in which they worked collaboratively with a recent immigrant to record some aspect of their immigration story that the interviewee elected to have documented. Upon completion of the assignment, students provided their interviewee with an audio recording of the interview, a transcript, and a copy of the final paper. Huisman Lubreski continued to teach this course for many years, striving to improve it with each iteration, drawing on the critical pedagogies of bell hooks and Paulo Freire with the intent of encouraging students to understand intersectionalities and inequalities, to focus on social justice, to see themselves as agents of change, and to increase the likelihood that participation in the interview would have meaning and relevance for the students' and participants' lives.

In addition to emphasizing service and reciprocity, the course also expanded to include the principle of *cura personalis*, which translates as "care of the person." It is a distinguishing characteristic of Jesuit education and emphasizes individualized attention to the needs of each student and respect for his or her unique circumstances. One option for integrating *cura personalis* into one's teaching at Georgetown is the Engelhard Project (see Valtin et al., 2018), which focuses on the development of a pedagogy of "curriculum infusion," based on the integration of college health and well-being issues into the content of academic courses. This approach was a very good fit for this course since students would be learning about the Jesuit approach to immigration justice in the classroom and hearing personal stories from immigrants themselves—in many cases, stories of loss and hardship, some from close relatives—outside of the classroom. It was essential that measures were taken to show care and concern for the well-being of the students and that they, in turn, felt a responsibility for both the care and well-being of themselves, the people they were interviewing, and for their fellow classmates.

Student feedback from written reflections on the course indicates the degree to which students felt the course addressed care of the person. One student stated:

> I appreciated the focus on self-care that this course allows because I think that it made the class more likely to stay with me as I move further into my college career ... I thought that the course catered to my needs educationally and well-being wise.

Another reported, "In addition to making me reflect on my own path, this course demonstrated to me that I'm not alone ... it helped me make connections between myself and the larger context."

Another aspect of the course that evolved over time was the use of technology. In the early years of teaching the course, it was fully face-to-face with students using analog cassette recorders to record the interviews. Over time, cassette recorders were replaced with digital recorders and phones, and online components were also gradually added to the course. The most recent iteration of the course, titled "Gender, Immigration, and Social Justice," was designed as a technology-enhanced course, using online components to supplement, but not replace, face-to-face time. In addition, the semester-long project was redesigned to have students create a three-part podcast rather than a final paper, in which they told their interviewee's story by placing it within the larger contexts of exit and reception. For the next iteration of the course, Huisman Lubreski will be moving from a technology-enhanced course where face-to-face content was supplemented with online components, to a hybrid course, where she is selectively replacing some face-to-face time with online time. A key element of the course redesign for the online space is the expansion of the three-part podcasting project that includes an introduction, historical background, and an interview with a recent immigrant that places the interviewee's biography within a broader social and historical context.[3]

The podcasting assignment highlights another key Ignatian principle, that of *eloquentia perfecta*, a Latin phrase that means "perfect eloquence" and emphasizes the importance of cultivating the whole person by using speech and communication for the common good. Pace and Merys (2016) write that *eloquentia perfecta* "calls us to use speech or communication that focuses on truth, accuracy, and comprehensiveness as a path into the world, especially used in order to stand for the silenced, excluded or impoverished" (p. 245). For the podcast assignments, students use writing and speech (their own as well as their interviewees) to tell their interviewees' stories, their truth, and connect these stories to the larger context. *Eloquentia perfecta* is similar to Freire's emphasis on the importance of "the word," which can be used to transform the world. Pace and Meyrs (2016) describe the connection between Freire's critical pedagogy and Ignatian pedagogy:

> The idea that speaking ... is the right of all, and that speaking evokes dialogue that has the capacity to change the world, which is to be transformed and humanized, especially for and from those who have been silenced, excluded, or impoverished, parallels what the Jesuit rhetorical tradition has been advocating for centuries. (p. 245)

Students described the podcast assignment as transformative and deeply meaningful for themselves and their interviewees, but due to IRB restrictions, podcasts could only be shared in the class and with the interviewee. Students uploaded their podcast components to the class discussion board and provided each other with peer feedback, which was rich and engaging. However, in order to further the commitment to *eloquentia perfecta*, steps are being taken to obtain IRB approval for students to share the podcasts publicly, in the interest of increasing the visibility of the stories and speaking for the public good.

In what follows, we walk through the five elements of Ignatian pedagogy, highlighting examples of how the hybrid course on Gender, Immigration, and Social Justice will be redesigned so that it is more deeply and explicitly grounded in Ignatian pedagogy. In doing so, we identify how moving some aspects of the course online carve out space for more hands-on work in the classroom. While each element is addressed separately, it is important to keep in mind Figure 13.1, illustrating the interconnected, complex web of elements with overlapping layers of meaning.

## Context

Like other critical pedagogies, Ignatian pedagogy emphasizes the importance of context by beginning with the question, "Who are the students?" and calling on teachers to become as familiar as possible with the world of the students (Tobin, 2012). As a sociologist, Huisman Lubreski viewed context as central to all aspects of the course, reflected in three of the current learning objectives, "Demonstrate a sociological imagination by examining the interplay between social context and biography," "Explain the Jesuit approach to social justice," and "Examine how race, class, gender, religion, and sexuality are interconnected and affect the lived experiences of immigrants." Student feedback illustrates that these learning objectives were largely achieved. The following quote from a student captures this, while also illustrating how context is interconnected with the other elements of Ignatian pedagogy:

> It was particularly meaningful to have a space to reflect on immigration, and how much it has influenced my own life and identity. This class encouraged a space of reflection with other peers on what role immigration has in each of our lives, and to further attempt to learn how this influences our well-being. The use of Mills' sociological lens in compilation with my peers' immigration narratives enabled me to understand my context in a greater light, and feel an overwhelming sense of gratitude for that context that I am in.

Context was central to all of the course assignments—students had to place their own story within the larger context for the sociological autobiography paper and their two-minute introductory podcast, and they had to place their interviewee's story within the larger context for the podcast assignment. Although these assignments provided opportunities to get to know the students and the contexts which have shaped students' lives, Huisman Lubreski is adding another learning objective to more explicitly address the classroom context, which will require students to "explore how context and positionalities impact relationships in the classroom and with interviewees." Students will also introduce themselves online during the first week of class by responding to a few questions about their background, the larger context, and also adding a pin to a Google map indicating where they are from. Students will also add their interviewees to the Google map along with a brief description of their background. The visual representation will further contextualize the background and diversity of students and interviewees.

## Experience

According to the ICAJE (1993) document, experience means "to taste something internally" (ICAJE, 1993, p. 12). In Ignatian pedagogy, learning experiences must engage students as whole persons and include activities that propel students to go beyond a cognitive understanding "because without internal feeling joined to intellectual grasp, learning will not move a person to action" (ICAJE, 1993, p. 12). In Ignatian pedagogy, human experience can be direct or vicarious, and in the hybrid course, students will have opportunities for both. The three-part podcasting assignment that students engage in brings students into direct contact with the lived experience of someone who immigrated to the United States. These direct experiences take place synchronously, whereas the indirect, vicarious experience of carefully listening to each other's podcasts will take place online, where students will not be constrained by the limited class time and can give each of their peers their full attention. The direct and vicarious experiences proved to be an emotional, moving, and in some cases, transformative experience for students that deepened some students' commitment to social justice. One student captured this sentiment when she wrote:

> This course has helped me understand how courses really should be. Learning can't happen in an environment where people are so disconnected from the material ... There is nothing really impersonal about learning—it's a process that happens internally and makes us grow, so it cannot happen without some sort of reflection or internalization about what is happening.

Listening to each other's podcasts was meaningful for students and furthered their understanding of the immigrant experience, as expressed by one student who said, "This class allowed us to delve deeper into the well-being of the immigrant and to better understand the intense emotional burden a migration journey may have on an individual." In the hybrid course, additional opportunities will be provided, in the classroom and online, for students to connect with each other to share and make meaning of their own experiences.

## Reflection

In this course, students were asked to reflect about their own lives and those of their interviewee, in relation to what they were learning in the classroom and what was going on in the world. One student stated, "Due to this course, I got a deeper understanding about myself ... I always thought I was alone in my experiences, but as it turns out, I am not."

In order to encourage even more reflection in the hybrid course, Huisman Lubreski is making two changes. First, each class will begin with a six-minute guided reflection based on the Jesuit Daily Examen of Consciousness. This secularized, audio version of the Daily Examen was developed by the Jesuit

Institute and gently guides listeners to pause and reflect about what they are grateful for, what feelings they have experienced throughout the day, and what they can do to be the person they wish they can be. The guided reflection will also be included on the online discussion board for students to listen to outside of class and reflect with their peers about their experiences doing the course project. Second, newly designed discussion questions will help students broaden their understanding about immigration and deepen their understanding of who they are in relation to others.

## Action

The Ignatian pedagogical paradigm reminds us that learning is made more meaningful when students are moved toward action and service. At the end of the semester, students combine the three parts of the podcasts into a unified whole and share it with their interviewees and classmates. This experience has compelled students to go beyond knowledge to action. One student reported that:

> Learning about the recent activism surrounding immigration allowed me to feel I was part of something bigger ... I began to learn about everyone else who came before me and their fearless abilities to continue the fight; it gave me strength and empowerment.

This student went on to get a summer internship at a nonprofit that advocates for immigrant rights.

In this hybrid course students and their professor also made weekly contributions to a shared Google Doc in Canvas, titled "Immigration in the News." It expanded to include video clips, documentaries, and local events pertaining to immigration. In addition to this page, another page on "Immigration Activism" will be added, which will include links to local and national organizations that are committed to immigration justice. Upon IRB approval, students will also have opportunities to share their work with a wider audience, allowing them to make their work and immigration stories public in digital environments beyond the classroom.

## Evaluation

For Ignatian pedagogy, evaluation goes beyond academic mastery to include student growth in mind, heart, and spirit. Student growth was evident throughout the semester, in the assignments, classroom discussions, and in their evaluations of the course. As an Engelhard course, students are reminded throughout the semester about the importance of reflection and evaluation and are asked to complete a reflective essay upon completion of the course where they self-evaluate the impact the course had on their personal growth. Three additional self-assessment activities are being added to the hybrid course that students will complete online, on their own time, and at the beginning, middle, and end of the course, to learn more about their process and evolution of their growth.

In sum, steps are being taken to more intentionally integrate the Ignatian pedagogical paradigm into the course and utilize the online learning space to allow students to stay connected and engaged in between class sessions—with each other, the instructor, and the course content.

## Conclusion

As these two case studies suggest, the parallels between critical pedagogy and Ignatian pedagogy can be leveraged in online course development to encourage students to engage at both the personal and social levels, as well as to achieve transformational learning. An Ignatian approach that took advantage of online affordances allowed both professors to ground their courses in social justice and lived experience, whether it was community activism or immigration reform. Yet the course design approach was also sufficiently flexible to allow for significant differences in terms of learning goals, disciplinary content, and assignment design.

We believe that an Ignatian-critical pedagogical approach can help mitigate what are often seen as challenges of online courses in which students are learning at a distance, especially in times when virtual learning is thrust unexpectedly upon instructors and learners, such as a global health pandemic. Ignatian pedagogy supports deeper reflection and action in context, which can lead to greater transformative experiences for students. Critical pedagogies will certainly look different in online spaces; however, as the case studies illustrate, thoughtful design can make an online course into a powerful transformative space for both individual students and larger communities. As more universities offer online instruction, whether in response to global events or demographic shifts, it is essential that we continue to offer transformative rather than transactional educational experiences that prepare students to serve the world.

## Notes

1. Authors are listed alphabetically
2. We candidly acknowledge here Ignatian pedagogy's patriarchal roots. This may be—at least historically—an irreconcilable difference between the two teaching paradigms. Exploring the theological possibilities and how these relate to the pedagogical ones is beyond the scope of this

paper. Within Ignatian pedagogy, however, there is an emphasis on the agency of the teacher, and the experience of the authors makes clear that teachers can employ Ignatian pedagogy without reinforcing hierarchical social norms, emphasizing religious commitments, or failing to focus on societal-level changes.
3. Students were also informed that if they were unable to or did not want to explore their immigration history, they could do an alternative assignment.

# References

Bernard, R. M., Abrami, P. C., Borokhovski, E., Wade, C. A., Tamim, R. M., Surkes, M. A., & Bethel, E. C. (2009). A meta-analysis of three types of interaction treatments in distance education. *Review of Educational Research*, 79(3), 1243–1289. https://doi.org/10.3102/0034654309333844

Boyd, D. (2016). What would Paulo Freire think of Blackboard: Critical pedagogy in an age of online learning. *The International Journal of Critical Pedagogy*, 7(1), 165–186.

Chubbuck, S. M. (2007). Socially just teaching and the complementarity of Ignatian Pedagogy and Critical Pedagogy. *Christian Higher Education*, 6(3), 239–265. https://doi.org/10.1080/15363750701268145

Foster, S. L. (2012). Engaging and empowering preservice teachers through Ignatian and Critical Pedagogy: Examples from the classroom. *Jesuit Higher Education: A Journal*, 1(1), 134–143. https://epublications.regis.edu/jhe/vol1/iss1/11

International Commission on the Apostolate of Jesuit Education (ICAJE). (1993). Ignatian Pedagogy: A practical approach. http://jesuitinstitute.org/Pages/IgnatianPedagogy.htm

Korth, S. J. (2008). Precis of Ignatian Pedagogy: A practical approach. In G. W. Traub, S. J. (Ed.), *A Jesuit education reader: Contemporary writings on the Jesuit mission in education, principles, the issue of Catholic identity, practical applications of the Ignatian way, and more* (pp. 280–284). Loyola Press.

Kreimeyer, J., & Huntington, J. (2018). Jesuit-infused online training to work with military couples & families. *Jesuit Higher Education: A Journal*, 7(2), 96–102. https://epublications.regis.edu/jhe/vol7/iss2/9

Merys, G. (2016, August). Ignatian pedagogy as critical pedagogy. *The Notebook*. https://reinertcenter.com/2016/08/31/ignatian-pedagogy-as-critical-pedagogy/

Mountin, S., & Nowacek, R. (2012). Reflection in action: A signature Ignatian pedagogy for the 21st Century. In N. L. Chick, A. Haynie, & R. A. R. Gurung (Eds.), *Exploring more signature pedagogies: Approaches to teaching disciplinary habits of mind* (pp. 129–142). Stylus Publishing.

Pace, T., & Merys, G. M. (2016). Paulo Freire and the Jesuit tradition: Jesuit rhetoric and Freirean pedagogy. In C. Gannett & J. C. Brereton (Eds.), *Traditions of eloquence: The Jesuits and modern rhetorical studies* (pp. 234–247). Fordham University Press. https://www.jstor.org/stable/j.ctt1bmzkwq.19

Rogers, S. (2019). Magis instructional design model for transformative teaching. *Proceedings of the Association of Educational Communications and Technology Annual Convention*, 457–465. AECT.

Rogers, S. A., & Van Haneghan, J. (2018). Online community of inquiry syllabus rubric. https://humanities-web.s3.us-east-2.amazonaws.com/college/chicagostudies-prod/s3fs-public/2020-03/Online%20Community%20of%20Inquiry%20Syllabus%20Rubric.pdf

Tobin, T. W. (2012). Transformative education in a broken world: Feminist and Jesuit pedagogy on the importance of context. In J. M. Boryczka & E. A. Petrino (Eds.), *Jesuit and Feminist education: Intersections in teaching and learning for the Twenty-first Century* (pp. 161–175). Fordham University Press. https://www.jstor.org/stable/j.ctt14brzh2.14

Valtin, L., McWilliams, M., & Ebenbach, D. (2018). Well-being in the curriculum: What faculty can do to address the mental health of our students. *Conversations on Jesuit Higher Education, 54*(8), 15–17. http://www.conversationsmagazine.org/web-features/2018/11/21/well-being-in-the-curriculum-what-faculty-can-do-to-address-the-mental-health-of-our-students

Verpoorten, D., Westera, W., & Specht, M. (2011). Reflection amplifiers in online courses: A classification framework. *Journal of Interactive Learning Research, 22*(2), 167–190. https://www.learntechlib.org/primary/p/33033/

CHAPTER FOURTEEN

# Educating Awarenesses in an Online Reflective Practice Course: Becoming Aware of Implicit Biases and Leaps to Judgment

ROBYN RUTTENBERG-ROZEN, SAHANA MAHENDIRARAJAH, AND BRIANNE BRADY

In their future classrooms many of the decisions our preservice teachers will make as teachers are in-the-moment (Mason & Davis, 2013), in fleeting instances, as responses to observations. At the root of these in-the-moment decisions and observations are assumptions about learners, learning, and other myriad factors. Because these assumptions are often supported by and intertwined with implicit biases (Welsh & Little, 2018), they lead to "leaps to judgment" (Frank, 1999, p. 1). Importantly, because most people are not aware of most of the thoughts they process (Staats, 2016), these in-the-moment decisions, and all the elements that led up to the decision, occur so quickly that teachers are not even aware of them (Mason, 1998). While some of these in-the-moment decisions may be innocuous and have little consequence, others may have drastic consequences with regards to issues of equity, especially when it comes to classroom management, discipline, and decisions around ability (e.g., James & Turner, 2017; Welsh & Little, 2018).

A significant contribution of bias within these leaps to judgments and in-the-moment decisions may be due to the regulation of systems, such as the classroom norms teachers establish for behavior management or scheduling subjects at specific times during the day, the very things teachers use to make their lives easier. It would be too labor intensive for teachers to constantly think of and respond to the minutiae of their systems. However, the in-the-moment observations, assumptions, and leaps to judgments teachers make are often entwined with the enactment of these very systems, but teachers remain unaware of their existence. The regulation of systems is thus used as a baseline for professional practice, and this comes with unnoticed stereotypes and biases. A result of this lack of awareness may be that teacher responses become reactionary instead of anticipatory, with leaps to judgments at the root of these reactionary responses (Mason, 2002). This has significant consequences for equity in the classroom. Reacting to classroom behaviors is one prevalent example of in-the-moment reactionary decisions that teachers can make based on their implicit biases. Teachers establish systems of norms for classroom behavior. And, because of the myriad of details to attend to in the classroom, it would be inefficient and time consuming for teachers to think about the minutiae of their system, causing reactionary responses based on unconscious bias of gender. For example, females may be responded to less often than males, and teachers may not respond at all in cases of harassment against gender-nonconformity (Meyer, 2008), and race, where children of color may receive harsher consequences (Skiba et al., 2002).

Because so much of what happens in the classroom is based on these in-the-moment observations, decisions, and leaps to judgment, it is important to build both an awareness in our preservice teachers of these small but powerful moments and an expertise so that our preservice teachers can fortify themselves against these leaps to judgments in their future practice. Mason (2015) (re)defines awarenesses as "form[s] of awakening: sharpening attention, enriching noticing, opening up fresh possibilities of action" (p. 110). Subsequently, preservice teachers should have multiple opportunities in many different courses to confront their own biases and develop their own awarenesses. Since these in-the-moment decisions and leaps to judgments occur in all different teaching spaces, including physical and virtual spaces, it is important that teacher education programs also provide multiple opportunities for pre-service teachers to confront their implicit biases in all these spaces. Whether they supplement their face-to-face teaching with online resources, interact with their students on online platforms, or are actually teaching in an online environment, one of the spaces where our future teachers will be making in-the-moment decisions is online. Thus, preservice teachers should be building awarenesses and gaining expertise in combating their biases and leaps to judgments while in their online courses.

In this chapter, we explore the burgeoning awarenesses of preservice teachers as they reflect on how an offline assignment in an online course brought their leaps to judgment into their consciousness. The preservice teachers in this study were all completing a four-semester Canadian teacher education program. They were enrolled in a compulsory online reflective practice and action research course as part of their fully online third semester. As part of the course, they learned about ethnography and conducted two observations (Frank, 1999) where they had to keep their leaps to judgment separate from their recorded observations and then reflect on the process of the activity and their growth from one observation to the next. In this chapter we ask the following questions:

(1) What is a critical awareness of these in-the-moment leaps to judgment?
(2) How do the preservice teachers understand and identify their own growth?
(3) How do preservice teachers see their future practice in light of their building awarenesses?

## Social Justice Teaching in Online Courses

Social justice pedagogy is a relatively new pedagogical framework (Ornstein, 2017) that augments already established subfields of educational research and pedagogy. Social justice pedagogy relies on a number of frameworks within critical pedagogy, in that it is rooted in the analysis of politics, deconstructing systemic structures, and understanding social phenomena as they are (Breunig, 2017; Giroux, 2004). Giroux (2004) argues:

> Any viable notion of pedagogy and resistance should illustrate how knowledge, values, desire, and social relations are always implicated in relations of power, and how such an understanding can be used pedagogically and politically by students to further expand and deepen the imperatives of economic and political democracy. (p. 34)

Giroux sees social justice pedagogy as the essential tether between acts of learning (thought) and actively creating change in the world (action). The aims of a social justice pedagogy, then, are twofold. On the one hand, the aim of social justice pedagogy is to empower the oppressed through developing an understanding of their experience and giving them a voice. On the other hand, the aims are to create an awareness leading to action through educating those in a space of privilege to be aware of how systemic structures of oppression operate, and then to be an active agent in combating these oppressive structures (Ornstein, 2017). Subsequently, social justice pedagogy is a highly political space (Breunig, 2017; Giroux, 2004; Ornstein, 2017) that one must learn to navigate.

Implementing social justice frameworks in teacher education courses allows preservice teachers to engage in critical discussions about problematic systemic aspects of education. Two important objectives within these pedagogical experiences are (i) to transform how preservice teachers perceive themselves as agents of social change, and (ii) to empower preservice teachers to further create agents of change in their students through transformative educational practices (Breunig, 2017). Significantly, preservice teachers should be able to view themselves in what they are learning in order to make their learning more impactful (Ladson-Billings, 1995). Ideally, through social justice pedagogy preservice teachers will be better informed of surrounding systemic marginalities and will then be empowered to problematize inequities and seek solutions with their students (Ayers et al., 2009).

Social justice pedagogy in teacher education has typically been developed for face-to-face classes. As online education becomes more prevalent in teacher education, social justice pedagogy is being integrated into online learning environments as well. However, there are a number of differences between pedagogy in an online learning space and a physically co-located learning space. One of the main differences is that online spaces have different affordances in supporting the construction of a transformative learning space than physical spaces have. For example, an online environment may be more flexible than an offline environment, and unlike physically co-located spaces, online learning students may be located in a variety of places during instruction time. The flexibility of an online environment means that learners may be distant from each other, may come from different cultural backgrounds, and may have had very different prior experiences. The multitude of different prior experiences and perspectives may be leveraged to enhance an online class with social justice as its focus; at the same time, disparate prior experiences might be an impediment to finding a starting point for discussion. Also, designers of online teaching environments purposefully have to plan for and design the community building interchanges that organically occur in the comings and goings of physically co-located classrooms. In order to create an online transformative social justice space, where learning goes beyond passivity and into action, instructors need to be purposeful with their virtual space and create an environment where learners understand that they are agents of social change.

There are examples in research of successful constructions of transformative online learning spaces. Caruthers and Friend (2014) discuss the *thirdspace*, a space in online learning where social transformation can take place. The *thirdspace* consists of two fundamental elements needed to construct a transformative space: (i) instructors and learners share authority, and (ii) the instructor purposefully becomes more aware of the strengths and contributions to shared growth of the learners in their class. At the root of both these elements, sharing authority and awareness of strengths and contributions, is sociocultural knowledge. Sociocultural knowledge is the social, cultural, political, and economic practices and beliefs that the instructor and learners bring with them to the learning space (Caruthers & Friend, 2014; Giroux, 2004). The support of critical pedagogy in an online environment, then, lies primarily on the sociocultural knowledge of all the participants—instructors and students. In *thirdspace*, once learners experience the key elements of sharing authority and making an awareness, there is then potential for self-transformation of the learner. Self-transformation occurs for a learner in *thirdspace* when using their sociocultural knowledge they confront, combat, and challenge the prevailing hegemonic powers, thus transforming their understanding and beliefs.

Guthrie and McCracken (2010) recommend four design components to implement a social justice pedagogical framework through an online learning platform:

- *Discussion Platforms*: creating virtual environments that have discussion platforms for ongoing conversations, which will then help foster organic relationships in the classroom.
- *Implementation for Critical Inquiry Engagement*: the design and implementation of methodologies and learning opportunities for critical inquiry engagement from students.
- *Developing Autonomy*: through critical engagement with the material in the class, including participating in meaningful and thought-provoking discussions, students should be able to develop autonomy in an online class.
- *Facilitating Discussion, Critical Inquiry Engagement and Autonomy*: the actual implementation of the above practices in order to foster accessible learning. These practices can allow an instructor to continue the effective ongoing implementation of a social justice pedagogy framework through an online platform.

## Implicit Bias and Leaps to Judgment

Think back to a prior experience that you know shaped you in some way. Can you describe the experience with details? How did the experience shape you? Why do you think the experience shaped you? Can you think of another experience that shaped you in some way? Can you describe that experience? Our guess is that you could probably name a number of experiences that had an effect on you. Something was so powerful either in the moment of or after the experience that allowed you to identify it and the way it changed you.

We are made up of life and personality shaping experiences. But unlike the experiences you identified above, we never get to identify and be aware of most of our experiences; they remain in our unconscious minds (Staats, 2016). Without our awareness, these implicit prior experiences can wreak havoc. These implicit prior experiences can make us do things that are the very opposite of our explicit belief systems, and worse, we often do not even know that we are doing things that are opposed to our beliefs. The problem is that our implicit takeaways from some life-shaping experiences do not always agree with our ideologies, yet we take them in anyway because we are completely unaware of them. Our implicit takeaways may be in the form of prejudices and stereotypes that are in direct disagreement with our explicit belief system. Consequently, we can espouse belief systems of equity and inclusion but might find ourselves experiencing knee jerk reactions that are the very opposite of equity and inclusion. For example, in our introduction, we shared two examples of how implicit biases may shape teacher responses to behavior. We noted that teachers may not respond at all to aggressive behavior against students who are gender non-conforming (Meyer, 2008) or may react more harshly to students of color (Skiba et al., 2002). In both these instances, the teacher's response, one of inaction and one of over-reaction, may actually contradict their explicit belief systems of gender and race.

These latent prejudices that clandestinely inform our actions are our implicit biases. No one is immune from implicit biases. We all have implicit biases because outside of our explicit control, we all gather implicit takeaways from our prior experiences.

Significantly, teachers are especially susceptible to their implicit biases because of the high cognitive load nature of their work (Staats, 2016). New teachers are even more at risk for activating their implicit bias because they have not had enough practice time in the classroom implementing what they have learned in their teacher education programs (Achinstein & Barrett, 2004). Implicit biases can be blamed for a number of inequities in the education system. The consequences of implicit biases include over referral to special education, over disciplining and more extreme punishments, underestimation of ability, and lowered expectations for learning, to name just a few. Some populations experience a disproportionate amount of biased behavior directed at them than others. One example of this is that young, black, males are more likely to be the recipients of disproportionate punishments for infractions because of implicit biases (Skiba et al., 2002).

If implicit biases are developed outside of awareness and wreak so much havoc on our students, it is imperative that we actively seek ways to mitigate their effects. One way is to educate an awareness (Mason, 2002) of implicit biases so teachers have more equitable and actionable alternatives to their biased in-the-moment responses to students.

## Educating Awareness

Reading this chapter, you might be aware that it is written in English or that it focuses on social justice pedagogy in an online course. You might be aware of your intentions for reading: maybe you are teaching an online course; or are interested in social justice; or are a graduate student researching these ideas. What we have just done by discussing your possible fields of awarenesses is to call attention to them. Essentially, through discussion, we endeavored to first have you notice an awareness, which in turn hopefully created a conscious awareness; then, through discussing your possible awareness, you created an awareness of an awareness. Gattegno (1987) calls the awareness of an awareness a "third awareness" (p. 27). A third awareness is "a knowing about knowing" (p. 28). Every third awareness is an extension of an awareness which itself is an extension of a noticing; you cannot have a third awareness without noticing something to begin with. Each noticing is a productive act:

> A world is brought into existence, or occasioned ... whenever questions are asked or something is noticed, for the disturbance which triggers a noticing triggers a collection of associated sensitivities, and hence also triggers a perspective, a way of seeing and of thinking about what is noticed. (Mason, 2002, p.167)

The thoughts that noticing produces for each of us depends on our individual makeup and experiences. The thought production of a noticing could be innocuous with little consequence, but it could also produce latent biases, assumptions, and leaps to judgments. Yet, these thoughts, this "way of seeing and thinking about what is noticed" (Frank, 1999, p. 1), does not necessarily lead to an awareness on the part of the individual. The thoughts and perspectives could remain in one's subconscious without them ever coming to consciousness. When bias laden thoughts remain in one's subconscious no action to correct or mitigate those biases is possible. Awareness does not automatically occur from a noticing; each awareness only occurs through a conscious effort. The effort for a third awareness is greater than for the original awareness. At the beginning, noticing happens after an event has occurred, but the goal of noticing is really to move closer and closer to notice the moment before an event, the moment when one still has a choice to make (Mason, 2002).

The degree of awareness a person may have, and the amount of effort expended, is related to expertise. Expertise allows a person to hone their noticing and draw from multiple connected experiences to interpret them (Mason, 1998). The more expertise a person has in the area, the more likely they are to be aware and to be able to access multiple prior experiences and inputs. However, at the same time, procedures can also become systematized with expertise and never lead to noticing or a third awareness (Mason, 2002). Therefore, there is a very fine line between having enough expertise to be able to develop an awareness of an awareness, and not allowing expertise to negate the possibility of developing an awareness through systematizing procedures.

In the teaching profession, noticing is ubiquitous; there is so much to notice, and it would be impossible to purposefully make an effort to be aware of all noticing. However, when our noticing is intertwined with our leaps to judgment, awareness is pivotal to noticing (Mason 2002). With this in mind, Mason (2002) and Mason and Davis (2013) recommend educating awareness. The ability to create an awareness about an awareness is itself an expertise that needs to be developed and nurtured. Educating awareness is educating about the multiple potential opportunities (awarenesses) that can result from one noticing. The opportunities for developing awarenesses from noticing can be socially-, equity-, teaching-, intervention-, or relationship-based, among others (Mason & Davis, 2013), with the purpose that those being educated in awareness develop ample experiences from which to refer and to connect. Educating awareness, then, is about becoming an expert about developing the ample repertoire of experiences that enable connections and actions from noticing (Mason, 2002).

Awareness is an activity that only occurs in the present. It cannot predict a future action. We cannot hypothesize that we will be aware of something. We may have intentionality, and that is important, but an awareness cannot determine future actions. However, an awareness can prepare us to be armed with the idea of multiple possibilities for both interpretation and action upon our noticings. Educating awareness through the idea of multiple possibilities is the foundation for change to occur. This change is extremely potent because it begins with the self and the educating of our own behaviors. A person practicing awareness chooses their behaviors and responses, instead of their responses being reactionary. Awareness involves moving beyond our own needs towards care and empathy to another's plight (Mason, 2002). This ability to see many different alternatives is one of the factors that enhances equity in the classroom (Achinstein & Barrett, 2004).

For noticing to result in an action, we need to first be sensitive to something; we need to experience a disturbance in the world around us. That is, we need to become aware of something that distinguishes that something from the background noise. A disturbance has no value—it is neither good nor bad. A disturbance is a state of being, a response to stimuli that causes us to alter our course. Growth occurs if we question our knowing and understandings as a result of experiencing the disturbance. These disturbances have to be small enough to be actionable and large enough to be noticed, but they must not be too large that they are debilitating. When the disturbance leads to growth, we feel a need for action and then think of and act upon an alternative action to what we are seeing. At each step, there has to be "intention and commitment" (Mason, 2002, p. 36). For action to result, it is not necessary that action be immediate. Action can occur at a later time. For action to occur at a later time, we take note of the noticing and create an awareness and then access it at a later time. The accessing can be done through an intermediary, like someone reminding you to revisit the memory, or it can be done through your own intentionality to remember.

## Description and Intention of the Online Course

The preservice teachers in this study were all completing a four-semester Canadian teacher education program. They were enrolled in a compulsory online reflective practice and action research course as part of their fully-online third semester. Out of the 126 students enrolled in the course, across six sections, eighty-nine completed ethics forms, and seventy-eight gave permission for us to use their student work. The instructor (Ruttenberg-Rozen) was unaware as to the status of permission for each student until well after course marks were submitted.

One of the intentions of the course design was to integrate transformative pedagogy into an online environment through encouraging the preservice teachers to unpack their implicit biases (Carter et al., 2017) through reflection. Rose (2013) states, "The essence of reflection is synthesis: the creation of new ideas, perspectives, and possibilities" (p. 8). Through synthesis, critical reflection can be transformative and mitigate reproductions of inequity that can occur through the learning of pedagogies that further certain social systems and dominant discourses (Boyd & Lagarry, 2016). Critical reflection helps to develop awareness of biases, which can help reduce the growth or furthering of stereotypes, dominant power struggles, and other discriminatory behaviors (Pitts & Brooks, 2016).

## Description of Activity

There were four parts to the assignment given to preservice teachers:

1. *Read*: The preservice teachers were asked to read chapter 1 of Frank's (1999) *Ethnographic Eyes*. The chapter explores using an ethnographic observation in order to bring leaps of judgments into consciousness. Frank (1999) explains the methodology of "notemaking and notetaking" (p. 10). In notemaking and notetaking, a researcher will keep separate sections

in their notes for what they are seeing (notetaking-observations without judgment) and what they are thinking (notemaking-thoughts about what they are seeing).

2. *Observe and Reflect*: Based on Frank's (1999) notemaking and notetaking, preservice teachers were asked to observe a familiar surrounding for 45 minutes to 1 hour and write their observations in separate columns: (i) for what they were actually observing (notetaking), and (ii) what they were thinking about what they were observing, or their leaps to judgment (notemaking). It was our hope that the acts of notemaking and notetaking would bring leaps to judgment into the awareness of the preservice teachers. Together with their observations, the preservice teachers then submitted a reflection about the process of bringing their leaps to judgment into their awareness and how they felt their new awareness might impact their future teaching practice.

The activity was designed for there to be little discussion about leaps to judgments and observations at this stage. We wanted to create a disturbance (Mason, 2002) in order to begin educating awareness. However, it is important to note about the vulnerability of our students and their own susceptibility to others' biases. Some members of the class, notably men of color and religious Moslem men, often noted in this activity an awareness of observing and being observed at the same time. We, therefore, also included a discussion, educating awareness, around the observer's own vulnerability and susceptibility to the biases and leaps to judgments of others. To mitigate some of our students' vulnerability, we suggested that students go in groups to observe, which leads to interesting conversations when students have different observations of the same area. Students could also stay on the university campus where it is more normalized for students to sit, write, and observe, or they could go to a place that they might frequent a lot anyway.

3. *Feedback*: The instructor gave feedback on each assignment, pointing out where there were leaps to judgments on the notetaking side, thus helping students develop more detailed notes without adding leaps to judgments. The instructor also pointed out where alternatives could be sought, instead of leaps to judgment on the notemaking side, and noted and modeled the power of asking questions.

4. *Observe and Reflect, building on 1–3*: The whole process was reiterated with the second observation assignment. Based on their feedback, students were directed to different venues for their second observation and were asked to reflect on their growing awareness between the first and second assignment and its implications for their teaching practice.

## Awarenesses and Growth

Especially since this was their third semester, the preservice teachers had a lot of practice in observing and reflecting on their own and other teachers' practices. By their own admission in the reflections of the course, prior to this assignment, many of the preservice teachers were "studenting" (Liljedahl & Allan, 2013) in their previous reflections; their acts of observing and reflecting were for the purpose of doing well in school and getting through assignments, not necessarily with the intention of developing their own growth. In light of this, it was unsurprising that some of the reflections on the first observation initially reflected the preservice teachers acts of "studenting," writing their reflections for the purpose of doing well on the assignment. In these often-well-written reflections, students wrote of reinforcing their beliefs about the benefits of reflection and being "accurate" in their observations for their future practice. These observations did not pay special attention to leaps to judgment, and the reflections did not problematize any previous actions or introduce any new ideas from either the Frank (1999) reading or any new learnings from the act of separating their leaps to judgments from observations within their written notes.

Like in similar activities (Strom et al., 2018), where people's implicit biases are brought to the fore of their awareness, at the beginning, students tend to be uncomfortable in becoming aware of their implicit biases. We wanted to leverage this "discomfort" because that discomfort is a disturbance (Mason, 2002), and the experience of a disturbance is what leads to awareness. We noted different types of growth and awareness and different types of disturbances across the two observation assignments.

Students noted developing awareness at a number of different points in the activity. Some students experienced a disturbance immediately with the first observation and then gradually grew their awareness across both assignments. For other students, their disturbance came from the feedback they received from the first observation. Still, others noted their disturbance came only upon their reflection of the second observation.

Some of the students claimed a critical lens to the activity from the first observation. In their writing, these students recognized the intention of personal growth within the activity and iterated their openness to growth through both observations. Students who brought an already critical lens were often surprised that they harbored implicit biases, even though their explicit beliefs were very different from what they were becoming aware of. Shiloh experienced this when her identity of being a feminist clashed with her implicit bias:

> this activity ... allowed some of my implicit biases (to) bubble up to my conscious awareness. For example, I assumed that one of the children's books that had a pink cover was about a girl, or some sort of needs a space "girly" topic. Despite being sometimes described by others as a "misogynist's worst nightmare," even I hold some of the assumptions and biases that I personally detest. (Shiloh, reflection on observation 1)

Shiloh was becoming aware that she held an implicit bias related to identifying "girly" items by their appearances that conflicted with her explicit beliefs around feminism. Like Shiloh's burgeoning awareness around feminism, other students wondered in their notemaking if they should be noting skin color in their writings and then if skin color is a notemaking (leap to judgment) or a notetaking (an observation). Other students did not question whether they should be remarking about skin color in their notes. Instead, they questioned why they paid so much attention to skin color in their observations.

Some students wrote about awareness that developed because of the juxtaposition of becoming desensitized to observations and reflections in their education program and becoming sensitized again through confronting their implicit biases. Although they had participated in numerous observations and reflections, some students felt these experiences had not been problematized for them yet, and they had not developed an awareness of the potential for inequities in observation and reflection. Shanti remarked that she thought the assignment would be "easy" because of her prior experiences and was "surprised" when she found it difficult. Jennifer shared that she was "annoyed" with herself because she kept trying to "assume" why people did what they did. It took her extra effort not to make assumptions.

Words that challenged singular perceptions like "truth," "culture," and "perspective" were common in these reflections. At the same time, there were also tensions with "accuracy" and "objectivity." Learners began to build awareness around accuracy and began to think about whether observations could be "accurate" and its relationship to "objectivity," as with William:

> Being objective while making notes can be useful because there are many different perspectives on a single situation and mine alone might not be accurate. How do we know that what we perceive is what is actually happening? (William, reflection on observation 1)

## The Role of Feedback

Instructor feedback often provided a powerful disturbance for the preservice teachers, especially when the feedback pointed out implicit biases within notemaking or notetaking. A number of students made assumptions surrounding relationships in their notetaking. For example, many students used the word "couple" as a descriptor in notetaking without realizing they were making an assumption or problematizing the label "couple." With feedback, we often drew attention to the overuse of the word "couple" for groups consisting of different genders and lack of use of the word "couple" for groups consisting of the same gender. For example, Neilah completed her observations in a restaurant. Each time she observed a man and a woman, she labeled them as a "couple" in her notetaking: "A couple is sitting and having lunch at a table by the window." Then, in her notemaking, Neilah would refer to each member by a role resulting from her reification of the two people as a "couple": "I wonder if her boyfriend will be able to get a word in. Is he annoyed?" At the same time, Neilah did not refer to same sex patrons sitting together as couples: "Two ... women are sitting by the window in a deep conversation." Nor did Neilah's wonderings in her notemaking refer to any sort of relationship between the two women. In the feedback for Neilah, the instructor drew attention to her use of the word "couple" when men and women were sitting together and her lack of the word when people of the same gender sat together.

Other feedback targeted creating an awareness of subjectivity in what observers choose and why they choose to be aware of certain things and ignore others. Tom came to this awareness through feedback on his first observation, when he developed an awareness that he was able to add more detail the more interested he was in what he was observing.

At some points, preservice teachers made assumptions early on in their notes, and then without realizing, they constructed an entire subsequent narrative around the original assumption. This type of feedback was shared with Shiloh after she had constructed a truth narrative around an early assumption:

> I tried my hardest to heed the advice (...) note(d) that in my previous observation, I based all my note-making around an assumption that I made at the very beginning of my note-making (i.e. I wondered if the children I observed were meeting with their tutors, and from that point onwards all my note-making was based on my belief that these children were, 100% without a doubt, meeting with their tutors). I was shocked (...) as I genuinely did not realize I had done that (...) I found it frightening that my brain chose a story so quickly and ran with it for the duration of my observation. I think that this was an important realization for me. Despite how passionate I am about promoting equity in the field of education, biases can sneak into any of your thoughts and actions very easily (Shiloh, reflection on observation 2)

Shiloh had become aware of how one leap to judgment early on in her notetaking had led to her constructing an entire truth narrative around tutoring students. We did suggest strategies in the feedback when this type of truth narrative occurred with students. We suggested that students ask multiple questions and suggest multiple alternatives (Mason, 2002) in their notemaking to mitigate the effects of their leaps to judgments. Shanti remarked that she found the strategies especially helpful for improving her responses from her leaps to judgments.

## Future Practice

As part of the assignment, students were explicitly asked to connect their learnings to their future practice. Three themes emerged from this aspect of the reflections: (i) Awareness of leaps to judgments in the classroom; (ii) awareness during assessment practices; and (iii) educating awareness in their future students.

**Awareness of leaps to judgments in teaching.** It was here that students noted how their in-the-moment decisions might be influenced by their implicit biases (Mason, 2002; Staats, 2016). Preservice teachers reflected on their growing awareness that what they would observe while teaching will not necessarily be the whole picture and that their implicit biases may influence how they interpret their observations during teaching. The level of awareness of leaps to judgments in their future practice differed for the preservice teachers. Molly wrote about striving to "be inherently unbiased and avoid adhering to quick or instantaneous thoughts and perceptions when documenting the behaviour of (her) students." Others, like Shea, became aware that biases are intrinsic to every teacher. Shea wrote about trying to "set aside" his biases and to "constantly ask questions" to confront and keep learning about his biases. Carlos developed this awareness even further, by noting the differences in being aware of his biases and actively deterring them during teaching:

> I am now aware that even when you are cognizant of your own misconceptions and biases it is a whole other intentional process to ensure that you are NOT allowing your biases to influence your teaching and/or the way you interact with your students (Carlos, reflection on observation 2)

Similarly, Reginald, also noting his own implicit biases, posited that "it is important that (he) recognize that the behaviour of (his) students is shaped by their previous experiences, as well as their personal interests and preferences." Like Reginald, Nathan noted "how easy it was to build up judgments and negative images of my students, when I do not consider more than just the actions I am able to see." For Samara, the awareness that she had inherent biases translated into her strategizing that she would need "multiple sensory levels" to observe and interpret her environment in her future classroom.

**Awareness during assessment practices.** Many of the preservice teachers made reference to gathering evidence in the classroom and their growing awareness as to how their implicit biases may affect their assessments. Noel remarked that they would use notemaking and notetaking in the classroom as they are assessing their students to help them be more aware of their own biases. Nayab shared that "it's inevitable that we're going to teach children who may give us a hard time," and this activity would help her to separate her biases from what she would be feeling as a result. Through this activity, April built an awareness around the logistics of doing assessment. April related her difficulty in choosing an appropriate spot to do her observation; she became aware that she would not be able to perceive everything, no matter what space she occupied for her observation. As a result, she noted:

> A noisy environment like the mall food court or an elementary school classroom also make it hard to clearly hear conversations being had, which is often where the majority of information can come from. This is why using a combination of different assessment strategies would be the best approach, as well as making sure, I observe from multiple vantage points or on-the-fly while I move about the classroom (April, reflection on observation 2)

**Educating awarenesses in their future students.** Some students saw the activity as something they could do with their students to help their students build their own awarenesses. Molly found the activity encouraged her to think while she was observing. She noted that as a future high school English teacher, she would teach her students awareness through teaching them to notemake their classroom notes. Ali also shared that he would use the concepts learning in notemaking to teach his students that teachers notemake, and that because of this, different teachers will focus on different things in their assessments.

## Critical Awareness and Growth

We found that through creating a transformative space, the online classroom can be a powerful conduit for learning about social justice issues. In our case, the online transformative space included an offline activity where preservice teachers began to build awarenesses of their own implicit biases and implications of these awarenesses for their future practice. The flexibility of the online environment afforded each preservice teacher to be on a different path and trajectory. Some awareness was just developing and some moved beyond the developing stage. Aside from the different paths, the preservice teachers also brought many different types of awareness into their consciousness. Thus, in regard to our question, "What is a critical awareness of these in-the-moment leaps to judgements?" we found that the type of critical awareness differed according to the starting point of the preservice teacher.

The perspective of each preservice teacher and their beliefs shaped not only how their awareness developed, but also what that awareness was. Shiloh admitted that she came into this activity with an already critical eye; yet, she was still developing a critical awareness through becoming aware of an implicit bias that contradicted her explicit beliefs. At the same time, and in a different way, Jennifer was developing her critical awareness because she was becoming aware that her observations were laden with her own assumptions. Shanti's awareness came as a result of her budding awareness that holding back leaps to judgments during observations is difficult to maintain, despite her previous experience with observations during her teacher education.

A critical awareness of leaps to judgments is a deeply personalized awareness—personalized in the disturbance (Mason, 2002) that leads to the awareness, personalized in the prior knowledge that the preservice teachers draw from, and personalized in the beliefs that shape the identification of the awareness. Importantly, it is only through awareness of their students' awareness that teacher educators can support different and personalized critical awareness.

## Critical Awareness, Growth and Future Practice

It is in the midst of their teaching practice, when preoccupied with a myriad of in-the-moment decisions, that there is the most danger that a teacher will be swayed by their implicit biases (Staats, 2016). There is really no way to eradicate these biases. However, instead of being reactionary, we can pre-empt the actions that would be as a result of our implicit biases (Mason, 2002). The only way to pre-empt our actions is to both educate an awareness of our biases and educate an awareness of the spaces where we might need to pre-empt our actions. This chapter ends with a discussion of our question: How do preservice teachers see their future practice in light of their building awareness?

The purpose of social justice pedagogy is to tether thoughts to actions (Giroux, 2004). For the students, through this activity, their budding awarenesses (thoughts) created a need for vigilance (action) in their future practice. Students were developing awareness around their implicit biases, and a number of students were surprised they harbored these secret and inequitable thoughts contrary to their explicit beliefs. Yet, the action that they could do in their future practice was still so far away. At the same time, awareness cannot predict future actions; an awareness cannot ensure equitable actions in the face of inequitable thoughts and beliefs (Mason, 2002) in the preservice teachers' future practice. Subsequently, through preservice teachers' budding awareness, their future practice was recognized as a space of conflicting beliefs. At the same time, not one of the preservice teachers despaired in face of an insurmountable task in combatting their implicit biases. They recognized that the strategies they were learning would be helpful in their vigilance. What type of vigilance was needed, and what the vigilance was needed for, depended on the student because the nature of the task and the nature of learning platform allowed each person to be on their own trajectory of developing awareness.

# References

Achinstein, B., & Barrett, A. (2004). (Re) Framing classroom contexts: How new teachers and mentors view diverse learners and challenges of practice. *Teachers College Record, 106*(4), 716–746. http://dx.doi.org/10.1111/j.1467-9620.2004.00356.x

Ayers, W., Quinn, T., & Stovall, D. (2009). Preface. In W. Ayers, T. Quinn, & D. Stovall (Eds.), *Handbook of social justice in education* (pp. xiii–xv). Routledge.

Boyd, A. S., & Lagarry, A. E. (2016). Moving from self to system: A framework for social justice centered on issues and action. *International Journal of Critical Pedagogy, 7*(2), 171–197.

Breunig, M. C. (2017). Critical and social justice pedagogies in practice. In M. A. Peters (Ed.), *Encyclopedia of educational philosophy and theory* (pp. 258–263). Springer.

Carter, P. L., Skiba, R., Arredondo, M. I., & Pollock, M. (2017). You can't fix what you don't look at: Acknowledging race in addressing racial discipline disparities. *Urban Education, 52*(2), 207–235. https://doi.org/10.1177%2F0042085916660350

Caruthers, L., & Friend, J. (2014). Critical pedagogy in online environments as Thirdspace: A narrative analysis of voices of candidates in educational preparatory programs. *Educational Studies, 50*(1), 8–35. https://doi.org/10.1080/00131946.2013.866953

Frank, C. (1999). *Ethnographic eyes. A teacher's guide to classroom observation.* Heinemann.

Gattegno, C. (1987). *The science of education part 1: Theoretical considerations.* Educational Solutions.

Giroux, H. A. (2004). Critical pedagogy and the postmodern/modern divide: Towards a pedagogy of democratization. *Teacher Education Quarterly, 31*(1), 31–47.

Guthrie, K. L., & McCracken, H. (2010). Making a difference online: Facilitating service-learning through distance education. *The Internet and Higher Education, 13*(3), 153—157.

James, C. E., & Turner, T. (2017). *Towards race equity in education: The schooling of Black students in the Greater Toronto Area.* York University.

Ladson-Billings, G. (1995). Toward a theory of culturally relevant pedagogy. *American Educational Research Journal, 32*(3), 465–491. https://doi.org/10.3102%2F00028312032003465

Liljedahl, P., & Allan, D. (2013). Studenting: The case of homework. In *Proceedings of the 35th conference for psychology of mathematics education North American chapter* (pp. 489–492).

Mason, J. (1998). Enabling teachers to be real teachers: Necessary levels of awareness and structure of attention. *Journal of Mathematics Teacher Education, 1*, 243–267. https://doi.org/10.1023/A:1009973717476

Mason, J. (2002). *Researching your own practice: The discipline of noticing*. Routledge Falmer.

Mason, J. (2015). Responding in-the-moment: Learning to prepare for the unexpected. *Research in Mathematics Education, 17*(2), 110–127. https://doi.org/10.1080/14794802.2015.1031272

Mason, J., & Davis, B. (2013). The importance of teachers' mathematical awareness for in-the-moment pedagogy. *Canadian Journal of Science, Mathematics and Technology Education, 13*(2), 182–197. https://doi.org/10.1080/14926156.2013.784830

Meyer, E. J. (2008). Gendered harassment in secondary schools: Understanding teachers'(non) interventions. *Gender and Education, 20*(6), 555–570. https://doi.org/10.1080/09540250802213115

Ornstein, A. C. (2017). Social justice: History, purpose and meaning. *Society, 54*(6), 541–548. https://doi.org/10.1007/s12115-017-0188-8

Pitts, M. J., & Brooks, C. F. (2016). Critical pedagogy, internationalisation, and a third space: Cultural tensions revealed in students' discourse. *Journal of Multilingual and Multicultural Development, 38*(3), 251–267. https://doi.org/10.1080/01434632.2015.1134553

Rose, E. (2013). *On reflection: An essay on technology, education, and the status of thought in the Twenty-First Century*. Canadian Scholars Press.

Skiba, R. J., Michael, R. S., Nardo, A. C., & Peterson, R. L. (2002). The color of discipline: Sources of racial and gender disproportionality in school punishment. *The Urban Review, 34*(4), 317–342. https://psycnet.apa.org/doi/10.1023/A:1021320817372

Staats, C. (2016). Understanding implicit bias: What educators should know. *American Educator, 39*(4), 29.

Strom, K., Haas, E., Danzig, A., Martinez, E., & McConnell, K. (2018). Preparing educational leaders to think differently in polarized, post-truth times. *The Educational Forum, 82*(3), 259–277. https://doi.org/10.1080/00131725.2018.1458361

Welsh, R. O., & Little, S. (2018). The school discipline dilemma: A comprehensive review of disparities and alternative approaches. *Review of Educational Research, 88*(5), 752–794. https://psycnet.apa.org/doi/10.3102/0034654318791582

CHAPTER FIFTEEN

# Reaching Critical Depths: Engaging Teacher Candidates in Critical Pedagogy Online

VICKI A. HOSEK AND JAY C. PERCELL

> Knowledge emerges only through invention and reinvention, through the restless, impatient continuing, hopeful inquiry we pursue in the world, with the world, and with each other.
> — FREIRE, *PEDAGOGY OF THE OPPRESSED*

Central to critical pedagogy is the application of critical theory to teaching practices. According to Darder et al. (2017), such pedagogy calls educators "to recognize how schools have historically embraced theories and practices that serve to unite knowledge and power in ways that sustain asymmetrical relations of power" (p. 10). Further, it calls educators to work to ensure that such inequitable power structures are challenged and dismantled. Essential to the understanding of critical pedagogy are dialogical opportunities between teacher educators and teacher candidates to both reflect about and critique real world experiences. Giroux (2017) explained that a critical theoretical approach to education necessitates "ongoing critique, one in which the claims of any theory must be confronted with the distinction between the world it examines and portrays, and the world as it actually exists" (p. 31). Also foundational to critical theory is praxis, where "activity is understood as emerging from an on-going interaction of reflection, dialogue, and action" and that such interaction "requires theory to illuminate it and provide a better understanding of the world as we find it and as it might be" (Darder et al., 2017, p. 13).

As teacher educators, our goal has always been the development of teacher candidates' critical literacy. This necessarily includes their deep, critical, and personal examination of experiences surrounding bias, prejudice, and stereotypes they have encountered or possibly have enacted themselves. An online course design focused on specific instructional strategies can facilitate this goal by providing opportunities and dedicated space for each student's story and voice to be represented, thus supporting the development of teacher candidates' knowledge of critical pedagogy (Giroux, 2017). Concurrently, as teacher educators, we have the opportunity to position ourselves as learners and create a reciprocal teaching environment where dialectical practices essential to critical pedagogy are invited (Freire, 1970). Such practices offer a "supple and fluid view of humans and nature that is relational; an objectivity and subjectivity that is interconnected; and a coexistent understanding of theory and practice" (Darder et al., 2017, p. 11). In fact, throughout the course highlighted in this chapter, the instructor, Hosek (author 1), found herself continually and critically examining her own pedagogical beliefs and understanding of critical theory, thus positioning her as a learner as much as an instructor with much growth still left to do.

We recognize that engaging teacher candidates in an examination of biases, prejudice, and stereotypes requires a classroom environment founded on mutual respect and trust. This led us to consider how teacher educators in online classes employ critical literacy practices and shape the online classroom community to invite, encourage, and support student engagement in critical pedagogy.

## Creating a Critical Online Space

In this chapter, we detail the experiences of Hosek who taught the same secondary education foundations course face-to-face and then in a fully online format. We begin by describing the course content, platform, and digital classroom environment, as well as the struggle this instructor faced transitioning the course format and delivery. Next, we describe her process for engaging online students in critical literacy practices. We include exchanges of critical reflection between the instructor and three teacher candidates in the online course. These are indicative of development of students' critical pedagogical knowledge and their newly developing praxis (Freire, 1970). We highlight each candidate's personal critical reflections that demonstrate an awareness of the social and political implications of their teaching decisions (Breunig, 2005). Finally, we present the key components of this online course design with suggested accompanying instructional strategies.

## Course Content and Format

The course examined in this chapter is a secondary teacher education major requirement entitled The Teaching Profession in Secondary Schools (TPSS). The university directory describes it as focused "on the social, economic, and political forces that influence the development, organization, and purposes of secondary schools" (Illinois State University, n.d.). Students take it in their junior or senior year. At the time of this study, the TPSS was offered in either a face-to-face or online format. Despite the significant difference in course venues, the master syllabus remained the same for both course formats.

Chiasson et al. (2015) found that developing and/or redesigning a course for online delivery requires thinking about learning in new ways, a process that changes the instructor as well. When Hosek was asked to teach TPSS online, she found the transition to be extremely challenging and overwhelming as she ineffectively and inefficiently dedicated time to identifying ways to modify face-to-face methods to an online format. For example, orchestrating a Socratic seminar online, either synchronously or asynchronously, proved to be logistically unmanageable due to scheduling constraints of both students and professor. This led to much frustration and doubt that she could accomplish the same objectives online that she did face-to-face with her students.

In Hosek's case, she found that circling back to the course description was key. To her, critical theory needed to be central to the online course design and assignments if students were to examine and understand the social, political, and economic forces at work in our education system. Importantly, she focused on the affordances of a digital environment as instrumental to developing a course that privileges student voice and experiences (Basham et al., 2016).

## Online Classroom Environment

There is an inherent personal quality that exists in face-to-face classrooms which cannot be replicated in an online classroom. For example, there is no specific requirement for physically showing up, and there is no eye contact during conversations in asynchronous online communications. The challenge is to ensure that personal connections and engagement are real, despite a lack of physical presence.

The physical distance between students and instructor can be virtually bridged in numerous ways. Consideration of the level of access students have to the instructor is essential (Chiasson et al., 2015). Hosek viewed online access as an opportunity to engage each student in deeply critical conversations surrounding their personal beliefs and pedagogical experiences. She implemented a virtual learning space that was decidedly different from a face-to-face course where there are constraints on both time and opportunities for individual interactions. Effectively using that individualized digital space laid the foundation for praxis to occur where reflection, dialogue, and action help connect theory with practice (Darder et al., 2017). The online platform facilitated this dialogical course design by allowing both instructor and students to continually re-center their pedagogical beliefs as impacted by previous personal experiences and course materials. Such dialogue takes concerted effort and significant dedicated time from the instructor to ensure the most impactful feedback.

### Aligning Online Teaching Methods with Instructor's Pedagogical Beliefs

Continual consideration and reflection about teacher candidates' personal pedagogical beliefs are as critical in online classrooms as they are in face-to-face classrooms (Hrevnack, 2011). Ensuring that methods reflect and align with those beliefs is integral to effective and meaningful engagement in digital environments (Ertmer et al., 2012). Essential to accomplishing this is an understanding about how to recruit pedagogical beliefs to digital environments (Hosek & Handsfield, 2019).

As critical theory is foundational to her pedagogical beliefs, Hosek recognized that honoring student voice needed to be foundational to her methods online. Each student was offered a personal online space within the university's learning management system (LMS) where there was an audience of only one: the instructor. The LMS used offered the option to allow for private journal entries where access was granted by the instructor. In addition, Hosek modeled critical pedagogy by continually connecting theory to her own teaching practices with course materials and providing constructive analysis of teaching examples to aid in the development of students' critical literacy practices. Such modeling has been shown to be an effective means for increasing teacher candidates' critical literacy practices once they enter the field (Urbani et al., 2017).

## Using the Online Platform to Connect Beliefs with Theory

Online classrooms are unique as they offer students and teachers both private and public opportunities to engage with the course content and each other. Hosek utilized different points of access provided by the course LMS to either share online spaces with the whole class, groups, or just individual students. We know individuals are less likely to share their personal opinions when they differ from those of their audience (Hampton et al., 2014). As an instructor, asking students to deeply and critically examine their personal beliefs in light of materials, resources, and authentic diverse experiences that challenge biases, stereotypes, and social injustice requires an acceptance and understanding that instructors will meet the students at exactly where they are or where they are permitted to be. Knowing this, she decided that critical reflection assignments would be central to her course design (occurring continually throughout the semester) but would also be kept private between herself and her students. These assignments were separate from normal course communications and other course assignments, such as group projects, where all students were provided access.

Research surrounding online courses shows that when engaging in online conversations and communications a student's level of interest in a topic directly impacts decisions about how much an individual shares (Hampton et al., 2014). Building students' trust through the design of a digital space where reflections would be thoughtfully read and respected and where growth of knowledge and experiences would be directly and personally beneficial to their development as teachers was Hosek's priority. By making each student's beliefs, perspectives, experiences, challenges, and biases (whether implicit or explicit) both the starting point and the re-centering element throughout the semester, the development of students' understanding of critical pedagogy was privileged in this online course. All of the reflections and feedback were easily accessible to each student in the LMS, making it convenient for students and instructor to see the formative development of each individual's critical pedagogical knowledge.

Students' critical reflections began immediately during the first week of the course, continued during authentic offline assignments where students engaged with diverse communities—"world as we find it" (Darder et al., 2017, p. 13)—which included secondary classrooms and community events, and ended with their final assignment. In those critical reflections, students were asked to examine and incorporate course materials which were purposefully selected to present diverse perspectives on social inequities present in K-12 classrooms. This provided opportunities—world "as it might be" (Darder et al., 2017, p. 13)—for students to reflect about how their pedagogical beliefs and practices may impact their future classrooms. In essence, critical reflections served as the dialogical center which was housed in the course LMS where each student and the instructor continually returned to before, during, and after all course activities.

Role of Critical Reflections in Learning Critical Pedagogy

Studies have shown teacher candidates struggle to understand how theory and practice are connected (Ertmer et al., 2012; Hrevnack, 2011). Critical reflections offer valuable means for helping students consider how the theoretical can become practical. In fact, developing the practice of critical reflection is considered key to best practices in teaching (NCATE, 2008). Operating from this premise, Hosek sought to learn about students' pedagogical beliefs to identify a starting point for each student to consider and incorporate critical theory by reflecting about specific assigned readings about critical theory in education and class discussions surrounding those readings. Guiding questions for online readings and materials were provided to the students to examine their personal beliefs and experiences in classrooms and to help them identify their subjectivities about teaching and learning. This included examination of their own experiences in light of implicit and explicit biases they encountered, witnessed, and participated in. Importantly, the dedicated and personalized online space provided a valuable means for students to have both the assurance of privacy and the freedom to express themselves openly. When followed with timely, constructive engagement by the instructor, this personalized digital environment supports individual learner growth (Basham et al., 2016).

Hosek utilized the online platform for student reflections to individualize each student's learning experience through immediate feedback that focused on support, encouragement, and provision of additional guiding questions and materials (Percell, 2017). Students were asked to push beyond summarizing what they read or experienced to include consideration and comparison of differing and multiple perspectives in order to develop reflexive critical literacy practices. Each reflection was worth ten points, and students were informed that they were a means of formative assessment of their understanding of critical pedagogy and an opportunity for the instructor to provide constructive feedback for further growth. Reflections and exchanges between Hosek and three students in this course are examined next.

## Illustrated Examples of Student's Critical Reflections

Excerpts of the students' work provide illustrated examples of both their comfort in sharing personal information about their experiences, beliefs, and cultural and socio-economic backgrounds and the development of the students' connection between critical theoretical knowledge and teaching practice. The students gave permission to confidentially share all information presented throughout this chapter. Demographic information is provided below in Table 15.1.

Table 15.1: Student Demographic Information

| Name | Identifies as | Ethnicity | Content Area |
|---|---|---|---|
| Caleb | Male | African-American | Art |
| Isabel | Female | Latina | Spanish Education |
| Kenna | Female | Caucasian | High School Science |

Source: Author

First Critical Reflection

The LMS was an invaluable platform as it housed all materials and reflections which built on each other throughout the semester. Students began the semester reading several articles containing three differing perspectives (administrators, teachers, and high school/college students) about the purpose of schools. In addition, they watched Sir Ken Robinson's Ted Talk Changing Education Paradigms (2010). These were presented as opinion pieces, and the students were provided with guiding questions where they were asked to examine and reflect about the materials in light of their own personal opinions, experiences, and beliefs. As seen below in their first reflections for the course, the students shared their pedagogical beliefs early on. This information provided insight about each student, and Hosek utilized the online platform to quickly provide constructive feedback and identify points that could be used to engage each student in critical theoretical discussions. Having that information so easily and continually accessible for reference and guidance was vital in developing students' critical pedagogical beliefs.

Isabel's reflection showed the value she placed in classroom opportunities for student voice and creative thinking. In the following excerpts, her critical perspectives were evident. Reflecting about Sir Robinson's (2010) video, she explained:

> As children grow up they are being told that there is only one right answer and that is making our children not to explore new ways of thinking and stops children from bringing value to a classroom setting.

Isabel focused on the significance of incorporating and embracing diverse cultures. She stated further, "School is the only place they can interact with different cultures and be able to overcome cultural differences." Isabel both valued and was concerned with structure, as she worried that the standardizing of schools left little room for incorporating cultural differences. In her response, Isabel was asked to consider how teachers might establish a balance between structure and freedom:

You explain that you saw the benefits of structure, schedule and rules in the preschool where you interned. At the same time you recognize the importance of freedom to learn without fear and feeling emotionally safe enough to engage in that freedom. I think this is a juxtaposition that many teachers find themselves in. How much structure is too much? How do you know where to place boundaries? This makes reflecting on personal experiences and on what other teachers and students think and believe so valuable.

Like Isabel, Kenna was greatly impacted by the readings and TED Talk. She connected her personal experiences and observed teachers' practices with the course materials when offering her perspective. She explained:

> I was most surprised when Sir Ken Robinson suggested we should become less standardized, don't categorize students by their age, instead by their abilities. Eisner (2003) mentioned this theory in his article as well. I genuinely love this idea ... When I observed in the special education classes, students of different grades were grouped together. The focus was more on their emotional, social, or physical abilities. Why do students of the same age have to be at the same level?

Kenna's response centered on inclusivity and showed she already was adept at connecting theory with practice. In her feedback, Hosek focused on valuing and encouraging Kenna's instinctive ability to incorporate her personal experiences, the teaching practices she observed, and current and future course materials:

> I appreciate the way you support your opinion with your personal experiences. You follow that with a clear explanation about how you would enact change in your own classroom ... your personal experiences combined with the resources you are reflecting about will continue to shape your pedagogical beliefs in positive ways. I also believe in the reciprocal relationship between student and teacher and appreciate the connection you make between teacher and student goals.

Another student who shared his pedagogical beliefs early on was Caleb. His reflection showed that he valued elements of Reconstructivism. He explained his understanding of the purpose of schools and education's role in society:

> Reconstructing society should always be the sole goal between the two. The author tries to make a case that both are necessary and balance the other out, but I do not understand their take because the end goal, as they also stated, is to improve and move forward in society which in turn reconstructs it. Reconstructing does the job of both, and also hopefully eliminates hateful practices and morals of certain members of the society as we move forward towards a common goal.

Although he did not yet recognize it, his reconstructivist beliefs showed Caleb's pedagogy to be grounded in critical theory. This was further evident in his reflection about the course reading (Powell, 2019):

> Two people mentioned that the school falls into the category of if it's not broke don't fix it, which I do not agree with at all. The school system is broken. This idea that the school system should not adapt with everything else around it is why the U.S education system is consistently questioned today. Society has evolved and grown over the years. The US education system was also made with white men in mind and forced to just include "the other" members of society ... If students learn how to approach social and cultural differences from those they are around and those they may eventually come into contact with then they are more well equipped in how they can better serve the society they live in.

To help Caleb think more deeply, Hosek encouraged him to consider how reconstructivist beliefs could look in practice:

> I believe Powell (2019) is suggesting that to secure a democratic society, or to ensure that reconstruction can take place without uprisings or upheaval of our government, developing democratic ideals or notions of citizenship is necessary. That said, your point is well taken. Powell assumes that democracy is equally benefitting all of society, when in fact, it isn't, which is a primary reason that reconstruction is needed and sought. It's similar to asking teachers to encourage creativity and embrace diversity while at the same time standardizing the means by which those same students are evaluated.
>
> You make a strong point about the value of students' opinions and the lack of student voice in the scholarly article. There is a branch of educational research that I think you would be interested in reading about—Youth Participatory Action Research (YPAR). Here is a link to it. Your comment "The students are speaking in the position of the receiver" could be largely the result of not having the opportunity to have a voice. That lack of opportunity results from teacher-centered, authoritarian methods so often used and/or resorted to by teachers.

These critical reflections where students provided their diverse experiences were easily facilitated on the LMS resulting in personalized teaching and learning opportunities. Prevalent in each reflection were students' critical pedagogical leanings which afforded opportunities for the instructor to encourage further growth and depth of engagement through constructive, guiding feedback that met students where they were while pushing each in different ways to make further connections and incorporate critical literacy practices.

## Second Critical Reflection

For the second reflection, the students completed a reading about educational philosophies (See Beatty et al., 2009) then took and scored an online educational philosophies survey (Educational Philosophies Survey developed by Oregon State University) which aligned each score with an educational philosophy. The LMS housed all of these materials, provided the platform for the delivery, scoring, and viewing of results of the survey, and gave students immediate and direct access to their personal digital spaces for their critical reflections. The instructor also had access to all of this data and students' personal responses online which enabled her to critically analyze and constructively provide feedback. After completing the reading, but before taking the survey, students were asked to identify and reflect about which philosophy they felt most closely reflected their beliefs. Then, they were asked to take the survey and reflect about how they felt about the similarities and differences between each. The students were also asked to consider whether or not their questionnaire scores reflected what they hoped or initially expected and why. The objectives for this reflection, which were easily facilitated through the design of the online platform, were twofold: to expose students to theoretical academic language and function, and to help them further examine and connect the theoretical to their personal experiences and beliefs.

Isabel explained that while she hoped she would be categorized as reconstructivist, the survey results categorized her as progressivist which she interpreted as "focusing on individuality" and not on students "growing as a whole." This troubled her:

> If I could change my educational experiences I would change how I felt in my 2nd grade class. I felt belittled when I went to a predominantly white school. As a Mexican, I remember my former teacher would get frustrated with me because my English wasn't up to par. … I can see myself focusing on race and how that divides us as a society. I would want my classroom to be knowledgeable about the impact race has on someone else and how hard it is to break free from that mentality and also that way of life. I would love to give my students facts as to why race plays a huge role in society.

She then offered very personal experiences as reasons for why she believed her questionnaire results were wrong:

> As a Mexican growing up in a predominantly white school it was really hard to find someone who would understand my way of life and not judge it. I was even sometimes embarrassed to admit that I came from a low-income household because I was scared how I would be perceived. I didn't want others to look at me as less … I can't see myself focusing on individuality because in my mind that doesn't make us grow as a whole. I want minorities to be heard and not be belittled like I was. I don't want anyone else to feel like they aren't important to the school system like I felt, this is why this hits close to home.

Isabel's reflection showed both worry about her questionnaire results and passion about ensuring her experiences and beliefs were heard. Hosek responded:

Reconstructivism shares much with Critical Theory—both seek the recognition of and need for change. I believe Progressivism includes active student voice and participation, paying attention to the individual's needs—where learning is by doing. A progressivist believes that curriculum content should be driven by student interests and questions. Your description of your beliefs does reflect the importance of respecting individual differences (which is progressive) but it is also highly reflective of a reconstructivist. You stated "a teacher who is a reconstructionist is going to focus on the role race has in our school system." A teacher who has progressivist beliefs may do the same—particularly if she/he sees that the interests of a student reflect what is wanted or is needed. It was honest and insightful for you to recognize that the names and descriptions that authors give to educational philosophies don't mean that there isn't room for the actual teacher with the beliefs to question. In fact, a reconstructivist would do just that! The fact that you are organized and approach your personal studies in a very structured way may have been why your score leaned away from Reconstructivism.

Similar to Isabel, Caleb reflected deeply about each teaching philosophy presented. His questionnaire showed his educational philosophy to be equally rooted in Critical Theory (how the education system considers the social, political and economic advantages and disadvantages of different members of society) and Humanism (emphasis on the potential value and goodness in all people). He adeptly connected the philosophies on both a theoretical and personal level:

When considering my connection to Critical Theory, it is ultimately about the outcome, and the outcome derives from Humanism. I have faith in the natural good in our youth, and the potential in them as well to shape a society more fitting for them in the future. Critical Theory acknowledges the reality of our society in regard to limitations and privileges each person holds in various communities and spaces we exist in, and how to approach each one, while humanism acknowledges the potential in each person that can be leveraged to benefit themselves and possibly others. My middle school was in "the projects", so teachers there all knew students attending the school did not come from communities with much resources and neither did the school, but that did not stop my 7$^{th}$ grade teacher from pushing me to be better at math. Without him, I believe I would still struggle greatly with math today. My 9$^{th}$ grade English teacher knew what middle school I went to, and also had a personal agenda to help black students with their reading levels and interest in literature.

Hosek's response to Caleb focused on the value of his deep critical thinking when not only naming pedagogical beliefs, but also understanding their origin:

I appreciate the time you took to deeply think about the readings prior to taking the questionnaire. That pre-thinking helped you reconcile your score with your initial understanding of your pedagogical beliefs. You can see how the lines get blurred and that's why just because an author names a philosophy something or categorizes beliefs into an organized table doesn't mean all of what's in that box, say in your case the Humanism and critical theory boxes, can't spill over into other philosophical understandings that then shape and sharpen your epistemological and pedagogical beliefs.

The first and second critical reflections provided students with a multitude of resources and opportunities to examine their pedagogical beliefs in light of both their personal experiences and teaching practices that they either observed or participated in before this course. Those reflections laid important groundwork for the critical reflections to come. They provided opportunities to learn about and encourage each student individually, which the instructor believed built rapport and trust. The reflections also served as a formative assessment of each student's level of understanding about how theory, beliefs, and practice connect.

## Third Critical Reflection

The third reflection the students completed centered on examination of the kinds of instruction they experienced as students and the impact of deficit thinking in teaching practices. For this reflection, the privacy that the online space provided for the students in combination with the personalized feedback provided in the earlier reflections created a level of comfort and trust which helped students speak openly and freely about their very personal experiences and hardships. Students critically reflected about the concept of the "apprenticeship of observation" (Lortie, 1975), chapter 2 of *Pedagogy of the Oppressed* (Freire, 1970), and Gorski's (2008) article "The Myth of the Culture of Poverty."

This reflection strongly resonated with each student in different, deeply personal ways. In her reflection, Isabel further opened up about her family's struggle with poverty:

> This hits close to home because this was my life growing up. For my parents it is still hard for them to find a living wage because they didn't finish college and that is why I have done everything that I've could to break from that cycle and give my children a better future. When I read this article I could identify with every point because these statements were so true. When I was in high school I wanted to attend extracurricular activities but I never did because my parents were working three jobs to put food on the table and they didn't have time to pick me up.

She explained how troubled and discouraged she was to be judged based on her family's income and to not be offered accommodations throughout her elementary and secondary education to help her feel more secure. She described ways she believed teachers and the community could help low-income students which showed her connection of theory, beliefs, and teaching practices. Isabel also connected the insecurity she felt growing up to her experiences thus far in her teacher education program. She felt unsure about expressing her teaching beliefs and forced to use and teach what she called "Spain Spanish":

> As a Spanish teacher in America, I felt compelled to teach Spain Spanish and I wish I could teach Latin America Spanish because I feel Latin America Spanish is more predominant in the USA but I am so scared to break free from what everyone else was doing. As a Mexican it just doesn't feel authentic to teach Spain Spanish I want to teach Latin America Spanish and be different from the rest of the Spanish teachers.

Isabel's frustration with our education system and her worries about privileging one dialect over the other were palpable in her writing. Hosek wanted to ensure that Isabel recognized that her reflection and suggestions were clearly grounded in critical pedagogy:

> I can't imagine how extremely disheartening it is to have your content area standardized at the expense of authentically recognizing and valuing Latin American language and culture. It speaks to how Euro-Centric our education materials and curriculum are and how important application of critical theory is to challenge those power structures. It seems very contradictory doesn't it? We know we need to apply critical theory to our practices, materials, and methods, but then we find ourselves in schools/classrooms where we are required to teach specific things that don't necessarily support or represent all voices. Because of your keen ability to reflect and recognize what it is that troubles you about our field where there is a promotion and privileging of certain methods and certain knowledge, you still are in a stronger position to incorporate critical theory into your classroom—even by explaining the differences and why it matters will be exposing this issue.

For Kenna, this reflection provided an opportunity to build confidence in her decision to become a teacher and in her ability to enact change. She explained:

> As I continue to read, I realized my lack of understanding of these students is why I have so much doubt. I don't know how to solve a problem such as this because I don't understand the nature of it.

Her reflection about Gorski's (2008) article further showed her understanding of critical pedagogy and how her teaching practices could lead to change:

> The quote, "In education, we often talk about the deficit perspective—defining students by their weaknesses rather than their strengths" really spoke to me. I forgot this is another reason why I want to become a teacher, I always see the good in any person or situation. At the end, he added different courses of action we can act on now, rather than waiting for this amazing educational revolution to occur. This finally eased my mind about my worries for teaching students in a nontraditional style … We don't have to wait for the revolution; we can begin it right now!

In her feedback, Hosek encouraged Kenna about her critical pedagogical beliefs:

> You have what so many teachers that revert to traditionalist, teacher-centered, banking methods don't have. You have the ability and desire to understand your students. That alone will lift you up in their eyes which will fuel you to provide opportunities to meet *their* needs. I believe teaching is about building respectful relationships with our students grounded on trust. By trust I mean a trust that you value their voices and experiences by learning about where they come from and respecting their experiences as knowledge. Thank you for taking me through your process of reflecting!

## Connecting Theory and Beliefs

At different points throughout this course, each of these students claimed a lack of opportunity as teacher candidates to deeply examine their personal beliefs and experiences in light of critical pedagogy. This reflects "a problem of enactment" (Kennedy, 1999, p. 70) where opportunities to develop functional language to explain ideas in a specific frame of reference are largely absent. In fact, Caleb stated: "I've never known that what I believed about teaching and learning actually had a name and that actually is a thing." In their reflections, they dissected their own apprenticeships of observation. That examination provided "a frame of reference that allows them to interpret their experiences"; however, without critical reflection about them, the "standards of expectation" (Kennedy, 1999, p. 55) can leave teacher candidates feeling confused when their personal beliefs do not match the standardized version. As their critical theoretical knowledge expanded during the course through readings, materials, critical reflections, and instructor feedback, all three students were able to critically examine and frame their personal experiences, beliefs, and subjectivities in light of the social and political powers at work in our education system. As a result, each student gained a deeper understanding of critical pedagogy. These positive results led us to offer the following suggestions for online course design and instructional strategies.

## Online Course Design and Instructional Strategies for Developing Critical Pedagogy

Through our examination, we identified several important online course design components and accompanying instructional strategies that can facilitate the development of students' critical pedagogical beliefs. First, an LMS that can centrally house all course materials and be used to facilitate the organization of the materials and critical reflections is essential. This supports the instructor in helping to develop students' knowledge progressively and cumulatively by building upon foundational readings and materials about critical theory in education from the beginning of the course to the end. Within that LMS, a personal and private dedicated digital space for each student is necessary to both individualize student learning and develop personal instructor-student connections. Such space can build the trust needed for students to be open about their personal beliefs and experiences, which is both essential for a student's development of critical pedagogical beliefs and indispensable for empathetic and constructive instructor feedback.

Additionally, close attention to the sequencing of the course materials and critical reflections is key for both the students and the instructor. Providing students with repeated opportunities through deep, meaningful critical reflections is essential as they draw upon their growing knowledge to further understand prior personal educational experiences and learn how to apply that critical pedagogical knowledge to future teaching practices. All materials and assignments should be organized in the LMS so the instructor can effectively and efficiently access the accumulating reflections to formatively assess students' progress and constructively guide students in the connection of critical theory to practice in a consistent and timely manner.

A critical theoretical approach to instruction is imperative if we want future teachers to recognize and challenge social injustices within our education system (Giroux, 2017). As such, to support the development of students' critical pedagogical beliefs, critical theory must be prioritized and central to instructor decisions about materials, assignments, and feedback. An emphasis on growth over performance when creating the guiding questions, providing feedback, and assessing students supports such an approach. Also key is strong instructor dedication to critical framing of feedback that is individualized and culturally responsive to each student. Equally important is a commitment from instructors to continually reflect about their own teaching decisions through critical framing and prioritizing critical literacy practices in their methods which can provide valuable modeling of critical pedagogy (Freire, 1970). All of the above online course design components and instructional strategies support a critical theoretical approach to foundational educational courses and can provide a means for helping students develop critical pedagogical beliefs.

# References

Basham, J. D., Hall, T. E., Carter Jr, R. A., & Stahl, W. M. (2016). An operationalized understanding of personalized learning. *Journal of Special Education Technology, 31*(3), 126–136. https://doi.org/10.1177%2F0162643416660835

Beatty, J. E., Leigh, J. S., & Dean, K. L. (2009). Philosophy rediscovered: Exploring the connections between teaching philosophies, educational philosophies, and philosophy. *Journal of Management Education, 33*(1), 99–114. https://doi.org/10.1177%2F1052562907310557

Breunig, M. (2005). Turning experiential education and critical pedagogy theory into praxis. *Journal of Experiential Education, 28*(2), 106–122. https://doi.org/10.1177%2F105382590502800205

Chiasson, K., Terras, K., & Smart, K. (2015). Faculty perceptions of moving a face-to-face course to online instruction. *Journal of College Teaching & Learning, 12*(3), 321–240. https://doi.org/10.19030/tlc.v12i3.9315

Darder, A., Baltodano, M., & Torres, R. D. (2017). Critical pedagogy: An introduction. In A. Darder, M. Baltodano, & R. Torres (Eds.), *The critical pedagogy reader* (3rd ed., pp. 27–51). Routledge.

Eisner, E. W. (2003). Questionable assumptions about schooling. *Phi Delta Kappan, 84*(9), 648–657.

Ertmer, P. A., Ottenbreit-Leftwich, A. T., Sadik, O., Sendurur, E., & Sendurur, P. (2012). Teacher beliefs and technology integration practices: A critical relationship. *Computers & Education, 59*(2), 423–435.

Freire, P. (1970). *Pedagogy of the oppressed.* The Continuum Publishing Company.

Giroux, H. A. (2017). Critical theory and educational practice. In A. Darder, M. Baltodano, & R. Torres (Eds.), *The critical pedagogy reader* (pp. 27–51). Routledge.

Gorski, P. (2008). The myth of the culture of poverty. *Educational Leadership, 65*(7), 32–44.

Hampton, K., Rainie, L., Lu, W., Dwyer, M., Shin, I., & Purcell, K. (2014). *Social media and the 'spiral of silence.'* Pew Research Center.

Hosek, V. A., & Handsfield, L. J. (2019). Monological practices, authoritative discourses and the missing "C" in digital classroom communities. *English Teaching: Practice & Critique, 19*(1), 79–93. https://doi.org/10.1108/ETPC-05-2019-0067

Hrevnack, J. R. (2011). Guided development of reflective thinking in the observations of classroom teachers by pre-service candidates. *Academy of Educational Leadership Journal, 15*(2), 81–94.

Illinois State University. (n.d.). *TCH 212: The teaching profession in secondary schools.* https://coursefinder.illinoisstate.edu/tch/212/

Kennedy, M. M. (1999). The role of preservice teacher education. In L. Darling-Hammond & G. Sykes (Eds.), *Teaching as the learning profession: Handbook of policy and practice* (pp. 54–85). Jossey-Bass.

Lortie, D. (1975). *Schoolteacher: A sociological study*. University of Chicago Press.
National Council for Accreditation of Teacher Education. (2008). *Professional standards for the accreditation of teacher preparation institutions*. NCATE.
Percell, J. C. (2017). Lessons from alternative grading: Essential qualities of teacher feedback. *The Clearing House: A Journal of Educational Strategies, Issues, and Ideas, 90*(4), 111–115. https://doi.org/10.1080/00098655.2017.1304067
Powell, S. D. (2019). *Your introduction to education: Explorations in teaching* (4th ed.). Pearson.
Robinson, K. (2010, October). *Changing education paradigms* [Video]. TED Conferences. https://www.ted.com/talks/sir_ken_robinson_changing_education_paradigms
Urbani, J. M., Roshandel, S., Michaels, R., & Truesdell, E. (2017). Developing and modeling 21st-century skills with preservice teachers. *Teacher Education Quarterly, 44*(4), 27–50.

# CHAPTER SIXTEEN

# Converting Research Efforts to Improve Equitable Student Achievement from a Professional Development Program to Online Course: GESA (Still) Works!

DOLORES A. GRAYSON

When I first conceived of GESA—originally Gender/Ethnic Expectations for Student Achievement, later renamed Generating Expectations for Student Achievement—I could not imagine that a teacher development program which was offered to hundreds of educators throughout the United States during intense three-day seminars would become an online graduate semester-course. A colleague of mine, Mary D. Martin, had developed a series of workshops on teacher expectations and student achievement, and she permitted me to incorporate twelve years of results and raw data from the implementation of her work in Los Angeles County into the initial version of GESA. While the inspiration for GESA, its principles and implementation reflected a commitment to critical pedagogy, neither Mary nor I ever used "critical pedagogy" to describe it. However, we wanted to address social justice, meeting the needs of students for whom schools were not working due to the impact of gender, race, social class, ability status, sexuality, and other variables. We wanted to empower teachers to make rich, knowledge-informed pedagogical decisions, and we wished to nurture dialogue-based school communities.

Our idea for creating a program to raise teachers' consciousness and shape effective action in their classrooms started in the wake of the Civil Rights, Title IX and the Women's Liberation movements, with deep concern for equity in education for girls and women and all students of color, whose numbers were expected to increase steadily in the next decades of demographic shift. We wanted to bring critical pedagogy to public schools by creating opportunities for teachers to engage in dialogue about their teaching, based on observations of each other's teaching following rigorous protocols. We wanted them to reflect, keep notes, make observations, gather data, and keep classroom equity in mind. In other words, we wanted to craft a program to develop teacher praxis—reflection and action—in classrooms that pushed the boundaries of professional development toward "viable unprecedented" results (Freire, 1970, 2003); that is, we wanted to create a meaningful, research-based program that had not yet been tried but was feasible, and we applied what is now known as an "action research" approach (Mertler, 2019) to accomplish this. Coincidentally, GESA was piloted and field-tested in the aftermath of a national report on public education in 1983 entitled, *A Nation at Risk*. The report was very critical and emphasized many negatives associated with teaching. Ironically, GESA was focusing on the things that teachers had done well over time in a positive manner with a specific portion of students for whom they had the highest expectations. Needless to say, GESA was well received from the beginning.

Then, as now, there are those who would have us believe that attention to equity and valuing diversity dilutes the efforts toward excellence in the classroom. The facts indicate that there is no substantiated evidence to support this claim. On the other hand, we have a wealth of validated evidence, both quantitative and qualitative, that when the concepts we developed in GESA are applied, and its research based-strategies are implemented, all students gain; in addition, the students identified as in greatest need gain at a greater pace, closing the performance gaps between the heretofore academic "haves and have-nots" (Beyerbach et al., 2009; Grayson, 2012). Education equity fulfills a society's vocation to "be more" (Freire, 1970, 2003).

GESA focused on emphasizing how some students, likened to Freire's "oppressed," are dealt out or are permitted to deal themselves out of the learning cycle, resulting in a lack of achievement, participation, and interest. In other words, they become part of the "culture of silence" in classrooms, schools, and perhaps even later as adults in workplaces and communities, these absent voices in the country's purported democracy. GESA's approach and the accompanying materials were designed to break this silence, taking advantage of what was established knowledge from studies on students' motivation (internal and external), persistence, resilience, locus of control (internal and external), and attribution theory. The themes of perceptions, expectations and achievement, all connected, are woven throughout GESA.

In 1988, I left the Los Angeles County Office of Education. Since I was the original developer and primary author, and a large portion of GESA had been developed by me on my own time and preceding my employment there, I left with an agreement that I could personally retain all production and distribution rights for GESA. As the demand for GESA increased, I realized that I needed to devote myself fulltime to this mission, and a partner and I established a private consulting business, GrayMill, devoted to training practitioners in educational equity and to publish and disseminate GESA and related materials. We did so for over thirty years, closing GrayMill in 2019.

This chapter is an attempt to share how by taking GESA online I have updated, revised, and built on an already solid research base that has spanned several decades and has been informed by literally thousands of educational practitioners, graduate students, researchers, and decision makers from all over the United States and several other countries. After all this work over all these years, I am more convinced than ever that given the appropriate resources, encouragement, and leadership, we know how GESA-informed teachers can provide an excellent education for all of our students. In spite of many barriers, I have seen it happen on multiple occasions in a variety of settings with diverse populations of students across socioeconomic classes, across subject areas and across grade levels, but mostly in isolated pockets of awareness and willingness. The question is: Do we, as a nation, really want to do so? The past professional development efforts, and now this online graduate course, continue to be committed to that goal.

## GESA: Generating Expectations for Student Achievement

### Development and Implementation

We designed GESA to assist teachers and other educators to address the predicted changing demographics across the country during the 21$^{st}$ century; to identify strategies to improve equity in achievement for all students; and, to close performance gaps of those who had been traditionally underserved especially due to the impact of gender, race, social class, and ability status (Grayson & Martin, 1985, 1990). As mentioned earlier, GESA was piloted in Los Angeles County, California, which formed a microcosm of the United States. In the eighties, the county included 95 school districts which served over 1.2 million students and varied greatly in population characteristics. It had urban, suburban, and rural districts, some dominantly White, others dominantly Hispanic/Latinx, African American, Asian and Pacific Islander. A few were wealthy enclaves, such as Beverly Hills and San Marino, while others like Compton and Baldwin Park served mostly low-income populations. According to the Los Angeles County Office of Education at the time, the public-school population was 44.3% Hispanic; 31.1% White; 14.8% Black; 8.0% Asian and Pacific Islander; 1.5% Filipino; and 0.3% American Indian. 512,839 students claimed a "primary language other than English" and spoke eighty-seven different languages.

In this complex educational context, the GESA program was developed, piloted, and field-tested to address the needs of a culturally diverse population. It was very well received immediately in cities such as Seattle, Washington; Portland, Oregon; San Diego, California; and Prince George's County, Maryland, where districts were dealing with issues of disproportionality and high immigration rates (Grayson & Martin, 1990). For example, all students of color and especially males were being reprimanded, suspended, and expelled at a rate that far exceeded their proportion of the student population; additionally, most students in advanced placement and gifted and talented programs were predominantly White.

As the program expanded beyond Los Angeles County, a formal validation study was conducted in San Diego. Following this study, methods for assessment were included in the GESA materials and multiple agencies continued to assess their own implementation. As a result, we continued to collect data and feedback and GESA became a vehicle for practitioners interested in action research in their own sites, using our components and methodology. The material has been revised and the research updated on regular intervals throughout the years and that process continues with the online graduate students today (Grayson, 2008, 2012).

During GESA's first twenty-five years, a major vehicle for dissemination was a three-day facilitator training coordinated for multiple district representatives by personnel in the state departments of education through the Title-IV Civil Rights Act and Vocational Education federally funded programs. In some instances, individual school districts opted to host their own trainings. By the late nineties, over 10,000 local GESA facilitators had been trained, representing 47 states—all but Alabama, Oklahoma, and West Virginia (Grayson & Martin, 1997; Parsons et al., 2006).

By 2008, all fifty states, Puerto Rico and the Virgin Islands had been represented in the three-day facilitator workshops. Additional participants came from the Netherlands, Australia, Canada, England, Israel, Brazil, Nigeria, China, Japan, Germany, and Mexico. During this time, GESA began to be disseminated through several states funded by the Teacher Leadership Quality Partnerships (TLQP). Authorized by the No Child Left Behind Act of 2001 (Title II, Part A, Subpart 3), New York State's Teacher/Leader Quality Partnerships (TLQP) program aims at improving the academic success of New York's students by improving the quality of their teachers. The funding cycle for the New York State TLQP program was split into two funding initiatives. The first was an initiative focusing on in-service professional development. The second was an initiative focusing on the enhancement of educational leadership with School Building Leaders (SBL). New York became a major area of systemic distribution and data collection for GESA and it was incorporated into university projects in the professional development schools (Harrell et al., 2006; Ramalho & Beyerbach, 2005).

## GESA Strands: Areas of Disparity and Instructional Strategies

The initial learning and teaching literature review that informed GESA findings spanned several decades, ranging from a landmark study on classroom interaction (Hurlock, 1925), to numerous studies (Flanders, 1964; Good & Brophy, 1978, 1987, 2007; Rowe, 1987; Sadker & Sadker, 1984, 1985) conducted from the beginning (Addy & Wright, 2012; Cohen, 1994, 1998; Hale, 2001; Kozol, 2006; Steele & Aronson, 1995) and continuing. The earlier studies were included to document the extent of the existing pertinent literature and to remind us that our work has been part of a continuum of effort in the critical field of study on teacher perceptions, expectations, interactions, and achievement.

From careful examination of the research and numerous classroom observations, we identified five major categories which we labeled *Areas of Disparity* that have persisted over time and specific *Instructional Strategies* and patterns demonstrated by teachers in constructive ways with students for whom they had the highest expectations. These components became the basis for the original GESA program and continue to be incorporated, but have been refined, expanded, and adapted as the need and research has informed us over the years. For example, the disparity of teacher attention has developed into expanded knowledge on instructional contact and engagement. The identified disparity in seating arrangements gave rise to exploration into student grouping and classroom organization. The study of initial discipline disparity evolved into the study of classroom management and discipline techniques. An identified disparity in personal regard statements from teachers grew into identified disparities in the areas of self-esteem, self-concept, and self-efficacy, and the fifth original disparity in testing became the basis for the evaluation of student performance.

We did not develop new instructional strategies. While some of the terminology had to be explained, most of the original *Instructional Strategies* were known by teachers and many have been identified in the literature more recently as "best practices." Some were strategies identified from the Martin data that teachers used differently with their students, depending on their expectations and perceptions of the student's ability. For example, more attention was given to certain students, length of response times differed with certain students, active listening and probing was limited to certain students, and higher order questioning and both the quality and quantity of feedback was limited to only certain students. In addition, we noted how teachers responded to inappropriate behavior, depending on the student. When we had teachers identify target students based on their perceived (high or low) expectations and identified the student gender and ethnic characteristics of these choices, the equity ramifications were overwhelming. Consequently, we put the emphasis on the positive manner in which the teachers demonstrated the behavior with the students for whom they had the highest expectations and had them practice using the strategies in the same manner with all of their students. A major part of our solution became to "act as if" you expect them all to achieve. As indicated earlier, the results were and are dramatic. These components have continued to resonate as priorities with the graduate students in my online course, and I involve them in selected research and observation activities during which they identify more recent studies and findings in each area.

The GESA components are listed in Figure 16.1 below and discussed in greater detail in the next section on the GESA online course.

| AREAS OF DISPARITY | INSTRUCTIONAL STRATEGIES |
| --- | --- |
| Instructional Contact/ Engagement | a. Response Opportunity |
|  | b. Acknowledgment/Feedback |
| Grouping and Organization | a. Wait Time |
|  | b. Physical Closeness |
| Classroom Management/ Discipline | a. Reproof |
|  | b. Collect Discipline Data |
| Student Self-Esteem/Self-Concept/ Self-Efficacy | a. Listening |
|  | b. Probing |
| Evaluation of Student Performance | a. Higher Level Questioning |
|  | b. Analytical Feedback |

Figure 16.1: GESA Strands. Source: Author

The framework was originally piloted using peer observation, reflection, and discussion with teams of teachers from five districts during the six-month pilot phase. Applying what we had learned during the pilot study and refining our processes, we field-tested for another six months with teams of teachers from ten additional districts. This resulted in a program that was designed with teachers, for teachers, and by teachers. As stated earlier, the research has continued to be updated on an on-going basis.

GESA Impact

When the national dissemination commenced, the GESA professional development program was among the first to attempt to apply solutions across parallel equity issues: the instructional *Areas of Disparity* and *Instructional Strategies* have proven to be applicable to teacher interactions despite differences in race, national origin/ethnicity, gender, language dominance, sexual orientation, gender fluidity, developmental or physical ableism, socioeconomic class, perceived ability—or any of the labels that tend to deal students out or permit them to deal themselves in or out of the educational system. The ways in which the disparities manifest themselves may differ within and between specific groups.

Many of the strategies which we first identified and described have become commonplace among recommended effective instructional practices and the identified instructional *Areas of Disparity* (instructional contact/engagement; grouping and organization; classroom management/discipline; student self-esteem/self-concept/self-efficacy; evaluation of student performance) remain among some of the most frequently stated root causes of lack of participation and success for certain students, especially in the areas of science, technology, engineering, and mathematics (STEM), as well as other curricular disciplines. Several years of successful implementation with thousands of practitioners and graduate students continue to reinforce the original work.

Based on continuing data collection, we drew the following conclusions:

- Students in classes taught by teachers who became more critically aware through GESA achieved significant personal gains in reading, math, and other subject areas as assessed by standardized achievement tests scores;
- Teachers who participated in GESA reduced disparity in their frequency distribution of attention and increased the quality of their interactions with all students;
- Teachers who participated in GESA reported an increased use of non-stereotypical and more culturally-relevant materials and activities and created overall more constructive learning environments for their students.

Beginning in 2008, GESA moved to the electronic stage, and I developed and began providing a series of instructional webinars for the National Alliance for Partnerships in Equity (NAPE) and for the Intercultural Development Research Alliance (IDRA), among others. During this time, colleagues at SUNY Oswego and the Chair of the Curriculum and Instruction department began discussing the possibility of my offering an online graduate course based on the GESA materials, procedures, and findings. This was the impetus for my designing an online graduate course and using the GESA publication as my text.

## GESA-Based Online Course: Instructional Strategies to Improve Student Achievement

Since the beginning of 2010 to the present, over twenty cohorts of State University of New York (SUNY) graduate students have used the most recent GESA materials and research in an online graduate course offered through SUNY Oswego and entitled *Instructional Strategies to Improve Student Achievement*, taught by the author. Averaging forty to fifty interactive assignments for each individual, every cohort has made major contributions to the GESA text and an updated Bibliography Addendum (Grayson, 2019a). They have done this through reviewing, updating, and informing the research and concepts in their responses, application, and practice of the strategies; through written and charted observation reports; through scholarly review, analysis and replication of some of the research findings; through discussion forums with peers and colleagues; and through in-depth written reflection. With their permission, some of their work has been infused throughout the GESA text and in the Appendix. Too numerous to list individually, online GESA students have been a tremendous source of feedback, validation, and suggestions for ongoing relevance and improvement of this coursework. In addition, this experience has inspired and prompted me to make the most recent edition of the GESA Book available through an E-format and the GESA Facilitator materials and visual aids to be distributed digitally.

### Course Description

In the spirit of critical pedagogy, the course *Instructional Strategies to Improve Student Achievement* includes pertinent information on GESA's instructional *Areas of Disparity* in the learning and working environments. It sets effective instructional behavior patterns and indicators for observing them in practice and guidelines on how to record and assess each set. Survey activities, observations, practical application, reflective written assignments, data sharing, and follow-up discussions are included in each module. In addition to the required text, all students receive an electronic copy of an updated GESA Bibliography Addendum (Grayson, 2019a) by course email at the end of the first week of class.

The students use conventional productivity software, such as word processors and graphic presentation tools. This would be any software that can be used to produce required items, assignments, and final presentations. Microsoft Word or Works and PowerPoint or Keynote are appropriate, or similar Google Forms or programs that can convert files to the RTF or PDF format. In addition, we use certain Internet plug-ins for using articles, simulations, or videos inserted in some documents of this course. The course is designed to be delivered through the Blackboard Learning system/platform (BBL) or Brightspace. The BBL provides user-friendly organization.

## Course Objectives

As a result of participating in this course, students:

1. Examine teacher perceptions, expectations, behaviors, and their implications relative to specific populations of students, depending on the school's geographical location, student characteristics, and representation in the classroom;
2. Review research-based instructional areas of disparity relative to the teaching and learning environments that affect or prevent student achievement and their explorations of nontraditional paths or pursuit of interests in a variety of topics, classes, and careers;
3. Receive information on constructive, supportive, and motivational instructional strategies designed to counter the areas of disparity and improve student achievement. These strategies are used as data sources for observation and reflective narratives and dialogues.

## Course Curriculum

The introductory discussion prompt, which establishes the first critical dialogue among participants, reads as follows:

> Though it may sometimes seem that you are going through this class experience by yourself, it is important to remember that there is a community of students in here with whom you will interact in the discussions throughout this course. To begin this discussion process, please take this opportunity to tell us a little about yourself and

begin to get to know your classmates. Once you have introduced yourself, take some time to review what your peers have shared about themselves.

The students are then instructed to submit an original introductory post and respond to at least two classmates, ideally two with whom they have discovered something in common.

Once the Icebreaker activities are completed, the student begins the text-related content folders, which include *Background Information* and *Module One* on *Instructional Engagement and Participation*, the first area of disparity identified in GESA. The title or theme for each consecutive module, two through five, focuses on the remaining areas of disparity that make up the first strand of the GESA components.

The course learning activities include:

- Completion of assigned readings from the text and/or additional research;
- Participation in discussion forums that provide students with an opportunity to interact and dialogue on the assigned topic with their peers and apply the concepts that they are learning in a practical setting;
- Reviewing, selecting, summarizing, and analyzing assigned research related to the topic;
- Completion of online assignments, polls, and/or surveys;
- Written reflections and reports on observations, practical applications, and practice of the information and research covered in the modules; and,
- Development of a written presentation, a visual presentation, and an action plan to apply and implement the acquired knowledge on equity and social justice for possible future use in a practical setting.

## Module Content and Activities

Each module includes a content discussion on the specific instructional *Area of Disparity*. Designed to encourage collaboration and collegiality among peers and build community, the discussion forum permits the students to develop personal and professional bonds through critical dialogue about scholarly information, the topics in the required text, and their experiences and opinions. Each module also contains a classroom observation practice assignment on instructional interactions, a selected research assignment, and a written reflection.

In what follows, the issue of classroom observations of instructional areas of disparity is discussed in greater length than the other activities. Classroom observation of instructional interactions, a central aspect of the GESA professional development program, is part of the online course's critical pedagogical approach. It supports the development of qualities and skills of an observer in the teacher and provides experiential data for personal reflections and, most importantly, for dialogues. An observation chart and examples of quantitative and qualitative insights are also provided.

*Module Two* instructs the students to respond to the following prompts relative to observations and encourages them to illustrate their narrative responses with examples:

> How is a classroom structured that is **least** effective and not conducive to all students being included in the learning processes? Where are the students seated? Where is the teacher located? Where does the teacher spend most of her/his time? Why do you consider this ineffective?

> How would you structure a classroom that would be **most** effective and that includes all students in the learning processes? Where are the students seated? Where is the teacher located? Where does the teacher spend most of her/his time? Why do you consider this more effective? Which of the two has been most familiar to you throughout your educational experiences?

The observable instructional interactions studied in *Module Two* are wait time and physical closeness. The term and concept of wait time in instruction was first coined by innovative science educator, Mary Budd Rowe (1972, 1987). A proponent of exploratory instruction and a foe of rapid response rote memorization, Rowe found that the periods of silence that followed teacher questions and students' completed responses rarely lasted more than 1.5 seconds in typical classrooms. She discovered, however, that when these periods of silence lasted for at least three seconds, many positive things happened to students' and teachers' behaviors and attitudes. She and many other researchers have replicated and extended her work (Grayson & Martin, 1990). The purpose of wait time is to provide the student with time to think and formulate a response. The length of time tends to be longest when the teacher asks questions that require the student to discover, interpret or reorganize the facts, to form an opinion, to respond in their own words, to respond in a second language, to give an example, or respond in a way other than to simply recall a fact.

In the eighties and nineties, Grayson and Martin found that the average time that a teacher waited for a student to respond to a question was about 2.5 seconds. The teacher waited an average of 5.0 seconds if a correct response was anticipated and curtailed the wait time to less than 1.0 second if the student was expected to give an incorrect answer or to not respond at all. In the eighties, the wait time studies were replicated by other researchers who also discovered that perceived low achieving students received an average of less than one (.9) second of wait time (Sadker & Sadker, 1984). During the implementation of GESA throughout the last several years, participating teachers have validated that they provide a period of wait time ranging from three to five seconds to students for whom they have the highest expectations. The goal is to provide a comparable amount of time for all students to process and respond.

The second interaction studied in *Module Two* is physical closeness. Teachers often organize classrooms in ways which determine where individual students will be located. Some students may be unconsciously kept at a distance. When given the opportunity to choose, this is one of the most obvious ways students deal themselves in and out of participating in a class. Teachers need to be aware of anchor points or hot spots in the classroom. These may include certain students, pieces of equipment, or areas of the room in which we tend to plant ourselves or pivot back and forth. In contrast, we need to be aware of *dead zones*, areas of the room where students tend to hide and into which the teacher seldom ventures. These are the most extreme patterns pertaining to teacher and student mobility in classrooms.

Physical closeness—in traditional face-to-face learning environments—is observed when the student and teacher are conducting their classroom activities near each other, within three feet, an arm's reach, or within the same quadrant of the room, at least for a brief period of time. This can depend on grade level, class size and structure, and whether the furniture is mobile or stationary. In formal observations, when the teacher stands or sits within an arm's reach in a stationary position, physical closeness is recorded for each student. Nothing is recorded if the teacher merely walks by a student. If a student approaches the teacher and stands within an arm's reach, physical closeness is recorded. The course text includes observation guidelines and sample forms that may be copied or adapted for the observation practice assignment, with instructions based on the research and information provided in the required reading:

> Practice and / or observe the interactions for Unit 2 in your classes and / or work settings. Who is getting called on and/or responded to? When someone is called on, do they get time to think and process their response? Who gets at least three to five seconds of wait time? What do you observe about the mobility patterns of the teacher and/or the students?
>
> Tally and record your observations on wait time and movement or physical closeness. Note the characteristics of the people involved. Are there any equity concerns evident? Look for examples that validate or contradict the research. Note who is sitting/working with whom.

Where is the teacher/leader/facilitator in relation to the students/participants? Can you identify "hot spots" or "dead zones?" Jot down any observations related to the research.

(Refer back to your Observation practice for Module One? Did you have any of these mobility patterns? Are there any correlations to the mobility patterns and the frequency of attention patterns you observed in your first observation assignment? If so, include comments in your report.)

Report the results of your observations/practice in a one-page document. You may add chart(s) if you like.

## Sample Analysis of Observations, Observation Chart and Equity Analysis

Classroom observations are sources of quantitative and qualitative data collection and analysis. The chart below (Grayson, 2012, p. 143) in Figure 16.2 is an example of a graphic to explain the statistical analysis by category of equitable distribution, with a "coefficient of equity," as described in the course's *Module 1*, which is also amenable to be applied to any category or student characteristic.

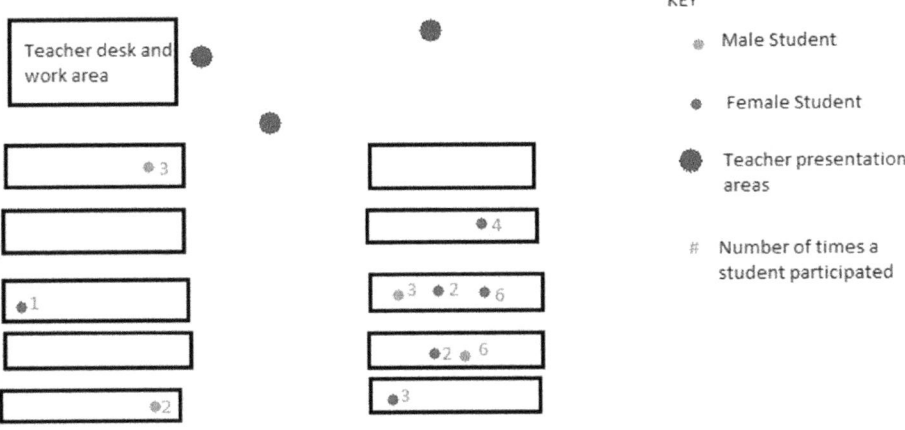

Figure 16.2: Observation Chart Based on Submission by K. Jacobson. Source: Author

A simple analysis of this chart is as follows:

There is a total of ten students (six females and four males). Consequently, 60% of the total interactions would optimally be allocated to females and 40 % would be allocated to males. These are the equitable goals.

There is a total of 32 interactions (3.125% each), with 18 (56.25 or 56%) distributed to females and 14 (43.75 or 44%) distributed to males.

Based on past experiences and data, we consider a distribution within three percentage points or less to be moving within an equitable range; consequently, this teacher is very close to being in an equitable range in terms of gender distribution.

The same proportional analysis above could be applied to any characteristic pertaining to social justice categories other than gender, such as students in poverty or students with disabilities, for example. Individual student scores could be calculated by multiplying the number of tallies received x 3.125 for the individual percentages. This is only one way of looking at basic data quantitatively. It does not have to be complicated and can be easily displayed. Course students also indicate critical insights in the narratives about their observations (Grayson, 2019b):

> I observed … a predominantly English language learner (ELL) class from my student teaching placement … There were 16 students present on the day that I completed this observation—only four of which were female. Six … were non-ELL students while the remaining ten were ELL students. During this lesson, the teacher was lecturing the students using a slideshow. There was a total of nine student responses to teacher prompts. Six of the responses were from the same male student (male student #1). One response was from a different male student (male student #2). Two responses were from a female student. These students were native English-speaking students. I noticed that no ELLs participated or seemed engaged during this lesson.
>
> In the high achieving class, the teacher spoke for about 30 minutes (75% of class time). In the low achieving class, the teacher spoke for about the same amount of time. However, six minutes of the teacher speaking in the low achieving class consisted of speaking to another teacher, not the students. In both classes, I observed that the only negative student/teacher interactions were between the teacher and black male students.
>
> Observations I made (on wait time) were eye-opening. … a teacher responded immediately after getting a response from her students almost every time. I am guilty of this as well. The (research) readings said that you need to allow students to finish their thoughts … I took that one to heart and have been trying to allow students to finish their thoughts completely.
>
> The teacher had one main hotspot that she stood in throughout the entirety of the lesson … consistently in the front of the room next to the Smart Board. The frequency of attention patterns that I observed in my first observation assignment correlate with the student participation during this observation. … the three students that engaged with the teacher were all seated in the front of the room while the non-participating

ELL students were closer to the back corners of the room. These back corners were the same dead zones that I observed in the module 1 observation practice assignment.

The most important topic … to me is the high-level questioning and analytical feedback section. … in my observation assignment, (the) teacher has struggled with questioning as a whole for many years. S/he chose to post question starters in the back of the classroom. This has caused (the teacher) to become much more effective in the questioning of students.

In these narratives, course students clearly identify equity issues in the classroom they observe. Insights not only highlight the number of teacher interactions with particular students but the absence of participation by others as well; they show disparate length of interactions favoring certain groups over others; disciplinary interactions focusing on young Black males; greater interactions with students sitting physically close to the teacher; and other inequitable dimensions of interactions in the classroom. Attitudes and behaviors that perpetuate inequity in achievement and outlook can be changed through teacher awareness and action, which are important critical pedagogical outcomes of the course.

1. *Research assignment*

The course text contains related research findings in each module on each component being studied. This assignment focuses on the assigned readings. The students are instructed to select, identifying by author and date, at least two studies that they find interesting and would like to read or know more about. They are asked to summarize the main point(s) and finding(s) for the study, add a scholarly analysis/ comment or two about their thoughts and reactions, and describe why they chose each one. They are instructed to add a recent/current study or article on the topic, which they identify through their own library or internet research outside of the text. They are to summarize, analyze, and describe their rationale for choosing this study, also, for a total of three studies.

2. *Written reflection*

For the end of the *Module Two*, students are instructed to write a one-to-two page, double-spaced paper on their readings, reflections, practical application, and experience with the information and research covered in *Module Two*. The main purpose of the written reflection paper is to indicate a summary of the extent of their learning, knowledge, and comprehension of the material, topics, and concepts covered and their scholarly analysis. They are to include any main points learned and applied from the text, assignments, and activities in *Module Two*. As stated earlier, these are examples of the types of assignments that are required in each of the content modules.

## Course Culminating Assignments

As final projects in the course, students are expected to complete a culminating activity of *Presentation Planning and Development* as well as an *Action Plan* for possible application of the course content in their future professional responsibilities. The assignments are in lieu of a final exam and include three required submissions. The first two consist of a written presentation on GESA and an accompanying visual presentation with a minimum of ten slides. These are for possible future use with their peers, colleagues, and other educators in a class or faculty meeting, or in a professional development, interview, or conference setting. The third item is an *Action Plan* expressing what they hope to accomplish as a result of their learning and participation in the course.

## Evaluation of Student Learning

Students are provided with a number of opportunities to assess that they have read and comprehend the assigned material throughout the course. These include their participation in course discussions, reviewing research and other selected activities, surveys, polls, assigned observations and practical applications, written reflections, the culminating assignments, and quizzes and tests on the required readings, as needed. When grading students' submissions, the following factors are assessed for maximum point value:

(1) **Content** of the original discussion posts and written submissions. Does the length and substance of the submission explore the assignment and demonstrate their personal understanding by providing personal experiences linked to the readings, with citations, as needed?
(2) **Reactions** to their colleagues and peers. Are their initial reactions substantive and do they contribute to the group discussion, as a whole? Does their additional reaction prompt more discussion, encourage peers, and receive responses from others?
(3) **Relevance** of the submission. Does it relate strongly to the module topic and required readings? Have the specific assignment directions been followed?

(4) **Expression and delivery.** Are the ideas and opinions in the submission expressed in a clear and concise manner and are they stated clearly, with connection to the topic? Are correct spelling and grammar used and indicative of academic and professional writing?
(5) **Promptness** of the submission. Are written submissions on time or early? Is an original post in a discussion forum submitted early in the module and are discussion reactions submitted shortly after the original posts (unless otherwise instructed)? Does the student log on and visit the discussions two or three times before the deadline (unless otherwise specified in the assignment instructions)?

## Student Feedback on the Course

In addition to the formal evaluations conducted by the Curriculum and Instruction department, feedback is elicited directly from the students at the end of the course. This is accomplished through an assignment in the sixth and final module, when the students are asked to write a final paper on their experience in the course. This may relate to the readings, observations, reflections, practical application, and practice of the information and research covered in the text, or an additional article or related research study they may have discovered. It may also be about something that resulted from their participation when they applied some of the concepts in their own classes or schools.

The following excerpts are from some of their most recent responses during the 2019 and 2020 sessions:

> NYS Common Core ... talks about (being an) effective teacher. To me, that tied in with GESA because it really encompasses practices done and established by effective teachers and teaching. An effective teacher assesses the students individually and meets students where they are to effectively bridge the achievement gap. If other teachers want to learn how to be effective, they have to be reflective and also be willing to learn from others.

> This course has taught me a lot about myself as a person and as a teacher. It has given me different ways to look at myself and at my students. I have learned many new strategies that have helped make my classroom a positive learning environment, such as wait time, physical closeness and analytical feedback.

> Being a school counseling student ... I'll be engaging with the students during one-on-one interactions ... I should be even more aware of my own bias and the messages that it sends to students ... it can have a huge positive impact on students in their future ... I'm so glad that I can apply these learnings in my own work.

The design and real passion for what is being taught is truly valued and contributed to how my students will succeed in the future. From this course, I learned the importance of making high expectations for all of my students but (also) supporting them and showing them that they are supported every step of the way. Thank you for all that you have done in this aspect ... never before have I left a class sad that it is over!"

There is a Zen quotation from Tibetan Buddhism (In Tao Te Ching by Laozi, 400 BC) that says, "When the student is ready, the teacher will appear." My experience with this course has been that all of these graduate students are ready and willing for the excellent teacher inside of them to appear—this critical pedagogy-informed course provides a mirror and tools for that to happen. The quotes above indicate the types and quality of feedback on the GESA-based online course that participants have provided since its beginning. They demonstrate that participants understand that teaching effectiveness requires identifying achievement gaps that result from often unconscious differential and inequitable treatment of diverse students. Teachers must reflect on their biases and make changes to ways of interacting with students. Hopefully this course is a vehicle to help them to achieve that goal.

## Conclusion

As I compiled and developed this chapter, it provided me with an opportunity to reflect on the evolution and growth, not only of GESA, but my own as a professional critical educator and researcher. Researching, conducting, and presenting the ongoing findings and results of this work has been the focus of a major portion of my career during the last several decades. Thanks to the support and encouragement of my colleagues and the opportunities provided by SUNY Oswego and the state of New York, I have been able to meet one of my most daunting challenges. That has been to convert a very interactive and successful professional development program into a constructive, productive, and critical online graduate course that could equip professional educators to make a contribution to our field, enhance their experiences, and improve the achievement and outlook of their own students.

GESA continues to work. It raises teachers' consciousness and shapes effective action in classrooms. GESA online empowers teachers to make rich, critical knowledge-informed pedagogical decisions, and engage in meaningful dialogues in school communities.

# References

Addy, S., & Wright, V. (2012, February). *Basic facts about low-income children*, 2010. National Center for Children in Poverty. https://www.nccp.org/publication/children-under-6/

Beyerbach, B., Burrell, M., Cosey, B., Evenstead, J. P., Grayson, D., Parsons, D., & Ramalho, T. (2009). Assessing the impact of GESA (Generating Expectations for Student Achievement) impacts on teachers, preservice teachers, and K-12 students. In R. D. Davis, A. London, & B. Beyerbach (Eds.), *How do we know that they know? A conversation about a social justice knowledge base* (pp. 189–210). Peter Lang.

Cohen, E. G. (1994). *Designing groupwork: Strategies for heterogeneous classrooms*. Teacher's College Press.

Cohen, E. G. (1998). Making cooperative learning equitable. *Educational Leadership, 56*(1), 18–21.

Flanders, N. A. (1964). Interaction model of critical teaching behaviors. In F. R. Cyphert & E. Spaights (Eds.), *An analysis and projection of research in teacher education* (pp. 197–218). The Ohio State University College of Education.

Freire, P. (2003a). *Pedagogy of the oppressed*. Continuum. (Original work published 1970).

Freire, P. (2003b). From pedagogy of the oppressed. In A. Darder, M. Baltodano, & R. D. Torres (Eds.), *The critical pedagogy reader* (pp. 57–68). Routledge Falmer.

Good, T. L., & Brophy, J. E. (1987). *Looking in classrooms* (4th ed.). Harper & Row.

Good, T. L., & Brophy, J. E. (2007). *Looking in classrooms* (10th ed.). Allyn & Bacon.

Grayson, D. A. (2008). *Generating expectations for student achievement*. GrayMill.

Grayson, D. A. (2012). *Generating expectations for student achievement: An equitable approach to educational excellence*. GrayMill.

Grayson, D. A. (2019a). *GESA bibliography addendum*. SUNY Oswego.

Grayson, D. A. (2019b). *GESA research summary report*. Western Educational Equity Assistance Center.

Grayson, D. A., & Martin, M. (1985). *GESA teacher handbook*. GrayMill.

Grayson, D. A., & Martin, M. (1990). *Gender/ethnic expectations and student achievement* (2nd ed.). GrayMill.

Grayson, D. A., & Martin, M. (1997). *Generating expectations for student achievement* (3rd ed.). GrayMill.

Hale, J. (2001). *Learning while black: creating educational excellence for African American children*. The Johns Hopkins University Press.

Harrell, M., Ramalho, T., & Beyerbach, B. (2006). Community, diversity, and social justice: Are we promoting an understanding of diversity? In J. E. Neopolitan (Ed.), *Where do we go from here? Issues in the sustainability of professional development school partnerships* (pp. 199–221). Peter Lang.

Hurlock, E. B. (1925). An evaluation of certain incentives used in schoolwork. *Journal of Educational Psychology, 16*(3), 145–149. https://psycnet.apa.org/doi/10.1037/h0067716

Kozol, J. (2006). *The shame of the nation: The restoration of apartheid schooling in America*. Random House.

Mertler, C. (2019). *Action research improving schools and empowering educators* (6th ed.). SAGE.

Parsons, D., Ramalho, T., Beyerbach, B., & Burrell, M. (Summer, 2006). Implementing GESA in Small Town and Urban Contexts. *AGELE Newsletter*.

Ramalho, T., & Beyerbach, B. (2005). Using GESA with practicing and preservice teachers to work towards equity in a professional development school. In I. Guadarrama, J. Ramsey, & J. Nath (Eds.), *Research in professional development schools, Volume 2* (pp. 163–187). Information Age Publishing.

Rowe, M. B. (1972). *Wait-time and rewards as instructional variables, their influence in language, logic and fate control* [Paper presentation]. National Association for Research in Science Teaching. Chicago, IL, United States.

Rowe, M. B. (1987). Wait time: Slowing down may be a way of speeding up. *American Educator*, *11*(1), 38–43.

Sadker, D., & Sadker, M. (1984, April 23–27). *Teacher reactions to classroom responses of male and female students*. [Paper presentation]. American Educational Research Association Annual Meeting, New Orleans, LA, United States.

Sadker, D., & Sadker, M. (1985, March). Sexism in the schoolroom of the 80's. *Psychology Today*, *19*(3), 54–57

Steele, C. M., & Aronson, J. (1995). Stereotype threat and the intellectual test performance of African Americans. *Journal of Personality and Social Psychology*, *69*(5), 797–811.

# CHAPTER SEVENTEEN

# Adjunct Online Instruction in Higher Education: Are Piece-Work Professors Able to Teach Critically Under Virtual Panopticism?

BATYA WEINBAUM

I am a spider
I just step right now
Onto another track
The rail I was walking along
For the last seven years
May or may not
Have just dissolved
Out from under me
So I rotate my eyes
Sockets to the right,
Looking down, 'til I find a strand
I can walk upon
And if there isn't one
I create one
I create my own road
My own path
A new one a new strand a new
fresh long glistening shimmering vibrating
pulsating wet silver
Drippy strand emanating from my own belly
my guts gushing throbbing this mass out
And I walk across to a new highway,

>  a new railway, or pathway, or runway
>  My own courses
>  No one watching me
>  No one telling me I have to give grades
>  Or how many pages
>  Of what I can or cannot
>  Ask the students who do not like to go to the library or read
>  To buy
>  No one telling me how to use
>  Rubrics
>  Which I can't understand.
>  I will just keep spinning.

I am watching a woman preacher on YouTube as I write this essay in the category of unyielding situations and issues in online teaching. I am trying to stay positive. Specifically, the situation is teaching from a critical pedagogical perspective to foster community in the interest of creating dialogue when discussing readings critically, while under conditions of virtual panopticism. The issue is how to do this while employed only intermittently as an academic piece-worker. While I describe my critical pedagogical strategies online here, I also argue that it is not easy to carry out critical pedagogy under these conditions and that this takes a huge emotional toll on the academic workforce, if unconsciously, undermining the kind of education that can be delivered, with the result of dumbing down America.

Is this coincidental? I would argue, probably not. Reducing the ability to think critically ensures the passing of democracy to underprepared people, as we have had the misfortune to witness in the election of Donald Trump and others in his wake. The bottom line is, when people feel fear, they do things you might not want them to do, including giving in to the banking model of education, using scripted curricula, intimidating rubrics, grading and testing, instilling fears of inadequacy even further into students beneath them in the rungs of the capitalist educational hierarchy, offering the academic piece-worker neither safety net nor security.

In a Microsoft search, piece-work is defined as a noun in which work is paid for according to the amount produced. The illustration is given that "workers did piece-work at home" the kind of work now commonly available in the academic labor market to those holding doctorates, such as myself, with an English degree. An institution where I had been teaching online reduced my students to 37 this year, from 108 last year, from over 200 the year before, which was closer to the quota or upper limit allowed to the adjunct online instructors, who the administration pays by the number of students who complete the course.

This is academic piece-work, a higher education system of employment rapidly replacing tenure, the effects of which I have written about extensively before (Weinbaum, 2017). Online work itself is not really the problem and even has become my preferred method of instruction because of the various advantages of disembodiment I was pleasantly delighted to discover (Weinbaum 2013, 2016). Yet, since academic piece-work often pays by the number of students completing the course, and/or by the course, the situation of work is not secure and does not lead to taking risks. Even if the instructor is not prone to taking risks, never in the future does the metaphorical cotton-bale picker foresee a more secure existence.

At another institution where I have worked as an adjunct online instructor since 2017, I expressed my concerns about installing cameras in the students' computers to watch them writing World Literature essay exams. This was a software device called Proctorio that instructors had to install with no extra compensation beyond the normal teaching duties because our contracts said we had to do whatever the administration asks. Being paid by the piece completed or produced, like a bale of cotton, or a delivery, or a dress, means *ipso facto* being paid regardless of time used in tasks piled on. And despite protests, at least in my class, the students had to pay for this too, beyond the cost of their regular tuition, although other institutions make other options available without passing the cost and time forward to student and professor (Distance Education Committee, 2017; Watson, 2017). Instead, I proposed to the Dean and got approval for a work-around where the students filmed themselves doing creative readings of texts illustrating themes of plays, and submitted videos for their assessments, holding up ID cards for identification at the start. This got me out of installing cameras and saved the students some out of the pocket expenses. I did teach successfully that way for one term. But that was that. I was never offered more work there again.

Some students teamed up and did their oral performances together. The challenge was to film themselves explaining their choice of the excerpt, do the production, and then explain all aspects of their choice, including decisions about location, elocution, costume, rehearsal, and what they learned by the live performances. Then, they had to apply the lessons of the pieces performed to our own times. Thus, Hamlet came alive, as did the Wife of Bath, Oedipus, and Ophelia, and so on, much more effectively than in a remotely proctored written exam. The students learned through a fun, creative experience driven by their own choice and agency and got the opportunity to work with one another.

At the end of the term, however, my course assignments stopped abruptly. Subsequently, the Director of Human Resources told me in writing that the Dean of Online Instruction had committed to hiring me later, for Winter 2020, with nothing in between, when I had been hired regularly summer, fall, and winter since 2017—That claim was made in an unemployment investigation, but it was false. I had never been formally offered any further contractual work. Actually, I never was. This means, after expressing my concerns about asking the students in my own classrooms to pay for the violation of their own privacy with Big Brother watching (which raised cybersecurity issues I documented with technical reports and scholarship from the field), I became employed intermittently, according to the Georgia Department of Labor. Consequently, the university did not have to pay unemployment tax, even though the intermittent employment would not have paid anything between June 3, 2019, and a check somewhere in October of 2020, **IF** said class had been actually assigned and **IF**, when it did, it filled and **IF** the students stayed registered at least through the first week of the class, which is how they write contracts for adjuncts. I could not collect unemployment compensation according to the appeals determination we were in the midst of when this announcement happened about *possibly* getting a course in 2020, after getting no guarantee or promise or even answer about a course since August of 2019, when I stopped asking until February 2020, when I finally got from the Dean that further assignments were highly unlikely at all.

No matter how I teach, critically or not, I cannot pay a car loan based on vague allusions to possible future intermittent employment that deposit nothing into my bank account. That is in Georgia. I later filed a claim in my state of residence, Ohio, yet was told unless I appealed at the Supreme Court of the State level in Georgia, after being already turned down at the local level, I was ineligible there as well. I did try again with the new "unemployment on steroids" Congressional bill. But what I experienced was that engaging in critical experimental pedagogy, which altered what I was told to do, was punished by the cessation of what had been regular term-by-term assignment of courses and then the cessation of any assigned courses at all. Criticizing the institutions in which we try to carry out critical pedagogy and the society those institutions are serving, we might end up not getting to do pedagogy of any kind in the first place, and society stays dumbed down, unless we minister through poetry, alternative networks we create on our own, or in churches.

Due to the encroachment of artificial intelligence into higher education, I have discovered that Big Brother is always watching. When I had a tenure track job, yes, I was observed, but the observing team theoretically had to tell me when planned visits were going to happen. I could prepare. I had some boundaries. Yes, things could go wrong. Someone could drop into a classroom unannounced, and if he happened to be hostile to feminism, he could write up something absurd, like that I refused to teach men, though the course he had been observing was on the Beats as a Multicultural Literature Movement, and Ginsberg, Kerouac, and Burroughs had been on the syllabus, and the class was filled with both men and women on the day this tenured white male professor dropped in.

But in artificial intelligence, supervisors and deans are always signed in, watching every move, like the panopticon of the prison guard Foucault (1997) described in *Discipline and Punish*, having the advantage of staring down into the cell or cubicle to the prisoner not knowing when he or she is being observed. Supervisors can and have asked me to remove posts, because said posts "violated the curriculum," or because I suggested to a student who lived locally that we might "meet for coffee" if he were interested, if he had any concerns, questions, or thoughts about the readings, discussions, or assignments throughout the course—my attempt to compensate for no direct office hours since we had no campus. The adjunct online instructor has the right to set no boundaries in such situations. If management does not observe forum posts, grading, or email correspondence in real time, all levels of supervision have complete records of class interactions stored to return to inspect on their own time.

Once, in an online course, I questioned the binary division between Western and non-Western, suggesting this might be racist. I indicated that others also felt these terms might leave the impression that those who did not live in the civilized West, or operate according to Western establishment values, could not think in a sophisticated manner. I argued, as well, that perhaps people within the geographic civilized West also thought in a non-Western manner, such as those labeled schizophrenic, but they were very much part of the Western society itself, a reality the terms confused. I also posted narratives of feminist anthropologists in the field, including within the U.S., to that effect.

My immediate supervisor instructed me to take those posts down. This request was followed up by the Dean, reiterating her request, and then shortly thereafter, telling me not to expect employment for the following year or thereafter. Her issue was that I was criticizing the syllabus. My job, even though in the early stages, I had been on the revision team that helped create the course, was simply to teach what got poured, not to criticize what appeared. She thought criticizing something the students had just been asked to read would confuse them, seemingly operating out of a different theory of education than I did. Hers, possibly, was that knowledge is simply, like the courses, downloaded, and poured—not to be stirred, or chewed, or mulled over, as I felt I needed to do when I taught—but just swallowed.

The interchanges just described demonstrate a clash between a more traditional teaching model that takes a syllabus as an endpoint, a product, not as a starting point or a beginning, and the style of Paulo Freire. Freire in *Pedagogy of the Oppressed* (1970) was critical of depositing information into students like a bank deposits money, while advocating a more liberatory educational practice of posing problems to ask the students to rethink again, as if they are moving around in new ways on a dance floor—improvising, not just focused on learning a step to goosestep to the other side. He did this to liberate the oppressed students from being objects, as he explains his philosophy of education in Chapter Two:

> Education is suffering from narration sickness. The teacher talks about reality as if it were motionless, static, compartmentalized, and predictable. Or else he expounds on a topic completely alien to the existential experience of the students. His task is to "fill" the students with the contents of his narration contents which are detached from reality, disconnected from the totality that engendered them and could give them significance. Words are emptied of their concreteness and become a hollow, alienated, and alienating verbosity ... (1)

Pedagogically, Freire attempted to reverse the flow.

Critiques have already been made of Freire's educational theory in that students may bring unconsciousness into their solutions or improvisational responses, and teachers may already have fixed agendas about where and how they want the students to go while appearing to offer the free space to move around without being directional about taking them to the other side of the room (Michelletti, 2010). Yet, the role of the administrators, seen or unseen, has not been introduced into the functioning of the dyad of teacher and student in the classroom, either virtual or brick and mortar. It used to be that faculty wrote their own syllabi, but adjuncts rarely do (Weinbaum, 2019). University-supported theorists have not, as far as I know, begun to identify teachers, faculty, instructors, and particularly adjunct online instructors, as the unconscious receptacles into which syllabi, rubric, teaching methods, and readings are simply to be deposited. Faculty in the position of adjunct online instructor are not considered to be conscious beings, or possessors of consciousness, but receptors of deposits from the world above. Adjunct online instructors receive syllabi and teaching materials from administration the way Freire identified students having received curriculum from teachers—they are given courses to teach which they have not designed.

In my courses, I was trying to create a community of critical learners, modeling how scholars debated with one another. I was also encouraging the students to feel like they could do that which we all did together in the virtual classroom. I suppose it was part of my attempt to do critical pedagogy online. I continued to teach in the way I had learned in graduate school, not being aware that by becoming an adjunct online instructor I had passed over a line from agent into a mere receptor mold. Due to the introduction of automated classrooms and of automated instructor selection, I am beginning to see the barriers for online instructors to carry out critical pedagogy-informed teaching as part of our job description. What we receive, we carry forward. We are only the tinkers of the cars as they drive through, not the instructional designers. Our evaluations, too, are specifically connected to how well do we carry out the teaching of the curriculum in terms of content and method, as poured.

Generations of students on the university level in growing numbers are increasingly taught by adjunct online instructors who are not allowed to teach as we would see fit; not allowed to select materials or methods of study; nor, able to criticize readings that we are presented to teach in the poured classrooms that we are so appreciative to be given, if we want to pay bills at all. We teach in terror every time we post an opinion that may be construed as radical or if we criticize a given reading. Terror when we invite a student or two to try to imagine criticizing the inherited thought of the society and culture in which we live, let alone to meet with us off-campus, if they have questions and want to discuss their ideas in person. Terror that a supervisor will slot into the algorithm that assigns our courses that we are to be black listed[1].

At the institution where my number of assigned students dropped exponentially from 216 to 108, then to 37—what happened? At first, I naively thought this was because two courses I had been signed up to teach and never been offered, African Literature and Latin American Literature, did not exist anymore as I had inadvertently discovered in a conversation with a previous supervisor just before she suddenly left, which most of the middle management people do. The new middle management did not give me two additional courses, so I went directly to scheduling and asked the assigner what the best courses were to add to my roster to increase my odds for getting more students. When I returned with five choices, management was upset and later told me I was on probation until my teaching had been observed and my ability to teach without gender bias ascertained. Unbeknownst to me, an older male student had complained about not feeling heard in my course. Management had agreed with him, making this determination without consulting me and taking disciplinary action.

I was suffering the results in declined student numbers and pay, without even knowing why. Then, I discovered that, all along, African Literature and Latin American Literature had been offered anyway. Officially, adjuncts are told that the algorithm assigns courses to the online instructor with the lowest number of students, once the full-time faculty have been fed. When I inquired why my low number of taught students for the year was not getting me other assignments, I asked what the algorithm factors were. I also asked if there was a drop in registration and if that could be the reason why the numbers of students I received were plummeting. I was told,

.... there are many factors that go into determining how and when task assignments are issued, including those you mentioned. The algorithm that is used in this process is proprietary and thus cannot be shared. We are also restricted from sharing any registration trends/info as this may result in insider trading (personal communication, on behalf of scheduling, 8/30/2019).

Since the factors by which it is determined what courses are assigned are hidden, those who are doing critical pedagogy online within institutions might find themselves being squeezed out and blacklisted without ever being told specifically why. If you want to keep a job in the increasingly neoliberal corporate culture of what was once academia, best practices might very well be to just treat administrators as bosses and students as customers. Recognize you have little to no power as an adjunct online instructor. You may be just wearing the apron in someone else's restaurant. Someone else designs the menu and prepares the cuisines. Keeping the customers happy and satisfied is your routine, not to be strayed away from under conditions of institutions supporting the values of capitalism. The fact is you can't even add salt.

In conclusion:

1. I might be very good at teaching from a critical pedagogy online that:
   - Privileges communication and generates discussion;
   - Stimulates student thinking by constructivist methods;
   - Encourages collaborative group work;
   - Values input by different kinds of intelligence;
   - Demystifies the process of making scholarship by being a gate opener rather than a gate keeper;
   - Creates space to put the students in the driver's seat;
   - Encourages original thinking that relates what we do in classes to the students' own bodies of knowledge and immediate worlds;
   - Criticizes the institutions in which we work and study;
   - Looks at the society which those institutions are serving; and
   - Closes binaries between East and West, indigenous and other knowledges.
2. Over the years, all of this has led to volunteered excellent course evaluation comments from both male and female students each term. Notwithstanding,
3. This might also mean that any male student, old or young, who is used to dominating in traditional structures in which he is more comfortable, may not get the attention to which he feels, and might resent the efforts of a female professor to create the space for females or for non-traditional students to get equal time.

The preacher I had been watching when I started writing this essay calls herself a prophetess. She became very animated and talked about finding the spark of god within, which seems to me to be what we try to do when we teach critically. We encourage students to think for themselves and to criticize the society they see, the institutions they are in, the hierarchical frameworks they are working in, and yes, even the books they are reading. We don't want to teach to the book, we want to teach from the book, once we get started teaching. If someone is watching us from a panoptic command tower and stops us when we do, how are we able to teach at all? Let me know how you fare when you do. Bottom line is, if we want to create a critical pedagogical community of scholars, virtually or not, by going around the room and asking people what they think, or what they know, or what movie they would like to discuss, this is so far from the cookie cutter top-down model of education, with its focus on depositing and testing, that it is best to take that kind of show out of any classroom and find, or even create, other kinds of virtual and real-life roads.

## Note

1. This is a reference to the list that was made in Hollywood of people in the film industry who were not allowed to work due to McCarthyism

## References

Distance Education Committee. (2017). *Distance education handbook*. Evergreen Valley College. http://www.evc.edu/AcademicAffairs/Documents/Appendix-1.6_EVC_DEHandbook.pdf

Foucault, M. (1997). Panopticism. Discipline and punish. In N. Leach (Ed.), *Rethinking architecture*. Routledge.

Freire, P. (1970). *Pedagogy of the oppressed*. Herder and Herder. http://accountability.qwriting.qc.cuny.edu/files/2016/08/Philosophy-of-Education-Chapter-2_-Pedagogy-of-the-Oppressed.pdf.

Micheletti, G. (2010). Re-envisioning Paulo Freire's "banking concept of education." *Inquiries Journal/Student Pulse*, 2(2). http://www.inquiriesjournal.com/articles/171/re-envisioning-paulo-freires-banking-concept-of-education

Watson, B. (2017). *Systems and digital technology departmental report: July 1, 2016 – June 30, 2017*. Library Department and Committee Reports. https://digital.stpetersburg.us.usf.edu/cgi/viewcontent.cgi?article=1089&context=npml_dept_committee_reports

Weinbaum, B. (2013). Expropriation of the professoriate: Special issue on contingency labor force in academic labor. *ADE Bulletin 53-ADFL Bulletin of the Modern Language Association*, 42(3), 82–91.

Weinbaum, B. (2016). Teaching feminism online: Possible benefits of disembodiment. *Femspec*, *16*(2), 12–52.

Weinbaum, B. (2017). Commentary: Disempowerment of the adjunct online instructor in educational institutions. *Journal of Interdisciplinary Feminist Thought*, *10*(1), 1–7. https://digitalcommons.salve.edu/jift/vol10/iss1/4?utm_source=digitalcommons.salve.edu%2Fjift%2Fvol10%2Fiss1%2F4&utm_mediun=PDF&utm_campaign=PDFCoverPages

Weinbaum, B. (2019). *Where has all the feminism gone? Teaching early twenty-first century "Women's and Gender Studies" in an elite southeastern American university*. Academia. https://www.academia.edu/40070656/Where_Has_All_the_Feminism_Gone_Teaching_Early_Twenty_First_Century_Womens_and

# About the Authors

**Yolanda Abel, Ed.D.**, is an Associate Professor and chair of the Department of Advanced Studies in Education at Johns Hopkins University School of Education. She is also a faculty affiliate with the Center for Social Organization of Schools and the Center for Safe and Healthy Schools. Her publications appear in *American Educational Research Journal, Journal of Negro Education, Education and Urban Society*, and *School Science and Mathematics Journal*.

**Maximillian Alvarez, Ph.D.** graduated from the University of Michigan with a dual-Ph.D. in Comparative Literature and History. He worked as an Associate Editor at the Chronicle Review (The Chronicle of Higher Education) before taking his current position as Editor in Chief of The Real News Network in Baltimore.

**John Bannister, Ph.D.** Educator, bridge builder and advocate of innovative ways to approach sharing knowledge, Dr. John Bannister has committed himself to develop learning experiences through his work as a professor, trainer and the Director of the Johnson C. Smith Center for Innovative Teaching and Learning. Holding degrees in business and education, Dr. Bannister is an advocate of using new frameworks to create engaged learning. His research interests include connectivism, faculty development, adult learning, educational technology and the development of learning communities. In addition to frequently presenting on these topics Dr. Bannister serves as a reviewer for the *International Review of Research in Open and Distributed Learning Journal* (IRRODL), is on the Board of the Association of Non-Traditional Students in Higher Education (ANTSHE).

**Lee Skallerup Bessette, Ph.D.**, is a Learning Design Specialist at Georgetown University's Center for New Designs in Learning and Scholarship (CNDLS) and affiliated faculty in the Learning, Design, and Technology MA program. She has written and presented about critical digital pedagogy, online learning, and digital fluency, among other things. Her current research is focused on the affective labor involved in faculty development and instructional design. You can read more about her work at readywriting.org.

**Anita Bledsoe-Gardner, Ph.D.**, is an Associate Professor of Criminology at Johnson C. Smith University (Charlotte, North Carolina). Professionally, Dr. Bledsoe-Gardner has worked as principal investigator and co-principal investigator to facilitate research projects in the substantive areas of cyber-intelligence, race relations, community safety (in concert with Charlotte Mecklenburg Police Department), victimology, and juvenile delinquency. Notwithstanding, Dr. Bledsoe-Gardner has served as a research consultant for the Minister of Education in St. Kitts, Basseterre, West Indies. With her educational experiences and business acumen, she also currently serves as a consultant for the United States Department of Justice, the Department of Health and Human Services, the Department of Housing and Urban Development, and the Department of Education. Dr. Bledsoe-Gardner serves on several advisory committees both locally and statewide supporting social justice reform. Additionally, Dr. Bledsoe Gardner has presented and published several professional papers during her tenure as a university professor from various publishing houses and professionally refereed journals. She has also secured grant funding ranging over three million dollars for non-profit organizations. Dr. Bledsoe-Gardner is also a member of several professional and social organizations, including but not limited to, Mid-South Sociological Association, American Criminal Justice Association and the American Sociological Association.

**Denise K. Bockmier-Sommers, Ed.D.** is an Associate Professor at the University of Illinois Springfield, where she teaches the online Social Services Administration concentration in the Human Services Department. Dr. Bockmier-Sommers has accrued over twenty-five years of rehabilitation counseling and evaluation, management, and supervisory experience in the human services arena. She obtained her bachelor's degree in Human Growth and Development from the University of Illinois at Urbana Champaign, her master's degree in Rehabilitation at East Carolina University in Greenville, North Carolina, and her Doctor of Education degree in Counseling from the University of Missouri in St. Louis. Her research focuses on the use of service learning in online classes, the development of multicultural competencies in Human Services training, and the use of empathy, genuineness and high regard to enhance engagement and success in online teaching and learning.

**Carey Borkoski, Ed.D., Ph.D.**, is an Assistant Professor at Johns Hopkins University where she holds a joint faculty appointment with the School of Education and the Bloomberg School of Public Health. Within the School of Education, she teaches research methods and advises doctoral students in the online Ed.D. program. Her research explores the role of communities, bridging media like podcasts and

TEDTalks, and storytelling in facilitating student onboarding, promoting deeper learning, and mitigating anxiety around learning and engaging in often unfamiliar academic spaces. Her research focuses on understanding the barriers and supports for cultivating our personal and communal sense of belonging. In particular she works to identify strategies that most effectively cultivate belonging in our learning communities and is currently working on research to understand the onboarding and development of first-year doctoral students in online programs.

**Drick Boyd, Ed.D.**, is Professor Emeritus in Urban Studies from Eastern University, St. David's, Pennsylvania. He is a community educator and restorative justice practitioner in Philadelphia, PA. He is the author of three books including *White Allies in the Struggle for Racial Justice* (Orbis, 2015), *Paulo Freire: His Faith, Spirituality and Theology* (with Dr. James Kirylo, Sense, 2017), and *Disrupting Whiteness: Talking with White People About Race* (Arch Street Press, 2021). He lives with his wife in Broomall, PA, and is the father of 3 adult children.

**Brianne Brady** is an Ontario Certified Teacher with a passion for inclusive education and advocating for equity, accessibility and students' needs. Brianne is a research assistant in the Mathematics and Equity Awareness Research Lab at Ontario Tech University in Oshawa, Ontario, Canada. She is interested in researching equity and disability specifically exploring awarenesses of teachers and their biases relating to disability.

**Eric Ruiz Bybee, Ph.D.**, is an Associate Professor in the Department of Teacher Education in the David O. McKay School of Education at BYU. He teaches courses in multicultural education. Dr. Bybee's research interests include the social and cultural foundations of education; Latina/o education; teacher education; and identity, agency and social movements in education and stem from his experiences as a former New York City public school teacher. Within teacher education, he has focused his research on exploring the ways that teachers are prepared (or not prepared) with necessary cultural knowledge to meet the needs of students from historically marginalized populations. More recently, he has also explored the role of teacher education in the identity productions of Latina/o preservice teachers from various racial, class, linguistic, and immigration backgrounds. He is particularly interested in Latina/o racial identity and whiteness and situates his ethnographic work within the broader cultural history Latina/o schooling in the United States.

**Ramona Maile Cutri, Ph.D.**, is an Associate Professor at Brigham Young University's Teacher Education Department. Cutri's research attends to the complexities of technology integration in higher education. Her work contributes a criticality to research on eLearning and highlights the tensions between the culture of academia and the potential and demands of online teaching. Additionally, Cutri explores how technology can facilitate the pedagogical and dispositional goals of critical multicultural teacher education. She has produced important work that documents the emotional work involved in multicultural education teacher education and managing affective polarization in ways that lead to changes in students' thinking and development as teachers.

**Maggie Debelius, Ph.D.**, is the Director of Faculty Initiatives at CNDLS and a Professor in both the English Department and the Learning, Design, and Technology MA program. She works with departments across the university on curriculum design, writing assessment, and faculty development. She publishes and presents on graduate education, writing pedagogy, and career development. She is the co-author (with Susan Basalla) of *So What Are You Going to Do with That?: Finding Careers Outside Academia* (University of Chicago, 2007 and 2014).

**Sara Donaldson, Ed.D.**, is an Assistant Professor of Education at Wheaton College in Massachusetts. She is the co-coordinator of the early childhood and elementary education programs and teaches mathematics, science, and special education courses. Sara also works as an online, adjunct faculty member in the School of Education at Johns Hopkins University in their Mathematics and STEM Leadership master's program. Sara's research focuses on examining the systems, structures, and cultures of learning spaces that enable critical colleagueship and promote deep learning, positive perceptions of efficacy, and empowerment for diverse learners in multiple contexts. Her publications can be found in the *Journal on Excellence in College Teaching,* the *Tennessee Educational Leadership Journal,* the *New England Mathematics Journal, and* NEFDC's *The Exchange.*

**Dolores (Dee) Grayson, Ph.D.**, is a nationally recognized researcher, scholar and leader in educational equity, action research and instruction. Her work has been presented to the American Educational Research Association, the American Association of Colleges for Teacher Education, the National Education Association, the National School Board Association, the American Association of University Women, the National Association for Multicultural Education, the National Association for Bilingual Education, the National Alliance for Partnerships in Equity and numerous other state and national organizations. As the developer and principal author of the award winning Generating Expectations for Student Achievement (GESA) program, she has made presentations for participants from all fifty states and twenty countries. Grayson holds a Bachelor of Science from the University of North Carolina, Greensboro; a Master of Science in Educational Administration from California State University, Fullerton; and an interdisciplinary doctoral degree in Educational Leadership and Social Justice from the Union Institute and University, Cincinnati, Ohio. Grayson has recently relocated from California to a community north of Atlanta, Georgia. She continues to teach and consult online, visit with friends and family and participate in golf and related activities.

**Mary Holiman, M.A.**, received her Bachelor's in Interdisciplinary Studies from Johnson C. Smith University where she was a peer tutor and mentor. Recently, she obtained her Master's in Public Health with a concentration in Community Health Science and Practice from New York University. She is also a proud member of Alpha Kappa Alpha Sorority, Incorporated. Inspired by own experiences, she has done research on the correlation between early childhood experiences and juvenile delinquency. Mary is interested in the intersection between the arts, the media, and public health and wants to take a more holistic approach to health and wellness. She aspires to start her own organization that provides free mental health counseling and creative arts therapy to at-risk youth and make it more accessible to disadvantaged communities. Mary has a passion for social justice and hopes this reflects in her work.

**Vicki A. Hosek, Ed.D.**, is an Instructional Assistant Professor of Education at Illinois State University in the School of Teaching and Learning where she teaches secondary methods, foundations and literacy courses. Her research focuses on educational technology and examining the technology integration practices of teacher candidates and practicing teachers and the role and value they place on student inquiry and student voice in digital environments. In addition, she studies the development of the critical digital literacy (CDL) of teacher candidates and the ways that teacher education programs can support this development. Recent publications include her examination of the Technological Pedagogical Content Knowledge (TPACK) of practicing teachers and the missing critical component of the TPACK framework, and also an examination of authoritative discourses at work in the digital citizenship policies of schools. Dr. Hosek earned her degrees from the University of Colorado, Boulder, Western Illinois University, and Illinois State University. She can be reached at vhosek@ilstu.edu.

**Heather M. Huling, M.Ed.**, is a clinical instructor in the Elementary Education Program at Georgia Southern University. She is currently a doctoral candidate in the Curriculum Studies Ed.D. program at Georgia Southern University with an emphasis in Multicultural and Social Justice Education. She was an elementary educator in the public school system for seven years before moving into higher education to work with preservice teachers.

**Delores D. Liston, Ph.D.**, is Professor of Curriculum Studies and Social Foundations at Georgia Southern University. She is author of Joy as a Metaphor of Convergence: A Phenomenological and Aesthetic Investigation of Social and Educational Change, Learning to Teach: A Critical Approach to Field Experiences (with Natalie Adams, Christine Shea and Bryan Deever), as well as Pervasive Vulnerabilities: Sexual Harassment in School and Promoting Social Justice Through the Scholarship of Teaching and Learning (with Regina Rahimi). She is also LCSW licensed through the State of Georgia.

**Kimberly Huisman Lubreski, Ph.D.**, is the Assistant Director of Learning Design at CNDLS, where she works with faculty on designing online and blended courses. She teaches in both the Sociology Department and the Justice and Peace Studies Program at Georgetown. She has written and presented about a wide variety of issues related to inclusive and critical pedagogy, social inequality, and immigration. She is the lead editor of Somalis in Maine: Crossing Cultural Currents (North Atlantic Books, 2011).

**Sahana Mahendirarajah** is currently a research assistant in the Mathematics and Equity Awareness lab at Ontario Tech University and a French Immersion teacher in the Durham District School Board in Oshawa, Ontario Canada. Sahana's research interest in social justice education stem from her varied teaching experiences including in a rural village in South Africa.

**Jennifer L. Martin, Ph.D.**, is an Associate Professor in the Department of Teacher Education at the University of Illinois at Springfield. Prior to working in higher education, Dr. Martin worked in public education for seventeen years, fifteen of those as the department chair of English at an urban alternative high school for students labeled at-risk for school failure in metropolitan Detroit. She is the editor of Racial Battle Fatigue: Insights from the Front Lines of Social Justice Advocacy (Recipient of the 2016 AERA Division B's Outstanding Book Recognition Award), and co-author of Teaching for Educational Equity: Case Studies for Professional Development and Principal Preparation, Volumes 1 and 2 (Rowman & Littlefield). Her most recent edited volume is Feminist Pedagogy, Practice, and Activism: Improving Lives for Girls and Women (Routledge, 2017).

**Mindy McWilliams, M.A.**, is the Senior Associate Director for Assessment and Programs at Georgetown University's Center for New Designs in Learning and Scholarship (CNDLS). She has written and presented on the importance of focusing on student well-being in the curriculum, as well as on developing learning analytics for analyzing reflective writing. Her current research projects include assessing the impact of infusing ethics into introductory computer science courses and whether including sustainability education in coursework can impact student attitudes and behaviors.

**Erin Mikulec, Ph.D.**, is a Professor of Secondary Education and the Associate Director of the School of Teaching and Learning at Illinois State University. Dr. Mikulec teaches general methods and assessment, as well as methods and materials for English Learners. She has developed clinical partnerships with several area schools and leads education abroad programs to England and Finland. At the graduate level, her coursework focuses on student diversity and educational practices. Her research interests include pre-service teacher education, working with LGBTQ+ youth, and teaching for global engagement.

**Brianne (Brie) Morettini, Ph.D.**, is an Associate Professor in the Department of Interdisciplinary and Inclusive Education in the College of Education at Rowan University. She teaches doctoral courses on research literature and analysis, and undergraduate courses on working with families and communities, inclusive education, and elementary education. She draws on a sociocultural theoretical framework to research beginning teacher identity development, beginning teachers' perspectives on teaching, and the use of self-study methodologies to uncover and acknowledge epistemological frames. She considers the intersections of theory and practice in her teaching and research. She has published her work in book chapters and peer-reviewed journals. She also presents her work at national and international research conferences.

**Carol Mutch, Ph.D.**, is an academic in the School of Critical Studies in Education in the Faculty of Education and Social Work at the University of Auckland. Prof. Mutch has held roles across the spectrum in education from teacher and educational leader to teacher educator and policy advisor and now university academic, but always with a focus on social justice. She has lived and worked in the UK, Canada and Japan and has been a frequent visitor to Samoa, working with the National University's Faculty of Education. She is a prolific writer with six books and over 100 articles and book chapters to her name. She teaches, researches and writes about educational policy, curriculum, social studies and citizenship education, and research methods. Over the last decade, Prof. Mutch has conducted research and published on the role of schools in disaster response and recovery across five Asia-Pacific countries. This research was recognized by her university with a 2020 Research Excellence Medal. She has won other national and international awards for her research, service and teaching and is a frequent keynote speaker and media interviewee. With the arrival of Covid-19, along with her research team, Te Whakatere au Pāpori (Navigating Social Currents), Prof. Mutch has been researching how schools are coping with the impact of the pandemic on their students, staff, families and wider communities.

**James Olsen, Ph.D.**, is the Assistant Director for Programs for Graduate Students and Faculty at CNDLS and teaches courses in Philosophy and in the Environmental Studies Program. His work in faculty development is broadly focused, with particular emphasis in inclusive pedagogy and graduate student pedagogical development. Both his teaching and research interests primarily revolve around issues in sustainability and environmental ethics.

**Jay C. Percell, Ed. D.**, is an Associate Professor in the School of Teaching and Learning at Illinois State University. He teaches secondary education methods courses for implementing literacy and technology across all content areas and serves as the course instructor for the ISU Secondary Professional Development School. He is also the faculty advisor for the ISU chapter of Educators Rising. His research interests include educational technology, digital literacy, and alternative grading. Prior to moving to higher education, he spent a decade teaching high school English in Arizona and Colorado and served for two years as volunteer in the U.S. Peace Corps teaching overseas. Dr. Percell holds degrees from Illinois State University, Northern Arizona University, and the University of Northern Colorado. His passions include teaching, writing, coaching, and spending time with his family. Follow him on Twitter @jaycpercell.

**Jessamay Pesek, Ph.D.**, is an Associate Professor in the Department of Professional Education at Bemidji State University. She coordinates an online/hybrid teacher preparation program that serves students across Minnesota to earn initial teacher licensure. Her areas of research are multicultural education, social studies education, civic engagement, and learning technologies. She holds a 5–12$^{th}$ grade social studies teaching license and has taught middle and high school students.

**Tania Ramalho, Ph.D.**, a Brasicana (Brazilian-American), is Professor of Education at SUNY Oswego's Curriculum and Instruction Department of the

School of Education, where she teaches Critical Literacy and Pedagogy in the tradition of Paulo Freire. She was educated in Brazil and the United States, studying the social sciences at the University of Rio de Janeiro and education policy and leadership at the Ohio State University. Her first steps as faculty in academia took place in Women's Studies. Critical feminist pedagogies have since inspired her research and teaching in teacher education, face-to-face and online, with a special interest in global education and global citizenship approaches.

**Robyn Ruttenberg-Rozen, Ph.D.**, is an Assistant Teaching Professor and Director of the Mathematics and Equity Awareness Lab at Ontario Tech University in Oshawa, Ontario, Canada. In her teaching and research Robyn explores growth and change, equity and access, and innovative practice.

**Yianna Vovides, Ph.D.**, currently serves as Director of Learning Design and Research at the Center for New Designs in Learning and Scholarship (CNDLS), Professor for the Master of Arts in Learning, Design, and Technology (LDT) program at Georgetown University, and Curriculum Director for LDT. In her role at CNDLS, she oversees the online learning, technology-enhanced, and development efforts. She focuses her practice and academic efforts in addressing how people learn within networked learning environments. She has worked on projects that emphasize individual and group learning, institutional programs that enable systemic changes, and research that examines how new technologies support teaching and learning.

**Tina Wagle, Ph.D.**, is a Professor, Chair of the Education Division, and M.Ed. Coordinator in the School for Graduate Studies at SUNY Empire State College. Her areas of interest include teacher education, issues of social justice, languages other than English, and bilingual education and has given many presentations and written publications in this area. She has been teaching online, blended and face to face for twenty years. She is the recipient of a SUNY Chancellor's Award for Excellence in Faculty Service.

**Batya Weinbaum, Ph.D.**, has written and published twenty books, the most recent of which is about the popular TV show Jane the Virgin, available in nine languages on Amazon, published by Scholastic Press. She earned her doctorate in English at University of Massachusetts at Amherst and founded and edits the journal Femspec (see femspec.org). Her papers are archived at Duke University Special Collections, among other places. She teaches feminist art and writing classes on zoom, operates a feminist retreat center in the Blue Ridge Mountains, and adjuncts in 2021–2022 at American Public University System, Kent State Stark, and Boston College. Her online video course Feminism in Popular Culture is offered on a continuing basis at UDEMY and Academia.edu. She has published award-winning poetry, fiction, and essays.

**Erin Feinauer Whiting, Ph.D.**, is an Associate Professor of Teacher Education at Brigham Young University. She is responsible for teaching multicultural education for secondary education majors as well as graduate courses related to socio-cultural aspects of knowledge and schooling. Her research focuses on understanding and alleviating social inequalities including a focus on school community and organization for the inclusion of all students. Her work has examined many aspects of equity and belonging in schools including an emphasis on cultural and emotional geographies and the socio-political forces implicated in teaching and learning. She has also studied the complexities of teaching a critical multicultural teacher education and what leads to changes in perspectives and dispositional development of social justice practices through emotional work.

**Heather Yuhaniak, Ed.D.**, co-founded and coordinates McDaniel College's Equity and Excellence in Education graduate certificate and master's degree programs (chronicled by Edutopia features "Can Equity Be Taught?" and "Reflections on Becoming More Culturally Responsive"). She also serves as a senior educational adviser and adjunct faculty member in the online Ed.D. program at Johns Hopkins University School of Education. Her research focuses on cognitive dissonance, White Racial Identity development, and the role of critical consciousness in multicultural teacher education. She co-authored "Creating Equity Warriors in the Face of White Fragility" included in Confronting Racism: Counternarratives of Critical Teacher Educators. In addition to teaching adults, Heather has served as a middle school general and special educator, team leader, department chair, and staff developer.

## Studies in Criticality

*General Editor*
*Shirley R. Steinberg*

Counterpoints publishes the most compelling and imaginative books being written in education today. Grounded on the theoretical advances in criticalism, feminism, and postmodernism in the last two decades of the twentieth century, Counterpoints engages the meaning of these innovations in various forms of educational expression. Committed to the proposition that theoretical literature should be accessible to a variety of audiences, the series insists that its authors avoid esoteric and jargonistic languages that transform educational scholarship into an elite discourse for the initiated. Scholarly work matters only to the degree it affects consciousness and practice at multiple sites. Counterpoints' editorial policy is based on these principles and the ability of scholars to break new ground, to open new conversations, to go where educators have never gone before.

For additional information about this series or for the submission of manuscripts, please contact:

> Shirley R. Steinberg
> c/o Peter Lang Publishing, Inc.
> 80 Broad Street, 5th floor
> New York, New York 10004

To order other books in this series, please contact our Customer Service Department:
> peterlang@presswarehouse.com (within the U.S.)
> orders@peterlang.com (outside the U.S.)

Or browse online by series:
> www.peterlang.com

www.ingramcontent.com/pod-product-compliance
Ingram Content Group UK Ltd.
Pitfield, Milton Keynes, MK11 3LW, UK
UKHW022238230426
12048UKWH00018BA/1324